MEMOIRS

D0880332

René Lévesque

MEMOIRS

Translated by Philip Stratford

McClelland and Stewart

Copyright © 1986 by Editions Québec/Amérique

First published in paperback 1995

Published by arrangement with
Editions Québec/Amérique, Montreal, Quebec.
Translation, English edition © 1986 Philip Stratford
Afterword © 1995 Graham Fraser

ALL RIGHTS RESERVED.
The use of any part of this publication reproduced, transmitted in any form
or by any means, electronic, mechanical, photocopying, recording, or otherwise,
or stored in a retrieval system, without the prior written consent of the
publisher – or in the case of photocopying or other reprographic copying, a
licence from the Canadian Copyright Licensing Agency – is an infringement
of the copyright law.

Canadian Cataloguing in Publication Data

Lévesque, René, 1922-1987
Memoirs

Issued also in French under title: Memoires.
ISBN 0-7710-5285-5 (bound) ISBN 0-7710-5286-3 (pbk.)

1. Lévesque, René, 1922-1987. 2. Quebec (Province) –
History – 1936-1960.* 3. Quebec (Province) –
Politics and government – 1960-1976.* 4. Quebec
(Province) – Politics and government – 1976-1985.*
5. Parti quebecois – History. 6. Prime ministers –
Quebec (Province) – Biography. 7. Journalists –
Quebec (Province) – Biography. I. Title.

FC2925.1.L48A3 1986   971.4'04'0924
F1053.25.L48A3 1986   C86-094695-9

Printed and bound in Canada
The paper used in this book is acid free

McClelland and Stewart Limited
The Canadian Publishers
481 University Avenue
Toronto, Ontario
M5G 2E9

Contents

Translator's Note

René Lévesque wrote this book; I translated it. He did not dictate it or have it ghost-written; he wrote it out longhand, calling on his journalistic skills to make an exciting story of his life and times and political career.

I translated his text; I did not adapt it, or assimilate it for English readers, or try to disguise the fact that it was first written in French for a French-speaking public. The present version is very slightly abridged where references seemed too local, and a few explanatory notes have been inserted for the same reason. Otherwise it is a faithful copy.

René Lévesque, whose command of the language is excellent, might have written this story in English himself, but then the slant would have been different. As it is, we are closer to the writer's intimate thought and feeling but must occasionally pay the price of a certain strangeness in content, context, and tone. When that happens, my suggestion is to take a cue from the translator: stick with the story and it will become clear. The reward is a livelier and more comprehensive picture of modern Quebec than any available, as well as a full self-portrait of the intriguing man who has played such a prominent role in our recent history.

Acknowledgements

In addition to the men and women to whom I have expressed my thanks in this book, I would like to thank all my old friends from before my political career. Their warm memories were continually coming back to me as I was writing this book. As well, I have not forgotten all my compatriots who had confidence in me over the years.

Several journalists and writers have taken the pain to record the role I may have played in the evolution of our society. I am thinking of Jean Provencher, François Aubin, Peter Desbarats, Graham Fraser, and Alain Pontaut, among others. Their work helped me remember many details as well as the context of events I had not personally had time to jot down.

I sincerely hope that my publishers, Jacques Fortin from Québec/Amérique and Avie Bennett from McClelland and Stewart, will not regret the risks that they were taking – not to mention my own – by throwing me into such an adventure. I am indebted to them for their patience. A special thanks as well to Anik Lapointe, Andréa Joseph, and François Fortin from Québec/Amérique for their kindness and availability.

A very special thanks to Philip Stratford, an efficient and exceptional translator, whose sense of humour and pertinent suggestions were of great help to me.

Finally, I owe ever so much to my wife Corinne who not only put up with me throughout all these months but who also had the courage to transcribe and often improve my scribbling.

Foreword

I AM EXTREMELY CONSCIOUS of the fact that when faced with the challenge of setting down, in little more than seven months, this life of a child of our times, neither more nor less agitated than the age itself, I have only been able to acquit myself, in some instances, in a less than satisfactory manner. So it always must be.

I know, too, that certain people are going to be disappointed, or at least a bit impatient, to discover a so-called "public man" evoking memories that are not purely and simply public, as if I hadn't first had another existence, just like everyone else.

Political life provokes a long and curious rootlessness. It steals the leisure necessary to situate oneself in one's continuity. So I felt the need to rediscover a minimum of perspective by remounting the river of time to the place the world began for me. This exercise brings out things from a year or two ago, and others that are farther back than I like to think about. The farthest ones reserved a surprise for me. They were the easiest to recapture, as if time in its crucible had cleansed them of imperfections and left me only the pure metal. This is so true that if I had listened to my inner voice, my book would willingly have lingered longer over my Gaspésie of the twenties, that prison for my parents but a paradise for my childhood where, more than anywhere else in Quebec, we lived happily on the margin of history.

To the general libraries of memoirs of World War II or of the birth of television, the trifles I add have the sole merit of giving a particular face to the two seismic shocks that rocked our generation just as we were reaching adulthood, and just before we were whirled away in an infernal acceleration of events that is with us still and always will be.

The rest, naturally, is politics, and consequently, eminently debatable. The only assurance I can give the reader is that I have tried to apply a very simple principle that has always guided me: one cannot, obviously, say everything one knows, and even less everything one thinks – otherwise one would never finish toting up one's enemies – but I have always forbidden myself to play with the facts or, worse yet, to pretend to believe what I don't believe.

To tell my story I go back to the autumn of last year and take off, exactly as I took off myself, at a time when, having come to the end of my road, as they say, I felt a real urge to travel and to be somewhere else, even very far away, not so much just to change the pain to another place as simply for a change of air, to air my brains after a quarter of a century in the steamy kitchen of politics.

I

LEAVETAKING

*"Emotion is always new and the same word has always been used
for it. Hence the impossibility of expressing emotion."*
VICTOR HUGO

1. Reflections

IT HAS BEEN BARELY A WEEK since we left and already I've forgotten completely. It's always been like that. Once the plane takes off or the border is crossed, everything is wiped out automatically.

I said every*thing*, though, not every*one*. On the contrary, things or people encountered constantly remind me of this or that person left behind. Together they made up the last team – a small one, but then the best kind never did run to size. It was small, but warm-hearted and tight-knit, with its own passwords and superbly undisciplined, a team in which everyone, even after so many years, was still able to put private wishes last. About ten of us all told were on that slowly rotting ice, our "bunker," and others were on the shore in this or that ministry, or in Montreal, or in different parts of the country, as ready to rally round as at the start, or almost. For a while yet it will be hard to do without them.

That, too, is the way it's always been, ever since I lost my first gang on leaving Gaspésie at fourteen. . . . How one wished each handshake could last forever, since they all ended in the same kind of unfair wrench of pain. There was no use saying, "I'll be seeing you," when you knew very well that life would soon separate and disperse you. Besides, this time I have a vague and utterly absurd feeling of guilt, like the captain abandoning ship and leaving behind on the rapidly sinking deck the last members of the crew, the peerless few. . . .

As for the rest, so long, and no regrets! Beginning with Quebec City and the sinister third floor of Block J, where I gladly pass on to anyone who wants them the drawers full of paper clips and the push-button communication system I inherited from Bourassa. And the gossip mills turning endlessly from the Grand-Allée to the Aquarium. And the journalists in the parliamentary press gallery feeding off them and feeding them.

So a week has gone by already. The plane took off later than usual when we left. In the west all the sky had to keep warm was a narrow mauve scarf dwindling to black, while the east was already swallowed up in the night. We didn't even get to see Quebec. And now, no more TV or newspapers to remind us of it, nothing but Europe until further notice. But how similar it all is behind the different facade!

October, 1985, and here in France the opposition, too, is already being declared the winner, the polls putting it light-years ahead of the government. At a recent party congress, the socialists have just managed to avoid catastrophe by plastering over once again the breach caused by Michel Rocard. "We have need of you, Michel," proclaims Emperor Fabius, "and you, Lionel, and you, Pierre!" Unless I'm very much mistaken I've seen and heard something like that not so long ago.

What does it matter ? The sun is shining in Paris just as it does elsewhere. On the sidewalk opposite the ladies of the night – younger than the last time, a new generation – ply their trade and bargain hard. The metro is as incredible as ever, the taxis as unfindable. It's almost ten years since I had the right, or at any rate the chance, to use them at will, or to renew contact freely with this city that is so unbelievably prissy.

"Oh, so that's it? It's the mild you want," she says, snubbing me snobbishly at Le Drugstore. "You might have said so."

I had asked for "lights," imagine that! And then for a little . . . bag . . . to carry them in.

"Monsieur means a pochette . . . ."

And so on. But just the same, there's the Champs Elysées, the

Boulevards, Saint-Germain-des-Prés and the Place du Québec with that admirable fountain by Daudelin called "Freeze-up." It's more like break-up, but it's a beautiful treat, sparkling in the autumn sun with all its spring-like jets of water playing.

But O treachery! I like London better still. Can't help it. In its own fashion it's just as splendid, and good-natured into the bargain. Above all there's the humour. Paris has wit to burn, granted, but without humour it sometimes grates on the nerves.

In London, there's that good old Cumberland Hotel across the street from Marble Arch and Hyde Park and just a couple of steps away from the barracks where we were billeted in 1944 but which I can't find any more. It was in the Cumberland that we used to take refuge to escape those kindly volunteer matrons who kept a puritanical eye on us while doing their best to give us all the comforts of home.

They were so perfectly, so terribly English. I'll never forget the Christmas they organized for us that year. Huge quarters of beef had arrived from the States, big enough to make you steaks as thick as you please. And what happened to them? Yes, sir! Beef stew! A stringy mess of meat floating in its own juice surrounded by potatoes and Brussels sprouts. From that day on, sprouts and I have gone our separate ways.

What a people they are, though, in their little kingdom! The buzz-bombs would come over grinding and groaning like trucks on a bad road. Then, suddenly – silence. Ten or fifteen seconds that would last an eternity. Finally would come the muffled explosion that would mean a house and a household had been hit. After that, uncomplainingly, stoically, life would begin again, and would still keep its chin up near the end under the V-2s (the first supersonic missiles, soon to be followed by the first jets, equipment that Hitler fortunately hadn't had before then). You only heard their whistling after the explosion. The destruction was freely commented upon by those famous soap-box orators thumping their wobbly stands and mercilessly vituperating perfidious Albion, which had had the strange idea of accepting them to her shores in the first place. There was one bearded Hindu in particular who, with his finger pointing vengefully toward heaven, would shout out: "Let the bombs come! More and more of them! There will never be enough to wipe out the crimes of your Empire!"

The audience for these orations was gravely attentive. Sometimes a few of them would even applaud a little. As for signs of disapproval, they rarely went beyond a shrug of the shoulders. "There'll always be an England . . . ."

Forty years later London is still London, though more run down, it seems. The little golden Eros is no longer there in the middle of Piccadilly Circus to inspire us. He took refuge somewhere else when they began a slow demolition process here, as in many other districts, before continuing their interminable reconstruction, English-style. Only the prices move fast; everything is horribly expensive. The Rolls-Royces and the Bentleys still announce the classical arrogance of the rich, whether of the heriditary or the Arab variety, and the working class still gets splashed and apparently still maintains its imperturbable equanimity, although outbursts of racist fever are getting more and more frequent. As the riots succeed each other, one can feel the temperature rising. It's as if the old Empire, heavy with the weight of colonial abuse, were sending back to its true source the ills suffered by South Africa, India, and all those ancient far-flung lands on which the sun never set.

Back to Paris, where things are calmer now. But for how long? The same virus is in the air. "Le Pen to the rescue, quick!" a right-wing poster yells. And this blind terrorism everywhere puts oil on the flames.

Luckily, we're not on duty this time. *Pariscope* (*What's On In Paris*) comes out once a week and, as in times gone by, we treat ourselves to an orgy of films, a thing we never do at home.

But look out! Here's the latest issue of *Québec en bref* (*Quebec Update*) sent to us by the Quebec delegation. It tells us that the Paris office will be widowed for a while because Louise Beaudoin has been nominated to International Relations. That, along with a lot of pre-election housecleaning that is duly reported, makes me want to . . . if I could only . . .

But I mustn't. Ab-so-lute-ly not. Things could very quickly degenerate into what I am determined at all costs to avoid: passing judgement on my successsors, or worse still, self-justification. I don't want these memoirs to turn into political Memoirs with a capital M, the kind that historian Jacques Blainville said "help present History in its falsest colours."

I'm glad to think I can leave my Sunday painter's political palette in the cupboard for a while yet. We've still got a dozen or so countries left to visit.

CAIRO, 29 NOVEMBER 1985

So here we are in full flight from north to south, like migratory birds.

I had never known Scandinavia except in books, despite talking about it through my hat many times. Now, with three days per country ($3 \times 4 = 12$) and three extra for Leningrad, I can claim to be an expert, almost as much as Lise Bissonnette is on the United States.

Your newest expert can report, then, that Copenhagen is very expensive, that the Little Mermaid has been the victim of a bomb attack, and that the sinful Tivoli Gardens were already closed for winter; that Stockholm is Sweden's Toronto or West Island built on an archipelago that makes you dream about what we might do in Montreal; that heroic Helsinki is so dependent on the Russians it almost manages to forget the past; and that even in the freezing rain Leningrad is very beautiful with its pink, beige, and green stones stretching away from the Admiralty to the banks of the Neva. Also, in Leningrad the statues of Peter the Great and the Not Less Great (or less bloody) Catherine see more Finnish "vodka tourists" passing by than Gorbachevniks.

But with the coming on of the cold season we took flight, or more precisely one of those night trains that would give a groundhog insomnia, a train from the Venice of the North to the real one. And here we found real May sunshine, but a torrential downpour, too, that during the night had so flooded the Piazza San Marco they had to bring out the emergency wooden sidewalks. Perched on these, tourists are sitting ducks for the pigeons, and for rubber-booted souvenir salesmen whose rising prices match the rising waters. From there to Florence, which usually brings out the sparkle in anyone, except in the off-season when Neptune himself contemplates his fountain with a scowl. Same thing in Rome, where the wintry blast blows your change away before the Trevi has had a chance to promise better things next time. And even two or three beatifications were not enough on Sunday at noon to prevent John Paul II from shivering at his Vatican window, which says how bad it was.

So we made the big mistake of leaving for Egypt, in search of heat above all! It was an error because afterwards Greece would seem only a faint copy, an imitator of the real beginnings of the world that you can find – between two hijackings – on the banks of the Nile at Karnak, at the Valley of Kings, at Aswan with its Manic-à-la-Nasser dams, and above all at the Temple of Isis, saved from the rising waters by UNESCO's Superior Court. It's striking to see those Nubians on muleback as in times before Christ. There are so few automobiles and industries and so little pollution that everything is still intact, that is, everything that hasn't been destroyed or defaced by the incredible parade of creeds and conquerors, each intent on leaving its mark. We stand in awe before those incomparable columns that comprise architectural ensembles that will be an inspiration forever, and upon which eminent Egyptologists from the nineteenth century had the nerve to carve their names. Beside us a fellow tourist exclaims, "*Baptême*! It's like one of us countersigning a Picasso!"

One Québécois among many. They are to be found everywhere nowadays: Québécois studying, working, on business, falling sick and getting treated over here, like that lucky fellow who chose to have a heart attack in Helsinki, the Mecca of cardiology. And those groups of youngsters seeing the sights, and that snooty dame, the epitome of the Haut-Ville at Quebec City, our parochial capital, who noticed me as she got off the cruise ship as we were waiting our turn to get on out in the middle of the Nile and disdainfully remarked: "Tiens, tiens! Finally got around to leaving, did you? Bravo!"

That's what you call being put in your place, eh? Any call for an answer? Not worth it. Nor complicated explanations either. Maybe if I could just tell quite simply, without malice, how it happened. . . . But I know this part isn't going to be easy. Why didn't I let a year or two go by before agreeing to write this damned book?

First, I was afraid to sit around twiddling my thumbs. That's the kind of thing I can't stand for more than a couple of weeks at a time. Second, it's the fault of old buddies of mine who claim I write even worse than I speak, even when I'm talking my best; they're responsible for my giving way to the temptation of putting things down in black and white, for better or for worse, at my own risk and peril, quite free this time from those "Superior Beings" who used to spend their time revising and correcting me until I became totally unrecognizable. Finally, and above all, I think there are things I have seen on my long journey that, if I'm not mistaken, deserve to be told and will perhaps prove interesting, if not memorable.

I have some old papers here to jog my memory, a faculty which in my case works like an oyster, springing to life on contact with the least particle of mother of pearl or sand, and we'll just have to see what the result is . . . a few precious pearls or cat mush.

Seventeen I-me-my's in the last fifteen lines. Decidedly, me-myself-and-I seem to be taking over centre stage. Ah well, there's always a first time.

2. The Beginning of the End

No beating about the bush: Quebec or Canada. . . . And anyone incapable of accepting this way of looking at things or of finding it the one appropriate, correct, desirable, in short the only possible perspective, had certainly better cast his vote elsewhere.

WHO COULD HAVE ALLOWED such a presumptuous statement? Well, yes, I admit it, those words are mine. Without trying to find excuses, I should also add that it was March, 1984, and a party convention was coming up. And Trudeau's conniving "repatriation" tactics still rankled.

So what never should have happened inevitably came to pass. In the hothouse atmosphere that so quickly settled over the June convention, as so often in the past in that shoulder-to-shoulder emotion, it's easy to slip into infallibility, and that's the way that most arrogantly exclusive statement came to be made. It was just one little sentence, but a complete aberration, stating that a vote cast for the PQ couldn't be anything else but a vote for sovereignty, and that the electors would have to like it or lump it!

The whole thing came about in part by my own grievous fault. I was there, so they tell me, the day that rotten little sentence came up before the executive committee of the party, and I didn't see it. I was also there, beyond all shadow of a doubt, when it came up again in one of the workshops at the convention where a belated objection on my part earned me a polite snub and at the same time helped galvanize the hard-liners who had taken control. And I was there again in the plenary session when Jacques-Yvan Morin stood up at the mike and almost singlehandedly tried to limit the damage and was attacked for his pains by the unleashed fury of the assembly.

I now remember that, stunned by such collective madness, I must have thought it wasn't so serious after all and that, sooner or later, as Jacques Parizeau would have put it, we could blow the whistle and end this particular little game. This, in fact, is what happened some months later, but at what a price – a price we couldn't calculate precisely until the end of the year, once everything had been, as they say, consummated.

As soon as the Quebec parliament reconvened in the fall, I could tell the session would be a hot one. Coming back fresh from a fascinating and fruitful trip to the Far East where at last I had my turn to discover China, I hadn't even the leisure to digest the adventure properly before finding myself caught between two well-entrenched camps. On one side were the do-or-die indépendantistes, "If only one remained, it would be me!" My colleague Clément Richard wittily nicknamed them the "cariboos" in memory of that unfortunate herd that drowned in the waters of the Caniapiscau, which solicited the immediate rejoinder of calling the self-styled moderates the "kangaroos" – jumpy creatures that carry the thing they hold most dear hidden in an abdominal pouch.

But it wasn't all that funny, quite the contrary, in particular for a certain individual who shortly before this had felt it wise, or more precisely, inevitable, to approve some revisionist-type statements that were bound to set off a debate. Now that it had begun in earnest, it was quickly and dangerously turning sour. In the background, among the swarm of sub-groups that constitute the "powers that be" in the PQ, one could make out, as always, a great variety of calculations. The shallowest sprang chiefly from acute pre-electoral insecurity. Others came from what are called "career ambitions," which by this time were quietly developing, with the help of certain go-betweens, into hearty appetites for succession.

That's perfectly legitimate. Many times during our sixteen years of joint political action I had said and repeated to colleagues of both sexes that since they were almost all younger, the time would come when they would have to take the place of one who "by accident" (as for every other detour in my existence) held the role I filled now. And many times I had taken the same opportunity to stress that in the meantime nothing would stand an eventual candidate in better stead than a number of concrete realizations yielding conclusive results, in the form of projects that might carry the name of the person who inspired and executed them. But people of that stamp, and there are some, generally give themselves so long and unstintingly to the task that when the time comes to enter the contest, they aren't ready; there are others, of course, who have scarcely thought of anything else for years.

Anyway, our own autumn hurricanes, storms that had been brewing longer and deeper than I had foreseen, finally fell upon us with destructive force and even risked to uproot us irremediably.

We at least had to try to patch up what was still salvageable. But we had reached the point – not exactly a precedent in the party – where major surgery was necessary.

Voices from every corner had been amply heard. Now it was my turn. "Too late," cried certain voices from the peanut gallery, "too late as usual." It might have been preferable to kill the debate in the egg, but I was instinctively aware, I think, that it was no longer possible to avoid that debate – not for someone who had shouldered close to a quarter of a century of active political life and the inevitable wear and tear of almost nine years of government, and not with the growing impatience in the wings, aggravated by the general feeling of incertitude experienced by so many others.

Having waited until I was almost summoned to act, I at last decided, on November 19, to throw into the balance however much diminished weight a "founding father" of the party could still muster. But I wanted to be sure at least that my stand was perfectly clear and precise:

> First off, it is quite evident that we must eliminate from our program, and as much as possible from our party strategies, the one thing that has ceaselessly insinuated itself these last few years, that is to say the thing that, from convention to convention, has ended up by becoming a persistent element of ambiguity in elections that take on a so-called referendum character. . . .
>
> In my humble opinion we must most certainly resign ourselves, at least for the next elections, to the fact that sovereignty shall not, in whole, or in parts more or less disguised, be an issue. . . . [Although it should, of course,] be kept in mind and in force as the ultimate insurance policy, one which our people will never abandon.
>
> [It was therefore important to maintain our faith in this option,] the option which, each in turn, every people worthy of the name have in the past, do in the present, or will whatever the multitude of metamorphoses the future holds in store, eventually experience. . . .
>
> As this evolution progresses, what form will our nation-state take, this state we believed so close and so totally indispensable when we drew up our plans for it in the sixties? I don't know any better than anyone else.
>
> But I remain convinced, as much if not more than ever, that from now on we are progressing more and more rapidly, and in a thousand ways we had never anticipated, toward a constantly expanding

"sovereignty" for the men and women of Quebec . . . for our creative people and for national enterprises.

Before the end of that same week a circular letter went out announcing to party members yet another special convention, for January, 1985. In hopes of rallying a certain number of those who hadn't lost a moment before rejecting my declaration, I now wrote:

> I can certainly understand those who would like to see sovereignty as the main issue of the next election. No one is more anxious to see that goal realized than I am.
> But between our desire to achieve that end and its fulfilment stand the people of Quebec, and they alone will decide. . . .

Now I am getting dangerously close to those Memoirs with a capital M that plead their cause after the fact. To sum up, what I sensed, rightly or wrongly, and God knows tardily, was that the majority of our people no longer had the exclusive "taste for Quebec" that we had worked so hard, and not unsuccessfully, to spread. After Trudeau's departure, and above all after the spectacular Conservative victory, one could sense people's minds tending once again to favour the rebirth of that legendary phoenix, the "last chance" for federalism. What could one do? Anything but swim against the current, anything but take a last ditch, do-or-die stand. . . .

Unless, of course, one was ready to give up power immediately and forgo the least chance of getting it back again. Were we ready to become the micro-opposition once again, or to be swept from the Assembly completely and be reduced to the status of "movement" as in the early days? It was certainly an excellent opportunity to start from scratch all over again! But I never could believe in the merits of suicide, in public life or in any other; nor that it is ever a very good idea for a party that thinks it is still alive and kicking to "move further on up to the back," as we were told to do in the old streetcars. The vital strength of a party, its very *raison d'être*, is threatened in that case. The time had come, it seemed to me, not to forget our basic beliefs – far from it – but to imitate the long patience of the Jews who throughout the diaspora went on repeating as long as ever was necessary, "Next year Jerusalem . . ."

But that's enough for now, while waiting for the sequel which will tell us in its own way who was right and who was wrong, and has already wasted little time in showing us that, until further notice, these things don't have the importance they once had.

What does remain true is that the idea of independence must learn patience, must learn to endure until the day it stems not just from a movement, however widespread, but firmly from the whole people. Pierre Vadeboncoeur, who had warned us of this before the referendum, now stepped forward to repeat it in different terms. I have always found him to have a devilishly keen eye, for as soon as he judges a situation to be serious enough, he focuses on it a regard of frequently prophetic lucidity, prompted by a passionate and profound concern for Quebec. He wrote in mid-December:

> We must rebuild on the most realistic base possible. Otherwise we will be reduced to practising policies based on imagination and abstractions.
>
> For that matter, the fate of the independence movement itself, though rising from a single, central idea, depends on a broad base of national feeling on every level and on wide popular support. For a time it was an all-embracing movement, economic, social, popular, administrative, political, constitutional, artistic, public, private, even up to a point, revolutionary. This is no longer the case. Independence, for the time being, is a lightweight concept. It will come back again. Stronger. Perhaps. But only on condition that it can stay alive in the meantime. . . .
>
> We live as best we can. But staying alive is the bottom line. We may have to make enormous detours. There's no guarantee we'll get back to the main road. But that is relatively unimportant compared to the risk of a much greater peril. Yes, we must take the chance of losing our way, for if not, we run the risk of the much greater loss of becoming frozen like statues – venerable, absolute, lordly, but dead. Dead of hunger most likely. . . .

And so on. That is the essential thought of a great writer and a great Québécois who has his two feet planted square on the ground and his eyes wide open on the reality of a situation that dictated to him, too, the following conclusion:

> A popular consultation on the independence issue is radically impossible for the next election. *Indépendantisme* mustn't kill

independence. . . . It must not become an imaginary policy that would stifle all real policies. Otherwise, realistically, what will become of us?

That's pretty well the question I was asking myself at the same time: what would become of us?

Striking different postures and taking different paths, but all in quick order, a good many people refused flatly to make the change. You could find them, and above all hear them, on every level of the party. Several MNAs quit the caucus, slamming the door as they went; others kept it half open while they took the time to think things over. And of course, as might be expected, it was in cabinet that the bloodletting was most conspicuous and painful. Here and there it did have its amusing moments: dear Denise Leblanc-Bantey, for example, turning up in my office with a letter of resignation complete except for the last page . . . the one with the signature. In the end the losses didn't exceed the calculations of the master-minds: half a dozen, more or less. This was small consolation, really, when among them we had to absorb the departures of Camille Laurin and Jacques Parizeau, indefectible old campaigners through storm and tide – and a good share of divergent opinions from time to time – although this time the break was definitive.

Once again, quickly, before the dust settled, we would have to plug these gaping holes, before the Christmas break. We could hardly wait for words of wisdom on the present mess – one could smell them in the wind already in preparation. There was no question, in the circumstances, of spending too many nights sleeping on the problem. Something had to be done; a new cabinet had to be formed immediately. For the sake of future historians I have found the hieroglyphs of the nearly final draft of what to all intents and purposes was to be my last big cabinet shuffle.

Then Dr. Lazure came back from a trip and immediately left again, for good. . . . And Robert Dean, a union militant lost in the accounting forest of the Ministry of Revenue (the place where those who are destined to be "moved up," no one knows exactly where, are often exiled), took on a new job in Manpower and Planning, thus realizing *in extremis* his dream of a socio-economic aposto-late. So two new ministers joined us, Elie Fallu to replace Denis Lazure, and Maurice Martel in Robert Dean's place as Minister of Revenue. Nor should we forget that remarkable non-elected mem-

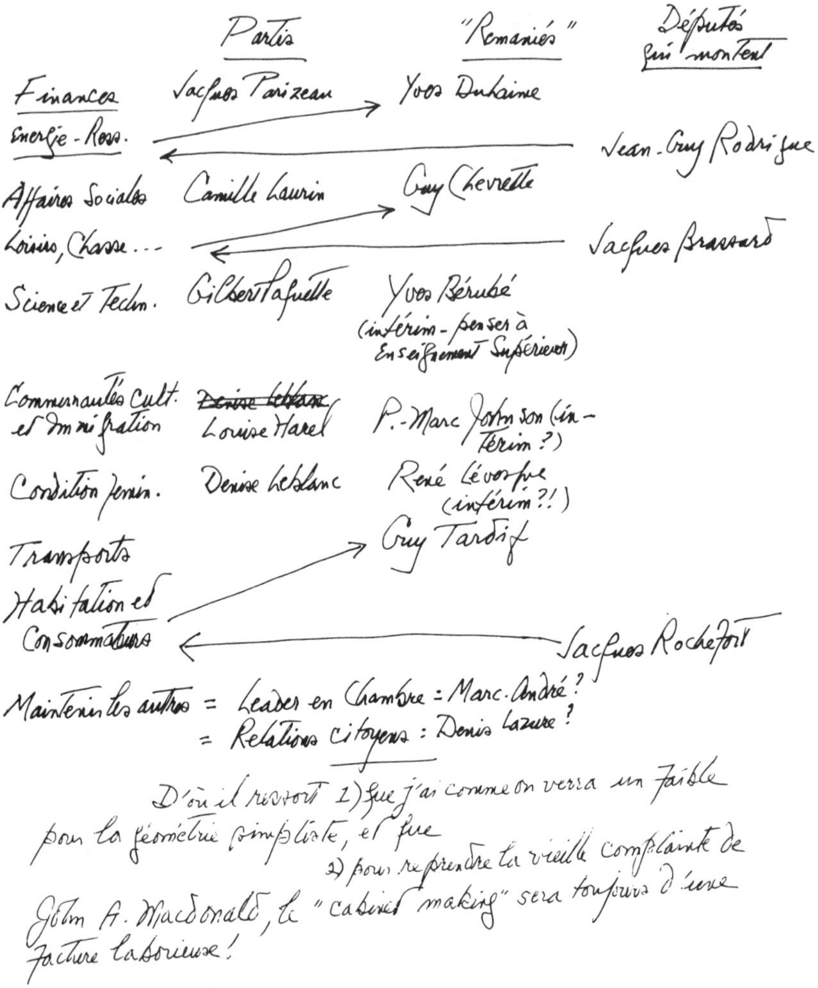

Handwritten chart:

Partis — "Remaniés" — Députés qui montent

Finances — Jacques Parizeau → Yves Duhaime
Énergie-Ress. ← ————————————— Jean-Guy Rodrigue

Affaires Sociales — Camille Laurin → Guy Chevrette
Loisirs, Chasse... ← ————————————— Jacques Brassard

Science et Techn. — Gilbert Paquette — Yves Bérubé (intérim - penser à Enseignement Supérieur)

Communautés Cult. et Immigration — ~~Denise Leblanc~~ Louise Harel — P.-Marc Johnson (intérim ?)

Condition Fémin. — Denise Leblanc — René Lévesque (intérim ?!)

Transports → Guy Tardif
Habitation et
Consommation ← ————————————— Jacques Rochefort

Maintenir les autres = Leader en Chambre : Marc-André ?
= Relations citoyens : Denis Lazure ?

D'où il ressort 1) que j'ai comme on verra un faible pour la géométrie simpliste, et que 2) pour reprendre la vieille complainte de John A. Macdonald, le "cabinet making" sera toujours d'une facture laborieuse!

ber, Madame Francine Lalonde, who rapidly showed her stuff both in Status of Women and in the by-election.

All of this shuffling, if I am not mistaken, left us with a cabinet of twenty-eight, that is, one less than the full capacity of the big table, thus leaving us plenty of room to manoeuvre! Seriously though, I was not at all displeased with the result. There were ministers anxious to try their wings – would they have time enough? – and a few veterans still young and perfectly capable of accepting a new challenge, as we were soon to demonstrate to anyone who had eyes to see.

I also think the cabinet was better structured, particularly on the side of Education. We finally decided to take the risk we had often planned, combining under one ministry all the vested interests in this domain that is the most important in any civilized society because it is the most fundamental. We grafted onto it the peak sector of Science and Technology in order to open the dusty edifice to the winds of change that were sweeping the world. Yves Bérubé was ready to do double duty at this task until the end, though unfortunately he also confirmed that he would not be a candidate in the next election.

Thus, as 1984 shaded into 1985 we had managed to put together and keep afloat a government that, by God, was a lot better than good enough, at least in appearance. The truth, though, was that the shocks of the past months had left cracks that nothing and no one could repair. Instead of standing together, the cabinet was little more than a heterogeneous collection of individuals. Only the fervour of some newcomers eager for the fray and especially the fierce loyalty of a small platoon of the old guard kept the whole thing from blowing apart. But what veiled looks, what mental reservations, what slips showing below our skirts every time, directly or indirectly, the question of the leadership came up in discussion. And what silences!

It had, indeed, become one of the hottest topics of the day.

3. The Great Fatigue of Mr. Lévesque

SO READ THE TITLE of a heartfelt editorial published on December 19, 1984. First one journalist, then another, found I looked exhausted. Immediately, the whole swarm of them started to buzz on this theme, gathering evidence through simple repetition. They got to examining my least words, trying to sniff out some blunder or other which, as everyone knows, is the sure sign of burnout. A little more of the same and I'd have begun to believe I was at death's door.

Tired? You bet! But more properly speaking, I was exasperated and feeling a desperate need of a change of air, so about New Year's I left, *en famille* with my sister and her husband, Philippe Amyot, both old hands at the tropics, for Barbados, which we would be seeing for the first time. We were located in a spot in the extreme south of the island, at the border between the Atlantic and the Caribbean. Before us the ocean roared in toward the beach in highly respectable waves; barely two hundred metres to the right, down a rocky pathway, was another fine sand beach on which nothing more violent was breaking than the tiniest whispers of Caribbean ripples. The water was warm, incredibly transparent. The burning sun was attenuated by the lightest of breezes bringing a few drops of rain every afternoon, always at the same time and barely formed before they had evaporated.

It was a true paradise. But how backward! There were only a handful of hotels and one or two little chain stores at Bridgetown, the capital, which was like an abandoned city. We met flocks of skinny goats on all the roads, but their milk, apparently, is never used. The population is almost exclusively black or strikingly mixed-blood, a pleasant, smiling people who seemed, wherever we met them – in taxi, restaurant, or store – to have remained under the yoke of the old colonial bosses who even after so many years of independence have hardly released their hold. But things are changing bit by bit: during our stay this little country, whose only riches are the sun and the sea, finally created a Ministry of Tourism . . . just like Quebec!

Though I had left for two weeks, I came back at the end of one. The reason was simple. The media virus had not spared my family and my poor state of health had them so worried that it was impossible to talk about it without having our conversation take a dramatic turn. Our holiday was becoming a forced rest cure rather than a vacation. The first evening back in Quebec I went to my office and there, while going through some dossiers, I had an experience the memory of which still today fills me with the sense of something bitterly unreal. I won't go into detail, but it was pure Molière with some Kafka on the side. To make a long story short, I was soon joined there by three persons who began to belabour me with friendly reproaches. The word "tired, tired, tired" kept coming back like a leitmotif. I finally exploded. It was too much.

And that's how I was hauled off to the hospital, an institution I hadn't set foot in since a bout of pleurisy when I was twelve, not counting a brief stay in a Belgian hospital for an almost un-nameable malady at the end of the war in 1945. As for medical examinations, my last one dated from 1951 at the time of the Korean War. How can I explain such an aversion? I really don't know, except that I had never forgotten that my father, who died very young, would no doubt have lived much longer if he hadn't gone under the knives of a couple of eminent sawbones in the thirties. So I have always felt that the less you fall into the clutches of the medical profession, the better your chances are of remaining healthy. Rightly or wrongly, and with all due respect, that's how I saw things.

On that January night in 1985, however, it didn't take me long to see that I wouldn't be able to resist any longer. During the next twenty-four hours, while a couple of sleuths from the press disguised as hospital employees kept watch to see if I'd be coming out on a stretcher or in a coffin, I had the opportunity to savour hospital care to the full, complete with auscultations, blood tests, and a trip through the scanner. "Better not forget anything while you're at it," I told them.

The upshot of all this was that before regaining my liberty (as discreetly as I had lost it), I learned with relief that as far as health was concerned I was in the top ten per cent of my age group. It's hardly necessary to add that this news didn't make the headlines. It was promptly smothered, like most other good news, and the caricatures and cruel editorials went on blithely running down the old crock I was taken to be. Once you get something started . . . . There was no turning them off, even if they'd known that appended to my clean bill of health was a note – obviously unpublishable in this non-smoking age – "lungs like a baby!" But since even medicine can make mistakes, I'm touching wood just the same.

As proud as if I'd been the object of some miraculous cure and delighted to thumb my nose at the doom-and-gloom prophets of Barbados, I was able to participate in the mid-January convention, which was quiet and uneventful, though one would have to admit there were a good many empty seats. It's a thing about political parties, ours at any rate, that after the big scene comes a sort of morning after the night before.

So we took the road south again and at last I was free simply to relax like anyone else. Deep inside, however, hadn't something changed? Hadn't the incredible avalanche of hard knocks I had taken caused a secret crack in my resolve? That, at least, was the observation made by one of my closest and most perceptive colleagues several months later when she said that from that time on I began to show signs of a certain detachment.

Until the end of the spring session, however, it was the same old rat race. On many specific points – the reconstruction of the Domtar plant at Windsor, artificial respiration for Pétromont, and this or that development agreement – the PQ's famous "brave risk" of attempting a rapprochement with the feds in the post-Trudeau period was paying dividends. The federal-provincial climate was becoming tolerable. We had taken on the laborious task of drawing up a text aimed at reopening constitutional negotiations. It was ready, as we had promised, well before Easter. But Brian Mulroney, who had so devoutly wished a settlement "with honour and enthusiasm," now turned out to be in much less of a hurry. Doubtless he still goes on talking about it from time to time, but it's just talk. He never does get the cup close to his lips when a dossier seems the least bit touchy. The constitutional imbroglio, like the question of transfer payments that is basically every bit as unspeakable, is a pretty thorny issue that essentially concerns only Quebec, which means, with the present federal regime, that it will be put off till the cows come home.

Regarding the parliamentary session, I have the deepest respect for the men and women who are sometimes called "simple" MNAs, especially for those on the government benches. For them the House is a frustrating place. They are there to swell the ranks and to vote and have precious few chances to shine. Big debates that really attract public attention are extremely rare, and when they do come, the ministers carve out the greatest portion of the performance for themselves. Even question period, that daily corrida, is mainly sport for the picadors of the opposition. What's left for the back-bencher, then, is his riding, the one place he can still feel he's somebody as long as he takes the trouble to keep abreast of his dossiers and in touch with the voters. At every election there are surprising victories won by obscure candidates who are never noticed in the Assembly but who have known how to hold their electors.

It's not that passing laws is unimportant. On the contrary, I can think of several bills whose effects have been eminently useful, although they are ordinarily enacted long after a need for them has been recognized. But that makes little difference as long as they finally get passed. It's not in parliament that the bulk of the work is done.

Bill 37, which we struggled with right up to the end of the session, is a case in point. In the public sector, unions have long since ceased to be anything but a way to incorporate the "always-more" principle, cashing in on both North American and European models but without assuming any of their constraints. The 1981-82 crisis had dramatized the ingrown abuses of this system, and the 1985-86 round of negotiations was scheduled to provide, at last, an occasion to put a halt to them. But how many different versions of the text, how much wrangling among ourselves, and how much sterile palaver with our "partners" had to be gone through before we could bring the project before the Assembly and have a vote on it! More often than should be the case, such efforts may even lead to poorly formulated laws, and this gives the members a chance to let off steam: "We told you so!" But it wasn't the case this time; all that was left to do was to vote.

Over the past few years we had undertaken reforms intended, among other things, to "revalue" the role of members of parliament: revision of House rules, strengthening of parliamentary committees, and the like. The main result of all this, it seems to me, was to increase the workload of the most active members and make the bureaucratic machinery even more cumbersome.

Why wouldn't we take up the idea advanced formerly by Jean-

Jacques Bertrand and try a presidential system? Members of the Assembly would find in it a new sense of responsibility and an opportunity for individual initiative that would be quite intoxicating – too much so at first, perhaps, but they would get used to it. As for the government, this would allow them to recruit ministers from outside parliament. Also, when one recognizes how political leadership has become a question of personalities, surely universal suffrage to designate the person who is to fill the top post in the country would have nothing particularly revolutionary about it. Every system has its peculiar faults and virtues, as everyone knows, but for a small and solidly democratic society like our own, I really don't see the risks of such an experiment, while the advantages are as plain as day – including the fact that it would be yet another way of stressing our difference.

That thought passed furtively through my mind on St. Patrick's Day when the President of the United States did us the honour to hold his little "Irish summit" at Quebec City. Acid rain, though a serious concern, didn't steal the limelight, nor even Brian Mulroney climbing up on stage to sing "When Irish Eyes Are Smiling." Previous to that there had been the occasion when Reagan, prompted by his advisers, had spoken of the unprecedented phenomenon of the veritable invasion of American markets by a flood of competent young Québécois sparkling with "French flair." It was striking recognition from an unexpected quarter of that vital energy which, far beyond any simple economic upturn, had been gathering steam year after year, making our people ever more sure of themselves and ready to meet any competition. The figures were there to confirm it.

Even more impressive was that quiet assurance to be seen, for example, in the representatives of Hydro-Québec in New York, or of the Montreal Stock Exchange in Boston, dealing as equals with their counterparts from south of the border and even on occasion calling the tune. One poll in February, 1985, showed the dramatic surge in self-confidence and faith in the future. "In your opinion are things in Quebec going very well, quite well, or not so well?" the question ran. The result: a rise of 8 per cent for quite well and very well.

Even more revealing were the replies to an old question that had been put on the shelf for several years and that I had asked to have tested again:

"Which government, according to you, should have full or chief responsibility in the following domains?"

	Quebec	Ottawa	Both
Education	71%	14%	9%
Foreign Affairs	35%	39%	13%
Regional Development	69%	10%	9%
Manpower	42%	25%	19%
Agriculture	49%	28%	15%
Fisheries	45%	34%	14%
Port of Montreal	51%	28%	9%

Now what does this table add up to if not a kind of secret attachment to something one might call, for example, sovereignty-association? . . . a concept, incidentally, that continued to rally "very" and "quite" favourable reactions from more than 40 per cent of those questioned.

But when asked how they intended to vote, that was another story. Barely 30 per cent for us against 55 per cent for the Liberals, which shows that even the greatest upswing, psychological as well as economic, can be taken as though it happened entirely disconnected from us, as though we didn't exist, as soon as people begin to feel they've seen enough of you.

An excellent subject for reflection over the Easter holiday of 1985.

4. The Last Card

I N REALITY, my reflection on this topic was already done, sub-consciously. All that remained was to draw up a conclusion for myself, which I proceeded to do on some scraps of paper, lining up the pros and cons as usual, and scribbling in between, for the fun of it, a few of those speculations where you let last doubts flicker over things you know to be perfectly clear.

Health required to continue? No problem there according to the medicos.

Did I still have a taste for the task? That was already more complicated. Yes, but . . . . Yes, very certainly I'd like to run another campaign and recapture the lost ground. I still felt sure of that, and there was also a whole raft of projects I was eager to pursue, and more that would turn up en route. But . . .

But in my heart of hearts, if I tried to peer in there without self-deception, did I really believe it was possible? I was already perfectly aware that some people were persuaded another leader would have a better chance against the new-old Liberal chief and would be able to come up with a refurbished image. (Ah, the precious image!) I had to admit they weren't necessarily wrong, especially since the idea had already occurred to me long before as a card I might be able to play when the situation required it. But what really clinched the argument was the way things were happening, and they were going from bad to worse: the accumulation of carefully anonymous little complaints, letters or memos often well orches-trated, saying very nice things about me but at the same time sug-gesting in more or less covert fashion that it was time, *n'est-ce pas*, to start thinking of . . . Most of them granted me the privilege, of course, to choose the day, and even the season, but they insisted on reminding me that time was passing. The whole business left me feeling more and more nauseated, a sensation that disappeared completely as soon as I had taken my decision, which is the best proof it was the right one.

So I was going to hang up my skates. Why in the devil didn't I do it, or at least announce my intention of doing it, immediately? I am often asked that question. However, it seems to me the answer is self-evident if you put things back in context. It was mid-April. The session was about to reopen for two months. If a leadership race had been announced, it would obviously have emptied the benches on our side of the House. It was clear that in that case not only the candidates but also their supporters, ministers and MNAs alike, would be thinking of nothing so much as getting out on the hustings. The Assembly did not enjoy an exactly glowing reputation as it was. Would it be wise to offer the citizens of Quebec the spectacle of a half-empty House and a tottering government forced to comb the corridors to survive the least vote? Perhaps I'm exaggerating the danger, but that's the way I was thinking. So I decided to wait till the end of the session, that is, the beginning of summer.

I never would have believed they couldn't find a way to shorten the interminable three-month campaign they had invented on paper to designate my successor. A shorter stint would have left the man or woman chosen all the time necessary to get broken in, prepare the election campaign, and, profiting from the old proverb, "luck to the new runner in the race," he or she could have chosen to call an election immediately or wait until after Christmas. It's hardly necessary to say that, as I was soon to discover, my opinions weren't worth much from then on.

I should also say that this wasn't, or more precisely no longer was, my principal concern. The future belongs to nobody, whereas the present was knocking at the door with great insistence. First and foremost we had a budget to bring down. It would be the last one for this term of office and the first since 1976 not to carry the signature of Jacques Parizeau. One inevitably recalled his talents in this domain, talents that often approached high art. Just before leaving he had left us that monumental work on fiscal matters that will be used as a reference for years to come since it was the first new exploration of that jungle since the distant Carter Commission Report. They were big shoes for Yves Duhaime to fill at short notice, and the challenge seemed daunting. But he rose to it in a way that I can only describe as masterful. The new minister began by clearing an atmosphere that his predecessor preferred to keep charged with mystery and even a touch of the apocalypse. His nonchalant manner disguised canny common sense and a vitriolic sense of humour, and he quickly managed to incite the remarkable team of the Finance Department to come up with the main lines of a budget that was at once realistic and reformist. As might be expected, first commentaries on it bore exclusively on the eternally obsessive question, were taxes going up or down? The answer: both down a little and up rather a lot, mainly up in the first instance, but with a promise of relief in the near future to restore some equity that had been lost in a mess we had tolerated for too long. In short, it was a last budget that I was, and remain, quite proud of.

If I insist on this subject a little, though I'm only a layman, it's that I've been in the business long enough to know that nothing is more important than the budget. Nothing indicates more clearly the government's convictions and intentions . . . or the absence of same. The throne speech at the beginning of the session is scarcely more than a sketchy itinerary, inevitably incomplete, sometimes stuffed with illusions and, very luckily, as malleable as you please. The budget, on the other hand, is a finished product, a carefully documented picture of the economic and financial situation and of perspectives for the future. A well-made budget, as long as one knows how to read it, is the most exact annual photograph that you can possibly have of a society, with all its bread and butter plainly visible. In retrospect, I can't help but compare our Quebec performance with the way this essential operation is generally man-handled elsewhere, and not too far away either.

Okay. So much for the budget. What else was left to do?

In leafing through the little dog-eared notebook I used to carry around in those days I rediscover the jumble of details that agendas usually get bogged down in. On paper the week would begin in orderly fashion, but within a couple of hours I was back in the atmosphere of a firehall that's just been summoned to a five-alarm blaze: calls for help, unexpected visitors (naturally each more important than the last), bitching backbenchers caught in the toils of the "machine," the daily trick-question period, the perpetual going and coming between Quebec and Montreal (I won't miss those trips along Highway 20), the all-too-rare touch-downs in my own riding, and then, no sooner damped down than breaking out again, those joyous, continual guerilla wars, over matters of moment or trifles, between ministries whose jurisdictions overlap. Then there would be those projects I had my heart set on but which would forever be slipping through my fingers just when they seemed to be on the point of completion. One example is the Concert Hall for the Montreal Symphony. After the sod-turning ceremony signalled the imminent beginning of construction, how many hours of discussions, telephone calls, squabbles, and patchings-up expended by Mayor Drapeau and myself! And how much farther along is it today? Not much.

All that is small potatoes, however, compared to the internal wrangling that now flared up at its best. It was sometimes so stupid that despite my firm resolution not to, I came within an ace of throwing in the sponge. One day in particular we received a stupefying report on the progress registered in nominating conventions "authorized and carried forward" in six ridings, three of which were those of ministers. . . . "Difficulties encountered in moving forward in the regions Abitibi-Témicamingue, Bas-Saint-Laurent-Gaspésie, National Capital . . . etc., etc. . . ."

It was systematic obstruction, anticipating a grand total of twenty candidates by the end of June, while the Liberals, if my memory serves me, had already lined up a hundred.

Nor was it very encouraging "either for me or for whoever is eventually going to replace me," I told the next meeting of the caucus. With eight months to go at the outside until the next election, probably less, the situation was suicidal. Never since 1970 had we been in such a state of unreadiness, yet there wasn't much use shouting fire: there are none so deaf as those who will not hear. The most troublesome aspect of the whole business was that it was all deliberate, planned in the wings by people whose only aim was to force you-know-who to leave. By losing precious time they were ready to risk self-destruction, which is exactly what happened in certain cases. In short, while thinking they were preparing mine, they were digging their own graves! I almost told them so, but they wouldn't have believed me.

I must admit I was beginning to care less and less. Faced by this fine menagerie I could feel myself, after so many years, becoming an observer. So it was in a blissfully serene frame of mind that I was able to turn my attention to that indispensable pile of paper we were to lug with us to Paris, briefing us on the last official voyage to see our French cousins. This was to return Laurent Fabius's visit of the autumn before, which had been very flattering for us since it was his first trip as Prime Minister. It was also important to keep up the excellent habit we had established of holding annual meetings. There is no more effective way to maintain pressure on dossiers of mutual interest, even economic ones, for our French friends are among the hardest-nosed bargainers (very close to their sous and penny-pinching for us, too) that I know in this field.

Take automobile manufacturing, for instance. Renault sells most of its Canadian exports in Quebec, but it's in Ontario, thanks to the merger with American Motors, that the assembly lines are located. Okay, I would say, that's the bottom line, we admit it, but couldn't you make a little extra effort here instead of seeing your last jobs in Quebec go down the drain? Yes, no, maybe . . . even when we remind them that their threatening rival Hyundai, with its Pony and its Stellar, is seriously thinking of setting up production here.

But I shouldn't exaggerate the difficulties. Twenty-five years of frequent meetings have brought results, the most spectacular to date being the Pechiney aluminum plant, though one should not forget a growing number of more modest enterprises, not only theirs, over here, but also ours, that have learned – and it's no mean feat – to penetrate the market over there. That's what these short-hand notes serving to jog my memory refer to:

Sinorg and Ideonic (Maisonneuve Hospital – consider tenders – laws of market demand).
Cascades taking over box-factory in La Rochette in Savoie: 300 jobs.
International Cutting Tools: Montreal acquiring Senoca, Garenne-Colombes-Minicut.
Electromed with Merlin-Gérin: Technological transfer.
Oxychem Canada, branch of Liquid Air: Peroxide/Oxygen factory (Bécancour. $50 million, $9 million in interest-free loan).
Lyonnaise des Eaux, squabble with the Squaw! . . .

I, too, get lost in such briefing notes, but one can see coming together behind this gibberish a rough sketch of the economic co-operation between our two countries, without which all other achievements will remain condemned to a certain fragility. For them, as for us, this must be imperative at a time when French, even in France, is menaced by the tidal wave of imperial American culture: a Disneyland installed so quickly outside Paris while we are still taking up again, for the umpteenth time, like Penelope her weaving, the problematic question of the Francophonie. Outside Europe the talk is about a club on the model of the Commonwealth, which would inescapably be something of a house of cards except for

Quebec, if we can add a vital minimum of profitability to those old and noble family ties one continually rediscovers upon escaping Paris to visit "our" parts of the country.

This time, at the end of the trip, we were invited to visit the Prime Minister's riding in the northernmost part of Normandy. Watching the checkerboard of fields and woods as we sped along the autoroute, I recalled the tiny settlement of Hautot-Saint-Sulpice near Yvetot where I had gone on an earlier occasion looking for traces of the Pierre Lévesque who was the first of this name to sail for the New World toward the middle of the eighteenth century. It was a deception: not the shadow of a Lévesque left in the area . . . but what warmth, just as in Quebec, in the welcome of the family of farmers who asked us to stay for lunch. It was a copious affair, abundantly accompanied with wine, served up by mother and daughter, the latter very excited at just having learned that morning that she had passed her baccalaureate. The father showed us around the house, a lovely little manoir beautifully kept up, surely old enough to be classified as a *"monument historique."*

"No, not that," he replied, "it's not big enough. And besides, it barely goes back to the beginning of the sixteenth century!"

All those centuries! They're really more than we can imagine, but the accent is so familiar it draws us together. You feel at one and the same time very far away and very much at home.

A similar impression of familiarity and distance was left by the port and city of Grand Quevilly where, like any French politician worth his salt, the head of government is at the same time a modest municipal officer. In the memorial park, le Parc des Fusillés, stood those dismal stakes the maquis were tied to when they were executed in 1944-45, and on the wall were carved the names of the martyrs . . . Morin, Pelletier . . . . We knew nothing of their combat. So they are strangers then? As much as that?

Certainly they are no more strangers than those representatives of English Canada we were going to find ourselves meeting on our return from France at the annual reunion with premiers and governors from neighbouring states: Maine, Vermont, New Hampshire, Massachusetts, and Rhode Island on the one hand, and from this side of the border Newfoundland, Nova Scotia, Prince Edward Island, and New Brunswick. It was the latter's turn, in the person of the incredible Richard Hatfield, to play host – plenty of lobster, and just as good as the Gaspé variety we had used to impress our

Parisian friends, but what a business to get hold of a modest twenty-six ouncer on a Sunday, even in the tourist "metropolis" of St. Andrews. And what a price: $115 (tax included)! Let that be a warning to anyone going astray down that way on a weekend.

It takes more, obviously, to explain how it is one can feel so lost, and even sometimes an intruder, in the rest of this country that is supposed to be ours. Language has something to do with it, that's sure. But Americans don't understand us either, and it never occurs to us to hold that against them. But that's just it, you'd expect something more in *our* country from our so-called compatriots. That's one of the ways (there are others) that it rankles. I've been speaking in the plural because I'm sure I don't speak for myself alone. But why resent it so much, you'll say, when you were practically born bilingual? That's only paradoxical on the surface. When you recognize and so often have seen oozing between the lines the superiority complex of a deep-seated, majority-bred paternalism, that's when you feel especially strongly the urge to be at last one day *"maîtres chez nous."*

But that's another story, or at any rate another chapter. As for this one, scribbled down in a white heat without waiting for the cool head of prudence to intervene, there's nothing for it but to bring it to a close.

5. Lame Duck

THE REALLY FINAL ACT of my public tenure was quickly put down in black and white several hours after parliament adjourned. A few days before that I had been obliged to show myself a good loser once again (it was getting to be a habit) by welcoming to the House the Liberal winners of the latest by-elections, including the new-old party leader himself making his re-entry just in time for the holidays. The commentator who thought he could see in me at that moment "a Lévesque revivified by Robert Bourassa" might better have written "amused," if he had only known.

For that matter, a little extra time was gained for amusement, and the hungry pack of those who always want to know more was kept off the track a bit longer by delaying as late as possible, to the evening of June 20, these two quasi-telegraphic paragraphs that need no further commentary:

June 20, 1985
Mme. Nadia Assimopolous
Vice-President of the Parti Québécois

Dear Nadia,

You doubtless have been expecting, like many others, that sooner or later I would be giving up my post as president of the party. After due consideration I am sending you this letter which constitutes my resignation, effective immediately. It is now your task, if I am not mistaken, to inaugurate the procedures for my replacement, as laid out in the statutes.

I would be grateful if, on my behalf, you would transmit to the National Council the following simple message: Heartfelt thanks to you, and to all those men and women – they will know of whom I speak – who for so many years have never spared their persons or their pocketbooks in order to build, anchor, and maintain this eminently healthy and democractic project we have drawn up together for our people.

Amicalement,
René Lévesque

As for commentaries, you can be sure I got my fill of them just the same: was it possible to imagine a more indecent withdrawal, so belated there wasn't even time for gossip? And what about the hallowed responsibility to observe media deadlines? This crime of lèse-media did, however, have one advantage; it constituted a subject in itself and one that allowed them to do a "job" on me, to the point of making a juicy contrast between my impardonably inelegant exit and the "style" of a Trudeau emerging one February night from an immemorial snowstorm. But at least they deigned leave me – to the very end, in my case – the essential title of democrat.

All this was served up, as you might imagine, with the usual pieties. "It's amusing," wrote André Rufiange, "to see the crocodile tears. . . . You'd think you were in a funeral parlor with the dead man's enemies coming around to tell the widow what great admiration they'd always had for the dear departed."

From outside the country, and also from the real grassroots, came the words that really touched me. Those of Elliot Fieldman of the *Boston Globe*, for instance: "Nothing more typifies René Lévesque's political leadership than his unprecedented leaving. We are not accustomed generally to such a voluntary surrender of power, but especially not from Quebec. . . . No premier has ever departed while entitled to stay." Always that much to the good. And Michel Rocard, the French minister, did me the honour also to interpret my departure as "a responsible act."

Then also there came messages straight from the heart and without media hoopla. For example, among many others: "As far as politics is concerned, I also wish to assure you of my unswerving fidelity to the objective of definitively affirming this country of ours, Quebec. My feelings on this subject go back very far, back to the time [. . .] when we advocated *in 1964* 'the sovereignty of Quebec paired with an economic association with the rest of Canada' . . . I am filled with hope and enthusiasm to see that we seem to be progressing in the right direction in this regard." How much juster such a perception of things was than facile obituaries for our dreams and for our projects. We would see what we would see. The future lasts a long, long time. . . .

In the meantime, I was no longer leader of the party. But I would have to remain in the government until the succession had been determined. Instead of the five or six weeks I had naively imagined, this process stretched out over the whole summer. With the bureaucratic rigour they are famous for strapping themselves into, the "powers that be" had thus decreed. Nor did they neglect to regulate the candidates' public meetings in such a way as to render them colourless, odourless, and without savour.

In other parties, where things move just as slowly, the bulk of the work is done in discreet campaigning, and the excitement of placards and balloons is saved for the eleventh hour. No such slyness for the PQ. Our duty to be "transparent" forces us to put all our cards on the table. So we kept laying them out, interminably, right up to the end of September, until every shadow of interest had been dissipated, until even the party militants were asleep on their feet.

Does this mean we would have been better off to reject our new formula of a vote by plebiscite for choosing the party leader? I don't think so. On the contrary, many observers see in it the beginning of a solution to the intriguing in the wings and recruiting in taverns that transforms so many leadership campaigns into ridiculous and often repugnant sideshows. But everything depends on the manner in which things are done, and in this regard we missed the boat.

So it was as a lame duck, like an American president at the end of his mandate (if one can compare great and small), that I "did" my last three months. As for the campaign that was running its course during this time, I've nothing to add. Perceptions formulated long before about how things were shaping up were simply confirmed. The absence of any surprise developments undoubtedly contributed to the general boredom, but that wasn't anyone's fault in particular.

No surprises in cabinet either, that is, several colleagues spent more time working for the party than for the government. Once again, if we generally managed to muster more than the quorum of five for cabinet meetings, it was thanks above all to certain veterans, in particular to those who were also preparing to quit the arena, and to a few new ministers who found the challenge of the job more interesting than the peregrinations of the leadership candidates. Somehow or other the principal dossiers seemed to progress a little, even during the summer period when productivity is never at its best. And with a couple of extra engagements I had to fulfil outside the country, time didn't hang heavy on my hands.

First I had to go to Halifax for the Premiers' Conference. It's an occasion for plenty of public relations, but it can also give rise to some very instructive sessions. One in particular, on free trade, a subject we were discussing together for the first time, became so heated we forgot to break for lunch. Based on several different assessments of the markets involved, we came up with a view of Canadian regionalism in a nutshell, stated with a brute frankness that was a lot more stimulating than all those maybe-yes, maybe-no attitudes that have been multiplying ever since. Put simply, our talks lined western free-traders up against Ontario protectionists, with Quebec somewhere in the middle, more open than one camp but more prudent than the other, for our economy still had some old "soft" sectors that would have to be given a last chance to adapt or be given a respectable burial. On the other hand, the future, especially the future of development in this country, is going to depend more and more on our ability to meet the competition, wherever it raises its head. For a people whose little home market absorbs barely half its production, the rule is to sell and export or die on the vine. What we need is skates good enough so we can get out on the rink and learn to play with the Gretzkys of world trade.

The discussion was getting so hot that to patch up differences it was quickly decided to perform a ceremony designed to ensure friendship – the presentation of little gifts traditionally offered to those who are leaving. Peter Lougheed was also on the point of stepping down. This Albertan, by far the most remarkable man on the Prairies in his time, is so passionately concerned about sovereignty in his own way that, even though opposing us, he can understand our position. We were offered two porcelain statuettes. His (prophetically?) represented a judge majestically cloaked in the ermine of some superior tribunal. Mine, on the other hand, evoked the past: at the feet of an old fisherman sits a small child whom you might take for a Gaspésian.

Then, *a mari usque ad mare*, from Halifax to Boise, little capital of the little state of Idaho, famous for its potatoes (only the baked variety) and its extravagant Mormon temple. Unfortunately, the place is less well known for those numerous traces left on the map that recall an America that might one day have been French. Boise, still pronounced with an acute accent, Laramie, Coeur d'Alène . . . .

We were guests at the annual Governors' Conference, a meeting which, it seemed to us, only the lightweight states took the trouble to attend. For New York, California, and most of the other mastodon-states, it's the minor leagues. But for us the reunion was interesting particularly because we once more came up against the very subject we had been exploring: trade and world markets, but this time seen through concerned and angry eyes. Here we discovered the great temptation of economic retreat, in some cases as much as a new isolationism, that was already sweeping the States. If we come to realize that to balance their books our neighbours only need to export 5 per cent of their production, this attitude becomes understandable. What works below the 49th parallel, however, is error above it. Just the same, it's disturbing to see the invincible ignorance that clouds some American minds. That's the way it was at the time of the Middle Empire when anything that was not Chinese deserved nothing better than disdain, and doubtless hostility when business was not so good.

At last September came, and, with it, final private meetings with Pauline Marois and Jean Garon, who were determined to go on, if possible. And I had similar meetings with others, too, who were asking themselves questions in this regard I wouldn't have trusted myself to answer.

Trying to counter the ingrained paralysis of the way we choose riding candidates, until the very last minute we tried to encourage first-class candidates, particularly among women. All things being equal, don't women show more boldness and determination than men? I believe so. On top of that, the time seemed ripe for a thrust in that direction. Lise Payette had been of that persuasion since springtime, writing, with a touch of exaggeration: "When a party is going down the drain, that's the time to invest in it . . . ." Without going quite that far, I must admit that at the time the horizon was rather gloomy. If I remember well, our monthly poll set the Liberal advance at a good fifteen points, if not more.

But time has a way of mending things . . . it's happened before now. So in provision for at least a partial session that might see the government through the autumn, we had prepared a short list of projects:

A Bill on municipal elections: simplification, etc.
A Bill on popular consultations (referendums): procedural improvements; introduction of private and parliamentary initiatives.
A Bill on voting practices: introduction of proportionality.
A Bill protecting the rights of . . . non-smokers!
A Bill on voluntary work-sharing programs.

The so-called "Return Bill" aimed at encouraging Franco-North-
Americans to emigrate to Quebec (a "Judeo-Québécois" invention
of the tireless and ingenious Guy Tardif).
A Bill on wildlife habitats.
A Bill (yet again) to simplify goverment house rules. . . .

In most cases, as a preliminary note prudently suggested, the list
was only intended "to signal the intentions of the government . . .
given the political conjuncture."

Indeed, things were happening so fast I barely had time to
attend the two extraordinary evenings that were organized for me.
One was given by the party where the little scamp from the film *Le
Matou*, Monsieur Émile, only had to stand up to steal the show, and
where, as a parting gift, I was offered a really excessive credit line,
enough for two or three trips around the world: "So you're really
that anxious to see me go!" The other brought together friends
from everywhere, so numerous that I'd never have believed it possible, or wished it so. "After the mean trick of the plane ticket," wrote
a journalist from *Le Devoir*, "one might have expected even worse.
What else could they contrive for René Lévesque?" There was a
meal followed by the usual send-ups. They were naturally quite
uneven and the *Devoir* journalist, that arbiter of elegance, found
them equally insipid. Her article was even headed up by Rutebeuf's
famous melancholy words, "And what has become of my friends?"
and she pretended not to have noticed that I had had the nerve to
edit the old master to read "fairweather friends."

Situation normal, *n'est-ce pas?* It was time to go. Mean trick or
not, the too-generous gift of the party militants made it possible,
for once, to leave without having to calculate the costs.

But first, and last, the handing over of the reins of power, a
fancy phrase to designate a simple half hour that was strictly business.
For the occasion a final briefing document was completed on September 29, the very day that a first ballot was to be enough to
indicate the winner clearly. Prudently, the document was simply
addressed to "The new Premier."

I've kept my copy. I hope Mr. Pierre-Marc Johnson has his, too,
for it was a precise résumé of the situation. It was even a pleasure to
read because for once the technocrats' jargon was reduced to a
strict minimum.

All things evolve, of course, and, like life itself, every problem in the end finds its solution: either by changing direction, and sometimes even appearance, or by disappearing from circulation. But time is rarely in a hurry. . . . As for the exercise of power, its limits are so quickly reached that often the only thing left to exercise is patience. And humility.

6. I Met a Little Power As I Went My Way

IF FÉLIX LECLERC, Quebec's premier chansonnier, had ever had a scrape with politics, he might have thought up something like that. Far be it from me, I hasten to say, to make fun of power or to give the impression that the grapes have now turned sour. There are other subjects I've touched on that I will return to later on, as I continue this tour of my garden. Power, however, is one that I have just left with a final farewell, so I feel free to talk about it one last time. For the first time, too, in fact.

To all appearances I have known it well, yet its true face, the quintessence of it, still eludes me. What is it exactly, this Power so easily written with a capital P? Philosophical profundities not being my cup of tea (in fact, they leave me cold), I prefer to reply in a simple, descriptive way. Here's approximately how I saw and lived my modest experience of power.

The first thing that strikes one is the apparatus of it all: the office that you imagine as isolated as an ivory tower; the bodyguards front and back; that aura that is supposed to float around power and that you can actually see in most people's eyes, except children's. Of course, what I'm talking about here is the post of Premier that I filled or was subjected to from 1976 to 1985.

To begin with, the head of government automatically becomes a captive, the prime captive, first in the cabinet, where he must learn to listen, to listen *ad nauseam* to the pros and cons while trying to spy the solution that is most often well hidden in a haystack of verbiage. If things continue to go round in circles the topic is "postponed to the next session, or the one after," just as it is in the House, except for emergencies, for it's never a question of taking a vote. You can see the cliques forming a mile away: "Tit for tat, you back me here, and I'll prop you up there!"

The Premier is a tireless listener, then, the only one who can't permit himself to go to the toilet as long as the agenda hasn't been exhausted. He is the only one, too, nearly always, to have taken the trouble to read and annotate every last dossier before the meeting. Grinding his teeth, he is obliged to sit there and watch others get up, wander around, hold huddles in corners, leave to make or take telephone calls, never listening to what the others are saying and only really coming back to the issue to defend *their* item of business . . . and taking offence when they notice that someone has ignored them in turn. It is not always so easy, this teamwork. What I've just described is fortunately not the general rule, but there are always the incorrigible few.

Then there's obligatory attendance at the Assembly at least once a day, with few exceptions, and frequently I would have to assume the role of conciliator to stop someone from stepping on someone else's toes. Every honourable minister that ever was is exposed to the risk of becoming a prima donna, and the ones who successfully resist this temptation are rarer than you think.

Finally, there's all the detail to be dealt with, as has been suggested in the preceding pages. In short, the exalted role of leader devours and empties whoever fills it while binding him more tightly than anyone else. The initiatives that a "simple" minister can permit himself, though more limited in appearance, all benefit from a degree of free will, for if need be he can take a chance. In the days when I was one of the juniors in the Lesage government, alone with my secretary-chauffeur, waiting my turn to speak, the scope to manoeuvre seems to have been much greater.

And then this poor thing, political power, is so partial, so inevitably truncated, so squeezed from every side, not simply because in the first place it is provincial, which is to say incomplete and extremely dependent, but because of its own dilution among a sea of middlemen who proliferate on every level. In other words, there are fourth and fifth levels of power and, why not, a twelfth, too. In the States they count some twenty different power blocs and pressure groups. *Newsweek* gives an annual breakdown of their relative weight. After the White House, which naturally remains at the top, the gang elbowing each other on the staircase is awesome: the Senate, Wall Street, Chicago, agriculture, General Motors ("What's good for GM is good for the country!") and other giants of industry, the media, the Pacific Coast, petroleum interests, even intellectual circles. On a much reduced scale and with no illusions of grandeur (if that's any comfort to our neighbours), it's the same business here.

So why this taste – still quite widespread though visibly diminishing – for an occupation that is less close to that of conquering admiral than to galley slave? Basically because, when all is said and done, it's a post that must be filled even if it no longer has the grandeur and prestige it once had. Everywhere, continually, there are decisions to make, or to see that others make, decisions that without exception are, or should be, useful to others and that sometimes meet an extreme need. It's a devouring job, as I said, but there's another side to the coin. I can't imagine any task that can give an equal feeling of being required to use one's strength and one's ideas to the maximum, to work regularly beyond full capacity to obtain, after terrific effort, that one step forward that you really believe in because you really believe it means progress.

At the same time there's the satisfaction of duty accomplished and the certainty that you have means completely disengaged from personal interest to help others. It is an opportunity to meet undeniable and urgent needs and to contribute to solid and tangible results, like a building or a bridge – those are the real rewards. And at the same time (at the risk of looking cross-eyed) the one in power must never lose from view a few grand objectives there on the horizon that must be sought, or at least never forgotten.

As a result of all this I positively cannot understand people who think of power without considering in the slightest the use they will make of it. Power for power for power, like a rose is a rose is a rose . . . . Yet power is not an end but a beginning, the beginning of a chance to move forward, not alone but with others, and to bring as many forward with you as you can.

That, at any rate, is the way I welcomed power when it presented itself to me on two occasions and at two different degrees of intensity. It sought me out when I wasn't expecting it. It wouldn't have been proper to turn my nose up at it then, but we were never wedded till death did us part, either, which is why the two of us, Power and I, could envisage an amicable separation.

I don't regret having had this encounter with power, any more than I regret seeing it move away. I simply remain quite pleased, proud even, that we were able to travel part of the road together – when you look at it, in fact, a good part of the road. Thinking of other Québécois who have been in touch with it, guys from Quebec City, La Mauricie, Les Bois-Franc, or now from Montreal again (Saint-Laurent), I tell myself that Power has had worse companions than the little guy from Gaspésie.

II

ONCE UPON A TIME...

"Ah! but the world is large in the light of lamps!
But in memory's eyes, Ah! but the world is small!"
BAUDELAIRE

7. A Wild Childhood

THE YEAR 1922 was an exceptional one – for the Gaspésie and for me. That was the year the diocese was founded. Having missed out on having a great seaport and an incomparable transportation network, which it might have had if Halifax and the Maritimes hadn't been there first, the Gaspésie had to settle for a modest place on the ecclesiastical map.

As for me, 1922 was the year I saw the light of day: a true Gaspésian, but born elsewhere. In fact, I had to go over to Campbellton, New Brunswick, to try my lungs out for the first time. It nearly proved to be my last, for I immediately caught a healthy case of jaundice whose only lasting after-effect was that half-breed tint that makes people ask if I've just come back from Florida. Officially, I was born on August 24th, but my mother was never too sure; nor am I. Maybe it was very late on the 23rd. Astrologers have often reproached me with this indecision.

According to my parents, I was a beautiful baby, though not as beautiful as a little brother who preceded me but didn't live. No matter how kindly they put the fact to me – when I reached the age to be told such things – this armed me with the valuable gift of modesty that has never deserted me.

This quality was strongly reinforced when, at about two and a half, I found myself shoved roughly to one side of the living room by a large woman carrying a bundle of blankets that let out vague whimpering sounds. It was my brother Fernand making his appearance in our lives, an event I had been expecting with a certain apprehension, and with good reason, as I had just discovered. I didn't hold it against him, but this memory stayed with me. It was my first.

I survived that, too, so well in fact that I rapidly became uncontrollable, which occasioned my second memory. I can still see myself, my left ankle imprisoned by a cord tied to the back-porch railing. This device prevented me from escaping anywhere very far, especially as far as the water's edge, which I could see from my window. By the same stroke it deprived me of a favourite pastime: stealing matches and lighting them. One fine summer afternoon when the hay was a superb incandescent gold, I managed to burn down the fence, and with a little luck the barn would have gone up in smoke, too.

As they used to say at home in New Carlisle, I was "a sad child," by which they meant difficult. So much so, and so often, that from that age on when I went beyond the limit, as I often did, I was sent to spend a couple of weeks with my grandparents at Rivière-du-Loup. I had nothing against that, far from it. My grandfather ran a general store whose specialty was those famous Hudson's Bay blankets, but I had my own special department, the penny-candy counter. Needless to say, when I was hired to help on certain stormy days, accounts quickly ran into the red. My grandmother was an impenitent old lady. I adored her unreservedly, most especially because she was a great card player and let me sit in on the game any time one of her cronies didn't show up. I had the right to a dollar in risk capital. If I lost, the debt was wiped out, but I was allowed to keep my winnings. Bridge and poker soon held no secrets for me.

As for the cord at the back steps, my parents finally got around to untying me, to entrust me, more or less, to the neighbour's kids. They were four Poiriers. Four boys, that is. The girls didn't count. There were Wilson, the oldest, then Bert, who was a bum in those days, then my gang, Gérard and Paul.

We never saw much of Wilson; he went to the seminary. He was the only one the family could afford to educate, and they put all their hopes in him. In 1939 he was one of the first to enlist in the RAF and in no time he had crashed into the Channel in his Spitfire. His father, a train conductor, turned white practically overnight, continued to age rapidly, and died not long after. Gérard, too, left for overseas, in 1941, but he came back a Squadron Leader in Bomber Command with decorations, mention in dispatches, and an English bride.

He was already a leader in those early days. He knew better than any of us how to set snares in the woods to the north of town up past the white house that belonged to the old notary. He had an instinct for sniffing out trails that were invisible to us, and next day, sure enough, there'd be a jack rabbit or two waiting for us, laid out all stiff in their wire necklaces. Officially – and I do mean officially – he was the only one who was allowed to handle the shotgun, and he was also the only one of us who could flush out partridge and bring them down. But what made us even more envious was that he alone knew how to roll a cigarette. Just big enough to risk asking for tobacco at the store, he would come out with a package of Ogden's fine cut and cigarette papers. Then, with those fingers of his that seemed so fat, in no time and with remarkable dexterity he would roll one for each of us. They inevitably made us feel so sick we forgot that we'd each paid our share. So he'd keep the rest.

From one season to the next we ran free between the forest and the sea. Galloping across the common fields and climbing up over the railway tracks, we would reach the dock and, on either side of it, the best beach in the township, which remains almost unknown even today. On the right the water was a sandy brown, that is, not too deep. Here, one after another, we learned to swim. The method was simple enough: we were thrown off the dock down to where Gérard and one of his pals took care of the lifesaving. We swallowed buckets but made it on our own just the same. Legs flailing like a dog's, thrashing and splashing, we finally grabbed the ladder. From that day on we were certified swimmers, soon to be called to the supreme test of diving off the other side into deep water, or even from the deck of one of the ships come to load our wood to take over to New Brunswick. These hijinks earned us the reputation, among the fishermen's kids, of being a bunch of happy morons. They thought of the sea as strictly a place for hard work and didn't have the slightest inclination to go back there for pleasure.

But the biggest thrill of all was to escape from our families and go over on foot as far as Paspébiac, where the bay closed down to a narrow neck and then opened out on a vast sandbar. As the tide came in the water would enter and heat up in the sun. When it withdrew a regular tropical sea would flow out, warmer and saltier than before. We would loll around here for hours drifting in the current that ran out to the open sea. And that was how I drowned. . . . Unable to reach shore, I swallowed the wrong way time and again and began to suffocate, as easy as that, while a magnificent kaleidoscope of brilliant colours flashed before my eyes. Then nothing. Drowning . . . what a spellbinder!

And coming out of it was even more irresistible, for who should be leaning over me but the goddess of the beach, a long-legged, flaming redhead who had saved me. She must have been about twelve and her name was Frances. I was her tongue-tied worshipper for many months after my day of drowning. Not daring and, for that matter, not able to imagine her in flesh and blood, I would drift off to sleep dreaming of her in the sound of the muffled rolling thunder of the waves breaking perpetually on the sand.

Like all good things, our life as "a bunch of savages," as we were innocently called in those days, came to an end. Eventually we were forced to traipse along to school and catechism.

As for the latter, all I can remember is that it pretty well made me lose my faith. It would be a marvellous morning in May or June, the warm sun beaming down, the birds singing cheerfully, and there, right in front of our noses, the groundhogs poking their heads up out of their holes by the bank of the stream, daring us to sneak closer. And there we would be, lined up against the wall of the church like so many penitents, repeating over and over, idiotically: "How many persons in God? There are three persons in God – the Father, the Son, and the Holy Spirit. Where is God? God is everywhere. . . . " I knew it all by heart, but we had to sit there without moving, going over it again and again. One time I suddenly felt a surge of revolt, threw my book down, got up, and left to see if I could steal any closer to the groundhogs. Monsieur le Curé saw me go but didn't say anything, undoubtedly unaware that he was witnessing the flight of a future parishioner, lost forever. And God, who sees everything, undoubtedly realized we had seen enough of each other.

That curé was a rather suspicious character. He had been duly praised for having invented, long before Their Excellencies the Bishops, the daily recital of the rosary on the radio. But this merit was thin enough, and it evaporated completely the day that he had the nerve to transform the church hall into a movie house to swell the parish coffers, especially since the first film (to which children were admitted) was *Jungle Princess* with Dorothy Lamour! There was hell to pay and his dangerous initiative came to a sudden stop, but not before I had a chance to admire Dorothy in a sarong cooing to some partner whose name has disappeared into the mists of time, "I belong to you, you belong to me, my looove . . . ." It was an obsessive little tune that I still hum on occasion.

The school, such as it was, was one of those one-room affairs, a miserable shack more than a kilometre from home. On certain winter days, with a blizzard whipping my face, I would walk all the way backwards. We would pile our scarfs and windbreakers around the red-hot stove in the middle of the room, and they would send up a cloud of vapour so thick the teacher could hardly see. Behind this screen sat the whole gang of us, jostling and joking and throwing paper airplanes, which made poor Miss Gorman jumpy and, by the end of the day, hopping mad.

Did we learn to count? A little. To write? Little enough. To speak? Yes, and in both languages at once. To read? It wasn't necessary, really. Electricity still hadn't entered our lives, but we had those beautiful oil lamps you can adjust by raising or lowering the wick, and it was by this soft light, sitting on my father's lap, that I learned my alphabet from a big red book published by Editions Mame. It contained generously illustrated stories by a certain La Fontaine, who, I discovered later, was a genius. So, one thing leading to another, I not only learned to read but developed an insatiable appetite for the printed word.

I didn't have to look far to satisfy my craving. Our house was bursting with books. My father was a young lawyer who, when the Spanish influenza came within a whisper of carrying him off, had to resign himself to a rural practice. As a student at the beginning of the century he was one of those young Liberals who thought Laurier was a god, and he had dreamed of leading an active political life. But since his health didn't permit him the rough and tumble of politics, he had ended up in this tiny county seat where for some years he was the assistant of an older colleague who, at least by local standards, was an important businessman who looked down on everyone from the heights of his ugly little château on the edge of town. He was an Irishman, Kelly by name, and I was threatened with his Christian name, John, because he had been asked to be my godfather. Only my mother's intervention saved me from the ignominy of being called "Ti-Jean" Lévesque for the rest of my days. Years later I was doubly glad to have escaped when my father, sick of shady dealings whose bad smells emanated from every drawer, brought the association to an end and opened his own office where he at last knew the respect and success he deserved. None of this, however, prevented the godfather from becoming "Sir John" and being named High Commissioner to Ireland, where he ended his life in an odour of sanctity.

Throughout this time, I was finishing off my ongoing meal of the library. Having begun with books sanctioned by the Catholic censor of the time, a certain Abbé Bethléem, I progressed to those on his index, for the family library contained both kinds, as well as the category between the two – "not for every eye."

Dear old friend Rostopchine, alias Comtesse de Ségur, you may be accused of crimes against childhood, but how you made me sympathize with *The Misfortunes of Sophie* and share the misadventures of good old Cadichon in his *Memories of a Donkey*! And you, immortal Jules Verne, whose Captain Nemo I accompanied on undersea adventures to the very heart of *The Mysterious Island*. And you, Abbé Moreux, who answered as best you could those existential questions, "Where do we come from? Where are we going?" It is undoubtedly thanks to you I caught the science-fiction bug so badly that I still remember my two first excursions to other worlds: *The Ring of Fire* by I can't remember whom, about a voyage to Saturn, and *The Giant Cat* by a famous writer whose name is on the tip of my tongue, who took us back in quest of fire and other fascinating rediscoveries (for we had experienced them all already!) to the time of the cavemen.

But these orthodox pleasures were quickly exhausted and I began feverishly to await my parents' all-too-infrequent absences so I could pay a quick visit to "hell" whenever I had a little time ahead of me. Quick, the key! Switch hiding places as they might, I always found it in a flash. Ah! those splendid prohibited books! I must admit I didn't understand much about them at that age, but is there anything like the pleasure of forbidden fruit? What dazzling satisfactions were promised in *The Flapper*, and what half-guessed voluptuousness with the demi-virgins of Marcel Prévost! My favourite book by this author, however, was *A Whiff of Cannon Shot*, which plunged the reader, if I remember well, into the bloody maelstrom of the Revolution and the Napoleonic wars. In those days I was more interested in adventures than adventuresses.

So what a memorable day it was when I first had the privilege of making the acquaintance of *The Three Musketeers*, and then found them again as fit as ever *Twenty Years After*, finally to see them in *Viscount de Bragelonne* slowly bowing under the weight of years, to disappear one by one, leaving me disconsolate. D'Artagnan, Athos, Porthos, Aramis: I have often returned to you, but never had the courage to accompany you again to the bitter end. And it's the same for all the characters I've become attached to: I refuse to leave them; I have a devil of a time getting into the last chapter.

To the orgy of life in the open air and the salt wind, then, cut with that horrible ritual of cod liver oil, was added this rage to read. Mine was an omnivorous madness that spurned nothing, not even the pulps, for example, those cheap-paper, ten-cent books that ran from *Nick Carter, Detective* and *Tarzan of the Apes* to future great writers like Raymond Chandler who used this sub-literature as a testing ground. My last resort was the veranda of the local MNA's house, for his daughter owned the whole set of Bécassine books, which I swallowed down without suspecting for an instant that they stunk to high heaven of Parisian paternalism. On the sly I inspected the rest of the house from top to bottom but found nothing else to satisfy my hunger. The family of this honourable member, who was on the way to becoming a cabinet minister, wasn't more curious than that. Obviously, things have changed a lot since then.

As for politics, we got vague rumours on the radio, but only during elections. The rest of the time we were too few and so far away. Yes, we did have the radio. We were not so isolated after all! But for a very long time it was "other people's" radio we listened to, first Charlottetown, and then, way off, WJZee, New York, coming to us across the water. Then one day my father ordered two huge poles, veritable trees, that were strung with wires to make us an antenna. To replace the original crystal set came an enormous Stromberg-Carlson receiver that took up one whole corner of the living room. From then on, picking up CKAC, "the pioneer French station of North America," we could take Fridolin's "Pleasure Train" and my brother and I could squabble over hockey (he was for Toronto, the traitor). This gave us a new feeling, the strange sensation that we were beginning to belong to something that might be Quebec. Or rather French Canada, until further notice.

It really was "once upon a time . . . ."

8. New Carlisle, P.Q.

"ANY FRRESH COD TODAY, Madame Lévesque, or some nice mackerrel?"

That roughness and the slight lilt in the voice is the Paspébiac accent. It belonged to the fisherman who came to peddle some of his catch to earn a little ready cash. All he would have got at the company dock, all anyone ever got, was a piece of paper, redeemable at the company store where these illiterates got taken, from father to son, for generations. We used to laugh at his thick accent and never thought for a second that there was anything admirable in the basic purity of his language. The man's name made us laugh, too: Antoine de la Rosbille. It was only later that I'd wonder what well-born ancestor from Angers or Brittany had provided the impressive patronym.

The shores of the Baie des Chaleurs share with many other lands' ends in the world a vocation for picking up the shipwrecked. When the Gaspé Peninsula first entered our history at the beginning of the French regime, it had already been a land crisscrossed for centuries by the Indians and also, in all probability, a place for occasional Viking landings. And those Portuguese names, what pirate ship did they arrive on? And that handful of black families, what distant plantation did they manage to escape from? As far as names from Jersey are concerned, on the other hand, there is no mystery there. These Robins, Lebretons, LeGallais, and Lebouthilliers were the people who took over business interests after the Conquest and redirected them to English markets.

But the main contribution to this patchwork settlement came from two groups of "boat people" strewn along the coast by two successive disruptions. First the Acadians. How had they been able to get away from the solicitous attention of those soldiers whose orders were to scatter them to the four winds? The Gulf is vast and its fogs are frequent. It's easy to get swallowed up in this pea soup. That's surely how a good many of the deported Acadians strayed to that cape that provides a shelter from the winds by the mouth of a river rich in fish. They called it Bonaventure and made it their new capital.

For me, it was mainly the capital of ice cream, the best in the country. Nearly every Sunday we would make the expedition, twenty miles there and back in the midst of a thick cloud of dust thrown up at the slightest acceleration.

"Faster, faster!" the passengers would cry.

"My word! What next?" my mother, the co-pilot, would reply. "We're already doing thirty. Be reasonable!"

And, ah! those cones that were the fruit of this weekly odyssey!

Afterwards, we would return home to Loyalist country, that is to say, to the land of the expulsers expulsed. Acadia had been ravaged and depopulated by order of His Britannic Majesty. Fair is fair, and shortly after this same Majesty was kicked out in turn by the Americans. This operation left behind some thousands of staunch supporters of the Crown, too committed to royalty to hang around much longer, or else physically incapable of breathing republican air. These diehards came north to shelter under the shadow of the monarchy in the Saint John River Valley in New Brunswick and in our Eastern Townships. But soon these places were full to overflowing. Where to put the rest of them?

This explains how, one day in 1784, a flotilla of three small brigs and four whaleboats not much bigger than lifeboats put to sea near Trois-Rivières with three hundred refugees aboard, men, women, and children. They had been graciously offered a chance to settle a stretch of coast uninhabited and anonymous at that time but which was soon to take the name of Carlisle, a fortified city in the old country on the border of Scotland. In this new home they could cultivate their nostalgia and perhaps perpetuate the clan.

As for roots, in their own way theirs were as resistant as ours. These ancient tribes of Beebes, Astles, and Chisholms, among others of Huguenot descent, had been steeled by countless forced displacements, from France to England, to Holland, to America. . . . And what about those whose ancestors had followed Cromwell on his campaign to "colonize" poor Ireland, which hasn't recovered yet? In short, they were a distinguished lot, knotty and tough.

As for nostalgia, you can guess that in no time it turned out to be not what it used to be. Leaving behind, or left behind by, the ex-Thirteen Colonies where their ungrateful kith and kin had just finished freeing themselves, here they were straight back under monarchical rule as true to itself as ever. And, to top it off, they were plunged in the midst of newly conquered and therefore brow-beaten natives who, to make matters worse yet, were of another "race" and thus incapable of understanding. What a life! You can imagine the ecstasy of some fighting cock of an ex-small-town boss from Vermont or New Hampshire learning that the seat of govern-ment was to be transferred (temporarily, thank heavens) from Gaspé to New Carlisle, complete with its courthouse and, "at the corner of the building, a whipping post." Around 1860 a government prospectus was even published citing New Carlisle (no kidding) as "an ideal spot whose climatic conditions compare favorably with those of New York, Edinburgh and London. . . ."

This was the town of less than a thousand souls where, involuntarily, I spent my first years. It thought of itself as the bellybutton of the world and was very, very WASP, the microcosm of a blissfully dominant minority. The whipping post had disappeared by the time I got there, but the courthouse was still there with its pint-sized prison under the rule of Sheriff G, who had come back from the 1914-18 war minus an arm but assured of job security. Caldwell's General Store stood at one end of the street and Legrand's at the other, with the Red and White Grocery in between considered rather suspect because its owner was also the preacher of some new turbulent sect, an American import, obviously. We certainly had enough Protestant churches and quasi-churches already: the United, the Baptist, the Presbyterian, the temptingly secretive Masonic Lodge with its second-storey windows (at the same level as the tree across the street, but we couldn't see anything), and, dominating this ecumenical jungle, the Anglican, the establishment church whose Pope or Popess lives at Buckingham Palace and whose local repre-sentative, the Reverend B, could keep an eye on the big yellow-and-white high school just next door.

In reality the school was not "big" at all but only a modest two-storey wooden structure. The same holds for the "enormous" this and the "huge" that strewn throughout the preceding pages. At an early age one is always so far down, looking up. For example, the "great" maple at the end of the yard was not so great at all. I used to climb it to show off to my brothers and sister and to drive my mother wild. "He's going to break his neck!" she'd prophesy, and I'd be as proud as Lucifer. But I've gone back to check it out since; it's a small northern tree somewhat on the stunted side. The same is true for our "immense" home, which isn't much more than a doll's house. And so on for all the rest.

The memory of that miserable maple reminds me of the admiration I felt at seven or eight at the sight of all those trees planted and so well cared for by the English in New Carlisle, creating an unbroken sea of green beneath which the village was practically invisible. To begin with, I never thought much about it, no more than I did about those "slash cuts" we would see at Bonaventure and elsewhere with not a tree left standing so all the building could be done on bare land, without the encumbrance of trees. But one day someone pointed out the difference to me, explaining that we Québécois didn't give a damn for our trees, whereas the English had brought with them from the old country via New England a respect for woods and flowers and a need to live surrounded by them. We've done some catching up since those long ago days, but when I revisit my home town or the beautifully shaded streets of New England villages, I can't help but think that we have a lot of replanting to do yet.

Another claim to fame was that New Carlisle was a railway centre of first importance . . . in Gaspé terms. With its marshalling yard and its repair shop, the local train, *"le p'tit train,"* was made up there. Never in a hurry, it would sneak around the cliffs on its narrow-gauge tracks, panting and puffing up the hills, glad to stop anywhere to pick up or leave off a package. What a humiliation to see her one day at Matapedia like a short-winded dwarf, completely overshadowed by that Goliath, the *Ocean Limited*, arriving from the Maritimes on its broad track in a titanic confusion of blinding smoke and screaming metal. At any age it's tough to realize just how small we really are.

In wintertime our puny little train would sometimes disappear completely for a couple of days, sometimes more. We would conclude that it had been snowed in and would wait patiently for the mail and the papers to turn up.

As to the latter, the old *Montreal Standard* was absolutely indispensable because its expert crossword puzzles provided the weekly occasion for a Homeric battle with my father. It always struck me as totally unfair to have to lose, as I did regularly, when I spoke English (though badly) as naturally as I breathed, whereas my father had a murderous accent and had picked up the language with great difficulty from one client and another. But he had a staggeringly rich vocabulary. He used it, as we discovered with admiration later on, in his replies to letters to him as "Dominique Lévesque, Esq." I was a little disappointed to learn that this abbreviation, quite commonly used then, did not designate at least a Squire in the lower echelons of nobility but was simply used to replace "Mr."

Although immersed in this English micro-climate, we were no less French for all that. Well, Francophone. Even a bit too much for my liking. Among the marvels that *le p'tit train* finally got around to delivering to us were the yearly catalogues: Eaton's, fat and self-assured, and the skinny little one from Chez Dupuis. They would come out near the end of fall, on purpose, we were sure, to keep us on tenterhooks till the holidays. Yet even here was an Anglo/French distinction, for those bright mysterious packages that arrived in December (which we soon discovered at the back of the cupboard) the English could open at Christmas and play with their skates, sleighs, and skis a week longer than we could, one whole precious week of holidays! We had to hang around waiting for New Year's Day – the French way.

But the time would come when this sort of half-survival would not be enough. I wasn't really bilingual. I spoke the most terrible brand of franglais. For "le phare" out on the point I would say "la litousse." The place we used to hang around in the afternoon was called "le" or "la post-office." And so on . . . .

The summer when I was eleven the barbarous decision was taken to uproot me from my carefree childhood and send me to boarding school.

9. A Seminary at the End of the World

MY FATHER was watching the director out of the corner of his eye; it had a twinkle in it. My mother was in a flap. No sooner had I set foot in the seminary at Gaspé than I had asked to visit the library, and I was barely over the threshold before I made my first request: "Do you have any Arsène Lupin? I don't see any." They'd gone and stuck me in boarding school before I had a chance to finish *Thirty Coffin Island*. I was hoping to make the two guilty parties feel a little remorse.

"Well now, I don't believe we do," said Father Mayer, as though he had just run out. "No Lupin. But there are lots of other things. Have a look around."

All Jules Verne, okay. Read them all. Léon Ville, who's that? And Karl May, don't know him. Ah! Walter Scott, the whole set. Hope they're as good as *Ivanhoe*.

Reassured, my father stepped outside with the young Jesuit, dragging my mother after him and leaving me planted there. When I was called for supper a little later the two rascals were already on their way back to New Carlisle and there I was, delivered up defenceless into the hands of the guardians of the prison.

At the age of eleven and a quarter (how impatiently we added each fraction on then) I was in no position to know how impoverished the place was. Poverty is always relative and is judged in comparison to others, and I hadn't yet met anyone who really belonged to the upper end of the scale. The library was barely better stocked than the one at home. The corridors were of a monastic nakedness. The Jesuits had "contracted" to run this little seminary for a diocese deprived of everything, even priests. It was as poor as Job on his dungheap, but that didn't strike me at the time. What would I have compared it to? Anyway, and this was the important thing, I didn't waste much time before becoming quite happy.

It did take a couple of weeks: learning to get up, or rather to be hauled out of bed with the mattress piled on top of me, at *5:45 in the morning* was terrible at first because I had been a night owl since birth. This was especially traumatic because it was not even to go down to the refectory but to the chapel. Luckily, if you masqueraded as being deep in meditation, you could catch an extra forty winks. Your stomach's complaining? Too bad – there's still an hour to put in, the worst one in the day, pretending to study upcoming lessons under the implacable eye of those sallow upperclassmen who are wearing the cassock already. Whether they would have a vocation or not, time alone would tell.

Breakfast at last! The nuns have prepared us their special mishmash: potatoes mixed with potatoes cemented together with a mixture of water, onions, and flour. This is accompanied right down to the "Deo gratias" by a reading from the lives of the saints. We noted in passing that a good many of these blessed individuals probably ate as poorly as we did. The sinister mishmash and the occasional dish of pork and beans is all I can remember, except that, as son of one of the professional class and therefore well off and able to pay a supplement, I had the right to an egg three times a week. The others, almost without exception, had to make do with the regular fare. They came from little fishing ports and for the most part were supported by curés who had discerned in them some call from the Almighty or simply a sign of talent.

All right, everyone outside! Fair or foul, like it or not, we had to evacuate the building. When it rained we milled around interminably under the covered part of the courtyard waiting our turn to play Mississippi or Rover-come-over. The smell of tobacco rose stealthily in the air. The supervisors, heavy smokers themselves, turned a closed nostril.

When it was nice, essentially in the fall, for in those latitudes spring wasn't worth talking about until June, you had a choice of activities: tennis, on condition that you kept the courts up yourself; handball; a workout on the antediluvian gymnastic equipment; or whatever else you could dream up. In winter, on the rink we shovelled off and flooded ourselves, hockey was king, naturally. One was either on the team or else hung around the boards ogling the girls from the village who had come to fawn over our two champions, the Duguay brothers from Anticosti – Sauveur, a real ace, and Ti-Phillipe, who would have been just as good if he could have made up his mind to grow a little.

There was no compulsory activity as long as we respected the incontrovertible bottom line: outside and keep moving! Behind that command lurked the evident fear of those special friendships that boys' boarding schools foster just as much as the navy or the penitentiary. But it is also true that we thrived on this enforced exercise, for boisterous physical activity is the mark of a healthy adolescence. Today, after so many years of reforms, and consequently of progress, when one sees those gangs of young flabby-asses hanging around school corridors rapping and smoking pot, one can't help but feel uneasy. What's the point of raising strong kids to let them drag around like that?

I'll go further than that. All of this "least effort" attitude, and the fad of permissive education that persists even after it's been shown to be totally ridiculous, with lessons you don't have to know, homework that's just for laughs, report cards that report little – what does it all amount to? It's just the slackness of adults spreading everywhere. They don't dare impose the least constraints on youngsters any more, not even on ten- or fifteen-year-olds, who are particularly wild and frisky young animals and are thus deprived of that minimum of discipline that would do them so much good. And deep down in a confused way the young people know it, and sooner or later they end up blaming us and despising us a little.

Old-fogey opinions like that will never make the good old days come back. But, yes, in this way and in several others, those were good times. That rigour we were flanked by from dawn to 8:45 in the evening – "Get into line! Watch out, Lévesque, you'll be left behind! What are you looking for, a detention?"– it corresponded admirably to a sort of natural order that we instinctively respected, though at the same time we publicly condemned it. It was conceived and regulated like a high-precision mechanism, so astutely it even allowed a few bits of freedom now and then.

Take that "inviolable" study period, for example. It stretched out every day for a long hour and a half before supper. Its strategic importance was heavily emphasized by the fact that the superintendents sent to watch over us were not simple upperclassmen but *real* fathers belted in rosaries whose clicking warned us of their approach. We were there principally to do our homework, but once this boring chore was over – it never took more that half the time and sometimes less (English for a guy from New Carlisle, for example) – we were free to invent whatever we wanted to keep ourselves occupied. Gainfully. Frivolous things like novels were excluded, even those by that Reverend American Father whose scouting adventures were notoriously dull.

And that's how we were underhandedly led, for want of anything better to do, to reopen this or that textbook, which to our great surprise suddenly turned out to be quite interesting because we were "at liberty" to go back to it again.

Such was the case for the *Histoire du Canada*, as it was then called, a very small and naively illustrated book that made an indelible imprint on a memory as fresh as it was insatiable. There we could see Jacques Cartier raising his famous cross at . . . what the exact spot was is still a mystery, not that it matters, though they were still looking for it at the 1534-1984 anniversary. And let me tell you, a lot of expert opinion was to be had from those of us who had been there for the 400th anniversary. What exact spot? At the site of the unfinished cathedral a few yards from the place they were supposed to erect that clumsy cross in grey granite? Maybe, but that answer seems too easy; it's surely just a tourist attraction. Farther down the hill somewhere along the one and only main street crossed by those poor alleys disappearing into vacant lots? A less orthodox guess and already more plausible. But my own answer to this question that has never ceased to trouble idle minds is Penouille – Penouille Peninsula, that meagre spit of sand that barely dares stick the tip of its tail out into the immense estuary. Why in the devil would a salt-sodden seadog go scraping his toes scaling a rock when there was an excellent opportunity to land soft as you please and dryshod on sand? And to be able to hightail it out of there if the Redskins (one never knew) refused to prostrate themselves or let them take that coppery savage hostage so they could put him through his paces in the court in Paris.

I should add that Penouille will have to take its place in history whatever happens because we elected it as the setting for our picnics and it's there that I made a name for myself as pancake-flipper. Besides, many years later, having noticed that a reserve of Anglophones had replaced the Indians and that a legendary crime had been committed there (it was my father who got the guilty party condemned), Anne Hébert decided to set her novel *Shadow in the Wind* there – though she will never admit it, I can tell you that. As one Gaspésian to another I sent her a letter of congratulations and had the nerve to add this important detail. She sent me a warm thank-you note but remained mum as to the source of her novel.

Champlain? Not very stimulating, the old founding father. His wife seems to have been a lot more fun. Poor guy, always stuck with the building of his *habitation* at Quebec with the English overrunning it time and again and all the while there was lovely Hélène living it up in those faraway palaces perhaps giving secret rendezvous to a certain young soldier from Gascony, or to Athos with the velvet eyes, or to that Jesuit so quick to hoist up his skirts, Aramis by name . . . .

O History! That inexhaustible storehouse of stories to be embellished infinitely. My favourite, the one we all preferred, was the story of d'Iberville, musketeer of Longueuil. From Hudson Bay to the Gulf of Mexico, he was a snowshoer like us and a buccaneer as we would have loved to be. Though the English might be hiding behind every spruce and in every gully, they'd better look out or he'd make short work of them. He was our man.

After him, with a short pause to salute the unknown soldier of Carillon, it was downhill all the way to the Plains of Abraham. It was all over. From then on somebody else's history began, the history of another country we didn't feel like learning, with the exception of Montgomery and his gang, and Arnold the turncoat, who came close to re-annexing us to the continent, which would have taken care of the question of free trade forever. Even Benjamin Franklin, however, had to give up on the idea when faced with our colonial loyalty so soon transferred to the British. . . . It was all over, all right. And for years to come.

Yes, but isn't history, as wise men say and fools repeat, a perpetual rebeginning? Who knows? Take that text *Antiquity* by P. Gagnol "For classes of the Sixth Form, A and B." Is it really possible we were entrusted with such explosive material? There can't be any doubt about it, for there it is in black and white: "History Course, J. de Gigord, editor, 1927." That's my period, all right.

At the very beginning of *Antiquity* one sentence caught my eye, and I encountered it again just a month ago while travelling, fifty years later. It's Herodotus proclaiming: "Egypt is a gift of the Nile." The flooding, the three seasons, the nilometer: everything was in this text, including, *nihil obstat*, the following passage that really took my breath away. The author is talking about the Egyptian religion, universally practised before and after the time of Ramses: "With regard to the divinity, their priests entertained sublime notions which one might often be tempted to relate to Mosaic revelation. They acknowledged a God who was of one substance but in three persons. This Trinity was composed of the father, the mother [no less], and the son. Their three-in-one God had all the attributes of the Christian God, immensity, eternity, independence, supreme will, and infinite goodness." So there's really nothing new under Ra-the-Sun. Good for you, Reverend Fathers, even if it slipped in inadvertently. When I think that today so many schoolchildren are left ignorant of the fact that Montcalm was a general before he became a street name . . . . O History! without you things know neither where they come from nor where they are leading us.

Back then, at any rate, they were leading us straight from Egypt to Greece. And to Greek – to classical Greek, which, along with Latin, was to accompany us just as far as French and farther than English. What remains today? Those roots that have a limited usefulness for someone who is not well versed in technico-socio-scientific jargon, which went drunk with Greek borrowings; scraps of Socrates and Aristotle and, though hazy, the touching face of Sophocles' Antigone. But Xenophon, that pain in the neck, I remember him, all right. We had to follow his *Anabasis* every step of the repetitive, dusty way. Luckily, old Homer was part of the company with his grand sagas, which from the very first page completely satisfied our delight in fine battles, voyages to unknown seas, and fairy tales (or nymph narratives), all permeated with the stuff of dreams. "Rosy-fingered dawn . . . " From those heights we were brought down with a hearty bump of vulgarity, very classical, too. Yes, that old Greek was decidedly resourceful, running up and down the scale from the most ethereal to the earthiest of the earthy. I wonder if schoolboys in classical times used Homer to joke and to tease their girls with?

For that matter, our own profs were not beyond using this venerable lingo to make fun of us. One long spring afternoon I was made victim of one of these practical jokers who ordered me to go and bring him his *ictus*. From classroom to study hall and from furnace room to the foot of the hill, I was sent from pillar to post and finally came back winded, crestfallen, and empty-handed just to be reminded that it was April Fool's Day and that *ictus* is Greek for fish (*poisson d'avril*). The worst of it was that the chief prankster was none other than the director.

Still, we were good friends, the two of us. I was the smallest boy in the school and a few weeks younger than my only and inseparable friend, Bourget, who, as luck would have it, was a day boy. I was the captive and had a great need to feel I belonged. So the director took me under his wing and, seeing that I had time to spare, exploited me shamelessly. Errand boy, in charge of the darkroom, sent to dust off bizarre instruments, I even became, thanks to my school-marm hand, scribe for the monthly report cards – from the pure gold of *optime* to somewhat tarnished but still acceptable *bene*, to . . . nothing at all, which contained the threat of imminent expulsion.

Not counting my close family, this director was the first grownup to leave a mark on me. A. Hamel, s.j. That brusque signature denoted a "late vocation." He had served for a time in the navy and had come out an officer, a scientist, a photographer, a jack-of-all-trades, and, when he took the trouble, a man of the world. He kept for himself the physics course in the top form but also kept a close eye on natural sciences taught to the smaller boys and made the profs take us out on field trips to collect rocks and plants. Short, broad, and bald as an egg, he possessed the gift of leadership, of quiet authority that could be cutting when necessary but was tempered with a smile, and the art of knowing how to put you at your ease. He loved life, and since frail health had closed any very grandiose plans for him, he had fallen back on simple things and showed us how to appreciate them. He had fun making fun of us, lips severely pinched but eyes twinkling maliciously. He was really a father, a substitute, but almost as good as the real thing.

He understood full well, for instance, the unspeakable horror inspired by the Saturday bath, and he tolerated the monumental fraud this ritual had turned into. In platoons of four to six we were marched up to the dormitory and, picking up a bundle of clean clothes, climbed on up to the Siberian attic where, in cubicles, there was a series of bathtubs that never gave anything but perfectly frigid ice water. From the pockets of our dressing gowns we would extract the books concealed there beforehand. With a shiver, plunging first one, then two toes into this polar pond, it was possible, for the regulation twenty minutes, to set up quite convincing splashing if we remembered to vary the movements a little to fool the warder outside. Then, having put on the changes of clothes and carefully wet the towels and our hair, we could come back downstairs with a feeling of duty well done. Needless to say, in no time we were all transformed into stink bugs. But as we all gave off the same perfume, including several of the fathers if the truth must be known, as far as we knew there was nothing abnormal about the atmosphere.

At the Christmas holidays I was soon given to understand what sort of attar of roses I was exuding. After a first kiss and a brief visual inspection that revealed the deplorable state of my health, my mother suddenly gasped, held her nose, and, in a tone that brooked no reply, said: "Before you do anything else, go and get washed. Anyone as dirty as that is a sure carrier of microbes. Quick! Quick, before we all get sick!"

That was only the beginning. The holidays I had so looked forward to held deception after deception. To a degree I would never have believed possible, my brothers and sister demonstrated a lamentable grade-school mentality. After Fernand, André had come along, then Alice. André was tallest of the four of us and only his stork-like legs saved him from a thousand deaths when, the summer before, he began to beat me consistently at croquet. As soon as he had gone through the last two hoops, he would throw his mallet at my head to slow down my vengeful pursuit and make a beeline for the house. Then there was nothing left for me to do but wait till after work when my dear little only sister – Daddy's pet and an awful tattletale, as they all are – would denounce me to Father for attempted murder. They were insupportable, the pair of them.

As for my friends, whether they had dropped out or gone on to the high school, I didn't fit in with them any more. Nor they with me. It happened so quickly; in three or four months we had lost our easygoing relationship, and the holidays were too short to catch up again.

Without admitting it even to myself, I waited for the vacation to end with a certain impatience. It was a relief to take the train back after Twelfth Night. I was going back, as I had just realized, to my new gang. But what a lugubrious trip it was, this return to Gaspé. In less than an hour night fell. In the interminable clickety-clack of the uneven rails we soon stopped listening to the bigger boys boasting about their conquests. Eyelids drooped in spite of the cold coming in through all the cracks in the antique coach car. When we at last arrived a little before midnight we were a snoring, half-frozen flock that the welcoming committee had to shake awake, muffle up, and convoy across the Monseigneur Ross Bridge. The wind congealed us again as we made our way through the sleeping village to the lights signalling a welcome to us from every floor of that mournful building, our college at the end of the world, our first opening on the world, too, and henceforth our home away from home.

68

10. The End of the Beginning

ELEMENTS, Syntax, Method, Versification, Belles-Lettres, Rhetoric, Philo I and II . . . those sonorous names, given the steps we had to climb for eight years of the old classical curriculum, had a lot going for them, a lot more, one must admit, than that monotonous ascent from grades one to two to three, or the reverse, as in Europe.

And in my humble opinion the content wasn't inferior either to that cafeteria menu of options so often presented prematurely and served up any old how to our young consumers today. To begin with, there were four languages we were expected to more or less master and that we had to work at assiduously. First was French, not as bad as it is nowadays, I think; then English, certainly a little better. Having wrestled for five or six years with Virgil, Horace, and their era, we could babble a brand of kitchen Latin that was quite adequate for chapel and for serving the fathers' masses (which gave us the right to eat in their refectory, where there was fresh fruit). But the important thing was that a bridge had been thrown across between Greece and Rome, and we could begin to guess how a civilization is constructed.

I will never begin to understand how the "core courses" of traditional education have come to be so completely eliminated, thus throwing the baby out with the bath water. This is particularly true with the study of languages. Faced with a shrinking world in which the descendants of our *coureurs de bois* will have to become *coureurs de continents*, the impoverishment of this field is nothing short of catastrophic. Why didn't they replace the dead languages, which admittedly have had their time, with one or two modern ones, not as laughable options – "bird courses" – but as an integral and compulsory part of the curriculum, complete with the study of the grammar of the language, its literature, and the whole cultural treasure it articulates?

But French, of course, must come before all else. It is a language that lends itself very poorly to the law of least effort and audio-visual gimmicks. Much more arduous than English, it can only be acquired by hard work at the very start and then must be savoured long and lovingly at the table of great authors. Settling for "instant French" is like accepting instant coffee, a feeble substitute without body or flavour. No doubt our concoction was far from a model of excellence, but at least they tried to equip us with correct speech, the indispensable instrument for clear and precise communication, without which thinking itself remains clouded.

There was one prof I remember in particular, one of those rare teachers who knows how to be unforgettably provocative. It was in Method, I think, or perhaps Versification. His passion was vocabulary and the romance, as extraordinary as any in literature, of the evolution of words and their family relationships, so complex and sometimes so deceptive. He spent one whole week, starting at the word "pride," and took us through everything that resembled it, far and near, without being exactly the same: dignity, vanity, egotism, self-respect, standoffishness, haughtiness, arrogance . . . a – Alouette! . . . which gave us a sketchy notion of the marvellously rich tangle of nuances. Then, starting at the dawn of time, we mounted our little Aryan steeds and galloped across Asiatic deserts to the borders of Europe through layers of primitive sounds that always had a certain family likeness to them, though they presented themselves in many different fashions: father, vater, pater, padre, père. Inescapably I have just demonstrated that we were neither philologists nor linguists. Nor was the prof, but he awakened us just the same to the magic of words.

And he awakened us as well to the sheer pleasure of "morceaux choisis," those selected passages from famous authors which the chore of so-called literary analysis never quite managed to spoil. Pages and pages of Victor Hugo's *Legends of the Centuries*; Lamartine returning to sigh on the shores of Lac Léman; Musset's pelican exhausted after its long flight . . . . But my first and most lasting passion was for poor Rutebeuf. Somehow or other I got my hands on *A History of Literature* by Kléber Haedens, not *the* history but *a* history, an exceptional one, thanks to which I grasped the fact that choice and appreciation are a question of individual taste, since no one can ever read all the books. Rutebeuf, that medieval poet who was the first personal voice to be heard in French poetry and always got short shrift in our textbooks, came up strong in Haedens's *History*, and he and his friends, "so closely held and much beloved," became mine, too, for life. I still listen to them sometimes, their words so nicely set to music by Léo Ferré, especially latterly when the winds were blowing stronger and stronger at my door . . . .

It's a curious thing, that instinctive return to the roots of the language. My true idols were and still are those pioneers of our mother tongue, perhaps because they knew how to sing so simply about simple things and were the first to do so: Villon and his "Ballad of the hanged men" whose skeletons still rattle in my memory; Du Bellay bringing his Ulysses back home with " . . . and make me a fire in the hearth"; and Ronsard's sweetheart fading like the rose, but, at the end of her days,

"Reciting my verse, marvelling at my ready rhyme,
You'll say that Ronsard sang your praises in your prime."

And I musn't forget Louise Labé, whose name was on the index but whose sonnets, particularly the most evocative and troubling ones, I could recite at length and with great feeling as soon as I had secured a willing female listener.

In short, we were growing up, becoming distracted, secretive, impossible. The summer holidays were spun out between the tennis court and the beach, especially the beach with its bordering bushes where we tried to inveigle our intended female victims. Or else, more exciting, we would take them to the top of Christie Rock, safe from prying eyes. But all those efforts unfortunately resulted in nothing more than painful frustrations. No one would consider the consummation of our advances – "No, stop! That's enough!" – not even S, who was said to be fast, but her reputation was overdone. The sense of sin hadn't completely disappeared and the pill would only come along much later. So we growled and groaned but in reality weren't so unhappy to have to wait till the cherished fruit offered itself for the picking.

But how could we go on being obsessed by such trivial preoccupations when the whole country was in the depths of the Great Depression? People who talk this way make me laugh, as if adolescents – disorganized, aimless, shiftless – were a breed apart they'd never met before, as if adolescence hasn't been the same since the beginning of the world. And that is precisely what it is, a closed world inhabited by tormented souls traversed by unknown currents and blind angst, a totally self-centred world testing itself cruelly on those outside it and then withdrawing immediately inside its shell. And only the storm or a passionate rallying cry will bring it out to march in the street. Peace and calm are not its inclinations.

While our Depression was not exactly peaceful, it hardly affected us. The papers from the city talked of it more and more, but those "camiliennes," public conveniences set up in Montreal by Mayor Camillien Houde, seemed to be something from another planet. Later I would mainly remember us keeping the same old car longer and thinking more about the poor. But everyone was more or less poor, except for certain foreigners like the Americans in their private fishing clubs, and even they became rarer as the thirties got worse.

In fact the Depression was there all around us, but permanent. For example, our next door neighbours died one after the other from tuberculosis, *the* disease of the period. (And how many others lurked behind it when it reached the stage of "galloping consumption"?) Thus, from one funeral service to another we became acquainted with death. It was nice, clean death, all painted up and tucked away in a coffin, and it didn't faze us because it was unreal. But the agony before death, even the agony of an animal such as the one those poor neighbours inflicted on us, that was another story. When other people's leftovers would no longer meet the bill, the neighbours dug up enough slow energy to raise some chickens and a couple of pigs. One day a terrible screeching, a real death cry, suddenly pierced our ears. Rushing over, we saw the poor pig crucified on the barn door, its throat cut, bleeding like . . . like a stuck pig, and screaming, screaming. He screamed like that all afternoon, taking a break once in a while, then starting up again but more feebly, descending the scale from sharp to flat. At last, at sundown, the death rattle. Death? There was nothing much to it. But dying . . . .

Because they drew so much attention, the unprecedented difficulties the outside world was experiencing finally had their effect on us, too. Misery and sickness were daily fare, but the shameless exploitation that went along with them became progressively harder to take. Often in the morning before going to school I would go down to the dock with my father to buy a lobster. The fisherman would throw some of his catch into a big cauldron, stir up the fire, and then sell us the steaming result. How much? Twenty-five cents for a big one? Not more at any rate, and the little ones were given away. My father would take this opportunity to tell me the story of the Robins of Robin, Jones and Whitman and the incredible servitude they subjected their workers to. They were victimized like plenty of others around the Gaspésie, like those lumberjacks that James Richardson and Hammerhill paid a handsome five-dollars-a-day during the brief woodcutting season. Go back to the land and live better? What land? Strawberries in July and blueberries at first frost . . . tiny plots where the cow got thinner by the day and the only things that grew well were those northern garden peas. Luckily there were plenty of sheep, the woods swarmed with rabbits and deer, and the waters teemed with miraculous schools of smelt and caplin. Certain nights when the moon turned the sea to silver, an enormous patch as black as ink would suddenly spread out, extinguishing the shimmering light. Everyone would grab a pail and run to the shore. When the fishermen pulled in the bulging net stretched between their two boats, we would all slither around in that sparkling tidal wave of little fish glittering and leaping and trying to scoot away to the safety of the open sea. But there always remained enough to gorge ourselves on the next day amid great debates about whose turn it was to get the eggs. Such feasts are unknown today. I suppose people have become too lazy to put themselves out for so little.

By then, however, nothing, not even those "colonies" where city dwellers were shoved in back-to-the-land movements, like refuse, could disguise the general situation that we perceived – better late than never – should not, could not, continue like that. Unprecedented rumblings began to be heard, behind which, hesitantly, swarmed still unstructured ideas about co-ops and unions.

Meanwhile, without really thinking about it, we were acquiring a sketchy identity. "Les autres," the ones on the other side, which included the majority of the bosses and exploiters, weren't they also the English conquerors? That had never bothered me when we chivied each other good-naturedly by exchanging stones or snowballs and countered their "French pea soup" with "English crawfish." One name was as silly as the other. It was all in fun and we had never taken it seriously. It was a family matter, so to speak, even those mornings my father would have to take me down to the corner past the house where that bloodthirsty tribe of Law kids lived. (Once in safe territory I would quickly take to my heels!) But now, slowly, regretfully, I was beginning to notice a difference.

Soon I was plunged into it up to my neck. First came, *noblesse oblige*, Lionel Groulx's *Our Master, the Past*, though he was so preachy I preferred him as Alonié de Lestres in his novel, *The Call of the Race*, even if to call Groulx a novelist is to give him the benefit of the doubt. But I was more impressed with Philippe Aubert de Gaspé's *Canadians of Old* and above all by *Born in Quebec*, the life of Louis Joliet somewhat romanced by the poet Alain Grandbois, which told of times when the whole of America was ours and might have remained so, and might perhaps become so again by the "revenge of the cradles." Then Ringuet, the Ringuet of *Thirty Acres* in which I had underlined and later extracted this passage at the place where Euchariste Moisan's hard life had taken its turn toward humble tragedy: "It was things that had decided for him, and people conditioned by things." Were we, too, forever destined to live this kind of life "conditioned" by others? It was impossible not to fear the worst when I read the traumatic *Taking our measure* by Victor Barbeau, a book that had been procured for our school library even if the biggest French daily, *La Presse*, refused to speak in any way, shape, or form of the author's malicious and all too accurate observations.

Most of the fathers at the seminary, in fact, shared Barbeau's enthusiasms and were not slow to inculcate us with them. Although they seemed to us to be almost ancestors, they were very young, twenty-three or twenty-five at the most, backed up by some "old-timers" in their thirties. Exiled by their superiors into this boreal solitude, they would return to Quebec or Montreal for the holidays to see their families and would come back to us pumped full of brand new nationalism. Very inflammatory and still very new it was, seeking its rhetoric and its path, like Olivar Asselin, the pugnacious journalist, hammering away at the most obvious evils, such as the association of sheep with Quebec in religious iconography: "Far worse than any religious symbol, it is the emblem of passive and stupid submission to every tyranny!" Would we ever be able to break loose? Or were we condemned like Emile Nelligan, the most famous nineteenth-century Quebec poet (it was taboo to speak of him though we all knew how pitiful and beautiful he was), "to sink into the abyss of dreams"?

Nevertheless, the air we breathed was a pretty strong tonic most of the time, particularly the fresh supply provided by the fiery, flamboyant Jesuit writer, Father Dubé, better known by his pseudonym, François Hertel. He eventually came to a bad end (defrocked), but in those days we were proud to boast his very own cousin as one of our masters. The honour was enhanced by the shiver of recognition we experienced in reading those literary portraits of ourselves as young Québécois, which he had collected in the volume entitled *Their Anxiety*. In reality he claimed to be writing a defence of self-confidence. First we had to follow him as he clumped through long analyses of famous worriers from ages past. Then – pow! – the introduction was over and there we were, targeted as the central subject. He wasn't yet thinking in terms of Quebec, but he did write about what he called "Laurentie," which at least had the merit of breaking the habit of speaking of French Canada or "French-speaking Canada," as Henri Bourassa and company always did. And above all he dared to envisage this solution: "One day separation will come to pass."

We were far from that, I must confess, even in our thoughts. I can remember registering that small cry of angry affirmation as one of my last emotions as a student, and it was quickly swallowed up in the desert of political thought and the uproar of political infighting of 1935-36. Even our prime model, the Action Libérale Nationale group and its generous and prophetic champions – among them Philippe Hamel, the purest of them all, a regular Don Quixote attacking the trusts – was to disappear without trace. To all appearances; for the day would come when . . .

Like everyone else, my father got caught up in the mêlée that in the end shook the fabric of the old Liberal temple to its very foundations. He was still a Liberal himself but hadn't been active for years. Like many of his contemporaries, his reference point was still the idol of his youth, Laurier, whose picture dominated our living room to the end. But in 1936 panic had broken out. Taschereau was in danger. Party organizers came over to the house to beg my father to help, even pushed him with a hint at blackmail, saying, "You were named Crown Attorney, you know . . ." But it was also well known that he was so widely respected no one else would ever have been chosen. He simply sent them away with the promise that he would think about it. What they wanted was a speech on the local radio station, just a quarter of an hour to give the party a boost. My father's thinking, which stretched out over a good part of the evening, was punctuated by slight altercations with my mother, whose lineage was Conservative. Because of this ancestral divergence I came close to never being born at all: "What, marry that Liberal? Over my dead body, my girl!" The old dyed-in-the-wool Tory had held out in such terms until finally, worn out, he had to resign himself to becoming my maternal grandfather.

Anyway, the next day, dragging his heels like a condemned man on his way to the gallows, my father left for the studio carrying a few pages on which he continued to scribble his notes. It turned out to be a superb quarter of an hour that my mother followed with the same enthusiasm I did, an eloquent, moving panegyric on the illustrious Sir Wilfrid, but not a blessed word about Taschereau and his shipwrecked colleagues!

It was an unpardonable affront but Father barely had time to register the shock waves. He became sick shortly afterwards. Loyal to local professionals, he went to be operated on, very badly, at the same hospital in Campbellton where I was born. On returning home he didn't improve. He was bedridden for weeks and grew progressively feebler. As a last resort he accepted to be shipped off to Quebec City. At the time of his departure it was a shrivelled man, suddenly grizzled and aged, who hugged me in his arms as he had when I was small. I felt a vague apprehension that, alas, was confirmed by a call from Quebec City. We would have to get there as fast as possible if we wanted to see him alive. A friend drove us along that breakneck coastal road at ninety miles an hour to Matapedia where the *Ocean Limited* was just leaving. In the middle of the night, when I had just fallen asleep, I was rudely shaken and extracted from the berth to be led outside to a station I recognized immediately as Rivière-du-Loup. At that instant I realized it was all over.

The morning of the funeral I was left alone with him for a few minutes in my grandparents' parlour. How sorry I felt that I had known him so poorly and appreciated him so little. I told him so under my breath. He had been a good man, perhaps more upstanding and discreetly dedicated to the service of others than anyone I have ever met. He was a cultivated man but never flaunted it; he had lost none of his idealism, only his illusions; and he was so honest that he died in perfect poverty.

As soon as he was gone, his presence began to mark me as no

76

one else's, to the point of mimicry. The fountain pen I hold in this odd way between the index and middle finger is his, and my signature will always be the double of his, too.

I kissed him on the marble forehead, then left the room without knowing that I had also just left behind my happy, heedless youth, nor that my naked, best beloved Gaspésie had already become my paradise lost.

11. By Way of Farewell

I WILL GO BACK to see my Gaspésie, more often now that I'm a private citizen once again. It was impossible to enjoy it when I had to go as Premier and could never let go of the big political questions without having to come to grips with local ones like: Who's looking after that sideroad? or, Isn't that game warden getting too big for his boots? Not to mention the eternal question of subsidies and the grave problem of the municipal budget.

Yet I've been back several times in the last few years, enough to see that here as elsewhere there's been an acceleration of history that has changed and modernized my Eden at the end of the world but without making it ugly, which doesn't surprise me, because it's impossible to uglify. I revisited the little seminary at the celebrations for the 450th anniversary of Cartier's landing because a homecoming had been organized for me. I had a hard time recognizing the worn, faded bricks of that first barracks where we were never more than eighty inmates. It was completely overshadowed now by the wings of a modern CEGEP that has opened its doors to hundreds of students from every corner of the coast and even the Iles-de-la-Madeleine.

At last they're getting true value for riches that had been wasted for years. And they're doing the same thing in the Ottawa region, in the Lower St. Lawrence, at Lac Saint-Jean, and in all those extensions of the country that are strangely enough called "resource regions" after people had ignorantly undervalued for so long the one resource on which all the rest depend, the one resource that, if necessary, can do without the rest – just look at Japan and Switzerland.

The human framework is at last in place, right down to the diocesan clergy who now have the manpower needed to perform a task that formerly was beyond them, even if their responsibilities have been shrinking recently. The same goes for doctors, teachers, technicians, the growing number of native-born men and women who, once their studies are over, have opted to return to the sea air. Beyond their professional duties these energetic young people are mayors, town councillors, union and cultural leaders, and creators of new businesses, in short, the yeast in the dough, a dough that is rising fast and well after many years of neglect.

Even our fishermen, left out of the picture for so long, are showing new confidence and a growing determination to get aboard the train for change whose name is progress. One of my last "official" functions, in August of 1985, was to go with Jean Garon to Newport for the opening of a new fish-processing plant. "An operation so modern," boasted my colleague, "it even puts us ahead of Iceland. And that's where we mean to stay!"

There was applause and good humour and, better still, a sense of pride one didn't used to see in such places. The same kind shone on the faces of those two captains whose brand new trawlers were to be launched after the ceremony. Giving us the guided tour, they spared no pains in showing us to the last detail the very latest in equipment and in explaining how ship and cargo will be kept meticulously clean. "Look at this, we've even got toilets!" said one of them. "The times when everything was dirty and smelt to high heaven, us as much as the cod, are gone for good."

This concern for quality product had already struck me in the Iles-de-la-Madeleine on a similar occasion. When I was visiting the renovated plant of the Madelipêche Company, a strapping big fellow insisted on showing me some sample packages. "It's written right there," he said pointing to the label. "It says this fillet came straight from Cap-aux-Meules, Iles-de-la-Madeleine, Quebec. And it has to be good because it's our own name that's going to make our reputation now. Before we didn't have any name, we were swallowed up in United Fisheries, and when somebody did dirty work, it wiped off on everyone."

After the visit to Newport we came back by helicopter. The August sun, always in such a rush to have its late summer fling, scattered its rays over the constant play of water and waves, the colours changing and mixing from ultramarine on the open sea shading to emerald just below us. Between the snowy whitecaps driving toward the shore I could make out the garnet-red bottom, giving way to the pink beach rising to incomparable blood-red cliffs, and above them, set in among the sombre green of the conifers, pale gold fields already announcing the coming of autumn. Flying back over New Carlisle, skimming the rock and the common fields, then the church spires of all those different sects, I turned around for a last look and saw the moon making ready to replace the sun and the blue of the sea beginning to melt into the blue of the sky. Or vice-versa.

I know that Charlevoix, too, is very beautiful; people from there never stop telling me so. And the fjord of the Saguenay. And the narrow gorges of the Saint-Maurice. And Old Quebec purring with pride at having been chosen as a "world heritage" site. And Montreal, which has no need of honours because it knows there is scarcely a city in the world that can match its non-aggressive vitality, the beauty of its islands (as long as they're properly kept up), and its soul of a sunny village in a metropolitan setting.

In short, all Quebec affects me this way, and I can't imagine how anyone could go away and never come back, even if sometimes one might feel he has to go to "move the place it hurts around a bit" or to see what's happening and how people live elsewhere.

III

TIMES OF APOCALYPSE

"We are a civilization that knows how to make war, but not how to make peace."
GUGLIELMO FERRERO

12. Departure: Destination Unknown

FROM 1943 ON THINGS had become pretty well impossible: unless you were in uniform you couldn't get a girl to go out with you, it was as simple as that.

As for law school, the courses had quickly become a colossal bore. Judge Roy delivered his course in Roman law in a tedious monotone, a course he had concocted a quarter of a century before and hadn't altered by so much as a sigh since, like Roman law itself. As for Professor Pigeon, later to be an intimate adviser to Jean Lesage and still later one of the esteemed jurists to honour the Supreme Court with his presence, he disgusted me. In his high-pitched voice he forbade smoking in his course, and when I kept on as though nothing had been said he threw me out of class. And so what? The days were long past when, if anyone asked what I was going to be when I grew up, I would puff out my chest and reply, "A lawyer like Papa, a lawyer, a lawyer." My father was dead and only my mother believed that any more. She had been obliged to rent the little office at New Carlisle but flatly refused to give it up completely. Her eldest would take it over one day, she was sure of that. Even when she became sure of the contrary, she kept on talking about it. I can still remember her, when I had been Premier for two full years, saying sadly, covering my hand with her own: "Poor little boy, I feel sorry for you. Politics is so cruel and so uncertain. Ah! if you'd only finished your law school!"

She must have been eighty then and many years had passed since that winter of 1943-44 when I found myself hunting around the port of Montreal for a certain dock and the ship that was to take me overseas for the first time. I had come up from New York the night before, equipped with a paramilitary job in the American Office of War Information and an A-1 health certificate that had been awarded me by an amazon in a white coat, the first and last doctoress ever to examine me from stem to stern. "Go on home," I'd been told, "and wait for orders. And not a word to anyone in the meantime." This silence was imposed by U-boats mounting their last desperate offensive in an attempt to stem the flow of arms and vehicles leaving America for what were to be the invasion beach-heads. I had gone to advise my family that I wouldn't be coming back to Quebec and then had waited patiently till that morning when my Montreal recruiting officer, an American doing duty in the Canadian colony, finally gave me the fatal phone call.

At last I tracked down the right dock and found the ship, a little multi-purpose freighter that in a pinch could put up a dozen passengers or so. She was called *L'Indochinois* and had rallied to the cause of the Allies like a host of other French vessels after the fall of France in 1940.

Germans marching into Paris . . . As we sailed past Quebec City in the middle of the night I remembered the historic day and how I had spent that fine June afternoon. We were coming back from class down the Grande-Allée in Quebec City and all the windows along the street were open to the soft spring air. As we walked along we could hear a voice, always the same, reaching our ears from house to house. In that way, word for word, we followed the sober and moving commentary of that excellent journalist Louis Francoeur.

The year 1940 was also when I found myself a refugee among the day boys, those black sheep the seminary mistrustfully parked at the back of the class, for I had left the Jesuits. Or, to be more accurate, *they* had left me when, in Philo I (also known under the name of Mathematics), I obtained a mark of one out of a hundred on the math exam. It was a well-deserved mark, earned for copying down all the problems without making a single mistake.

"Don't you think a change of air might do you some good?" the director asked with his typically Jesuitical humour.

The next year I took my revenge by getting an unheard of 19.5 out of 20 on the alternative baccalaureate, a program that served up plane geometry, the only basic science I have ever felt any sympathy for. So out of filial loyalty I subsequently went into law and began to regret it immediately. Luckily, on the rue Couillard there was a nasty little dive, the old students' club, where habitués as notorious as Robert Cliche, Jean Marchand, and other celebrities used to hang out, although unlike me they were slated to make the grade and get their degrees. Once engaged on the slippery path, I gave myself up to sliding. One of the most noisy agitators was a certain Lussier who, disguised as Father Gédéon, was to turn out even worse than I did.

To make ends meet I sometimes did work, and even quite hard, at the noble and influential trade of journalism. I had already won my spurs the summer I turned thirteen. Fed up with seeing me twiddling my thumbs, Father had pulled some strings to get me a job as translator of news releases at the local radio station. Things were so slack there that when the regular announcer went on vacation they let me air some of my own texts. These heady pleasures left me with such an incurable case of nostalgia that after law school I eventually ended up at Radio-Canada as "temporary wartime employee." And now here I was on this tramp steamer slipping down the river past the sleeping city of Quebec on my way to Halifax.

Why? What was the motivation? I would have been hard-pressed to answer. It was all very confused. How I envied that fourteen-year-old girl, Bernice, who had adopted me as soon as we got on board and who was now leaning on the rail telling in her excited voice about her teeming memories and hopes. For her everything was clear. She was going home, to Yorkshire, along with five or six other English kids who had been evacuated to Canada at the time of the Blitz. The rest of the passengers were a mixed bag: Yankee mechanics, radio operators, electricians, and technicians on their way to work on the infrastructures of the upcoming invasion, plus a few European refugees, among them a multilingual Pole who had already begun to smell the sweet air of home. As for the French crew, kept on their toes by their choleric captain, a bearded giant, they were taking bets on the date of their first leave in liberated Paris.

But what the hell was a little twenty-one-year-old provincial doing lost in this cacophony? As far as I remember, the answers to that would have been fragmentary and dictated more by instinct than by reason. Roughly, they probably went something like this: no wish to fight to kill, but a ravenous hunger for war experience, to see it close up, to learn what it was all about. Perhaps, as well, there was a desire to "defend democracy," as the saying goes, but it was very vague and I felt no special fervour for England, our first line of defence. If I did have such a purpose it was more likely directed to France, and at least in part out of a spirit of contradiction. Thinking people in Quebec had been ecstatic about Mussolini making trains run on time and had flirted with the strong man of the Reich who was sometimes proposed as a model around 1934-35. Then, after 1940, they had swung in a block behind Pétain, whose slogan, "Honour, Family, Patriotism," Duplessis himself would not have disowned. At that time there was still only a handful of De Gaulle supporters around, and they were reduced to talking to themselves or, making use of the only communications channel open to them, to listening to the weekly mini-broadcast presented by a Madame Simard, whom I generally had the honour to introduce on the airwaves. Was that the site of my conversion? One thing is sure, toward the end I became one of the rare defenders of the General in those interminable debates where we weighed the pros and cons of our own somewhat ambivalent commitment. But the cons always ended up winning, thanks to the sledgehammer argument: "What, help the maudits Anglais? Not bloody likely. And if Ottawa is stupid enough to bring in conscription like they did in 1917, we'll take to the woods!"

As a matter of fact, conscription was just beginning to loom on the horizon. "Conscription if necessary," that inimitable old Mackenzie King had craftily declared, "but not necessarily conscription." Necessary or not, it wasn't far off. And the least I can say is that the prospect of going to Valcartier to be ordered in English to peel potatoes in the name of His Majesty hardly turned me on. With the Americans there were no problems, and above all, no complexes. If I really wanted to get involved in this conflict that was the great adventure of our generation before it was too late, it was with the Americans that I should make my move. So, quite frankly, that's what was going through my head at the time.

In Halifax transport ships of every description squeezed up to one another in the chilly port watched by the warships preparing to escort them; strident sirens pierced the freezing mist; self-important tugs and launches bustled here and there. It was our convoy, or rather what was supposed to be our convoy. Our captain, who did not hide his scorn for this duck-like type of navigation, had gone ashore with one of his officers to look for information, not instructions, as he was quick to tell us. He was soon back on board and even before they'd hoisted his ship's boat out of the water he was busy issuing orders salted with choice remarks about those "brainless idiots of assbackward experts" who were supposed to be organizing the convoy.

"This is the captain speaking. We're sailing. Yes, alone. Yes, right now, before we get stuck with those lame ducks at the end of the line who are a sitting target. Look alive! Get those engines started and get us out of this Godforsaken hole."

He was furious as usual after some on-shore squabble he didn't condescend to tell us about. Nor Pat Cooney either. But Cooney had figured it all out. "What'd he say? We're leaving without a convoy? Not me, brother!"

Brooklyn Irish, and a specialist in communications equipment, he was a great little guy, short and stocky, feisty and full of beans. But right now it was a speechless, pale-faced Cooney who dove into his cabin to emerge five minutes later with a suitcase in each hand.

"I'm getting off, " he said simply.

"Oh no you're not, espèce de con de Yankee," roared the captain. "Just to go and shoot your face off in the first bar you stumble into? The walls have ears, German ones. We'd all be goners. Take him back where he came from and keep an eye on him."

Shouting Brooklyn insults that were fortunately Greek to the captain, Cooney disappeared between two sailors. He remained locked up till the next day. In fact, we were all locked up for the next twelve days on this solitary hulk whose least creak, especially at night, made everyone break out in a cold sweat. It was worse by day. Ocean, ocean, everywhere, as far as the eye could see, day after day, full of enormous waves charging toward us with the possibility of a periscope in every trough. It was the only time in my life I didn't really like the sea. We must have eaten two or three

85

times a day, but I can't remember. At last, far off, we caught sight of something solid sticking up out of the water – the Azores. We'd made a long detour to avoid any unlucky encounters. Cautiously, we began to creep north. Gaining confidence we congratulated the captain – "Well, what did I tell you?" – who, the last day, with something approaching a smile of satisfaction, announced that our ex-convoy had been badly mauled, with two or three ships torpedoed and lost.

It was only on coming into port that I realized I hadn't got completely undressed a single night of the entire voyage. Nor had any of the other passengers either, if I'm not mistaken, at least little Bernice confessed as much to me.

The memory of those transatlantic emotions didn't last an hour under the spell of London. It was the magic of my first great European city, a very special and very specific magic that has stood up to every comparison I have been able to make since. The frightful climate is an integral part of it. It was the season of permanent fog with the muffled cries of phantom ships arising from Thames-side. In the street I bumped into people I couldn't see coming. In those big, chubby taxis that are so wonderfully practical, the driver would apologize for just missing certain ignorant pedestrians carefully looking *to the left* before crossing the street. And then there was that politeness everywhere, perhaps simply the side-product of the superb indifference of an imperial race, now focused on tolerating that mixed salad of escapees from the whole of occupied Europe, plus swarms of not very quiet Americans. And the V-1s arrived so regularly you could set your watch by them.

With all that monumental history to explore I "forgot" to report for duty and spent my two first days rushing from Westminster to the Tower to Buckingham Palace to Trafalgar Square, where from a distance you could contemplate Churchill's bunker emerging from the depths like the point of an iceberg. Then I would return again to my room by the last tube, stepping out into the blackout after carefully straddling most of the neighbourhood settled in to spend the night on the platform.

Eventually I presented myself to the madhouse where they were supposed to be waiting for me. My arrival caused so little stir that I kicked myself for not having played hookey for a whole week; no one would have been the wiser. This tower of Babel was called ABSIE, "American Broadcasting System in Europe," but it was American in name only and employed just a tiny handful of American overseers to keep the record straight. It was the propaganda network that Uncle Sam had acquired to supplement, and occasionally to contradict, the solemn BBC and its Big Ben newscasts. In every language of the immense dungeon Nazi Europe had become, we broadcast a continual stream of news severely mutilated by the censor, commentaries of a monumental insignificance, interviews weighted from the start with the Belgian minister in exile, the head of the Norwegian party in exile, the little Yugoslavian king in exile. . . . But above all we sent out those famous nonsense messages – "A friend will be coming tonight . . . . The carrots are cooked . . . ." They at least never sank into banality, for one could imagine a member of the underground somewhere in an attic over there decoding these idiotic phrases that seemed to be getting more urgent day by day, especially the ones beamed to France.

In the French section we knew, like everyone else, that Operation Overlord would soon be unleashed across the Channel. The interminable suspense helped stir up the band of hateful, bickering, lovable freaks we were to the boiling point, and soon the editorial office was transformed into an indescribable bordello reigned over by the most impossible character of us all, Pierre Lazareff.

He was already famous. He was scarcely out of knee socks when he had become the Parisian Péladeau, pushing that impossible and essential daily rag, *Paris-Soir*, to the top of the heap. As a Jew, he hadn't hung around when the Germans came but fled to the States. He was the one who had auditioned me in New York, in French only, leaving the English to a subordinate, for the very good reason that he was absolutely impermeable to the language, and though he had been soaking in it up to the neck for three years its mysteries continued to escape him for the rest of his born days. A stubby little guy, losing his glasses perched on his bald dome a dozen times a day, shouting, storming, spluttering, he never left his office without adding a little more confusion to the general disorder. We adored him, and that is the only possible explanation for his success, inconceivable otherwise, a success that was to burgeon out anew several months later.

Quite by accident, in a folder full of yellowing mementos, I recently discovered an obscure sketch, unfinished and undoubtedly deservedly so, in which I had traced the following little audio-portrait, practically nothing caricatural about it, of the phenomenon in question. The title referred to the expression we used to make a piece of news seem absolutely trustworthy:

And We Quote . . .
    Monologue.
    Music: Funeral March
    Time: 7:55 p.m.
    Who the hell's been messing around? . . . We'll never be ready on time . . . No no no, not that – Yes, fine, O.K. get it to the censor. Quick! Get going! . . . That's crazy, completelyabsolutelyidiotic! Take it over again. Hey, Coco! No not you . . . Coco! Not you! . . . Coco, you there, get over here. The show's at eight, it's a quarter to and nothing's ready! . . . Do I have to do it all alone? Things can't go on like this! (The pencil flies in the air) . . . Ah, there you are, Coco. Take that script there, no not that one, not that one, not that one either . . . Did you ever see the like? I haven't got fifteen hands and feet, things can't go on like this! . . . What? What's that you said? Why no! You're crazy to say that, Coco, crazy crazy crazy! (Kicks someone's ass) Can't go on like this!
    Time: 9:05 p.m.
    Verrry good, messieurs dames, a great show, magnificent . . . Very good Balbaud. Ah! Diana, verry good Diana! Etting, Lévesque, Sauerwein, perfect my Cocos. Perfect! Just give me more of the same, keep it up boys!
    Music: "It's so good to be together."
    Cut

It was this same overheated little dynamo who, without giving it a second thought, passed around the hat a few weeks later to pay for his return trip to Paris. I lent him my last five-pound note and never had news of it again. But in no time *France-Soir* hit the newsstands and, just as disreputable as its predecessor, eventually came a cropper, too, lasting just as long as Lazareff himself.

As far as we obscure other ranks were concerned, we put in the last hours of the long wait endlessly repeating our skimpy news bulletins from "somewhere on the eastern front" or from that legendary pincer movement somewhere in Asia that was forever on the point of "cutting off Mytkina." (I looked the place up in the atlas; it's not there any more; probably pulverized by the pincer.) It got so that we were spending more time playing cards than working, diving under the table every time a buzz-bomb seemed to want to stop at our address, then, first come first served, picking up the money scattered over the floor. After, we would go over to Chez Auguste, a little French enclave in the midst of cosmopolitan Soho, for a coffee and croissant that were not too bad, considering, and chat with the girls just finishing their night shift on the sidewalk opposite, also recognized as French territory. One ate fairly well at Chez Auguste; it was even quite remarkable to see what Auguste could turn out compared to the culinary bankruptcy of the Anglo-Saxons. His "civet de lapin" was a specialty, though he confessed to me after the victory that the rabbit was almost always helped along by alley cat.

We did occasionally have preoccupations that were a little more elevated. Buried in that boring proliferation of patriotic literature where God was always on our side, occasionally you would run across something like Georges Duhamel's *The Pasquier Chronicle*, which stretched from before until after the war, or that extraordinarily pure story, *The Silence of the Sea*, in which Vercors managed to create an oasis of beauty in the midst of barbarity. And there was also that song by Joseph Kessel, perhaps the most immortal fragment of all his work, that we heard Anna Marly sing one night in that wonderful grave voice of hers:

Friend, if you fall,
A friend will step forth
From the shadows
To fill in your place. . . .

At last it was D-Day, that day when hundreds of friends were to fall together. On the eve of the day we still didn't know for sure it was the eve, but one could feel the suspense ending. The whole southern part of the country had been sworn to secrecy, so naturally hundreds of people knew what was up. Snooping around the periphery on the outskirts of Southampton, I stumbled across a bunch of guys in uniform, soaked to the skin by rain, whose attitude let me guess that if they weren't part of the first wave they wouldn't be far behind. Their curt outbursts and forced laughter were punctuated by long silences that spoke louder than words. These men seemed to be marked with an invisible stamp that made them larger than life. Even their "goddammits" and "fuck yous" took on a resonance beyond mere triviality. Perhaps they would be their last words . . . .

I wouldn't be with them, though I was their age. That bothered me, made me vaguely ashamed. I was relieved not to be storming those bloody beaches, but at the same time I felt a mixture of envy and regret at the fact that I would miss seeing what was to be the apotheosis of our times. Maybe they'd miss it, too, though. From the look of that abominable sky I'd have sworn the hour of destiny wasn't scheduled to strike that day. But at that very moment in all the ports of the south coast the ships were casting off.

Later I would get a taste of it, and even sup my fill. But it wasn't the same thing. All we would be doing then was mopping up, as deadly as that could be on occasion. I had missed the big rendezvous.

13. Neither Valkyries nor Werwolves

O N THAT SIXTH OF JUNE the end of the war began. It would drag on many interminable and bloody months, but we knew then it wouldn't last forever. After the success of the landing, the slow, costly expansion of the Normandy bridgehead, and then the sudden breakthrough at St.-Lô, which General Patton (that cowboy with all the faults and qualities of the trade) quickly turned into a mad gallop, it seemed evident that the western part of the Nazi empire was about to crumble. Already GIs were promising themselves to be home for Christmas.

What can one say about this time of epic movements that hasn't already been said a hundred times by the bit players as well as by the big stars of the drama? As for myself, I have only a very slim album of impressions to show: to begin with, my first encounters with death, in particular that of a dear childhood friend whom I had to identify. He was one of many more than were ever acknowledged who were smashed by our own bombs. Once the anger and disgust had passed, you began to become hardened, because you had to.

As far as one could tell from hasty exposure, the whole of France was like a dismembered body in those days. Of course, everyone I met had belonged to the resistance! That was categorically true for the Communists who had fought as much, if not more, for Little Father Stalin as for Big Charles De Gaulle. This gave them the title to advertise themselves unchallenged as the army of the future in charge of quite a different "liberation." It was a time, luckily quite short, of excess and hypocrisy. Among the judges of those poor women with their heads shaved for having fraternized with the enemy and of those corpses hanged as presumed collaborators or war profiteers, how many had still acclaimed Pétain three months earlier?

Then, in August, Paris was liberated. French troops from the

Leclerc Division were first to enter. The Americans had stepped aside at the gates of the city to let them through (and I met plenty of GIs who grumbled about that long afterwards). But the free champagne ran out, the war moved east, and it seemed certain the curtain would soon be coming down.

When autumn rolled around we had to change our tune. As the front moved closer to Germany, the supply route, that famous "Red Ball Highway," became unduly long and military operations disrupted the provisioning of the civilian population. Some went so far as to say that shortages were worse than under the occupation. Then, suddenly, everything went wrong. The German resistance stiffened; they turned around and bared their teeth like cornered animals. It is sometimes claimed that the error that galvanized them was committed in Quebec. It was here, in September, 1944, that the Morgenthau Plan was adopted, according to which Germany was to be stripped bare, emasculated, its claws pulled, condemned for all eternity to a purely pastoral future. To accept the idea that not only Hitler's Reich but the fatherland itself would be condemned to death was more than a great people could bear. They determined to fight to the end, and nobody would be "Home for Christmas" . . . .

Apart from those whose careers were advanced by war and for whom a return to peace spelled mediocrity, I was among a few other rare birds to welcome this extension of hostilities. Otherwise, there wouldn't have been time for me to be sent, at last, to cover my small share of the combat. So there I was in my tank, hunched in the bottom of the cab, jerked around by incessant bumps projecting me from one metallic protuberance to another, shivering under the rough uniform, a trench coat, and two blankets, swearing with retroactive vision that they'd never get me in a place like this again. A terribly bitter wind, cold as the Arctic, whistled off the peaks of the Vosges Mountains through which we rumbled toward Alsace. Like dozens of others, my tank was chained to a flat truck in a convoy on its way to beef up some combat unit designated to reopen the offensive. As for me, I kept wondering if I was going to survive until tomorrow.

One survives everything at that age, and I managed to get through the winter without too many big problems. We lived like squatters in the cellars of some ruined houses "somewhere" near Metz. Rats kept us company; they had a big majority. We washed down those foul K-rations with beer, "liberated" wines, and once even a whole case of Cointreau. Thank God there were always a few cigarettes with them, and a piece of very hard black chocolate that was so nourishing one could often use what was left over in barter to keep up good relations with the civilian population, particularly the female side. The only noticeable damage I suffered, from bronchitis via laryngitis, was to lose all but a feeble trickle of voice, which was only to be restored to full force by a miraculous intervention some fifteen years later.

We would make a sortie every day or so, just long enough to put together a news story, usually – with slight variations – to the effect that in the west *Nichts neues*. There was only one thing of terrible banality we might have added: wherever we went, fear was usually there at the rendezvous.

The first real fear was the sound of bullets whistling over, or the wind from a mortar shell. The only one that's really dangerous, they say, is the one you don't hear. Just the same, your guts tie themselves into knots and your hands grab at them so, you begin to wonder if the seat of life isn't in the intestines. Some soldiers vomit continuously, bent double, going on when there's nothing left to throw up. The incurable ones are sent to the rear and put to work in the kitchens or repair shops. Nobody gives them a hard time; their trouble is purely physical – visceral in the strict sense of the word – and they can't help it. Are the ones who don't experience this reflex, or manage to control it, any more courageous? If you want, or perhaps more daring or foolhardy, but I continue to believe that what counts the most is to be several working together. Team spirit, the sense of belonging to your unit, that's what holds everyone in place, fitting into the scheme of things like so many pieces in a puzzle. Occasionally some solo Rambo may rear his head, but I never saw one. The general rule is the one that applied to the cemetery at night when we were kids: when you were alone you cautiously went around the outside; in a group we'd cut right through the middle, whistling "Dixie."

Ever since the arts of war were invented, they've been a young man's business, for the young, they say, are less afraid of death – of death, perhaps, but not of dying, I'll never believe that. To see and hear someone die, someone badly cut up who goes on and on, that's absolutely intolerable, all the more so because you put yourself in his place. In my book the real heroes will always be those front-line doctors, nurses, and stretcher-bearers who pick up and patch together as best they can those pieces of living debris left on the battlefield . . . although they, too, must harden themselves.

So with fear as companion we visited Haquenau, Bitche (unforgettable name), Sarre-this and Sarre-that, and other places. The back seat of the jeep had been replaced by a heavy generator, a very ornery piece of machinery that had to be charged constantly to juice up the recording apparatus, the whole shebang the latest in "portable" audio equipment at the time.

Here and there we would run into little groups of Germans making their own probes into no-man's-land. More often than not we would exchange a few gentlemanly bursts of fire and that would be that. When things did turn nasty, I would leave my operator to shelter behind the armour plating of the vehicle and, microphone in hand, give the world an account of this lively brush with the enemy from under the jeep, an account that would be boiled down to a couple of sentences in the day's communiqué. As second lieutenant assimilated rank – that is, non-combatant – I wasn't authorized to carry a weapon, but to make myself seem more important I had acquired a revolver, which I would have quickly ditched in case of encirclement. Once or twice I did fire it, not at but toward some vague silhouettes, and I can guarantee that I did them no harm, as anyone will confirm who knows anything about the range and precision of small arms in those days.

As winter drew to a close, the front began to move again and withdrew toward Germany so fast we barely had time to read the signposts. By Easter the enemy had fired its last shots in that mad campaign in the Ardennes that for a time around Christmas had sown panic in the Allied ranks and had created a multitude of temporarily missing men, who one by one came back to the fold. But on the other side losses were irreparable. They scarcely had more than a skirmish left in them, just to show their teeth, like that one in the graveyard of an Alsatian village where they held us up for an hour or two. After this the German company commander, a white-haired veteran of less than thirty, had two of their men laid out side by side in front of the charnel house, and we added two of our own. Nothing in such engagements, however, could slow down the advance that soon took us to the banks of the Rhine.

The crossing of that great frontier river was another historic moment. Opposite us, behind a light screen of morning haze, lay German soil. One might have expected some sort of Gotterdammerung where clouds of warriors escaped from the caves of mythology would drag us off with them to Valhalla. Nothing like it. Without the slightest Wagnerian accompaniment, little landing craft plied quietly back and forth and by noon a bridgehead had been established that was solid enough to allow the general staff to come across.

First among them, in big moustaches and leather pants, and with an air that was at once conquering and vengeful, came a French general, De Monsabert, who thereby launched the counter-occupation. He was followed by a jumble of Frenchmen, Moroccans, and Senegalese, amalgamated to form the First French Army and thus assure the tricolour a place at the victors' table.

This was the occasion of my first Franco-American liaison job, quite a modest one but invariably interesting and often pretty amusing. Back in London the almost total absence of the Free French from our ABSIE studios had been conspicuous. Here it was quickly apparent there was no love lost, as they say, between the Americans and the French, these faithful but intractable allies. Long after friend Lafayette, but well before the Roosevelt-De Gaulle chilliness, a love-hate relationship had set in that a humble little liaison officer could do nothing about, except observe and hope not to get his fingers caught in the gears – and remind others of the fact that under the American uniform beat a true heart of New France.

The smouldering animosity that today's Rome on the Potomac is confronted with on a world scale is nothing compared to the gleeful hatred that possessed the French invaders of the Reich. I have only retained a few vague images of the cruelty that marked those first few weeks, among them that of a large city, it must have been Stuttgart, where there were only old people, women, and children left; they had survived, but not before they had paid the price.

Of course, things weren't much better elsewhere. Everyone knows they were a lot worse on the Russian front. Then, in February, opening the floodgates of misfortune on the heads of the vanquished, came the Anglo-American bombing of Dresden. It was only much later that the truth came out about this raid that pushed barbarism beyond all imaginable limits. Call it just retribution if you will, for Hitler and his hordes had stopped at nothing when they had the upper hand. But the sight of those troops that were only a wan shadow of the supermen of 1940 and 1941, skeleton units made up of adolescents and veterans of the 1914-18 war recycled in the Volkssturm (the People's Army), in the midst of a people decimated and resigned to their fate, soon made one feel that enough blood had been shed.

For that matter, as we moved toward the south and the spring, shirts open to the sun, we began to feel more like playing hookey than waging war. We had to be constantly called to order: we were in enemy territory, we musn't forget that. The deeper we penetrated, the more likely it became we would run across the Werwolves, those ferocious, last-ditch Nazi guerillas that Berlin had often announced were being organized in impregnable strongholds that were said to have turned Bavaria into a fortress.

No such encounter occurred. It was a fiction, the terminal delirium of a mad regime. We had to advance cautiously just the same, for the same delirium could still catch people's minds and make them dangerous. That's exactly what happened to us in Nuremburg. In this holy city of the Nazis we were looking for the road to the stadium where we had so often seen on film der Führer thundering at the faithful by torchlight. We had nearly reached our objective when two grenades flew out of a basement window. One rolled harmlessly into the gutter, but the other smashed the front of one of our vehicles. A conditioned reflex sent us sprawling behind a wall. After two or three shots fired in the direction of the cellar, out came first a piece of rag more or less white, then four kids, three boys and a girl, in their Hitlerjungend outfits. The oldest wasn't fifteen. What could we do with these kindergarten assassins who could easily have finished us off? Each one of the dangerous prisoners was frisked, knocked around a little, and then requested, in English, French, and unmistakable gestures, to get the hell out of there schnell!

Not many Germans, however, were ready to fight to the finish. It was rather their fawning attitudes that struck us. They had been conditioned for so long to hold still and blindly obey – and to work with incomparable diligence. We actually saw industrial plants partly in ruins that had been repaired piecemeal and whose machines had been running the day before or the same day they were captured. After twenty years in prison Albert Speer, first Hitler's favourite architect, then his Minister of Munitions, related that at the very end of the conflict Germany had even managed to beat its own production records.

Titre d'ascendance

Levesque

	Première génération	
Robert	22 - 4 - 1679 L'Ange - Gardien	Jeanne Chevalier

	Deuxième génération	
François-Robert	7 - 11 - 1701 Rivière - Ouelle	Charlotte Aubert

	Troisième génération	
Dominique	19 - 7 - 1745 Rivière - Ouelle	Dorothée Bérubé

	Quatrième génération	
Dominique	29 - 10 - 1781 Saint-Roch des Aulnaies	Angélique Pelletier

	Cinquième génération	
Zacharie	3 - 9 - 1812 Rivière - Ouelle	Isabelle D'Anteuil

	Sixième génération	
Dominique	26 - 3 - 1845 Rivière - Ouelle	Marcelline Pearson

	Septième génération	
Zacharie	19 - 1 - 1879 Saint - Pacôme	Célina Levesque

	Huitième génération	
Dominique	4 - 10 - 1920 Saint - Patrice	Diana Dionne

	Neuvième génération	
René		

Authentifié par François Beaudin à Québec, le 3 juillet 1978
Conservateur des Archives
Nationales du Québec

La Fête du retour aux sources

Denis Vaugeois
Le Ministre des Affaires Culturelles

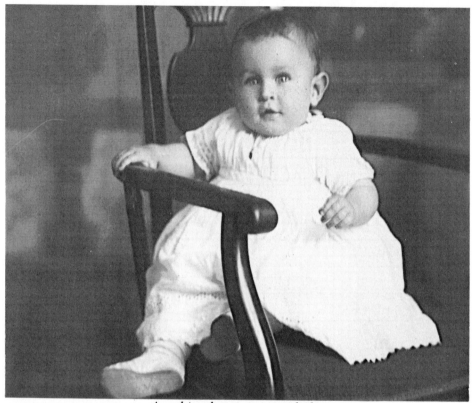

Anything but a starving baby!
René Lévesque — 10 months.

The house in New Carlisle.

Mother, Diane D. Lévesque, 1925.

Dominique Lévesque with his son, René, 1925.

Back from the war, 1945.

Just out of jail. CBC strike, 1959.

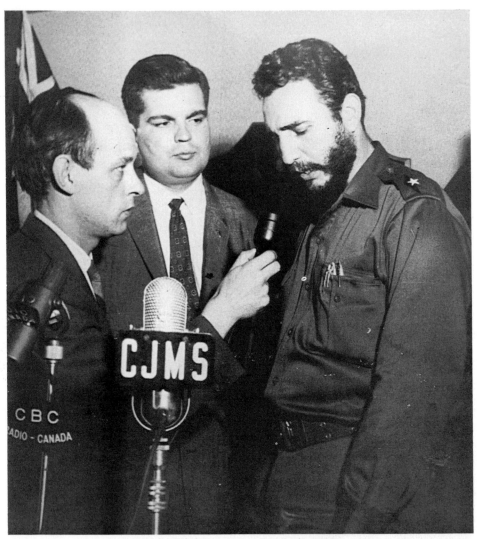

With Fidel Castro in Dorval, 1959.
(with president of Junior Chamber of Commerce)

Lévesque and Yves Michaud, 1967.
"Did he really say: Vive le Québec libre?"

The night before his death, Daniel Johnson with Jean Lesage
and René Lévesque.

We saw these traits of character displayed in a remarkable way in the little town of Donauworth near the source of the Danube. A column of tanks had just occupied it, knocking over the shaky old city gate on the way. The centre of town was demolished. All that was left of the main street were gutted, blackened buildings and scattered stubs of walls over which floated the acrid smoke of ashes and decay. Suddenly a group of elderly persons appeared and, bare-headed, approached the *Burgermeister*, that is, the officer in charge of the tanks who was filling the role of chief justice until the administrative team got there. They greeted him, identified themselves, then presented their request, which in substance ran as follows: "If you don't see any objection to it, *Herr Offizier*, we could begin to sweep all this up. That would clear a passage for you, and at the same time we could put to one side anything that was still good and . . ."

They were thinking about reconstruction already, starting from zero. This was what would eventually transform an unprecedented evil into a miraculous recovery. By strength of discipline and driven by necessity, Germany and Japan, Korea, Austria, and a few other countries were forced to rebuild, completely or in part, and in doing so became more modern and efficient, which soon allowed them to overtake and pass countries that had crushed them, particularly ones that had come through the war unscathed and had thus let many essential sectors become obsolete or outmoded. Among such countries now experiencing a slowdown in development and standard of living, Canada holds a prominent place. One might have wished (without the war or the carnage) that we, too, had "profited" from a good dose of destruction.

14. The Truth
Stranger Than Fiction

THE REST OF MY WAR is a series of sketches that runs from burlesque to horror by way of melodrama.

The last days of the Third Reich, with its leader preparing his own exit under the rubble of Berlin, were paced by capitulations all over the place as Germany finally spewed up those millions of prisoners, slaves, and living dead who formed the human plunder of so many cruel raids.

One sunny afternoon a thin, athletic man approached us, running at an unhurried pace, jogging before the invention of the word. Being a tennis buff I recognized him almost immediately: it was Borotra, an all-time champion. He was hardly winded and told us that he'd just walked out of the château-prison of Itter a few kilometres up the road. The garrison there had melted into the landscape, leaving some pretty fancy prisoners ripe for the picking. We found them in one of the ground-floor rooms sitting around in little groups seeming very disinclined to talk to one another. We had stumbled on the almost forgotten upper crust of pre-war Paris society: the union leader Léon Jouhaux, General Gamelin, Commander-in-Chief of the defeat of 1940, and, each in his own corner, the last two prime ministers of the ex-republic, Edouard Daladier and Paul Reynaud.

The chance to interview these ghosts was a real godsend. Respecting chronology, I began with Daladier. The old "bull of the Vaucluse" had thinned down a little, but he was still a rugged customer, though he had a hesitant look as if he might be worried about awkward questions. As far as that went, he'd had plenty of time to prepare himself.

"Monsieur le Premier Ministre," I asked him after we'd been formally introduced, "would you mind sharing with us some of the reflections that time and distance have certainly given you a chance to elaborate?"

"Cher Monsieur," he replied, "I have indeed many things to reveal, and above all a great many things to set straight. I intend to publish a full account as soon as I return to France. But here, you understand," he said lowering his voice, "there are indiscreet ears belonging to certain individuals who will be unmasked in my memoirs as they deserve to be. I can hardly say more."

Saying these words, he shot a murderous look at Paul Reynaud, who sat at the other end of the room affecting the most complete indifference. Hoping against hope, I now approached this dry, pointed little fellow and was summarily treated almost word for word to a repeat of the preceding scene. He, too, Reynaud said, had plenty to expose and certain people – same murderous look – had better watch themselves! Not only were they not on speaking terms, they could hardly wait to carve each other up. None the wiser, I had to settle for a simple statement of our discovery without further adornment.

Fortunately, another chance encounter made up for the scoop I had been cheated of and earned me a host of compliments, which just goes to show that a reporter is only as good as his luck. As we made our way along, eyes riveted on the gigantic rampart of the Alps sparkling in the sun, the bushes at the side of the road parted and out strode a large man who planted himself before us. We recognized him immediately as Hermann Goering. For his surrender he had once again donned the grand pastel blue uniform he had apparently exchanged for a simple khaki outfit on his escape from Berlin. Against the vast natural setting, the resplendent epaulettes of this Reichsmarschall who had been fired by Hitler, as well as a chestful of decorations, shone in the sunlight. But in less time than it takes to tell, our platoon leader, in a couple of passes worthy of a fencer, ripped away all that glitter. A few buttons popped off, too, and became souvenirs along with the rest of the paraphernalia.

Shaken, Goering lost his hesitant smile, came to attention, and without a word let himself be roughly shoved onto a bench standing in the field. During the next few minutes he silently endured the scatalogical inquisition the GIs reviled him with, for example (with expurgations): "So that's the great Marshal, huh? Great? That thing? Hell, he's just a great pile of shit!"

Taking advantage of a pause in these proceedings, he made a short speech in quite acceptable English, which ran more or less as follows: "You can do what you like with me. I have no illusions and nothing to complain of. I just find you very ill-bred. But I beg you, don't make our people go on suffering, They have already more than paid for whatever the world, rightly or wrongly, may hold against them. If there is more to pay, it is I and others like me who should pay the price."

At that particular moment one couldn't help finding him impressive, if not exactly convincing. Under the carcass of the old ruffian there still lurked a spark of the heroic young pilot of World War I. It was doubtless this resurgent pluck that made him a leader of the impossible defence at the Nuremberg trials, cynical but fearless right up to the very last choice – cyanide instead of the rope.

As for us, we didn't commit any hanging offences, but we weren't angels either. Nothing of any value escaped being "liberated," and then would be dumped if something better turned up. Among the NCOs in particular there were some real mafiosi running the plunder network; at the end of hostilities all they had to do was recycle themselves and turn up as managers of the first PX stores. From this point of view armies have always appreciated entrepreneurial initiative, so it seems. Shall I say what a single package of cigarettes could get you? With a carton one became irresistible. Thinking back on it, it's nothing to be proud of, but it's less embarrassing than the memory of what happened toward the end of April in a suburb of Munich.

I was accompanying a handful of Scouts from General Patch's Seventh Army. He could be a hard driver when he wanted to be, but he was mainly miserly when it came to spending the lives of his men. The few times I saw this big gangling guy with his worried look, he reminded me of young Gary Cooper. (Come to think of it, Cooper was young, too, in those days!) Anyway, we were rolling along pretty quietly down this middle-class street that had suffered very little damage when rifle fire broke out from a crossroad about fifty metres ahead. It didn't sound all that friendly, no more than the orders barked out by some individual who was still invisible but was definitely not American. Realizing we'd just blundered into something, we abandoned the jeep and the command car and took off up the nearest alley, down the next street, and into a courtyard on the other side of which a friendly door stood open. This led down a staircase to a basement room where the walls were hung with pictures and lined with shelves of valuable books; it obviously wasn't just anyone who lived there. There was no noise overhead;

the owners had fled. But through the window came those dangerous, easily identifiable voices discussing the situation, first further up the street, then closer, and sometimes so close we wished we could sink into the walls. We spent a long hour of eternity there before silence returned and finally the sound of good old Yankee accents.

Before rejoining the others, though, we had to get decompressed and release a little vengeance for having had such a scare, if not against someone, then against something. One of us had a great idea, everyone concurred, and the fireworks didn't stop till we had emptied the last magazine.

"Take that, rat-tat-tat-tat, you lousy Krauts!"

When we left, not a single painting and very few books remained unscathed. It was an understandable way to work off steam. And inexcusable.

Yet this sin against property was nothing, absolutely nothing, compared to the hell on earth we were to get our first sight of the next day or the day after. In the outskirts, at Dachau, we knew there were mysterious places called "concentration" camps. Rumours had already reached us, first from Poland where the Russians were telling incredible stories that we took with a grain of salt, and more recently from French units over by the Black Forest who had also been speaking of things to make our hair stand on end. Now it was our turn to see what it was all about.

We passed neat rows of pretty little Bavarian houses each with a niche over the door with a statue or image of a patron saint in it. In their shady gardens stood pleasant-looking old people who at a sign from us would come timidly over and very politely show us the way.

"*Konzentrazions Lager? Ja, ja,* over there. Five minutes at the most. *Danke. Bitte.*"

Our first sight of the camp was freight trains on a siding, two lines of boxcars with some cadavers hanging out the open doors, and more scattered on the embankment. A torrid sun shone down and the smell was atrocious. We quickly entered the town, for that's what it seemed to be: behind low walls interspersed with watchtowers there was some kind of industrial complex with small factory buildings and repair shops. But this first impression was dissipated at sight of the indescribable crowd that rushed toward us. Riddled with questions in a dozen languages, pulled here and there by hands of frightening thinness attached to translucent wrists, we stood there stunned, staring at these phantoms in striped pyjamas who were staggering out of the huts where they had been hiding until we had arrived on the scene with some of the members of the first health services. In fact, the last traces of the German garrison had taken to their heels less than a quarter of an hour before.

A man who was still young but who was nothing but skin and bones told me in excellent French that he had lived some time in Montreal and, like everyone else, asked for a cigarette. I felt in my pocket; the package had disappeared. I discovered that all the pockets of my jacket had fared likewise. The depths of misery and hunger sometimes bring out the hero and the saint, at least that's what they say, but more often they debase and bring out the bird of prey.

This was illustrated by the following spectacle. Holding each other by the hand as though in some kind of children's game, a group of prisoners, surrounded by others watching them avidly, came toward us. Suddenly, savage cries of joy broke out when, from the middle of the circle, a young fellow was cast forth. He had plenty of meat on him, for he was a "Kapo," one of the prison guards who hadn't been able to escape and who had been lying low waiting for the right moment. They forced him to kneel down, held his head up straight, and a big Slav with a toothless leer came up with a stick and methodically, chuckling with pleasure, smashed the lower part of his face and jaw until it was nothing but a mass of bone and bleeding flesh.

One couldn't do a thing. We wouldn't have known what to do anyway. And wouldn't have wanted to do anything when we learned it had been literally a case of an eye for an eye and a tooth for a tooth. Before putting their prisoners to work the Germans always stripped them of all their possessions, including their gold teeth. Then they worked them to death, especially the last year when rations were becoming scarce. At the end of the road they were sent to the "baths" (*Baden*), shabby-looking sheds linked to a reservoir by a couple of pipes. When the baths were full to the seams they opened the gas, and then, when the last groans had ceased, the bodies were taken to the ovens next door.

When news of this reached Quebec, and for some time after, people refused to believe. Heavy scepticism greeted such stories, which surpassed understanding. And even today, so many years later, it's sometimes worse. People who have the gall to proclaim themselves neo-Nazis, knowing that memory is a faculty capable of forgetting, go so far as to maintain that none of this really happened.

I can assure you that it was real, all right, that the gas chamber was real in its nightmarish unreality. The loaders had gone, trying to save their skins, leaving behind their last load of corpses, naked as worms in their muddy pallor. Near me was a cameraman whom I had promised a few words of commentary; he had to come out twice before he could film his ten seconds. On seeing it, the American Brigadier who had turned up on the scene took his revolver out of its holster and strode around with haggard eyes, muttering that he had to kill some of those bastards. His men had all they could do to calm him down.

Deloused and covered from head to foot in DDT, we retraced our steps to our billet in the harmonious-sounding village of Rosenheim. On the way, passing through the quiet suburb with its kindly old people, we asked each other with our eyes, "Did they know? How could they not have? What was behind those good, old, pious-looking faces?" But what was the use questioning? We were beginning to wish we hadn't seen anything ourselves.

To change our ideas we took a tourist detour to see Berchtesgaden and Hitler's eagle-nest retreat. But our friends from the Leclerc Division had already gone through it with a fine-tooth comb. In a pile of garbage I at least turned up an autographed record (signature illegible) of "Lili Marlene," that imaginary pinup of all the camps. Then we made a side trip as far as Milan only to discover that Mussolini, that Caesar so acclaimed and then so spat upon by the Italian crowds, was no longer hanging in the street. There was no more war, no more German army, just the residue pouring back over the Brenner Pass toward Innsbruck.

And there, in that Tyrolian oasis, thanks to some very superior radio equipment left behind for us by our escaping predecessors, we heard the news of V-E Day on the eighth of May, 1945, as we came in from winter sports.

15. Between the Wars

IT WAS TOO LATE for the mountain air to cleanse the legacy of so many unhygienic weeks. I had caught an ailment that makes people laugh when they don't know how maddening it can be: the mange, to call a spade a spade. Not everyone contracted it, but a goodly company ended up with me in the same wing of a Brussels hospital where they looked after our complaint and the whole range of venereal diseases. In those days penicillin was the cure-all, so they stuffed us with I don't know how many thousands of units and, knocked out by the wonder drug, the itch disappeared as if by magic. I regained health thanks to large doses of steak and French fries that the ingenious Belgians were already beginning to fill up on again, now that their port of Antwerp was open, while Paris was still constrained to a lenten diet.

Paris, as well, suffered from a rash of Americans. With their pushy *nouveau riche* manners, they fell into disfavour pretty damn quick. I remember a game of poker, for instance, where so many different kinds of bills were in circulation that everyone had to have his own currency conversion table in front of him. If a greenback happened to drift into this jungle of multi-coloured paper, an arm would immediately extend and a voice from below the 49th parallel would drawl out: "Ha! Real money!"

In July I was sent south, where troops that had been stationed in Germany were being assembled in Mediterranean ports in preparation for the inevitable invasion of Japan. I took the opportunity to make a leisurely exploration of little towns and villages in Provence, that other France that is so welcoming compared to Paris. But the American shock was lying in wait again on the Côte d'Azur, where many American troops were gathered. At the entrance to Cannes, a city reserved for officers, and again outside Nice where other ranks were billeted, stood huge billboards carrying crude cartoons supposed to be funny and the warning: "Beware! VD area!" I couldn't believe my eyes. But I was obliged to believe my ears one of the following days when, thanks to the incognito of my American uniform, I heard the barman at the Miramar, thinking he was safe to explode in French, exclaim: "*Nom de Dieu*! Now we've got these ones on our backs, give me the Boches any day!"

Yet a certain admiration hid behind this hostility. Like uptight parents trying to deal with teen-agers, the Europeans couldn't help feeling envious when confronted by the self-assurance and outspokenness of the New World. They were envious, too, when faced with American know-how, the supreme manifestation of which burst upon the world in the form of three large black words filling the front page of the U.S. Army's *Stars and Stripes* one August morning: A-BOMB ON JAPAN. What was this A-Bomb? We didn't know. But we guessed pretty soon that the sailing for Japan had just been put on the shelf indefinitely.

My own sailing late that summer was on board the *Normandie*, which hardly lived up to its reputation. We were some twelve thousand packed in like sardines, and rather than suffocate in the cabins we preferred to sleep, or at least spend the night, on deck. Since my two Atlantic crossings were decidedly short on comfort, and Progress soon after condemned me to air travel, I've always had a hankering for a beautiful first-class cruise awash in voluptuous luxury.

For the time being, however, I would have to settle for small potatoes in the modest job of jack-of-all-trades for the International Service of Radio-Canada. I rediscovered there something of the cosmopolitan climate of the studio in London, minus the madcap tension of 1944. Canada had now become a "middle power" and was blowing its own horn on short wave in several not-much-listened-to languages. It didn't take me long to see that I'd been relegated to the ghetto of radio. But what claim did I have to a better fate? With a voice not much above a whisper, almost non-existent in fact, I would never be called on to do those commercials for private stations that brought fame and fortune to Balu, Bertrand, Lecavalier, and other golden-voiced colleagues. Cast as a reporter, a job that no one took seriously in those days, I not only remained unknown but laboured under the additional handicap of having "come up" from the States.

Stripped of illusions, then, I earned my two or three thousand a year, a bonanza that allowed me to enter into wedded bliss with the girl who had had the patience to wait for me and with whom I lost no time in contributing to the Baby Boom. Two children soon appeared on the scene and I immediately became a classically gaga papa. Nothing can surpass the fascination of watching new eyes discovering the world but not quite sure they are ready to accept it. Pierre, for example, refused to go to bed and, like a little Joshua crying his eyes out, ordered the heavenly orb: "Sun not go! No! Pierrot say no!" Pierrot was what we called him until one day, after we had shouted and hunted for him in vain and were on the point of alerting the police, he turned up and announced coldly, "My name is Pierre." Whereupon his younger brother, who was still afflicted with his nursery nickname, decreed that for his part he was no longer "Baby Lévesque" but Claude. We took good note of it.

This rebellious spirit was compounded by gluttony and a staggering growth rate. We had to find ways to make ends meet at the end of the month. Bilingualism came to the rescue and I took up translation, a task that is generally underestimated, although it is among the most exacting professions if practised with care. It can even become as exigent as goldsmith's work, for example, when you are required to render the text of an English film into French with each phrase and if possible each word precisely marrying the natural movement of the lips. You must turn your work and yourself with it twenty times upon the muse's anvil, especially when the mirror obstinately reflects a slack-mouthed "a" instead of the pucker of an "o."

I was on the way to becoming a veritable lip-sync wizard and I would have continued quietly exercising this noble profession if the guys of the Van Doos hadn't taken it into their heads to get a piece of the action in Korea. The CBC was summoned to find someone to keep them company and send news back home. People weren't exactly trampling over each other to get the job; in fact, the person they chose for it was someone who had already occasionally been stuck with assignments nobody else wanted.

Korea didn't interest me particularly but I wanted to get to know Asia. The hardest thing was getting there. . . . From Montreal to Tacoma, Washington, was a breeze. Our North Star pumped along valiantly like those other indomitable veterans, the C-47s, the Caravelles, and others of that ilk that still service remote areas despite the ubiquitous and unnerving jet. It was more panic than nerves, however, that I felt the next morning, and I came close to scramming right out of there when I saw our pilot weaving up to the plane after a binge that had lasted until the small hours of the morning. The navigator didn't seem to be in much better shape, but luckily the co-pilot just looked tired. And after all, Hawaii would be worth the risk. . . . Hawaii, my foot! It was doubtless a stopover reserved for the great manitous of the Air Force. We commoners were sent over via the Aleutians.

Besides the beat-up crew, the passengers included a sergeant coming back from leave, myself, and a huge spare engine that sat in the middle of the stripped-down cabin area and took up all the space. Squeezed into our seats on either side of this bulky travelling companion, the sergeant and I dozed off while gazing at the infinite monotony of the ocean. After several hours there was nothing to see but a thick fog into which the plane began to make its interminably slow descent, seeking out Attu or Kiska, one of those minuscule rocks we were supposed to land on. Lower, and still lower, then suddenly the plane picked up altitude with the roar of an angry beast. The same scenario was repeated twice over. Frozen in our seats, the sergeant and I exchanged looks that betrayed a common preoccupation: would our three flying hangovers have the strength to stick it out? At last, a crack in the fog revealed an inch of airstrip, the plane dove down on it, and when it finally consented to come to a stop, we could make out the sound of waves breaking a few feet away.

Headlights emerged from the mist and we were taken by jeep to a narrow door. Above it a solitary lightbulb shone feebly. This must be the visitors' dormitory, I thought. But behind the door, stretching away for a good kilometre, ran a corridor crossed by innumerable halls, without a sign of a window. Along the entire length of the walls, however, the plaster was broken by countless holes. We were told that these were caused by furious blows delivered by men whose nerves were shot. Ever since the Japanese had stuck their noses into the area in World War II, thousands of Americans had passed through here to stand guard on this rocky, deserted promontory perpetually drowned in the frigid mists of the North Pacific. Only dice and cards and the risk of ruining yourself for life, or the chance of ruining your neighbour, helped more or less to make this caveman existence endurable.

All things considered, I concluded I'd probably prefer Korea.

16. Night on Bald Mountain

KOREA, OR CHOSEN, means "country of the calm morning." At the turn of the year 1952 the old poetic name applied again to the whole of Korea, except on the banks of the Imjin River where the demarcation line between North and South still runs today. Fifty kilometres further south, Seoul was in ruins after changing hands two or three times in the mobile warfare of the preceding years. The bulk of the population had fled still further south, leaving behind a dreadful number of lost children and orphans hunting through the rubble like little stray dogs. We had adopted one called Chung – they were all called Chung – and he had become our batman.

On this campaign I was a veteran who knew his way around just as did our fellow roommate, Bill Boss, a top reporter for the Canadian Press. In the midst of this urban desolation we had found a pretty reasonable pad for ourselves where our technician, Norman Eaves, set up a makeshift studio that I shared with McBain, my counterpart for the BBC. The degree to which I had become a battle-hardened veteran with initiative and cunning is illustrated by the following insignificant detail. For their food, which wasn't much better than in 1945, the international amalgam known as the UN Forces depended on the Americans. Shortly after our arrival there were nine hundred and one of us receiving a weekly bottle of tabasco with our rations to burn off the taste: the Thailand battalion and yours truly!

Our life would have been a nine-to-five routine except for the final spasms of the conflict that dragged us week after week into a guerilla war more vicious and disheartening than real war. After a peaceful drive through the suburbs we would reach the Imjin snaking around in its valley. On the opposite bank Koreans, dressed in black and wearing those curious shell-shaped hats, would be working away in the rice paddies. Friend or foe? Just try to find out. It's never easy to guess what's going on behind a face of another colour.

Beyond the flooded fields was a zone of bamboo and grass taller than a man that stretched away to the hills whose naked crests disappeared in saw-toothed ridges toward the enemy positions. That's where we were headed, across the river, through the rice fields where the impassive peasants paid so little attention to us it was nerve-wracking, and on into those damned hills. It took half an hour just to get up, more to come back. Once more into the breach, dear friends . . . and then once more. I was pushing thirty, an age when the legs aren't what they used to be. On top of that we had to be bloody careful not to step on one of those little mines, assuredly one of the dirtiest devices ever invented, that on slightest contact would send a charge of shot up between your legs, with curious consequences, as one can imagine. Add to that a collection of particularly charming insects. One day on a peak where we were bivouacking, I had just dropped off for a well-earned forty winks when I felt something moving on my forearm. I opened one eye and lay there paralysed. It was an enormous velvet spider, its stomach distended by a brownish, evil-looking pouch. Someone had the courtesy to give me a healthy kick, which got rid of the monster but almost broke my bones.

Of course, even more evil-intentioned than that was the enemy prowling around us. We had to keep our eyes peeled, especially at night. It was easy enough to stay awake, though, because the Chinese always began by treating us to a cacophonous concert of horns, first in the distance, then closer and closer, a roaring that was supposed to freeze the blood in your veins. Then, generally, they would launch their attack on the hill; from the top would come the UN riposte, and at last they would fall back, carrying their dead with them. Never once, if I'm not mistaken, did we come across an enemy corpse. There weren't too many bad casualties on our side either. It was nothing more than an unimportant little war, but terribly dirty, sad, and depressing. In fact, the worst victims were the men who ended up shooting themselves in the foot or the leg in hopes of being evacuated, or, worse still, ones who attacked an officer – then they had really had it.

But I did know some exceptions who swam and even frisked through that chaos like fish in the sea. One was Sergeant-Major Juteau, a thirty-year-old Montrealer affectionately nicknamed "Pipeau" by his comrades-in-arms and considered by hundreds of Koreans to be their Providence. Cool and composed as if doing his former day's work at the weather office in Dorval, he performed one of the most dangerous jobs done by the battalion. The first time I encountered him was well ahead of the front lines. Twenty minutes earlier I had left behind the bulk of the unit, who were marking time in the mud waiting for an order to advance. Between two flooded rice paddies I was following the tracks of the Pioneers, that is, the guys who carry the shovels and dig the trenches. But the path was becoming narrower and narrower, the mountain opposite higher and more threatening, and, above all, the silence was getting deeper and deeper.

Increasingly less sure of myself, I was just about to retrace my steps when suddenly I noticed a strange-looking character. A man stood there alone, terribly alone, alone as only a man can be in a hostile country, in the driving rain, at the mouth of a tortuous pass with God knows what at the other end. He was motionless, lost in his greenish poncho as though peering out of a tent, and all I could see were a pair of bright eyes, a mocking smile, and, between the two, the superb moustache of a Sicilian bandit. The glistening muzzle of a rifle stuck out from the folds of his cape. At his feet a police dog sat patiently in a puddle, its tongue hanging out.

"You going far like that?" he asked in a sarcastic voice.

I gave a quick, shamefaced reply: "I'm looking for the Pioneers. You wouldn't have seen them by any chance?"

He looked at me pityingly. Then, turning to his dog: "Say, Pancho, you wouldn't have seen the Pioneers go by while we were hunting Chinese, would you?"

Man and dog exchanged a long look. I had the distinct impression the animal was making fun of me, too!

"There aren't any Pioneers here. No Chinese either, luckily. I mean, there's always a few around, but they stay in their holes waiting for night."

"And you, what are you doing here?"

"*Nous autres*," he replied quietly, "we're scouts and snipers. We stay up ahead turning out Chinese. You can't see them, but my men are out on either side of us combing the place clean."

For two or three days running Pipeau would do this murderous job. Then, back at camp, while the others drank and tried to forget, he would go around with his even-measured stride giving conferences to explain his "Khaki Charities," a relief organization he had founded. He was an orderly and logical man, this sergeant-major, and he wasn't going to let himself be put off by the indescribable misery of the Korean people any more than by the ambushed Chinese. So to the best of his ability he set out to help them. He remembered the day and the hour the idea came to him: "May 29, 1951. Rain. In the front line."

These brief notes written in his journal, a school exercise book, were the beginning of a story that I eagerly transcribed with all the respect due a man with a big heart, though who perhaps was a bit short on schooling.

"A few seconds ago I was looking at a little Korean girl seven or eight years old. It's raining, she's barefoot, wearing a long robe that comes down almost to her ankles. Her jet-black hair is plastered down by the rain. She's looking for something to eat and she smiles in a frightened way as she walks among the soldiers and the trucks. Looking at her I was hit by a really strong feeling of remorse. I just ate two chocolate bars. Without thinking about it. I was hungry and I ate. Now I feel miserable. I should have asked her to come and sit with me in the truck. I could have put these three or four blankets around her and tried to get her warmed up. . . . What strikes me most is the egoism there is inside me . . . Pipeau."

Since he had decided he was an egoist, he determined to reform himself. From that day on he spent all his free time "bugging" people, begging chocolate, goodies, and all the old clothes they could pass on. When he had a truck full, he would go to the civilian hospital at Uijongbu, a pitiful tent city at the gates of Seoul where they parked the refugees: emaciated children looking for their parents; old people with wounds gnawed at by gangrene; women about to bring fatherless children into the world; and, lost in this sea of misery, a few doctors and volunteers trying to spin out their dwindling stocks of food and medicine.

"When I brought them my first load," this Good Samaritan said, "the doctor who received me had tears in his eyes. It was the first time somebody from the army had paid any attention to them. And for me, it was the first time I was glad to be in Korea."

But apart from him, everyone had had it up to here and dreamed of the next chance to escape to the charms of "R and R," that is, a period of rest and recuperation, which translated into army slang as "rape and ruin." With a little luck one could work in a few days' holiday in Japan. It was an "occupied" country in both senses of the word, living under foreign occupation and frenetically occupied in rebuilding cities that had been almost entirely flattened. In certain quarters of Tokyo that had miraculously survived – Ginza, the bustling commercial avenue, and the red-light district on the other side of the port – the locals worked hard to entertain the soldiers and others while fleecing them with a smile. It was only a couple of hours to Kyoto, heart of Japanese Buddhism, which the bombing had luckily spared. Everywhere else, like an anthill of crazy activity, the country was rising from the ruins before our very eyes. Even in Hiroshima reconstruction had made giant strides.

Standing before the only concrete reminder of that apocalyptic instant, the blackened carcass of a building that is to be left that way *in memoriam*, I was able to imagine the surrealist spectacle of thousands of crippled and dying Japanese lifting their heads from the ruins to listen to the voice that had come over the loudspeakers seven years earlier, the hitherto unknown voice of the Mikado, Son of Heaven, ordering his people to lay down their arms. Whatever the inspiration that subsequently dictated such generous terms and gestures to that famous megalomaniac Generalissimo Douglas MacArthur, things developed remarkably well after that. Once the collective despair had been purged by a vast wave of suicides, a peaceful atmosphere settled in that had nothing artificial about it. One could get lost after midnight in the dark, anonymous streets of Tokyo without more risk of danger than in Montreal, and less risk than in New York.

The détente was infectious and it reached everybody. Take, for example, the day I finally resigned myself to return to Seoul (I didn't have much choice) only to find that the plane hadn't waited for me. Seeing me hitchhiking on the side of the runway, a sloppy-Joe of a pilot took pity on me, at least so I thought, and beckoned to me to follow. His aircraft, with its turrets dismantled and its windows blacked out, was as shabby as he was and should have made me think twice. Inside I found a cargo of oranges destined for "the boys" in Korea. It was stiflingly hot, so I really appreciated the breeze that ran through the fuselage on takeoff. At three thousand metres I was beginning to think differently. It was like flying over the Pole. After two hours of shivering in that deafening windstream I was so quick-frozen I couldn't even tell we had landed. I came to when my pilot friend asked me sarcastically how I liked the air-conditioning. I left him without a word.

"Without a word" is also an expression that suits those first strange encounters that began the interminable palavers over the ceasefire. We would fly over the Chinese lines by helicopter, landing in a fortified area surrounded by barbed wire. In the middle was a small building with a pagoda roof. The press was parked near the door reserved for the UN negotiators. On the other side a bunch of Oriental soldiers with red stars on their caps kept close watch on their own territory. They spoke among themselves in low voices, but if one of us made so bold as to approach, he would be greeted by a deathly silence. Even the most pleasantly put question would be met with an enigmatic stare. Fortunately, a crack finally appeared in this wall in the person of a British journalist, Wilfred Burchett, an original and talkative Communist who for many years had been installed in Peking acting as the "white voice" of the regime. We had several discussions and I remember particularly the one about the recent expulsion of our missionaries. As serious as a pope, Burchett advised me that the Jesuits in particular deserved severe punishment, for they took in children not only to convert them but to turn them into slaves. Remembering all the pennies collected in bygone days to be sent to the *Brigand*, a mimeographed bulletin that used to come to the college urging us to "buy" one of the poor starving little Chinese, I wagered that despite all their faults the Jesuits would never stoop so low. Humour eventually won the day when Burchett confessed with a malicious grin that he was only giving me the official line.

As for the negotiations, they continued just as officially to mark time day after day. At least they lasted long enough to let me complete what was for me the most unforgettable assignment of the campaign. Perched on one of those abominable peaks during a night of driving rain, half a dozen Québécois had taken refuge under canvas, telling themselves the enemy would never be so crazy as to come out in such lousy weather. It was dark as pitch, the rain pattered relentlessly on the walls of the tent, and a sea of muddy water was gradually spreading everywhere. What else was there to do in such a hole but talk? From the depths of the shadows came heavy sighs punctuated by angry, melancholy phrases speaking of home, back there so far across the seas. It was fascinating. I crept out silently, and just as discreetly the operator, Norman Eaves, helped me slip a mike under the tent. All I had to do then was catch this homesickness as it overflowed, in terms I hesitate to reproduce but which remain a hallowed part of our vocabulary. It went something like this:

"*Baptême*! Are we ever going to get out of this *calîsse* of a country of *cons*? When I think I could be up on the North Shore, *tabernacle*, fishing salmon! Ah! that North Shore salmon, you don't know it, eh? Well, it fights *en hostie*, boy, it's really something! *Maudite merde de Christ* but I can't wait to get home again! . . . "

When I had half an hour of this moving testimony on tape, I quickly left for Seoul where all that was left to do was to relay the masterpiece home after tidying it up a bit. There we ran into a slight snag, however, for Norman Eaves didn't know a single bloody word of French, and most of the salty expressions on the tape were absolutely forbidden on the airwaves. Scissors in hand, we replayed the same passages over a dozen times, eliminating the most resonant oaths one by one.

"No, no, Norman, 'North Shore-*nacle*' isn't good enough. You'll have to cut the *nacle*. . . . Hey, did you catch that? '*stie*-boy' has a *stie* too many. . . ."

The sun was up before we got to bed. When I woke I found a second spool of tape on the foot of my bed. Norman was so fed up he'd taken the trouble to stick together all the scraps of tape we'd tossed on the floor. "Here's your goddam French swear-words," his note read. "You know where you can shove them!"

The enemy undoubtedly felt the same, for I'm told that the Van Doos' secret communications code was never cracked, and they always spoke the purest brand of *joual*.

17. I Am a Federalist

I T'S HARD TO WRITE ABOUT WAR. The bits of it I saw and have just described are only fleeting images perceived through the small end of the binoculars. But how, after all, can one do justice to such widespread folly played out in a hundred acts. Only the great historians sometimes manage it, and when they do, what they show us is the incoherence and the perfect absurdity of each of these capitulations to collective savagery.

Some writers conclude in their wisdom that all great wars are the midwives of history, delivering social upheaval and revolution. But you can't lose sight of the state the patient is left in. The forceps of the 1939-45 war left Europe, Germany, and the city of Berlin cut in two. They remain so today. Crushing Japan opened the road to Mao and Chinese communism. Great Britain and France became nothing more than very middling powers, and two new empires divided the world. Then Korea split into two new fragments not soon to be reunited.

To achieve this tortured result cost millions of deaths and shattered lives and the most blindingly barbarous holocaust ever offered History by this animal endowed with reason. To my knowledge, no other species is so mutually self-destructive unless in dire extremities, and none takes the morbid pleasure in killing that the offspring of humankind bring to the exercise. Like the fifty founding nations of the United Nations, in 1945 we wanted to believe that excess of horror would administer a salutary and durable shock. Five years later the UN itself had taken up arms in the Far East. Since then have we known a single day without organized butchery? The two superpowers described by Churchill as a couple of scorpions enclosed in the same bottle at least let their own terror hold them back from the brink, sometimes only by a hair's breadth. That does not prevent them from ceaselessly adding new devices for planetary suicide to their more than ample stocks. Will one of them finally yield to the temptation of using the ultimate weapon, and then, of course, both? Unfortunately, the inconceivable is not impossible – we know that only too well.

In the meantime the most pernicious effect of living under this sword of Damocles is to diminish all other conflicts in comparison, making them banal by attaching the adjective "limited" to them. How banal the war in Vietnam was, so expertly limited that in two and a half years more explosives were set off there than during the *whole* of World War Two.

Unless they find a Baby Doc or a Marcos to personify evil, how quickly, by dint of repetition, all these civil or tribal wars, the invasions, the coups d'état, and the assassinations become insignificant, briefly holding our attention between breaks for commercials! The worst of it is, war, too, is commercial. How many American cities and Soviet production centres or European, Brazilian, and Canadian factories would be reduced to idleness by a serious threat of peace? The war business* creates innumerable manufacturing jobs and stimulates research behind the mask of "defence spending" and sovereignty issues, and can even, as we saw in Montreal recently, hide areas of stagnation behind fat contracts for military equipment.

As for those powder magazines we keep on the verge of explosion by plunging countries up to their necks in debt in three continents out of five, their people are generally the poorest of the poor. Yet everywhere, in Central America, from Cairo to the Cape, and from the Middle East to Cambodia, we pressure them to sell their bread for rifles. If they were deprived of those arms shipments their sponsors stuff them with, wouldn't small nations manage to settle their problems just as well as now without resorting to bloodbaths?

What an extraordinary revolution it would be if once and for all we decided to melt down our swords for plowshares and turn all that sophisticated hardware into development funding. What we are talking about are annual budgets that total close to one trillion ($1,000,000,000,000) dollars. One small tenth of this wastage would multiply aid to the famished nations by six or seven and increase the contribution of well-off countries to a less shameful level. The Scandinavians, who are the most generous, do not yet give one per cent of their income to this cause.

Is all this just dreaming in technicolour? Until further notice, no doubt it is. But aren't dreams the source of most worthwhile projects? And couldn't our new generation, brought up on missiles and Star

---

* See George Thayer, *The War Business* (New York, 1969), a classic on the subject.

Wars, be the spearhead of a crusade for peace and true fraternity? If such a force could spread throughout the world as thoroughly as military bases and occupation armies have, little by little we could replace the business of arms with productive farms. From jungle to civilization is one short step, which calls to mind the evidence that on this shrinking terrestrial globe of ours, where North cannot live without South and South dies without North, the few in comfort cannot for long go on living off the hunger of the many, nor can life itself ignore the fact that too many unnecessary deaths are a virus whose incubation period will not last forever.

All of this means that on two or three absolutely essential levels, the nation-state has had its day. It must give up part of its powers and resources to an authority that would be a Security Council for humanity at large. It's not for tomorrow, of course. But if we want to count on a tomorrow, no other solution is in sight.

There, at any rate, is what I think, and what I repeat every time I get a chance, and what I'll risk saying again here: to put an end to the massacre of innocents, to give children everywhere a minimum of equal opportunities, one cannot be anything but federalist . . . at least in world terms.

IV

OUR FAR-FLUNG CORRESPONDENT

"Happy the man who like Ulysses . . . "
DU BELLAY

---

18. Two Superpowers: The Camera and the U.S.A.

KOREA – and my gallant hilltop swearers – presided over my coming of age as a journalist. Returning home I discovered that commentators as hard to please as Gérard Pelletier were referring to me as "the revelation of the year."

In high places they were also beginning to catch on to the fact that sport isn't the only human activity capable of holding public attention. Without ever equalling the magic of the stadium, the presentation of other sides of life still has the advantage of costing only a small fraction of the television budgets gobbled up by soap operas and variety shows. In addition, the years 1939-45 were the crucible in which the metamorphosis of the new Quebec society was forged.* Thousands of young men had left the country and

---

* One might also point out that during this period the Godbout government (otherwise unmemorable because it gave in to Ottawa before being forced to) put in place three essential features of a viable society: compulsory education, the vote for women, and the start of a long-range development policy (creation of Hydro-Québec).

had, like me, changed without quite realizing it. Thousands of women had been shunted by war from offices to factories and were no longer the same as they had been. This unprecedented turmoil was responsible for the rapid disappearance of the old traditional and isolationist Quebec. One of the effects was the awakening of a new curiosity about the distinctiveness and originality of our own people. In song, in theatre, in our first films, we began to discover in detail who we were and to find ourselves interesting.

Whatever the causes, that was the context for the creation of a "feature news service" that I was placed in charge of. It was a mini-department destined to remain microscopic, but a lot of heart was shown by the little team that worked on putting out a daily radio-magazine called *Carrefour*.

The other members of the group will forgive me if I single out one exceptional colleague whose talent was in great part responsible for our modest success. It is more important than it might seem to recall that Judith Jasmin spoke and wrote a French that was not only correct but as pure as spring water. A perfectionist, she expected the most of herself but was always available if a sloppy piece of work had to be rewritten or if someone had to be replaced on short notice. But there was nothing soft about her. Her mind was ceaselessly alert and its foundation was an ordered structure of experience and well-assimilated culture. Her knowledge of art, and especially of theatre, combined in an astonishing way with her deep concern for precision and frankness in reporting facts. Besides, I never knew anyone rubbed so raw by injustice. She had her faults, if it's a fault, for example, not to suffer fools and hypocrites gladly. In short, Judith Jasmin, comrade and friend for a few fine years, was a great journalist and an exceptional woman. When her career was cruelly cut short by sickness, she had reached the pinnacle of our profession.

At that particular moment our trade was just being sent back to school to learn the ABCs of television, the appearance of which threatened to put us all on the shelf. For the actors especially it was a disaster. They had been used to playing their parts script in hand for so long that many had completely forgotten how to memorize a role as required in live theatre. After the initial blow had provoked a period of self-examination, little by little there was revitalization and a new public appeared for quality radio. (The other kind, alas, simply continued to fight over the lowest common denominator.) I think I am not alone today in preferring sounds that create their own decor and leave a place for silence to the omnipresent image, the image at any price, of which it is false to claim that it is invariably worth ten thousand words, or even ten seconds of peace.

But let's get back to the fifties and that first generation to slump down for life in front of, or behind, the flickering screen. It was a mass infatuation, such as we've never seen, creating a drug-like dependency that few escape even today because it hits its victims at any age. Our eldest child was three when the thing first erupted into his life. Coming into its presence with that senatorial walk of his, he saw an airplane buzzing across the screen. As soon as it disappeared on the left, he went over to that side of the set, then walked right around it, coming back to us with: "Where'd the plane go?"

What will be the long-term impact of all those images that generations of kids have been served up endlessly for the last thirty years? You'd have to be pretty smart to evaluate that with any degree of certitude, or pretty presumptuous to claim accurate results. One thing is certain, though: almost nothing has escaped this alchemy that hasn't always turned base metal into gold. Education, household routines, the extravagant overpersonalization of politics and sports, all those fields have been affected. How does the dazzling technical evolution represented by these strange windows on the world stack up against the herd-minded superficiality spewed out of them day after day? The danger is particularly grave in a little society like ours where the monster makes short work of subjecting everyone to the same wavelength, with a menu that becomes more imperious than the dictates of any Academy: the next episode of the daily soap (Grignon's *Un homme et son péché*), *Hockey Night in Canada* ("Over to you, Jean-Maurice . . ."), and so on.

Here's a memory from those prehistoric times. I had been filling in a little on TV news when one day, in the middle of a blizzard so thick you couldn't see the end of your nose, a Good Samaritan gave me a lift. I soon began to notice him looking at me in a most curious fashion. Finally he couldn't contain himself any longer: "It seems to me I know you from somewhere, but I can't think where."

Not knowing either, I sat in silence until he was struck by a sudden revelation: "I've got it! It's simple. I'm sure I've met you at my house!"

Similarly, Victor Barbeau, an elegant old gentleman whose temper grew shorter as his years grew longer, once reproached me for my lack of good manners in appearing in his living room with a cigarette hanging out of the corner of my mouth. . . . In those days TV was decidedly a family affair.

As for the mutations that our perspectives and even our senses were to undergo, as early as 1948 I had a striking preview of that. It was in Chicago where I was covering the Democratic convention for the radio; south of the border television was already in power. It's hardly necessary to say that we Canadians were the poor relations relegated to the far end of the table, left to beg for crumbs from the feast that had been laid on for the grand seigneurs of the camera. On the rented set that allowed us at least to be not completely out of it, the day was winding down with the roll call of the delegates. They had reached Missouri and, in alphabetical order, the letter T:

"The delegate from Independence, Missouri . . . "

At these words an image bobbed up on the screen of an airport in the Middle West where you could make out a little man hurrying toward his plane.

"President Harry S. Truman!" the announcer intoned triumphantly. If I'm not mistaken, it was the first time two sides of a single news event were spliced together live on the screen. It's old hat now, but that day we found it mind-boggling and my report home was full of the wonder the future held in store.

This was also the beginning of what I might call my American period. It was the politics that interested me first – from Truman to Eisenhower to Kennedy – but also, as often as a chance or pretext occurred, I would cover any other aspect of that enormous cultural stew bubbling away just over the border. Our strikes teleguided from Pittsburgh or Washington, the blood ties that prevented Franco-Americans from completely forgetting us, the German presence whose beer was the Milwaukee flagship, the discreet infiltration and multiplication of Orientals on the West Coast: in short, everything fascinated me in the perpetual movement to the south of us whose rhythm invaded our lives and dissolved the frontier in floods of Coke and tires and V-8s.

Given the fact that my own frontier had been fixed long ago at the Ottawa River, it was easy for me to follow the natural slope of the continent that runs north and south instead of the unnatural east-west line along which Canada is built.

My wartime contacts had only reinforced this preference. Coming back to Quebec in 1945, then again in 1952, each time the temptation had been strong to follow in the footsteps of certain American comrades going home to New York or Boston to carve themselves out enviable situations in the U.S. media world, where the growth potential was geometric. But I realized then that I would never be an export commodity. I was condemned to remain Québécois. This feeling only grew stronger when, on several occasions, I was offered more or less golden opportunities of exile, among them at least one that would have seen me in the federal arena – on the wrong side of the river.

But as much as Canada outside Quebec seemed to me, generally, to be a sad collective grey, the United States never ceased to fascinate me, and this double impression has remained to this day. I had discovered and was belatedly reading up on the Roosevelt years. I don't believe one can ever find, in any place or time, a person who can serve as a model for one's own life, but close affinities often develop with people we admire. Without for a single instant thinking of political action, I began an intensive diet of FDR. In the first place I had been struck by his great communications skills. Listening to those "fireside chats," his lilting voice that scanned the sentences as if they were prose poems, I envied him his gift for capturing attention and creating suspense while using everyday words with chiselled precision. And he used humour so well to disarm or confound his adversaries, for example, during a wicked campaign when he was led to exclaim with just the sigh that was needed, "Good heavens! Next they'll be after poor Fala!" (his little dog, an inseparable companion). Above all I admired the incomparable instinct that permitted this aristocrat to maintain for so long a coalition made up of minorities, blue-collar workers, and the poor. In 1932, thanking the members of his brain trust for the monumental work they had done drafting the complete program of the New Deal, he asked them to resign themselves to seeing their chef-d'oeuvre condensed and reduced to its simplest expression, as concise as a manifesto.

This was what doubtless came to my mind when in 1967 I was writing the text that was to launch the Mouvement Souveraineté-Association and in 1968 *An Option for Quebec*, the second part of which, entitled "A Country that is Feasible," opened with the quotation, "We have nothing to fear but fear itself." These words, which Roosevelt had used to try to exorcise the panic caused by the Great Depression, seemed to me to apply every bit as well to our own colonial apprehensions and complexes.

The time is the fifties, the decade that saw the Cold War settle in permanently while the Americans elected another invincible president, the well-liked, weak-charactered General Dwight D. Eisenhower. While Ike was spending more time on his golf than on his dossiers, one of those crises developed that our neighbours know so well how to amplify to incredible excess. It was the shameful period of McCarthyism. I remember the hearing when the witch-hunter stood up and waved a piece of paper on which he claimed to have the names (he prudently kept them to himself) of all crypto-Communists from the Atlantic to the Pacific. With his oily look, his shifty eyes, and his vulgar, rasping voice, Senator McCarthy was one of those men who makes you think spontaneously, "I'd never buy a used car from someone like that!" Like others before him but less scrupulous, and with perfect cynicism and frightening success, he exploited the wave of anti-Communist hysteria sweeping the country. Unlike other parliaments closer to home that refuse, as we will see, to make a proper act of contrition, the U.S. Senate finally cornered its black sheep and put an end to the chase, but only after hundreds of reputations had been destroyed and valuable careers scrapped or forced to begin again in Europe or elsewhere.

During those dark years, however, a star named Kennedy began to gleam on the horizon. It was first seen in 1956 when the Democratic Party was trying desperately to find a couple of candidates to run serious opposition to the unbeatable Eisenhower-Nixon duo. When the second member of the Democratic team was being decided, everyone was talking about the ascending fortunes of this brilliant son of an elegant and wealthy Massachusetts family. He was a war hero into the bargain who, thanks to a hard-hitting speech, had become the man of the hour. But at the last minute they chose the veteran Kefauver, a pseudo-hillbilly whose Davy Crockett hat covered a crafty and progressive mind. He was the sworn enemy of the infamous racket the drug industry had become* and it was he

---

* Isn't it the same today? It has recently been disclosed that the price of drugs in the U.S. has risen twice as fast as inflation, generating profits three times the industrial average. A congressional committee has been told by senior citizens that their prescriptions cost them up to one-quarter of their incomes. "Either we are given a satisfactory explanation," declared a California congressman, "or we will have to conclude that we are in the presence of record greed." Are things much better here? Yes, certainly, since citizens of modest means don't have to pay anything. But it's easy to forget that "free" medication, which has made us the top pill-poppers in the Western world, costs the government, and hence the collectivity, a fortune.

who inspired me, at the time of the Lesage government, to lead a campaign, unfortunately too singlehandedly, against the same exploiters.

As things turned out, Kefauver and his presidential running mate, Adlai Stevenson, were defeated and Kennedy remained on the sidelines until his victory in 1960. If he had won an obscure vice-presidential nomination four years earlier, would he be alive today? The future belongs to no one. . . .

I was in a fair way to becoming transformed into a "Yankébécois." South of the border attracted me so strongly I invariably spent the holidays down there, always by the sea, to be sure. At first we went by train to Hampton or Old Orchard Beach to rent one of those vacation shacks whose only merit was that it was two minutes from the beach. Then around 1955, when my salary had reached the stratospheric heights of five thousand dollars a year, I was able to buy a car and expand our horizons. That finally led us to Cape Cod, that eighth wonder of the world whose southern beaches are washed by the warm currents of the Gulf Stream and whose entire shoreline has been wisely turned into a national heritage park, which spares it the disfigurements of so many other incomparable sites from Capri to Acapulco and Miami to Percé. It was there that our three children – Suzanne having joined the two boys and established her reign over the family – acquired a taste for salt water and seafood while learning English the painless way. And there I return faithfully every year for two or three weeks of thalassotherapy that my Gaspésian organism can't do without, but also to bathe in that society that is so close yet so profoundly different from our own.

Nothing is closer, indeed, than that American democracy one might almost call innate, which springs, like ours, from simple, unpolished people untrammeled by class division who knew how to make the most of the limitless space of a new and almost empty continent. This is the source of that fundamental egalitarianism that gives everyone the conviction or, if you prefer, the illusion that he is as good as his neighbour or, why not, the president. It is also the root of that habit, which puritan virtues have preserved better with them than with us, of working hard without asking for the moon (or even without expecting services as essential as health insurance and a reasonably priced educational system). In every-day life all this makes average Americans the most sympathetic "foreigners" you can imagine, and people you can identify with better than any other.

But this closeness that goes far beyond geographical bonds tends to camouflage the fact that History has given us traits of character that are markedly different. Children of a France obsessed with Europe and rich enough to live unto herself, we were only a handful of settlers at the time of the Conquest. On the contrary, England was poor and seafaring and had shipped a multitude of immigrants to its own colony. On the Plains of Abraham the weight of numbers won the day and eventually won control of the whole of North America. This was accomplished in the United States in the course of interminable campaigns against the Indians marked by a violence that gave rise to the racism and the revolver culture that remain a blight on the country to this day. Independence wrested with the bayonet, followed by a civil war more deadly than any previous conflict, served only to anchor this propensity to rule by force even more solidly.

Pass over a century and wars with Mexico and Spain, 1917-18, 1941-45, and Vietnam, and look at the situation in 1986. American society continues to secrete such violence that its crime rate is the highest in the world. The very strength of the country engendered what Eisenhower called the military-industrial complex whose chief interest is to maintain tension with the Soviets, thus justifying the insane budgets swallowed up in so-called defence – "so-called," because as far as we can see into the future, the U.S.S.R. will never have the temerity, much less the means, to pass to the attack. Russia is poor, and in our day wealth leads the world, not the flag as in times past. At this rate Tokyo and soon the whole of the Far East will be taking over from New York and Chicago. After the transplant that in the recent past removed the heart of the world from Europe to America, another transplant will see it removed again.

Running the risk of turning Central America into a new Vietnam or of locking himself into the unreality of Star Wars, President Ronald Reagan is only disastrously masking this evolution and delaying the need to come to terms with it, a task that will be anything but easy. The inevitable transition will doubtless call forth the greatest of any demonstration the Americans have ever been asked to give of their proverbial powers of adaptation. Scarcely less challenging will be the partial abandonment of the melting-pot philosophy, which may be forced on them yet by bi- or tri-culturalism, as witnessed particularly on the Pacific Coast. The internal evolution of the United States and the relative diminishing of its international importance will reserve shocks and surprises for us that a small neighbour will have to follow very attentively. And it will continue to be a fascinating spectacle.

19. From Elizabeth
the Second...

DURING THE FIFTIES everything was fascinating to me and begged to be seen, heard, and reported as faithfully as possible and by every means possible: microphone and camera, of course, but also the written word, which I was occasionally permitted to perpetrate and which, with your permission, I will reproduce here and there to give the flavour of the times. Knowing full well one can never reach such a goal, I earnestly wished that nothing human would remain foreign to me, which sparked a second period of globetrotting, this time in civvies, starting off with a trip to the mysterious universe of the Far North.

It was 1952 and the assignment was to accompany their Royal Highnesses Elizabeth and Philip as they discovered Canada from sea to sea, and then to yet a third, the Arctic. It was a discovery for me, too, for I had never seen the country coast to coast. What with all the national unity propaganda that is constantly being pumped at us via CN, Petro-Canada, and so on, I will spare you my impressions of Toronto the Good, which is not so good any more, of Greater Winnipeg, which has swallowed up St. Boniface, of the Rocky Mountains, and of Vancouver, which pressed us so insistently to see its Expo. I won't even tell you about Powell River, B.C., a little northern town where I remember our fifteen-year-old hostess called, let's say, Pauline Lamoureux, who let two big tears run down her cheeks when I made the mistake of greeting her in French. "I don't speak French," she admitted with a sob, adding that if I could come back that evening her father, a worker imported from Quebec, would show me that he at least hadn't lost his mother tongue.

No, let's move on rather to the Yukon and the Klondike, two regions and also two turbulent rivers that meet at Dawson City, the gold rush capital that was more of a ghost town when we went through it, where Charlie Chaplin would really have had to eat his boots!

It was right up at the top, at Coppermine, that we came upon the true North, especially in meeting the Inuit, or Eskimos as they were called then and would continue to be called for another generation. It was Arctic summer. As soon as we stepped out of our Canso a few metres from the shore we were attacked by unbelievable squadrons of flying insects of every size and colour imaginable. Each year these few brief weeks of warm weather hatch an ephemeral animal and vegetable life that develops feverishly, as if knowing that time is of the essence. The Inuit struck us as a bewildering swarm of another kind. Massed on the shore so close to the edge that we had to force our way to get by more or less dryshod, they formed a circle of laughter and rough monosyllables around us. An old woman, purposefully pointing to a damp butt hanging off her lip, indicated she wanted a cigarette. As soon as the package appeared, her hand shot out like lightning and at the same instant she melted into the crowd with her booty. Everyone had a good laugh. Suddenly I got the picture. With our leather shoes and our thin skins that were such easy prey for the mosquitoes, we, not they, were the rubes, and this primitive clan was making good-natured fun of us. This went on throughout the visit – chuckles when we tripped over one of their innumerable dogs luckily knocked out by the heat, jolly thumps on the back as they heaped our plates with meat that was as oily as the fish.

The princess and the duke got to taste it, too, which brought out Philip's true colours, revealing a character we had suspected from the start. Contemplating people and things from his exalted heights with a disdainful pout, he would only condescend to speak to his immediate entourage. He was beginning to get our goat. Eddie O'Neill, the cameraman, was particularly put off. A republican and a Free-Stater with a heart of gold but a quick temper, and one who had never lost any love on the English from the start, he ran straight into a wall of arrogance every time he dared suggest this or that pose. The day we were at Coppermine he took an irreversible decision: from then on His Highness had better be on his best behaviour, or, more precisely, he could behave however he liked, for O'Neill was reserving special treatment for him. Until the end of the trip his film exclusively recorded princely grimaces or Philip's feet!

One of the last stops of our long journey was at a construction site in New Quebec that didn't yet have a name on the map. Paddling around in the mud, we followed the trace of the hint of a chocolate trickle that bubbled up and disappeared, seeking its way as it went and redrawing the hypothetical border with Labrador as the spirit moved it. This was Burnt Creek, which finally disappeared altogether the day the place earned the right to be called Schefferville for a quarter of a century.

We spent the last day in a tiny outport on the Avalon Peninsula not far from St. John's. The royal yacht was pitching on high seas a few cables offshore. Hastily, for fear the motor launch might founder, the princess braved the storm and came ashore to honour us with a first and last handshake and to thank us all, O'Neill included, for our good and loyal services. She was quite slight in those days, almost dainty, with that translucent peach complexion that is the gift their execrable climate makes to young English girls. Holding down her skirt with one hand, which didn't prevent the wind from revealing a shapely pair of legs, she performed this small duty with the studied application of a schoolgirl. One was almost inclined to feel sorry for her.

The next year I really did feel sorry for her. Now that we were old friends, what could be more natural than that I be chosen to describe to the world at large the coronation of Elizabeth, second of the name, by the grace of God, etc., etc. Judith Jasmin and I, cheek by jowl with French and Belgian colleagues like some little Francophonie before its time, stood bunched behind the barricades at Trafalgar Square at the foot of the Nelson Column. We had arrived at dawn and were surrounded by good folk who had stayed up all night to get a place in the front row. What followed was one of the great performances in the history of radio. For five consecutive hours, until the procession passed by on its way back from Westminster going to Buckingham Palace, we had to invent fill-in, talking about the church bells in the distance, about the pigeons too close overhead, about the dense crowd from the midst of which, periodically, some woman who had fainted would be delicately extracted and passed from hand to hand to the waiting ambulances, great care being taken to see that her skirts remained discreetly hobbled. So we talked on and on about cabbages and kings for an eternity and then, in one minute, came Horse Guards, coach with an invisible sovereign inside, and the whole world's high society right up to that smiling monument of flesh and flamboyant robes, Queen Salote of the Tonga Islands (even more impressive than her independent kingdom of 90,000 souls), and the spectacle was over. Between the five of us we each had time for one well-turned phrase. We were completely bushed; never had so much work been done for so little.

To recover, we decided to make a jaunt to Paris, which we had to justify, of course. Brainwave! In three days it would be the sixth of June, the anniversary of the Normandy landing. One of our good pals, only an obscure free-lancer at the time, was Léon Zitrone in Paris. A quick call set up the trip: "Don't worry," he said, "I'll fix everything. All you have to do is get there."

At noon on June 6, Judith and I were at Courseulles-sur-mer, standing around like a couple of storks. It was the first port liberated by the Allies in 1944. The town hall was resplendent in its shrubbery; the military cemetery faced the Channel; the sun danced on the waves: the scene was set, and all that was needed was the cast. But there was no sign of Zitrone, not a hair. We were just about to damn him to hell when suddenly a miniature motorcycle hove into view, groaning and backfiring under the weight of a gargantuan driver complemented by that of a luckily tiny Madame Zitrone in tandem.

"Tut, tut," he said, cutting short our recriminations, "I told you I'd look after everything, and I'm as good as my word."

And he disappeared into the town hall. Less than a quarter of an hour later we were invited to sip champagne in the garden while the municipal band chimed in with all the favourite airs of two world wars, from "Madelon" to "Lili Marlene," not forgetting "Mademoiselle from Armentières." After that, a banquet studded with speeches to eternal friendship lasted well on past four in the afternoon, and when the last red-faced guest had left, steadying his Calvados on a companionable arm, Léon had effectively kept his word, so well, in fact, that later I was not in the least surprised to find him at the top of the heap in television entertainment, always managing to make something out of practically nothing.

With the words, the music, and the atmosphere, we came away with a magnificent broadcast that won us all kinds of praise. And we had our three days in Paris. It was, may I remind you, the sixth of June, 1953. Since that day there have been other fabulous anniversaries, for example the 370th of Quebec in 1978, but nothing will ever quite equal for me that remarkable *ninth* anniversary of D-Day.

20.   ...To Nikita the First

LET'S GET BACK to the world at large and more serious things. The place, the U.S.S.R.; the time, 1955, shortly after the death of Stalin. Trailing along on the skirts of Lester Pearson, Minister of External Affairs, our little press team was making its first incursion behind the Iron Curtain. We started at Prague where, at the foot of the Queen of Bohemia's castle, the Czechs were getting some of their own back by breaking the enormous statue of Little Father Joseph into smaller and smaller pieces. Then we went on to Poland, which for its part was reconstructing The Old Warsaw stone by stone. We also saw Leningrad and the imperial suite in the Winter Palace where, bashfully hidden in the attic, was an incomparable collection of those great bourgeois decadents, the impressionists. Later we were taken to a suburb almost within rifle shot of the city centre to gaze upon the carcass of a German tank that had penetrated that far when the famous city was surrounded and refused to surrender. Since they were sure they could take the prize any time, the Nazis spared Leningrad as a trophy, thanks to which I rediscovered it a few months ago as beautiful as ever under Gorbachev. Strangely, though, it is tenser, more haughty, and less welcoming than thirty years ago, or so it seemed to me.

On our 1955 trip we were anxious to get to Moscow, where the action was . . . or rather wasn't, as it turned out. In those days it was a city without suburbs emerging suddenly from steppes as richly coloured by an autumn palette as our own landscapes are. We were royally welcomed, given a great spread, and treated with an exuberance that couldn't be explained just by the recent end of such a long reign of terror, for Slavs are naturally very generous. At the Bolshoi Theatre we saw a wildly extravagant *Don Quixote* in which all Spain seemed to have been given rendezvous on stage. At intermission, students bought glasses of champagne and slices of bread and caviar for a few kopecks, then hurried back to their seats to pour over books while waiting for the curtain to go up again. Then in the enormous reception hall of the Kremlin the heirs apparent stood grouped together on one side of a long table with us on the other, and it was caviar again, this time mountains of it. There we saw the big earthy hands of Kaganovitch, Stalin's brother-in-law, unconsciously crumbling his black bread, while Malenkov, provoked by some inoffensive remark, went out of his way to demonstrate that at least in one area, the treatment of minorities, we weren't in any position to talk.

"Just remember how you treated your colonial subjects," he said, "and your blacks, and your Indians, and then take the trouble to find out something about the people of our republics who have been left their own languages, cultures, and ancestral traditions." He was red as a beet and had tears in his eyes. Apart from the fact that he had us mixed up with the Americans, was what he said true, false, or half-and-half?

We were trying to take the measure of this extraordinary character who, rumour had it, would be the next tsar, when, as everyone clustered around a ravishing beauty, a rising ballerina soon to be famous as the star, Maia Plissetskaia, a functionary approached Pearson and whispered to him that *someone* was waiting for us in the south of the country, someone whose invitations were orders. And so we ventured forth again.

The tiny plane, stripped down to military nudity, was equipped with a hostess who served us tea and allowed us to smoke as soon as the engines were turned on: Nitchevo! The cowboy crew got us down safely on the runway at Sevastopol, though we had had our doubts, and there a fleet of antediluvian limousines awaited us. On our way through the hills rolling down to the Black Sea, the chauffeur turned off the ignition each time we got to the top of a rise, letting his museum piece coast down in silence, then starting up again with a roar for the next ascent – to save gas, he explained. The jolly oaf also confided to us that he hit it off to perfection with his wife, who was a doctor.

Toward the end of the day it was an equally curious amalgam that we discovered assembled in one of the most impregnable sites of Yalta. Before the huge white villa with exquisitely elegant columns stood a couple more black jalopies, somewhat the worse for wear, and a gang of bodyguards, peevish louts in thick uniforms, like some archduke's modest personnel who had been briefly released among the petunias.

Nikita Sergeivitch Khrushchev was a typical moujik, too. The thickset peasant stuffed into a well-cut suit received us in the salon and sat immobile, letting us approach as if in royal audience. But his bright, shifty eyes suddenly came to rest on the little tape recorder I was carrying by a strap over my shoulder. Not even waiting for the end of the presentations, he asked me what it was.

"It's for the radio."

"Ah! radio, da, da, horosho!"

Brushing aside his slightly nervous bodyguards with an imperious look, he made me unload my gear onto a small table and asked me to turn it on. After which, like a well-trained boxer, he literally sprang at poor Pearson.

"So you come from Canada, the American colony. And you have the nerve to criticize what you choose to call our satellites!"

"But, er . . . but . . ." spluttered our crestfallen minister.

"And this organization," shot out Khrushchev, rushing his interpreter, "the one you have baptized NATO, this means North Atlantic, no? And doesn't it move outside the Atlantic and come dangerously close to our frontiers?"

"Er, but, it's for defence . . . "

"Well, you really make me laugh! Defence against what? Against us? Ridiculous! Talk about defence, we know something about that, let me tell you, and what it costs, and something about aggression, too. We haven't the slightest wish to get into that again. It's you who are threatening us, and I'd be much obliged if you'd tell your partners that."

Pearson was on the canvas. Collecting his wits again he asked to have the diplomats, one of whom was George Ignatieff, later delegate to the United Nations, shown to their rooms. The media contingent, myself included, was put up in a superb suite on the ground floor. In fact, there were just two journalists, Bob Needham of the *Globe and Mail*, the Anglophone scribe, and me, for audio-visual coverage and French. Due to the smallness of the plane and the hurried departure, the main group had chosen us to represent them and we were charged to pool everything we could pick up when we got back.

Our harvest had already been exceptional. Cracking a bottle of Caucasus champagne, we couldn't get over the good luck that had brought us to spend a night on the home turf of the master of All the Russias, living it up like kings into the bargain. And what a windfall that bout of verbal fisticuffs with Pearson had been! Tickled pink, I stepped out on the balcony with my sausage sandwich and my glass of Georgian bubbly. The sea looked wonderful, so I swallowed down my snack, dropped my pants, and jumped in. It was almost the end of me. The water was treacherously mild for a full stomach, and a very strong current carried me out beyond the promontory behind which the villa was hidden. Seeing that I was being transported into a vast bay that stretched away to the horizon, I made a supreme effort and managed to struggle back until finally a wave threw me up on a rock, nearly skinning me alive.

Some cognac brought me round and then we slept the sleep of the just, or would have if it hadn't been for the noise of flushing toilets that kept waking us up every half hour all night long. The explanation came next morning when we saw our pale diplomats coming downstairs on rubbery legs, hanging on to the bannisters. What had happened was quite simple. Since he had got his message across as soon as we arrived, Khrushchev arranged with his gang to have a little fun at the Canadians' expense in his own particular manner, which didn't always obey the rules of etiquette. All during dinner, at the least pretext, he or one of his aides would raise a glass in a toast with the express aim of getting Ignatieff in particular (a White Russian and therefore a degenerate to his hosts) dead drunk and rolling under the table.

We didn't breathe a word of this second federal Waterloo on our return to Moscow. Pearson was in such a vile humour that we feared for our visas. It was on this occasion we noted that the boyish half-smile and incontestable diplomatic skill hid a very touchy character that the least check would set to pouting and issuing cutting words. Well, we couldn't do anything about that. Our report from Yalta contained new material that, as all our colleagues in Moscow agreed, relegated everything else to the back seat, and the story of the sudden emergence of Khrushchev together with my interview made the front page in Brussels, Paris, and London.

As soon as I got back to Montreal I modestly inquired how my dispatches had been received at home. "What dispatches?" they asked. "Did you really dispatch something? We thought you'd been sent to Siberia."

"Wait a minute. What about the stuff I sent from Moscow, and especially from Yalta?"

"Never saw hide nor hair of it, man. Better go try to look it up some place."

As you can guess, this is exactly what I immediately did, only to run into surprised expressions and excessively evasive explanations. I ended up hammering on the door of External Affairs, where the cat finally came out of the sack. My very excellent interview, as I would surely appreciate without too much difficulty, had just one flaw: it was rather hard on the Honourable Minister, to the point that it might have caused him some embarrassment. So, as I would certainly understand, *n'est-ce pas*, they had taken the liberty to put a temporary embargo on it, though by now, of course, nothing stood in the way of my taking it up again.

Thanks a lot. There's nothing deader than old news. I blew my top, blasted them as they deserved for political censorship, and came out of there feeling like jumping over a cliff and with a solid and enduring antipathy for that cautious collection of Canadian mandarins. Under my fellow journalists' bylines I'd been able to read my story everywhere, but here at home the most colourful scoop of my career had been suppressed to protect the dignity of Lester Pearson. It was enough to make one . . . separatist!

Sadly, I transformed my red-hot news story into a straight documentary, served up cold.

21. "Daniel Johnson, perhaps, but Duplessis, never!"

RUE BONAVENTURE. A narrow brick house of modest bourgeois appearance. There's some hesitation about opening
the front door. No wonder. With all the heavy equipment,
the suitcases, the tripods, and the wires hanging out everywhere,
the radio-television squad looks more like a team of demolition
experts. Gathering up her courage, the discreetly distinguished
woman, who, we are told, is his sister, finally lets us penetrate the
Duplessis home, but only to send us straight to the basement.

It's June, 1956, and we've just finished another election. One
more, one less, I've stopped counting. I've followed, described,
commented on so many, in the States, in Canada, federal, provin ial,
not to mention the municipals in Montreal. I've covered them on
the hustings and in the studio because they're always using me as a
jack-of-all-trades. But this time, I must admit, it's something special. To be here at Trois-Rivières in the home of the little provincial
lawyer who for a dozen years has been the big boss of Quebec
politics, and, well, yes, of the whole of Quebec for that matter.

While waiting for the election results to come in, I examine this
office they've got us cooped up in. Passing over the dusty shelves
with their sleepy collections of old law codes and revised statutes,
my attention focuses on three objects, the only ones in the room
that are not strictly utilitarian. On the wall behind the leather
armchair the first thing I notice is the portrait of a smiling woman
dressed in turn-of-the-century finery. It's the mother of this inveterate
old bachelor who will never marry, though he has a well-known
weakness for the fair sex. (For example, he cordially detests Radio-
Canada, which takes the liberty to criticize him, so he invariably
tells its male reporters to get lost but always reserves a more than
unctuous welcome for Judith Jasmin and never refuses her an
interview!) Then, on the corner of the desk, I see a little bust of
Bonaparte, later to become Napoleon, his right hand stuck into his

137

waistcoat. And finally, on the windowsill opposite, a statuette of Brother André. Filial piety, unscrupulous power, and devotion to St. Joseph . . . that's the whole man in a nutshell. And it's certainly all intentional. Quite a man, our Maurice!

He suddenly appears to inform us that the first projections put his Union Nationale party far ahead of the Liberals, as usual. As far as he himself is concerned, he is as good as re-elected in his home riding.

"Monsieur Duplessis, could we have a word for our listeners, please?"

"Your listeners? What listeners?"

"Radio-Canada, sir."

"Naw-naw-naw, haven't got time."

This, of course, doesn't prevent the old rapscallion from replying courteously to a journalist from a private station. Then in that hoarse, thick voice that always smells of the soil, he reminds us that he's saving his first commentaries for his own electors, whom he is going to join at the Parc des Cèdres.

It's on the other side of town. By running a few red lights we get there before him. As night falls, several hundred citizens of Trois-Rivières crowd around the bandstand transformed into a stage. They're shouting and singing and not paying much attention to the man with the microphone who is doing his best to keep them waiting patiently. But now a black automobile is approaching slowly and the acclamations resound while Duplessis waves through the window.

"And now, Mesdames, Messieurs," the orator trumpets, sweating heavily, "here is the man we have been waiting for . . . the great defender of French Canada, the man who knows how to stand up to Ottawa, the man who protects our autonomy, the man who gave us Crédit Agricole, the man who . . . "

Duplessis reaches the stage just as the emcee is about to run out of breath.

"The man who is the new Member of Parliament for Trois-Rivières, the new Premier of the province, and whom I now have the honour and pleasure to prese . . ."

Raising an authoritarian forefinger, Duplessis signals the man at the mike to keep on talking and, taking out a cigarette, goes and sits down in the front row. He fumbles around in his pocket for a light. In a flash a good dozen lighters and matches are thrust forward.

Who'll be the lucky one? Impassively, le Chef examines these offerings shining before him like so many altar lights, takes plenty of time to think it over, then, pushing aside the most insistent hands, chooses a light from the second row of devotees.

". . . and in just a minute you'll be hearing from the man who . . ."

Mopping his brow, the poor announcer burbles on until the smoker deigns to butt out.

Because he had seen so much of it, Duplessis had become somewhat sadistic. Simple folk rather liked it because his claws were directed only against court favourites and classy adversaries. Nonetheless, an equal scorn, betrayed by the methods he used, was applied to the electorate as a whole. Here, for example, is what was described to me as the ABC of by-elections, Duplessis-style.

"Hey, boy," the boss would say to the organizer, "the purse is ready. Take it and use it smartly. Spend but don't waste."

The purse was the campaign budget, in bank notes, to be used for the case of beer or the occasional forty-ouncer, with the fridge or the paving job for the bigwigs. Almost invariably the candidate was elected and the triumphant organizer would return to recount his exploits and hand back what was left of the purse.

"Good going, my boy, you did a fine job," Duplessis would say, giving him a slap on the back. "The purse is yours. You earned it, you keep it."

He was totally indifferent to money himself, but he knew its power and used it shamelessly. In fact, he spent freely only when trying to counter or crush such vile opposition as trade unionists and progressives of all kinds, especially intellectuals, whom he called "piano players." As for the former, they were purely and simply Red Communists, likely to blow up the bridge at Trois-Rivières or run down our reputation by killing Americans, like Wilbert Coffin supposedly had, that obscure Gaspésian who was sent to the scaffold after a sham inquiry and trial that would never hold water.

Like his predecessors, though neither more nor less, Duplessis didn't hesitate to use public funds as a means of blackmail. We'll give serious thought to your road, he let it be understood, if you vote the right way. If not, your road has about as much chance as a snowball in hell! One riding between Quebec and Montreal, Saint-Hyacinthe I think it was, had the gall to turn a deaf ear to his pressurings; the TransCanada Highway remained unfinished there until the sixties. Worse still, at the very gates of his personal fiefdom, the riding of Saint-Maurice stubbornly persisted in re-electing the Liberal René Hamel. Mad as a hornet, Duplessis fumed at the heretics: "So you want your bloody bridge, do you? Well, you'll get it one day, I promise you – the day you get rid of that René Hamel."

Saint-Maurice stuck to its guns; Duplessis, too. So in 1960, when Jean Lesage briefly entrusted me with the Public Works portfolio, the first call for tenders I issued took on a symbolic importance: we were finally going to replace the old Shawinigan bridge that had been a deathtrap for twenty years. Every time I pass by there, even today, I expect to see a furious ghost springing up. . . .

And yet the old cynic believed in something, in something very deep and very narrow at the same time: in his kind of Quebec, a French Catholic Quebec, even "improved French," which meant schooled but not too much because "education is like liquor, there's some that can't hold it!" This rural Quebec, as prudent and penny-pinching as he was, had to be absolutely protected against the evils of the age. Hence that key word that describes a besieged nationalism: "autonomy." Freedom? Never in your life, for however small the dose it could give people ideas, like Philippe Hamel's project to nationalize hydroelectic power that three words, repeated in session after session of the Assembly, quickly turned to ridicule: "Electors . . . electresses . . . electricity . . ."

His Bible was autonomy, the Maginot Line behind which nothing was supposed to change. Yet this did not exclude occasional incursions into enemy territory, such as the fiscal counterattack of 1954 that saw a beaming Duplessis emerge from a knockdown fight with his federal counterpart, Louis St. Laurent, to announce that he had just regained the right to levy his own income tax. I remember that at that moment I felt a certain pride despite myself: our bantamweight battler had floored the Goliath of Ottawa.

Otherwise I belonged to those who, though we had to laugh at some of his best jokes, basically hated his guts. Everywhere you could feel the need for change that he, like a tight lid on a boiling kettle, stifled with all his strength, preventing even the least expression of reform. And the most maddening thing was to know there was nothing you could do about it. He had three things going for him – money, an infernally good sense of organization, and that unshakeable third pillar, the Church.

Did he really make that remark that is so often ascribed to him? "The bishops? They eat out of my hand." One thing is sure, there was no one like him for putting the clergy in his pocket. Many years afterwards his ex-chauffeur told us the following anecdote, a model of applied psychology that also reveals the secret of a memory reputed to be infallible.

Duplessis is making a pastoral visit to a distant corner of the country. Beside him sits his faithful secretary and open on his knee he holds the famous little black book. At the entrance to the village the chauffeur heads instinctively in the direction of the church, while the secretary consults the notebook.

"Yes. Well, here we have Monsignor Latulippe. Yes, that's right, Monsignor, he's been made domestic prelate since your last visit, which dates from two years ago. Don't forget, *Monsignor* Latulippe, and it's ten years that he's been curé here. Okay Monsieur? . . . "

"Well, well! Now isn't it nice to see you again," exclaims Duplessis as he mounts the steps to the rectory. "It was about time they showed you some recognition after, what, nine, ten years' service in this fine parish? . . ."

Up on the veranda the priest swallows with pride. The village gossips exchange knowing looks and admiring commentaries: "Say! Even the Prime Minister knows our Monsignor. And what a memory!" The sermon will be especially good next Sunday . . . .

Shortly after his death a statue was made of Duplessis, but they never dared set it up – too many bad memories, they used to say in Lesage's day, and too fresh. The memories remained so under Johnson, and Bertrand, and then under Bourassa I. At long last it was the left, if I may venture to call it that, which, exercising its paradoxical power, applied a political decision on the right, and your humble servant ordered the miserable statue released from the dungeons of parliament. The day of its unveiling, a stone's throw from the Grande-Allée, several hundred old supporters turned up from every region in the country. Leading them, painfully bent over two canes, was the Honourable Judge Ti-Toine Rivard. There was nobody under seventy-five, nobody whose eyes were dry during the brief ceremony. Afterwards, each made it a duty to shake my hand and tell me in a shaky voice such things as: "It's a fine deed you've done there, and the Good Lord will reward you. We thank you from the bottom of our hearts, and we'll pray for you . . . ."

All at once I saw that I hadn't understood the essential thing.

For these good folk and all others who followed him, Duplessis was truly the incarnation of the Quebec of his day, with all its faults and weaknesses as well as certain qualities. For better or for worse, they recognized themselves in him, which made him invincible right to the end, and afterwards matchless in the minds of those who survived him.

One day, finishing one of those political biographies he was so fond of reading, my father-in-law, a humble labourer from Alma who had to start work in the lumber camps at age eleven and hadn't learned to read till he was past twenty, floored me with this irrevocable judgement: "Yep, if you go on the way you're going, some day, perhaps, you'll be as good as Daniel Johnson, but Duplessis, never!"

22. A Prophet in His Own Country

S UEZ AND THE CANAL: What's going on there? Why is everyone talking about it? How did it get to be such a powder barrel? Instinctively, all the old topics of college came back to mind together with their end-of-chapter questions as I put my subject through a preliminary inquiry. It was to be the first treated in a series of television broadcasts Radio-Canada had commissioned from me in the fall of 1956.

In preparation I had to take a leap in the dark, abandoning job security and pension scheme for the precarious existence of the free-lancer. I had a first contract, a phenomenal one for those days, something like fifteen or sixteen thousand dollars! But what would happen after that? God alone knew, but the adventure was too promising to worry about that. To say it presented certain risks would be euphemistic at least. According to the experts in program planning, it was hard to imagine anything more stillborn than my idea to introduce real stories from far-off lands into the family living room after the local soap opera.

Absorbed as I was with Suez, I was inclined to agree with them. Sure, there had been plenty of talk about it ever since the Egyptian chief, Nasser, had had the effrontery to nationalize the legendary watercourse. The French and the British, owners by divine right, were frothing with rage. As for the Israelis, it was obvious to them that these Arabs were getting too big for their boots and that one day someone would have to put them in their place. All that was fine and dandy, but it was nothing but embassy tittle-tattle. Not a drop of blood had been shed; therefore there was no really bad news; consequently, according to the iron law of broadcasting, there was no news at all. How to reanimate this bloodless subject, that was the question, only moderately helped by the fact that things had been heating up in the Middle East over the past few days.

Since this was a first broadcast and there had been lots of time to prepare it, I had really read everything on the subject. Too much. Riffling through a mountain of notes, I was desperately trying to find the clue that would lead me through the maze when suddenly I saw the light. Everyone was crazy about our little family dramas perpetuated on TV from one series to the next. As distant as they might be from Saint-Denis and Sainte-Catherine streets, couldn't the crises of world events be made just as captivating, given that the cast was made up of highly dramatic characters and the plot was fuller of jolts and surprises than anything Grignon or Lemelin could invent? The main thread was there. Of course, some explanation would be necessary; we would have to set it up and provide the facts, trying not to falsify them, and then tell a story with some suspense in it.

Take Suez, for example. Wasn't it the joint tragedy of colonial empires and their humiliated subjects, of the unconscious arrogance of the rulers and, finally after years of resignation, the angry revolt of the subjugated? The whole drama was played out on a tiny strip of sand where History had witnessed parading before her, with arms in one hand and a shovel in the other, Pharaohs, Persians, Turks, and Europeans, all equally obsessed by the idea of a canal that would link oceans and continents. It was one of the most congested spots on the planet, and one of the most coveted, too.

The next thing to do was to show this strategic corner of the global village as if it were right next door. I had always been mad about geography ever since I was a kid, and I took great and endless pleasure in hunting up detailed maps, almost an inch to the mile, and organizing them in relation to each other. So here we had Suez situated in its desert and flanked by neighbours even more hostile than the arid environment. All that was left to do was to people these foreign parts and show the kind of life that was lived there. For hours the producer, Claude Sylvestre, and I locked ourselves up in the CBC morgue going through kilometres of film, from the oldest to the most recent footage, so we could place the actors of this exotic drama in their true setting. In reality, though, that drama was not so far from us and our big cars. If we were unlucky enough to see this narrow waterway obstructed and oil tankers blocked in southern ports, we would certainly feel the pinch of diminished oil supplies.

Was the explanation sufficiently clear? Was the storyline tight enough to hold the viewers' attention? We had to make choices and drop out huge chunks of our material. Did what was left fit in properly with the essential facts? It was rather late to be worrying about that because after the rehearsal we discovered we were running ten minutes overtime. Thankfully, I was inspired to do without a script, for that can really tie you up. Slashing into my shorthand notes, I revamped two or three transitions, making each one different so I wouldn't dry up on camera, hoping the words would "come trippingly to the tongue."

That night, signing off, I risked saying to the TV audience that from the look of things we'd soon be speaking of Suez again. The next day or the day after war was declared. Israel attacked, the British and French landed in Egypt, and then the UN took over the business and our friend Pearson was awarded the Nobel Peace Prize.

For my part, on a more modest level I was considered to be something of a sorcerer. Or better still, a prophet in my own country, however minor. Needless to say, our program, called *Point de Mire* (*On Target*), got instant high ratings that assured it a relatively long career. In fact, it lasted two years, until the spring of 1959. Week by week we would focus on hot spots on the international scene, coming back home occasionally to cover a violent strike by loggers in Newfoundland or the Liberal convention that elected Jean Lesage.

The weekly half-hour of TV time, and sometimes more, transformed each trip into a race against the clock. For instance, in 1958, in order to cover De Gaulle's first referendum, the one where the General voted in his presidential constitution, we had to take the Montreal-Paris flight on Monday, jam meetings, interviews, and the filming of atmospheric footage into two days, then come back to Montreal and, after spending the whole night sifting through the mess of material we had accumulated, turn up next evening in the studio with bags under our eyes that required a good thick make-up job.

Luckily, we were a very small team, and very mobile, a trio consisting of the producer, the assistant producer, Rita Martel, and myself – completed, when necessary, by a cameraman and a sound engineer, who were usually recruited on the spot. The choice of subjects, the research, and what you might call the scenario were exclusively my job, one I never delegated to anybody. Having to work solo as a "one-man show" and without a safety net, for in those days broadcasting was done live, I preferred to have no one to blame but myself if I fell flat on my face.

All in all, it was one of the most hectic and rewarding periods in my life. I became what you might call a full-time student. To communicate the meat of a story without error and deal with all of its ins and outs, I first had to know ten times more than I could use. Elsewise, I might miss the necessary peg to hang the story on. It meant a minimum of seventy to eighty hours' work a week. But how satisfying it was to have the taxi driver tell you that China and Formosa weren't quite as simple as all that, or to hear an argument break out at the corner restaurant about problems in Central America! The supreme tribute was to have a good number of our fans protest vehemently the year the Stanley Cup finals drove us off the screen for nearly a month.

I really began to believe we were doing a useful job the day Michel Roy wrote in *Le Devoir*, in words that are rarely used lavishly in the brotherhood: "Certain journalists claim that it is impossible to interest the masses in political and international questions. They are categorically wrong. One only has to consider the extraordinary popularity of Point de Mire, a program in which the commentator, René Lévesque, in half an hour accomplishes the work of popularization that our newspapers have been neglecting for the past ten years."

Indeed, although Québécois had been presented as being turned in on themselves, and too systematically isolated by the regime and by their intelligentsia to care very much about the rest of the world, in fact they turned out to be as curious as raccoons, and not only open to others but singularly eager to put themselves in their skins. The only condition was that the "others" be presented simply and as people like them, which, in effect, behind the mask of differences and inequalities, they are. In my attempts to familiarize people from here with people from elsewhere, I came up with comparisons that constantly astonished and delighted me. And speaking of societies that are open, spontaneously fraternal, and ready to share their sorrows and their *joie de vivre*, nowhere had I ever met one to equal ours.

An aphorism that I read many years ago remains engraved on my memory as a trenchant reminder of the journalist's responsibility: "To be well informed is to be free." To my mind, that's the heart of the matter. The citizen who doesn't stay fairly well abreast of what's going on in the world and know something about the ever-increasing number of things that may affect his destiny is little better than a slave. His ignorance delivers him up, bound hand and foot, to all forms of exploitation. He becomes subject to the most brazen type of propagandist, who can make him salivate or tremble at will.

The danger of being lulled and plundered that threatens consumers, voters, and taxpayers alike is what the "fourth estate" has a mission to combat. If the journalist refuses the challenge, as is too often the case, he becomes an accomplice to the abuse, journalism becomes nothing more than a stunted, ostentatious trade, and one is obliged to ask, just what and whom does it serve?

For it does serve. That's the key word André Laurendeau stressed in one of those personal essays written between 1961 and 1966 and published in *Ces choses qui nous arrivent*, which remain a model of their kind. Talking about the profession he had been practising for twenty years, he wrote: "It does have its moments of exaltation. It gives to the person who follows it seriously the impression that he is *serving others*."*

To my knowledge, no one better illustrated this fundamental requirement than Laurendeau himself. He was a man whose culture was more polished than broad. His thought was at once serene yet quivering with excitement, and his judgement became surer and better balanced as passion threatened to take it over. While my type of journalism was basically reporting, his was a journalism of opinion, though he was every bit as conscious as I was of the sacrosanct nature of facts. To tell the truth, he was the main and sometimes the only person I would willingly accept criticism from, even if it occasionally became quite biting.

"Just who's speaking now," he asked one day when I was sounding off in all directions, "the media star or the politician?"

Yes, he could be quietly merciless in his observations. He was a man of profound convictions and knew how to convey them in a luminous language. Yet he had a vein of corrosive humour that can be discerned, for example, in these thoughts on commitment: "To take sides is a risk that in my view is necessary, a prerequisite to true

---

* The essays from which this and the following quotation are taken can be found in *André Laurendeau: Witness for Quebec*, translated by Philip Stratford (Toronto, 1973).

journalism yet one that must be weighed judiciously, *for otherwise you end up taking your own opinions for important news.*"* To know that your first function is to serve the public, and to believe in what you say or write without ever taking yourself for somebody else: it's a deceptively simple formula. But I often wonder if today's communicators follow these criteria as well as yesterday's, and all I would venture to say is, no better.

I might even add that there are reasons for that. In today's media context, televised news clips make up nine-tenths of the people's intake of public affairs, and written journalism also tends to deteriorate, just to keep in line. In a world swept by innovation and change from the most trivial to the most fundamental, and where heart-rending human dramas are sandwiched in between aspirin and deodorants, ours certainly isn't an easy métier for someone who strives to exercise it conscientiously.

Nevertheless, journalism is still, together with education, its close relation, not only the finest but also one of the most indispensable of public services. To inform comes from the Latin *informare*, that is, to form, or to shape. One would have to be very frivolous indeed not to see the exciting and sobering implications of that.

In Quebec in 1959, a great many swallows were announcing a change in season. Despite the wraps that had kept the country so cut off from the twentieth century, Quebec was visibly preparing itself for a spectacular awakening. In a confused way I felt a desire to be part of it rising in my blood. As attached as I was to journalism, I had a vague longing to become for a while an actor rather than an observer. Yes, but in what role, I asked myself, when I only knew one trade?

Whereupon, in the nick of time, there occurred another of those accidents in my life that settled the question.

---

* Italics mine.

V

THE SO-CALLED
QUIET REVOLUTION

"From now on . . . "
PAUL SAUVÉ, 1959

23. If Only One Remained...

ONE EARLY SPRING EVENING in 1960 four potential candidates sat in a hotel room in Montreal wondering what to reply to the big question. Jean Lesage was waiting for us in the Windsor Hotel, a few blocks from the Mount Royal where Jean Marchand, who had come down expressly from Quebec City, had asked us to meet him in his room. As was later to be the case on the federal level, Marchand was the party's first-choice candidate. A front-line union leader, he had the advantage of being known to the provincial Liberal organizers more or less as the living incarnation of resistance to Duplessis's Union Nationale. My old buddy was a populist orator and possessed other precious qualifications for political success: the common touch and a happy-go-lucky attitude he has never lost. Nearing forty, as we all were, he had reached a fork in the road. As president of the Canadian Catholic Federation of Labour, a job of enviable stability, he no doubt feared he might stagnate in relative ease now that Duplessis was no longer around to drive him to surpass himself, as he had during the Asbestos strike and on other occasions. He was ripe for a new challenge.

Gérard Pelletier was not so close to me. I thought of him as a highly esteemed colleague. He was also committed to social reform as much as, if not more than, to his journalism. I found him as reflective as Marchand was instinctive, and his thought processes grew proportionately more strict and precise as Marchand's waxed ever more lyrical. Together they made me think – in an admiring way, I hasten to say – of Don Quixote and Sancho Panza.

As for Pierre Elliott Trudeau, the fourth of these musketeers and one who was not marked out for the same adventures, how can one define the undefinable? He was extremely cultivated, certainly, but almost exclusively only in matters of jurisprudence and politics. I had the impression that, except for show, the additional baggage he had accumulated from studies in the humanities left him supremely indifferent, like seed fallen on rock. Even in conversation his thought constantly took on a dialectical twist, and to have the last word he would stop at neither sarcasm nor the most specious argument. In its written form his thought was dry and typically technocratic, as exemplified in the pages of *Cité libre* where he recommended "borrowing from the architect his concern for 'functional' discipline." It was thanks to this little review he masterminded that we first met, some time in 1954 or 1955, I think. I had gone along with Pelletier to meet Trudeau in the cafeteria of Radio-Canada and offered to contribute the occasional article.

"Very good," he said in that drawling tone he affected, "but allow me one simple question: Can you write?"

You'll have guessed by now that we didn't exactly hit it off.

All three – Marchand, Pelletier, Trudeau – felt strongly attracted by politics, by the risk involved, and also, I think, by the career opportunities. This wasn't the case for me, even if TV exposure had given me more notoriety than any of them. In those days, with a fine disrespect for genres, anyone who appeared regularly in public was known as an "artist," a phenomenon, as we shall see, that nearly cost me my first election. But it hardly made me seem serious enough. I was badly bitten all the same and had a strong urge to do something else after the painful interruption of a strike that had severely shaken the little world of Radio-Canada and left behind a poisoned atmosphere.

At the beginning, on December 28, 1958, the confrontation between the administration and a little group of program producers was supposed to be nothing more than a skirmish that would be settled in a couple of days. Even so, it was a cruel blow, for my own striking producer was obliged to cancel a trip that would have taken us to cover one of the chief news events of the day. Our bags were packed and reservations made on the plane for Havana where the triumphal arrival of Fidel Castro and his *barbudos* was predicted for January 1, 1959, now that he had come down from the Sierra Maestre, driving out the enemy at Santa Clara and putting Batista and his Cubano-American mob to flight.*

But the couple of days stretched out to weeks, and we had to put water in our wine. The strike turned nasty, as they inevitably do when questions of principle are involved. The producers had dared to set up their own union. But the fact that they had to direct others, no matter how small the groups were, made them management, that is, part of the administration, and the right to bargain had never been accepted or even seriously envisaged on that level. The airwaves were under federal jurisdiction, and the poor devils of strikers ran into another legalism, a typically Anglo-Saxon one this time: where is the precedent? There wasn't any. I remembered, several years before, the former boss of the International Service of Radio-Canada, good old Ira Dilworth, dismissing the handful of budding union members we were then by saying, "But, my friends, it just isn't done," because it had never been done before.

So I knew that the producers at this time weren't out of the woods yet. And we were in there with them, because soon hundreds of authors, actors, singers, technicians, and other "artists" took up their cause. Thus, while I was weighing the pros and cons of this situation, with that inborn deliberation I have always been famous for, Jean Marchand projected me back into orbit by setting up as general-in-chief and calling me to that hotel room where he had established his command post.

The strike dragged on for ten long weeks, following the familiar pattern of stormy meetings, broken windows, police raids, and

---

* As a slight consolation I had a chance to meet Castro the following spring at Dorval airport where the Junior Chamber of Commerce felt called upon to offer him . . . toys for the children of Cuba! He had just come from the States where he had got the cold shoulder, the sugar lobby having killed any chance of dialogue. Like a shipwrecked sailor hanging on to his lifebuoy, he insisted, with a kind of anguished sincerity, on clinging desperately to a single ideological tag: *Humanismo*. But he foresaw clearly that the American attitude would leave him no alternative but that other "ism" that rules Cuba today.

brief interludes in jail, while the scabs holed up inside kept the programming going with news, documentaries, and many films, superb feature-length stuff of a quality never seen on television, which enchanted viewers so much they weren't in any hurry to get back to normal. And just to think, we grumbled, gnashing our teeth, it's the money we're losing that's paying for this film festival!

I have two indelible memories of this period. The first concerns a stage show entitled *Temporary Difficulties* that we put together with bits and pieces from here and there to build up a strike fund. Everyone was trying to dig up some stopgap job, like the one I had found on radio, but many were in dire straits in this milieu that is generally free-spending but also capable of astonishing generosity. Hence, all those who were still making both ends meet came forward to offer their services and their spare time and were incensed if by chance there wasn't room for them on the program. There was no question of accepting a fee; it was really from everyone according to his means, and to everyone according to his needs. I proudly agreed to prepare and deliver short "Point de Mire" commentaries each night, giving updates on the situation. My reporting, I must admit, was somewhat biased and became more so the more we learned about the systematic intransigence of the federal government.

My second memory evolves from the first. Seeing the conflict settling into a gloomy routine of stalemate, several hundred of us decided to go to Ottawa to plead our cause. Our delegation had the honour to be received by the Minister of Labour, Michael Starr, and the surprise to discover that the paralysis of the whole French network was for him like something happening on the planet Mars. A worthy disciple of his chief, Diefenbaker, whose ideal was "one language, one nation," he let us know in his friendly way that he wasn't going to budge an inch. On the other hand, the federal Liberals, as irresponsible as any self-respecting opposition always is, were predictably heaping upon us their warmest, not to say most incendiary, encouragement.

On the way back I couldn't help but think of the rapidity with which the least Anglo-Canadian brush fire mobilized the whole of Ottawa, while they would sit back in the greatest calm when it was our house that was going up in flames. The more I thought of it, the more furious I got. This became so apparent in my commentaries over the next few days that André Laurendeau, who fully supported us from the start, said to me one night: "You know, listening to you I have the impression you're headed straight for politics."

"Hmph! First I've heard of it," I replied with total sincerity.

Even the worst calamities don't last forever. In March, completely worn out, the two parties consented to sit down together and the strike ended. Our honour had been saved: the first management union had been officially recognized. We could go back to work with our heads high. But our mood and morale were abysmal. The two clans weren't on speaking terms and would hardly look at each other, while underhand squaring of accounts kept the wounds fresh. With great difficulty we struggled through until summer. It was almost a relief to learn that *Point de Mire* wouldn't be back in the fall. I was told later that, over and above the very understandable resentment felt by the administration, they also feared the excessive "power" that such a platform might bestow upon the broadcaster who occupied it.

Now I was again as free as a bird on a branch, and I spent several months wandering from station to station and from radio to television, but my heart wasn't in it any more. Without really recognizing it, I was, as might be said today, hanging loose, at the precise time that events were rushing to a head. The ice jam in Quebec politics had been dynamited and the way was opening to currents of renewal that had been boiling beneath the surface for ages. Duplessis had died in Schefferville. Paul Sauvé scarcely had time to issue his famous slogan – "From now on . . ." – when he, too, expired after a hundred days and his successor, Antonio Barrette, called an election. A political thaw, clearly, was under way. One could feel it, but it was still hesitant. And just as, when winter is ending there's still danger of frost, so it remained possible we would have to put up with a full four years of this threadbare regime.

. . . At the Mount Royal Hotel the hour was getting dangerously late and it was in these terms that I put the case as best I could. Don't we believe as much and even more than the Liberal Party, I said to the three others who were being sounded out, that it's "time for a change"? And if men like them, who were so well prepared, refused to put their shoulders to the wheel, would that change ever come? Even if it did come, would the resulting government, a new one but the product of an old party, be strong enough to enact its program and put life into democratic structures so recently conceived?

I am referring to my own memory here, which won't necessarily agree with what some of the others might recall. What I seem to remember, though, is that Marchand was more tempted than Pelletier, who was much warmer than Trudeau. In fact, the latter was hardly attracted at all, scenting in Liberal speeches and commitments emanations of a nationalism that was his pet aversion – Quebec nationalism, that is. That argument, along with others I've forgotten, plus the Olympian disdain he manifested for the provincial arena we were being offered a chance to enter, finally carried the day. Though I didn't feel it myself, I had to admire the influence Trudeau already exerted on those around him. So Marchand remained at the CCFL waiting to make his move, and Pelletier likewise held back from the fray of Quebec politics.

It was after midnight when I went over to the Windsor to tell Jean Lesage that only one remained, and it was me. Struggling against sleep because he liked to retire early, Lesage made the best of it and offered me a choice between two uncommitted ridings (they were getting very scarce as the election gathered steam), either Laurier or some riding in the West Island whose name escapes me because I didn't consider it for a second.

24. The Journalist and the Artist

AS OFTEN HAPPENS IN BIG CITIES, the riding of Laurier in the northern part of Montreal was a curious patchwork: Italians, Greeks, and Jews in their respective quarters and, from Saint-Denis to Christophe Colomb, a French heartland divided into villages, each huddled around its parish church. It was also the site of Plaza Saint-Hubert with its string of little shops and its lively crowds, where I had been going for years to interview "the man in the street" for my broadcasts.

So I didn't exactly consider myself a stranger there. But at the corner store they weren't exactly killing the fatted calf either. Hadn't I been parachuted in when several local sons might have expected to be chosen? They let me know about it. I was also that "lefty" described by the propaganda of the other camp as smelling strongly of borsch since I was almost in Khrushchev's pocket. These were heavy handicaps that weighed against me at first, for the good folk of the neighbourhood were rather suspicious and were feeling their oats, too, with this new internal democracy that had given them their say in the running of the party.

Under the inquisitorial eye of Mr. Alfred Reynolds, printer of Liberal publications, of Mr. Achille Renaud, a pillar of Sainte-Cécile parish, and of Madame Siméon Gagnon, president of the Wilfrid Laurier Club, I had to pass a strict oral examination, and then, thanks to directives from Jean Lesage that had their due weight, I was conditionally accepted.

I continue to believe, however, that what swayed the balance was the treasurer of the local association, "Doc" Hector Prud'homme. He was a grand old fellow, amazingly fresh for his seventy-five years. He bragged that he'd delivered every woman in the riding, and when he became my official guide and remained so right through to the end of the campaign, the joyful old rascal always took advantage of our door-to-door visits to check up on the most attractive of his ex-patients with an exuberance that was quite unprofessional. I was not surprised to learn later that he had remarried. Later still, in 1970, I was completely dumbfounded to see him turn up in my committee rooms. By then he was extremely frail, but he was determined to wish good luck to "the separatist" as long as I could keep it under my hat. After ten years I was like an adopted son to him, and the others, too, became much more than supporters – they were friends of unshakable fidelity. That's why I've always thought that the most important and, humanly speaking, the richest role one can play in politics is not to be a minister or premier but to be an MP. It is a role, alas, that in a quarter of a century of politics I was never free to play as fully as I would have wished.

The forced absenteeism I was condemned to began, in fact, with this first campaign. Since I was a media star and a "new man" in the party, I had to be seen. The day after my nomination I was already on the road to Chicoutimi. As youngest member of the "Three L's" – Lesage, Lapalme, and Lévesque – I was stuck on the wearisome grand tour, travelling from one riding to the next in every region of the country.

It was during the final sprint that excess of fatigue, perhaps in concert with the offices of Good Saint Anne, got me back the voice that had been all but extinguished fifteen years earlier during the winter of 1944-45. Examinations, inhalations, Desmosthenes-type exercises, and God knows what else: after the war I had tried them all, but without the slightest success. I didn't speak; I whispered, until that June evening when, in the feverish pace of the last campaign trip, after a speech at Beauport in the suburbs of Quebec City, I was whisked by convertible from the overheated hall and delivered, shivering, to Beaupré, a few steps from the famous basilica dedicated to Saint Anne, where I was to repeat my number. This shock treatment had an extraordinary effect. Next morning on waking up I noticed an unexpected sonorousness penetrating the usual aphonia, and in three days this adolescent change of voice had given me back the whole scale. Friends at the Faculty of Medicine claimed learnedly that the effort of the previous few days had undoubtedly freed some nodules they had never been able to see that had been stuck to my vocal chords. Personally, I prefer to think it was a miracle. Whatever it was, I now could speak above a hoarse whisper.

Our itineraries were designed in such a way that we all went everywhere but never at the same time, so I don't think I saw Lesage again once during those crazy weeks. I only remember late one evening telephoning from Rimouski or somewhere and managing to reach him at Trois-Rivières or somewhere to tell him my worries about the effect my too-intermittent presence might have in Laurier.

"Don't worry, my friend," he reassured me in a sunny voice, "your riding is in good hands. Azellus and his boys are looking after it."

Azellus Denis had been an MP with Lesage in Ottawa. Despite a fleeting career as minister and then being put out to pasture as senator, he was really made to be a backbencher. He excelled at organization. A great joker with his slaps on the back and his state secrets that were nothing of the sort, he had an inoffensive appearance that disguised the cunning and limitless cynicism of the expert electioneer. Brought up in his school, his "boys" knew all the shadiest tricks in the business, too. I was as innocent as a lamb and felt about as secure as one would if protected by a bunch of panthers purring while they sharpened their claws. For better or for worse, however, my fate was in their paws.

Luckily, besides these big felines of the electoral jungle, there was also a milder species of fauna in supporters who came from every corner of the city. Their noisy presence animated our local meetings and gave me back a minimum of confidence in the democratic process, even when their brilliant amateurism threw sand in the gears of the party machine. But our most precious recruit was a "little guy from around the corner" who was so broad-shouldered he could hardly get through the committee room door.

Jean Rougeau was an idol of honest wrestling fans everywhere. Beyond that, he was one of the most perfectly upright men I have ever had the privilege to know and had a courage that never failed him right up to death's door. Maybe, as must happen to every man, he had his weak moments, but for my part I never saw in him the least suspicion of pettiness or meanness. As for his courage, he had to show it only a few days after he joined our team. He was told there was someone at the door who wanted to see him urgently. When he came back an hour later he was white as a sheet and trembling with fury as much as from anxiety. The man who had sent for him was one of the big bosses of the party in power and the undisputed "Godfather" of that part of town.

"Johnny boy," he had hissed while driving Rougeau around the neighbourhood in his limousine, "you're making a big mistake, you know. There's still time to get yourself straightened out, but it's getting short. Think it over if you ever dream of being a big promoter one day . . . " Though his career was on the line, the champion told him to get lost. It is hardly necessary to add that one doesn't often have a chance to admire that kind of guts.

But that was just one banal little incident, for those were the methods used at the time. More flattering, if I can put it that way, was a new gimmick invented especially for me. On the ballot slip all the candidate was allowed to have after his name was his profession, so I appeared as "René Lévesque, journalist." One can well imagine my stupefaction on discovering that right after my name came a "René Lévesque, artist"! In those days all anyone had to do was supply a list of names and pay the deposit – it helped, obviously, to be on the right side – and a phantom candidate was thereby created. As a result of this fraud the last days of the campaign were spent driving around with this insistent message flying from every one of our automobiles: "Vote for the *real* Lévesque – Lévesque, journalist."

But voters are such a distracted lot that on the morning of the 22nd one of our staunchest party militants, who had been very upset by these tactics, confessed to us, a little late: "O my God! It's not possible! I think I voted for the artist!" And she burst into tears.

All day long, wearing as well as I could that falsely calm mask the candidate is forced to assume, I visited the polls collecting horror stories. Here's one example.

> . . . In Poll No. 168 (6797 rue Drolet), four plucky women managed to put to flight six hired thugs who had come to stuff the ballot boxes with marked slips. Mme. Rosaire Cloutier (whose arm was hurt), Mme. Arthur Michaud (an upstanding woman representing Union Nationale candidate Arsène Gagné), Miss Yolande Memme (representing René Lévesque), and Miss Denise Couilard (clerk) resisted the wrongdoers and prevented them from committing their crime. The men were forced to flee when the police, alerted by the shouts of the four women, arrived on the scene.

Such were the time-honoured criminal practices still current in isolated polls dispersed in various locals where the electoral mafia could usually call the tune.

One such scene almost occurred in mid-afternoon. Over on rue Dante in the Italian quarter a bunch of hoodlums had started raiding the polls. As soon as I heard about it I jumped in the car and went over. Luckily, Rougeau was with me. When they saw this living legend, the mobsters backed off a little, hesitating to bite even though they still showed their teeth. It seemed a long time before the municipal police got around to coming and hauled all these fine birds off to the station. Thank God our S.O.S. had been sent to the municipal force, for one of the first crooks to be picked up turned out to be, under his black shirt, none other than a captain in the Provincial Police.

Then all evening long and part of the night we were constantly thrown up and down a roller coaster: a few votes ahead, a few behind, sliding hour by hour from elation to depression until finally the official result was announced: I had won by 129 votes. By drawing off nearly a thousand votes that animal of an "artist" had almost done us in!

There were tears and laughter, kisses and shouting. In our "secret" committee room in the basement of the Azellus house the ceiling threatened to come down, and I thought that was what had happened when a heavy, dull thud was heard at the back of the room. It was our chief organizer who had just passed out, stiff as a board. The tension had been too much for him. He must have been wondering if our side had been able to stuff the ballot boxes as well as the opposition . . .

The results from Laurier came in late to complete a narrow Liberal victory: 51 seats against 43, plus the invincible Irish independent, Frank Hanley. Coming within a hair's breadth of that return of winter we had feared, the voters had chosen, but they had maintained the curious stance of the man wearing both suspenders and belt, just in case. Since we were blue in Ottawa, we could afford to be red in Quebec.

Several days later, drawing breath a little, I reread the statement I had made at the time I announced my candidacy:

> . . . I remain convinced, like the majority of Québécois – at least I
> hope they see this, too – that the leaders of the Union Nationale no
> longer constitute anything more than the remnants of a regime. For
> the good health and even the dignity of the province and every one of
> its citizens, it is more than time for a change . . . .

Now that had come to pass.

. . . Men like Lesage, Lapalme, Gérin-Lajoie, Hamel, and others have proven by holding out stubbornly, by making the structures of the Liberal Party more democratic, and by adopting the remarkable platform they have drawn up, that they are the replacement team we are in such urgent need of. . . .

But how in the devil, I was asking myself now, can a newcomer without experience help in any way whatsoever to move things forward? I hadn't the slightest idea.

Suddenly the telephone rang.

"Monsieur Lévesque, it seems you're expected at Saint-Jovite."

I recognized the raw tone of a permanently flayed sensibility. "But Monsieur Lapalme," I replied, "what's it all about? Why do they want me up there?"

"Maybe because you're the only one who hasn't telephoned yet," he grumbled, hanging up.

When I got back from Saint-Jovite I was Minister of Public Works. Since I wasn't exactly overwhelmed by the post, I had also persuaded Jean Lesage to give me those bare bones of a ministry called "Hydraulic Resources," where I would be Daniel Johnson's successor until a full-fledged ministry could be formed that would take the fine-sounding if somewhat parvenu name of "Richess Naturelles."

25. Apprenticeship

JULY, 1960: one newspaper spoke of the next month as the thirty days that shook Quebec. At the frantic rhythm I was living, getting my training "on the job" and at the same time participating in an avalanche of decisions, I was scarcely aware of the shock. When someone asked me which direction we were going, I replied: "Well, I'm not too sure, but we're certainly getting there fast!"

That might sound frivolous, but it was the exact truth, and it reflected a feeling I think we all had that we were being carried by an irresistible whirlwind of enthusiasm, appetite for life, and limitless confidence in our own capacity to move things forward. One evening I went to consult Father Georges-Henri Lévesque, the man who was the liberating conscience of our generation, in his cheerful retreat at La Maison Montmorency, and we walked together to the edge of the falls. Probably inspired by the deafening roar that seemed to fill one's very being, my companion turned toward me: "Hurry up!" he shouted. "What's happening is a revolution. Don't let it slip through your fingers."

It was the first time I had heard this expression that was later to be so abused when someone, doubtless because no blood was running in the gutters, attached the qualifier "quiet" to it. But doesn't any rapid and profound transformation of the established order – even if, as is nearly always the case, it has been brewing a long time – deserve to be called a revolution? If so, we were in one up to our necks.

Those first few weeks were absolutely staggering. No Quebec government ever innovated so much in such a short time. Thanks to his past experience as parliamentary secretary and junior minister in Ottawa, Lesage was the only one to have a certain knowledge of the workings of the state. As for the rest of us, we were just sorcerer's apprentices and didn't know what we couldn't do.

I should add that at each cabinet meeting we did have before us an itinerary that was an essential part of every dossier. Taking a page from the old Action Libérale Nationale, the party had come up with a printed program that was tolerably precise and which now had become a contract with Quebec citizens that had to be respected. From that time on I have always tried to avoid speaking of *promises*, which are just words in the air, preferring the term *commitments*, the nuance being that the latter must pass the test of being written out, which makes them last.

The lasting effect of this inaugural month, then, was nothing short of the political launch of what was to be modern Quebec, of that Quebec that seems today to be self-evident, but which for us took on the character of a society in full renaissance. Even if we were often only following in the footsteps of others who had gone before, for once things were happening here at home and at last we were catching up.

The first place to start was in education, where we had so much ground to cover there wasn't a moment to lose. "It is in the Province of Quebec," our program read, "that school attendance is the lowest in Canada. *Fifty per cent of Quebec youth leave school before they turn fifteen.* Recent studies show that 76 per cent of unemployed young people have not gone beyond the eighth grade and thus seriously risk finding themselves unemployed for the rest of their lives." This was due to the system that Duplessis had the nerve to claim was the best in the world, one he had let stagnate to such a degree that we had to start out our reforms with such measures as free textbooks in all provincially controlled schools and mandatory school attendance until age sixteen.

To move ahead, however, we needed clear authority and adequate instruments. All the splintered educational sectors that had been wilfully scattered in various corners of Duplessis's lackadaisical state were now regrouped under Paul Gérin-Lajoie, Minister of Youth. From then on he also became Minister of Education in all but name. For some time yet, the fear of such a ministry and of the power it would wield in opposing religious authorities remained so strong that Lesage felt obliged to declare: "As long as I remain Premier, there will never be a Ministry of Education!" On this point, as on several others, Lesage was to learn that one must never say never, and in 1964 the dreaded ministry finally received the official right to exist.

If there was a revolution, that's where it really happened. From year to year we could see public secondary teaching growing, free courses spreading, and the university sector begin to expand to fill the place it holds today while waiting for the CEGEPs to come along and link the two levels. UNESCO has recognized that of all world societies none supplied a greater effort than Quebec during the sixties to improve the educational opportunities of its youth. If we are a reasonably well-schooled people today, capable of meeting all the challenges that come our way, it is to the parents of those days that we owe this accomplishment.

After education there was public health to look into. That, too, was something out of the Middle Ages. There was no problem for people who were well off, but the poor had to go via the riding patronage boss to get that infamous passport to the hospital, the *pink card*. So very early on negotiations began with the federal government to set up, starting in January, 1961, the hospital insurance plan that the previous government had obstinately refused to consider. After that, a good ten years more were needed to exhaust the medical profession's opposition to health insurance. In the end we equipped ourselves with health services that are costly and there-fore must be administered shrewdly, but on the whole we have a plan that is certainly unrivalled in North America.

As for administration, it was during that same month of July, 1960, that a Treasury Department was created to replace The Prince's traditional fantasies with an accounting system of the strictest kind. And the Civil Service Commission undertook reforms designed to give us a professional civil service instead of that arbitrary lottery described in this famous quip: "Civil servants?" Duplessis is reported to have said. "Bah! You can always get a couple not too bad for the price of a good one!" This formula had been applied especially to the Provincial Police, which was rotten to the core. A small group of ex-RCMP officers was borrowed from Ottawa and given the task of rebuilding the outfit from top to bottom.

I could go on at length talking about this period that was incontestably the spring-cleaning of the century, but this is more properly the job of historians, I think. For my part, I prefer to concentrate on my own impressions and personal souvenirs. Laboriously, I was learning the ins and outs of the obscure Ministry of Public Works which, as a journalist, I had entered as unprepared as Daniel walking into the lions' den. To take on the engineers and the contractors, certain wiseacres suggested with knowing smiles that I should make a special novena to Good Saint Anne.

"I don't know," I said to myself, "in the first place, I'm no dumber than the next man; in the second, money doesn't keep me awake at night; and third, I'm lucky enough to have friends who haven't got too much of it either."

Indeed, in those days there was a lot of money floating around under those bridges I had become responsible for. Construction was also my department, but since nothing much was going on there, bridges had all the sex appeal – all kinds of provocative bridges, from the monsters to the pipsqueaks. What about the roads? Well, roads were somebody else's worry. It was still quite a while before good sense prevailed and the two pieces of road and the bridge that joined them came under the same minister! Incredible but true.

The Union Nationale had spent its last days in office distributing enough contracts to its friends to swallow up the whole budget. Declaring a moratorium on all that, Lesage ordered the contracts annulled or at least renegotiated. Time was getting short, for we were in midsummer, work was at a standstill, and protests were rising from every side. I had dreamed of doing a thorough house-cleaning with all the windows open, but I was now constrained to haggle like a cautious carpet salesman, feeling my way as I went into the bargain.

"Tell him to lower his price by 20 per cent," Marc Picard suggested. "Whatever you do, don't settle for less than 15 per cent."

Marc was an old classmate whom I had asked to guide me through this unknown universe. He was an engineer with a rigorous cast of mind and had his doubts about the highly unorthodox operation that lack of time had forced upon us. The sight of our first client was enough to reassure him, however. He was a fat, ruddy-faced little fellow who sparkled from head to toe. On the fingers of each hand, all around his gold watch case, and even to his tie pin, he was rippling in diamonds. "Gentlemen," he declared, looking down his nose at us, "this comedy has gone on long enough. I've got contracts signed and sealed here, and workers who are getting impatient. Something's got to give."

We didn't have to look far for the explanation to this superb creature. In the kingdom of Duplessis, budgets were carefully divided among the barons of the regime and this individual held exclusive rights to all construction and repair of bridges in the lucrative west metropolitan region. He was so sure of himself that when he heard me emphasizing that his contracts were obviously based on inflated estimates, he ventured to reply: "Well, well! What do you think! That's the very reason we should be able to get along! There's plenty for everybody, you know!"

Cutting him short before he asked me how much I wanted, I answered, raising my voice: "I've only got one thing to say to you. If you want to hang on to those contracts, you're going to have to bring your price down, say, 20 per cent."

"Twenty per cent? You want to ruin me?"

He pleaded, stormed, and swore we were throwing him out of business, and having finally consented to a 15 per cent reduction, left the office looking relieved.

"You might at least have looked over my way when I was making signs to you," Marc said in a reproachful tone. "At 20 per cent, and maybe even at 25 per cent, the big crook was still making a killing."

Since corruption was contagious, it wasn't enough to clean it up; we also had to prevent it from spreading in our own ranks – as much as possible. In my own riding, where I had to throw some customers with fat bribes out on their ears, I noticed that when I wasn't right there Azellus's boys kept up the custom of minting permits to sell beer in grocery stores and that from 1960 on the colour of the beer was red. I was obliged to make a clean sweep and without further ado found a riding secretary who came from outside the parish.

In this respect the two old parties resembled each other at the grassroots like identical twins. Here's an amusing example. In our modest Montreal headquarters of Public Works two employees worked side by side, a minor boss in the bigger office and his assistant next door in a smaller one. They had worked there since 1945. Formerly, under the Godbout government, the assistant had been the boss and vice versa. Every morning for the past fifteen years they could be seen arriving each with his own badge: *Le Devoir* for the Liberal and *Montréal Matin* for the conservative. When I took over, *Montréal Matin* went into eclipse while *Le Devoir* was very much in evidence. Seeing that I didn't seem to understand a thing about their system, the poor assistant finally screwed up his courage and explained that for him, too, it was high time for a change! So we put him back in his post and office of 1945. His partner didn't seem overly surprised and, as far as I know, they were both as happy as pigs in clover. Life had returned to normal.

An encounter I had with one of our defeated candidates was far less amusing. He was a member of the reform wing of the party and had come to talk to me about his riding, where he had narrowly lost the election and where he intended to go on "working" for the next time. To this end he wanted to keep an eye on the adversary to prevent him from filling his pockets again. "All you have to do," he told me virtuously, "is put me in charge of handing out the jobs you control to the people I choose. You know you can trust me."

He was clearly expecting to take over the gravy train in his sector. I told him that although I'd appreciated his campaign speeches, that kind of thing wasn't being done any more and that contracts were now going to the lowest bidder. My little democratic speech was in vain. He flew into a rage, called me a naive idiot, and left, slamming the door.

By far the most instructive experience was one that occurred well before that. Even before joining cabinet I had been called to a very curious meeting with a director of Hydro-Québec. Still on his guard after so many years of believe-or-die, he didn't want to meet me in public, preferring to see me in a little hotel near the Windsor Station that has since disappeared. Coming into the room, I first saw two maps spread out on the bed.

"This," said my host, "is the region of La Côte-Nord and here are two very important rivers, the Manicouagan and La Rivière aux Outardes. In a year or two you will see the greatest hydroelectric development in our history begin here. It is absolutely essential for Hydro itself to take charge of the project. We can handle it, but on one condition." Moving to the other map, which showed the site of the Carillon dam across the Ottawa, he continued his demonstration. "Carillon is already laid on. Construction starts this summer. It's a middle-sized operation that will be an excellent dry run for our engineers."

"So?" I said. "What's the problem?"

"It's simple. The main contract has already been promised to the Perini Company in Boston. They've always had a monopoly on all our major projects. That's got to change, or else our own Quebec skills will always go on serving under foreign orders."

But why, I wanted to know, was he confiding all this to me when I was only just elected.

"Rumour has it you may become a minister. And as you don't have a partisan political past, I thought you might still have an open mind on such matters."

I warned him not to entertain too many illusions, thanked him for his confidence, and promised him that should the occasion arise . . . Shortly after that I did indeed become a minister. At the first opportunity I recounted this story to my colleagues, stressing that as the one politically responsible for this sector I found it entirely appropriate for Hydro at last to be given effective control of its own construction sites. Considering the complexity of the question, it was decided to put off studying it until the following week. But no sooner was I back in my office than I received an urgent call.

"My dear, honourable, young friend," an unctuous voice greeted me, "it is my duty to let you know a few things about the Perinis . . ."

"Good God!" I replied. "News certainly travels fast! What about them?"

"Well, you should know," the voice continued, "that the Perinis are our friends, too. They have shown themselves to be as generous to us as to our predecessors."

I hung up on him and immediately called Lesage. Either this business of contributions to party funds was cleared out of my dossiers, I told him, or I was packing my bags. Lesage promised it wouldn't happen again. He kept his word, and ever since Hydro-Québec has been able to manage its own big projects.

This incident also persuaded me not to neglect Hydraulic Resources, the poor little afterthought that was my second ministry. I was soon to discover that under the afterthought hid the goose that laid the golden eggs.

26. Nothing Ventured...

IN QUEBEC, when people can't get along, they're sometimes told: "If that's how it is, go do a Lac-à-l'épaule."

For an expression like that to make its way into the language, it must have had its hour of glory. It was in 1962 that the little lake in question suddenly stepped out of obscurity. It is situated in the Laurentians, five minutes from the southern entrance to the park. On its shore, at the end of a winding road half-hidden in underbrush, is a handsome log chalet with huge stone fireplaces, a few plain but comfortable bedrooms, and a dining room where they serve incomparable smoked trout. It's one of a few "clubs" the state has set aside so ministers, senior civil servants, and MNAs can relax while working, or work in an unstressful atmosphere. What happened twenty-five years ago at Lac-à-l'épaule remains memorable because it was the Lesage government's "brave risk" and at the same time the real beginning of the economic reconquest of Quebec.

Imagine yourself back in those days when, in resignation rather than in anger, it was commonly said that Québécois weren't born to set the world on fire, not the financial world anyway. Money matters were carried out strictly in English. All strategic resources, as we would call them nowadays, were also in English hands. One could see that dramatically in those "company towns" in the mining and pulp and paper industries where the best-situated quarter with its tidy, shaded streets invariably went by a name that wasn't Québécois – a whole troop of little regional Westmounts and Hampsteads where not only fortune but also influence and, above all, control resided. Two figures summarize the situation: with 80 per cent of the population, French Quebec held barely one-tenth of the economic control, a feeble fraction, and this was restricted to the least dynamic sectors.

With the creation of the Ministry of Natural Resources in the spring of 1961, I found myself right in the middle of this collective insignificance, facing off with the top brass of those external interests and their local flunkies. They had added the mining sector to my Hydraulic Resources portfolio, but though I asked to have forests added as well, arguing that water has a much greater natural affinity with trees than with minerals, it was to no avail. I learned afterwards that the pulp and paper companies had flatly refused to have anything to do with the troublesome lefty I was reported to be then. It should be said that these enterprises held uncontested sway over vast forest concessions, rights that were so-called renewable but which in fact were perpetual, and that their contributions to party funds were among the most lavish.

Evicted from this colonial empire, I fell back on my two other domains. In the mining sector, Noranda called the tune, to the point of considering government services as one of its branch operations and *rewarding* the ex-deputy minister by naming him to the board of directors when he retired! The whole sector was literally under foreign occupation, and with laws, regulations, and frequent confrontations with the potentates of the business, we tried little by little to repatriate parts of it.

But as important as they may be while they are productive, mines are inevitably condemned to close one day or another, whereas water is inexhaustible, like the energy it carries. I had always kept in mind the memory of the campaign waged against the electricity trust by a few bright lights during the thirties, but quashed, as I mentioned earlier, by Duplessis. And before that again I had lived through the tardy electrification of the Gaspésie and knew that there, as in other remote regions, it still cost a pretty penny to get a minimum of current.

So I undertook to tackle this aspect of our economic subordination first. To this end I assembled a small team, a tiny nucleus of brilliant young men, that we pompously called "The Planning Directorate." There was Eric Gourdeau, an engineer and humanist who was soon to dedicate himself to the cause of the Indians and the Inuit and who would eventually become known inside and outside Quebec as one of the most faithful and farsighted friends of native peoples. André Marier, who was later to leave his mark on the Caisse de dépôt and other public enterprises, was also one of the group. The leader of the team was Michel Bélanger, chairman of the Banque Nationale after having been economic adviser to the government and president of the Montreal Stock Exchange. His precocious efficiency had already been put to the test in the federal Finance Department, but he was mainly remarkable for his perspicacity and a sense of logic that was quite exceptional. I sought him out with the avowed intent of "springing" him from Ottawa, offering him an opportunity to help us draw up a plan to decolonize the hydroelectric sector. He took his time to think things over and then, like a good many others, he must have perceived that in those years Quebec was the place where the action was going to be.

Several ministries, for that matter, saw the arrival of young men full of pep and projects, who before reaching the top of their various ladders began their careers as tireless dynamos working for change. In Education there was Arthur Tremblay, the strategist of so many upheavals who today is a Conservative senator! Committing themselves to government service in their early twenties, Pierre Marois and Bernard Landry were later to become pillars of our own Parti Québécois government. The same was true of Claude Morin, who started out writing speeches for Lesage, and Jacques Parizeau, who was soon to bring his talents to bear on economic matters. All of them were conscious of the fact that to move ahead we would have to shuck off the old shell in which public power had been confined, a little like polite children who were permitted to come into the living room so long as they were seen but not heard. We wanted the right to speak in our own living room.

"But the state is on our side," I dared assert one day. "It's even our strongest ally."

This remark set me up with certain right-minded citizens as an out-and-out socialist, yet in reality it was a most pragmatic observation. In the energy field, for example, none of our home-grown mini-magnates would have been able or would have dared to grapple with the system the whole of Quebec was divided into: a dozen different principalities, including Gatineau Power Co., Northern Quebec Power, La Compagnie de pouvoir Bas-Saint-Laurent, Saguenay Electric Co., plus three or four little local outfits and, last but not least, covering the whole central part of the territory, the empire of Shawinigan Water and Power with its two branches, Southern Canada Power and Quebec Power Co., the latter serving the provincial capital but not condescending to use a bilingual name. Only the government had the strength and means to take on these heavyweights, provided it also had the will to act.

As reformist as the Liberal Party was in many respects, it remained chronically timid in economic matters. For instance, its whole energy policy was contained in the two following sub-paragraphs modestly appended to the part of the program devoted to the Ministry of Natural Resources:

Assure Hydro-Québec the ownership and right to exploit all hydroelectric energy not yet conceded wherever development is economically feasible.

Normalize hydro rates throughout the province and lower them where they are too high. . . .

It didn't take long to see that what we were being asked to do was to square the circle. On the one hand Hydro-Québec was being guaranteed what it already had – not the right but the duty to produce, at Bersimis, at Carillon, and shortly at Manic, enough energy to meet a demand that was doubling every ten to fifteen years. Since most of Hydro's direct customers were situated in the metropolitan region, our nationalized company would have to go further and further afield to build extremely expensive installations from which to transmit power across the lands of private companies. And since the energy requirements of these companies were constantly expanding, part of Hydro's production would have to be passed on to them at price so they could resell it to their own customers at a profit! It is scarcely necessary to add that in the circumstances we could hardly fulfil our second commitment to reduce rates that were too high, except by offering an additional subsidy to this bunch of feudal barons.

In short, either we crossed our arms and let things go on the way they were, or we rolled up our sleeves and tackled the job head on. As easy as it was to make the choice among ourselves, it would require deep and solid backing the day I made our decision public and would have to face opposition from within as well as from outside the party. We worked on our presentation for months. Finally, by February, 1962, we were absolutely sure of ourselves, at the precise time I was scheduled to give a routine speech on the subject of energy. I let slip just one little sentence, something to the effect that "The future in this sector is state business."

The next morning all hell broke loose. I was told that Lesage was beside himself. Instead of lying low, the Great Manitou of the private companies, a certain Mr. Fuller, choked up an outraged declaration shot through with sovereign displeasure. This was a providential error, for it provided us with an opportunity to display in great detail the situation of electrification in Quebec.

It was a hair-raising picture. The output of our resources served to pay dividends mostly outside and taxes to Ottawa, so the bulk of our net profits was exported. The distribution system was piece-meal, poorly linked up, and in places had become completely decrepit. And it was in the poorest regions that people were paying the most. Reigning over this fine mess was a clutch of bigwigs, mainly from the West Island and Ontario, who were happy to accept money from our shareholders and consumers but who hewed to the line that outside the "family compact" there was no chance of promotion by merit, and even less of anyone having a say in running the shop.

This crude picture produced the most classic response, exactly like one that can be observed in any colony where the idea of emancipation is beginning to make its way. On the one hand, the elite of the new generation stood shoulder to shoulder with veterans of old, tenacious resistance organizations like the Saint-Jean-Baptiste Society. On the other were ranged the defenders of what is always called the established order, meaning the order of vested interests, the monolithic bloc of Anglo-Quebecers and, sticking to them, that part of French Quebec that can never conceive success, even its own, except in the role of satellite. Between these two extremes lay the bulk of the population, not knowing too well which side to choose, and a few outstanding figures like Trudeau, who tossed off the following scornful judgement in the pages of Cité libre: "The province has now reached the verbal boiling point, the maximum verbal development, the full thrust of verbal progress. . . . "

What he was really afraid of was the mobilizing potential of the word and its power of acceleration, a force one felt might be able to go very far in a society that took a stormy turn. Perhaps this force might even go as far as independence, a damnable perspective for this intellectual whose cold, devouring passion was exclusively reserved for federalism, a federalism that, to be sure, would concern itself diligently with the linguistic fate of minorities, but which, beyond this fatherly concern, would remain intractably supra-national for all the rest of our society's concerns. Or better still, and I don't think I betray his thought suggesting this, supra-tribal.

And wouldn't this step I was proposing go precisely in the direction he detested? I must admit he saw more clearly than I did in this regard, as is often the case when people's perceptions are sharp-ened by dread.

Laurendeau, Marchand, Pelletier, Trudeau, and I had got into the habit of meeting more or less regularly, usually at Pelletier's place. I would give them a backstage view of public life, telling them how the government was getting through its day-to-day, and they in turn would give me their unbridled comments, and plenty of blunt advice, too, that was often very useful. As keen observers they shared a strong sense that the awakening of our people was an important step in our development that should be marked by multiple, concrete achievements, among which the plan to nationalize hydro met the requirements perfectly.

All seemed agreed on this point – all but one, that is. The very mention of the word "nationalization" was enough to make Trudeau's hair stand on end. (During the next election campaign I had occasion to observe the same kind of reaction among many Anglophones who, nevertheless, found nothing abnormal in the renationalization of Britain's steel industry. What was good for the mother country was error in the colony.)

"You say it's going to cost something like $600 million," Trudeau would argue, inviting others to register the enormity of the thing. "$600 million, and what for? To take over a business that already exists. It's just nationalist suspender-snapping. When you think of all the real economic and social progress you could buy with a sum like that!"

"Yes," I'd reply, "but a sum like that doesn't just drop out of the sky for any old project. In the case of electricity, the present assets and the perpetual productivity stand as security. Try to find an equivalent to that."*

And to all the other arguments I added another that had just occurred to us. The control of such a vast sector of activity that would be vital to the development of every region in Quebec would constitute a veritable school for skills, a training ground for the builders and administrators we so urgently needed. My efforts were wasted, however, for my interlocutor remained as immobile as marble. At least, I may say without malice, these discussions gave me a chance to sharpen my weapons for the debate to come . . . the debate with the business world, I mean.

There, too, we were happily surprised to discover many exceptions. I could mention a lot of businessmen who, discreetly since they could not compromise themselves on a question that remained

* These two quotations are not meant to be textually accurate but serve only to reconstitute the correct context.

highly uncertain, not only encouraged us but, better still, let us profit from their experience. So I was able to ascertain that outside the Anglo-assimilated breed there still existed in our teleguided economy some brains solid enough to deal with Big Business without first completely uprooting themselves.

The case of Roland Giroux deserves to be singled out. One day he was brought along to the office by Jacques Parizeau, who had been stressing that to establish the true value of the various hydro companies we would have to get more precise information on the number of their shares and their market performance, which would require the specialized know-how of someone from Saint James Street. "Roland Giroux is an important stockbrocker who is going to help us," said Parizeau. "But I should draw your attention to a possible risk. Giroux is also a friend and very close adviser of Daniel Johnson!" Johnson had become leader of the Union Nationale and we would be squared off with him at the next election.

"You'll have to decide if you can trust me," said Giroux as soon as he came in. "I've got Quebec in my blood, too, and I'd like to see your project succeed. What I have to propose is quite simple: whatever my business is with you, Daniel will never hear of it, no more than you will ever learn anything about my relations with him. All right?"

"All right!" I said. *

A little later on, the summer break slowed down my office work but not the province-wide travels I undertook so that when the time came to meet the cabinet I would have as much support as possible from public opinion. After having wished me in hell at one time because of my ideas on hydro, Lesage had curiously enough avoided opening the subject again. Since the others were thus prevented from expressing their opinions, I was left free to sell my wares. But certain ministers were growing more and more nervous, and others didn't hesitate to say I was taking up too much room and should be

---

* We never had to regret this arrangement. On the subject of electricity Johnson got way off base in the 1962 elections. It was only after the vote that Giroux told him what had been going on, which caused a certain chill between the two of them. But five years later, when Johnson had become premier, he called me up to tell me that he was thinking of naming a new president for Hydro-Québec. "A man whose discretion is above suspicion," he said, "as you are in a good position to know. Guess who?" I didn't hesitate for a second.

shut up or such talk would eventually put the government in danger. When the fall session came, then, suspense had built up even more. It was becoming urgent to put our cards on the table.

Thus, on September 3, cabinet was summoned to a special meeting in the chalet at Lac-à-l'épaule. Driving up there I reviewed all the elements of the dossier, including some last-minute figures that seemed to me to clinch the feasibility of our plan. But could one ever know? In politics so often there are reasons logic has nothing to do with.

The first night reinforced these doubts. The atmosphere was heavy. Most of my colleagues were in an ugly mood. Some really had it in for me, this nobody, this black sheep who was the cause of all their woes. Discussion seemed to start up, only to fizzle out again in back-room bickering. Some had taken a glass too many, and since Lesage was one of these, it soon became apparent that the evening was a write-off. It was so depressing I wondered if I hadn't better let the whole thing drop. But I had promised the team not to come back without a clear decision one way or another. So I stayed on and passed a very bad night.

Next morning things didn't look much better. Mornings after the nights before are always gloomy. At last, about eleven, Lesage decided to call the meeting to order and, to get the ball rolling, gave me the floor. After distributing copies of our last memo, which certain members shoved disdainfully aside, I made a special effort to be as concise as possible, just hitting the highlights.

In rebuttal George Marler did his best to demolish me. An old Liberal leader returning to Montreal after a tour of duty in Ottawa, he had been named to that little provincial senate called the Legislative Council, and it was from here Lesage had invited him to join the cabinet as his right-hand man in financial matters. He was reputed to have a very tight grasp on the purse strings. Speaking French as well if not better than us, this superbly attired gentleman represented with exquisite courtesy the most upper-crust circles of the dominant minority, the very ones whose empire would be shaken by nationalization.

That day Marler was not the eminent and phlegmatic notary who never raised his voice. I perceived a great tension behind his words, a kind of stiffening that reflected marvellously well the general attitude of Anglophones. Insisting on the cost of the operation, on the danger of isolation Quebec might be exposed to, and on the opposition that was being manifested, particularly by the Chambers of Commerce, Marler had the bad idea to conclude by suggesting he might possibly resign. Lesage sat bolt upright and indignantly adjourned the meeting for lunch.

Chaos reigned for an hour. So-and-so began talking resignation, too, and went off to brood darkly by the edge of the lake. Lesage sent a couple of emissaries over to reason with him. Somebody else hunted me out to ask in a troubled voice if I really thought it was possible. The atmosphere was a mixture of uncertainty and confusion. One would have thought we were all on board a sinking ship.

Then suddenly everything was back on track again when early in the afternoon Lesage reopened the session and, after briefly summarizing the proposition, turned to Georges-Émile Lapalme, whom we hadn't heard from yet. "Well, Georges, haven't you got anything to say? What do you think of this business?"

Lapalme took his time. As usual, behind those heavy glasses with their black frames that made him look like an evil owl, he stared long and without indulgence at the man who had taken his place. He had been leader of the opposition during the last Duplessis years until he was replaced by Lesage in 1958, just on the eve of that string of events that at long last brought the Liberals back to power. Although he had consented to remain in the government, he was serving under a successor who would always be a usurper for him. This visibly gnawed at his vitals, and even though he adored the Ministry of Cultural Affairs that had been expressly created for him, he was too sensitive and deeply embittered to carry on much longer. In a few more months he would be gone. But for the time being he was saving a surprise for us.

"Well, yeah . . . " he said, stretching his pauses, " . . . is the project a good one? As for me, I'd say yes. . . . Is it feasible? . . . Yes, again. . . . But how should we go about it? That's the question . . . "

"Do you think," Lesage continued, "that we could make it an election issue?"

"Well, . . . it's a big deal. . . . Before we get involved in it, it wouldn't be a bad idea to go for a new mandate."

"Good. Well, let's see now," said Lesage, leafing through an agenda he had just pulled out of his pocket. "How does November 14 strike you?"

At first I was as astonished as the others. Then, seeing that a date had already been chosen, I realized that for once the two enemy brothers had been as thick as thieves. From the first, Lapalme had been in favour of nationalization. What I didn't know, however, was that Lesage had also rallied little by little without breathing a word about it; indeed, he had gone so far in private as to sound out certain American financiers we would have to approach if the project went through.

As if by magic, the climate improved. As soon as there's talk of an election most politicians react like race horses at the starting gate, especially when the stars seem to be smiling. It was clear that in throwing ourselves into a campaign that would be in large part a referendum based on a question that was likely to stir people's imaginations, we had every chance to carry the day. So everyone began to toast the eventual victory, and to bet on majorities to come. There was only one graveyard face – Marler's, as he sat there sombrely in his corner. Lesage took good note of it. After swearing us all to secrecy for the two weeks he would need to prepare the campaign, he dismissed us, but arranged things so Marler and I would be the last two to leave. Taking me aside, he slyly asked me to take Marler in my car and to use the occasion to make my peace with him. Doubtless, he also figured we would be seen together and that way curious persons would be kept guessing.

True enough, under the pouring rain dashing against the wind-shield we didn't notice the journalists until we turned out on to the highway. They saw Marler sitting beside me and tailed us all the way to Quebec City, where my companion, who had scarcely opened his mouth during the whole trip, said, getting out of the car: "You know, René, I'm very upset. I think what we're undertaking is very dangerous and I'm not sure I can go along with it. I'll have to think it over."

Realizing he wasn't really addressing these words to me, I passed them on to Lesage, who assured me that he'd take care of the matter (which he did, since Marler stayed on, albeit passively) and recommended that I turn all my thoughts to the battle that loomed ahead.

For this, as was the custom, we had to invent some banner-like slogan to snap in the wind over the heads of the crowd, so before I started campaigning I was required to participate in the hunt for the magic words. From early until very late one evening four or five of us sat around brainstorming until Jean-François Pelletier, one of the best publicity men of the time, recalled an expression he had, I believe, already used for some other purpose: Masters in our own house! "Maîtres chez nous!" Eureka! we all cried in unison.

Except that, deep down, I couldn't help thinking it was perhaps a little strong. Masters of a huge new sector, okay. But masters of everything else? On top of a decision that was going to downplay two years of government in favour of a single spectacular project, this exaggerated slogan gave me a feeling of uneasiness, which has, for that matter, never entirely left me. But as slogans go, "Maîtres chez nous" was a fine one, and seeing as it was getting very late . . .

27. The Apogee

SO THE "THREE L'S" hit the campaign trail again.

Lapalme was a powerful speaker and his oratorical flights often reached an extraordinary intensity. He used this campaign for a last fireworks display, a particularly spectacular one because our objective of reconquering economic control was a theme he had preached in the desert for years.

Lesage was the same champion debater he had been at university and this time he surpassed himself, speaking with the conviction of the recent convert. Even his most pompous tremolos came across: "I tell you, my friends, *ouiii*, I tell you. It's now or never. Maîtres chez *nouuus*!"

As for me, following the prudent advice of the strategists, I withdrew from centre stage. Playing second violin for a while would help people forget somewhat the pressure I had subjected the party and the government to. So I dusted off my modest television skills and assumed the role of demonstrator with blackboard and chalk, completed by a map showing our electrical dislocation. All this helped flesh out our electoral manifesto, which ran:

> Serious study shows that the unification of Quebec's hydro networks – the key to the industrialization of every region in the country – is essential as the first condition for economic liberation and a policy of full employment.
>
> This important step necessitates the nationalization of eleven companies that produce and distribute electricity.

It was a great campaign, one of two (the other was in 1976) when I had the certainty that in breaking our shackles we really moved forward and made minds open. It was intoxicating to see crowds of young people flood into our meetings and, under the glowing eyes of old nationalists grown grey under burden of so many frustrations, chant the slogan, "Maîtres chez nous!" till they were out of breath. The chant acquired a powerful thrust, but one that was slightly disturbing, for in the uproar I sensed aspirations for a future that, for my part, I was not yet able to imagine with any precision.

I wouldn't have had time to spend on it anyway, because very quickly the fight turned out to be much more arduous than we had expected. We kept running into a nervous conservatism that in the long run was part and parcel of the colonialized mentality. How many times did I have to remind people that in Ontario electricity had been nationalized for a good half-century. And what was good for Ontario, n'est-ce pas? . . . Yet how resistant that taboo proved to be that maintained Big Business was a closed door to us! Despite urgent promptings from pioneers of economic thought like Esdras Minville and Edouard Montpetit to "become involved nationally" in our natural resources, the demands made by this complex world continued to seem to many to be black magic, and all one could do seemed to be, at best, to trail along cautiously after someone else, and at worst, perhaps to lose one's soul.

This ancestral mistrustfulness was most deeply rooted in the rural regions, where in those days the Social Credit Party was its most impressive manifestation. In the federal election that spring Réal Caouette and his candidates had picked up 26 of 75 seats in Quebec by promising to fight to the death for such radical proposals as getting bilingual menus into the parliamentary restaurant in Ottawa. There was no question for them to go any further, let alone use the state to foster "socialism," which in their Bible was the deadliest of mortal sins. It was no doubt with them in mind that the Union Nationale issued a little communiqué in which, slyly, they congratulated Lesage – get this now – for having outsmarted "the manoeuvres of the Lévesque clan which was preparing to throw into the fray a socialist ally, *a comrade M. Lévesque met in Moscow* a few years ago."

Despite their deplorable simplicity, however, the Créditistes were solid country stuff, could be as tenacious as the devil, and had an uncanny populist instinct. Jean Marchand, who had gone to ask his union flock not to vote for them, had learned that to his own cost. When the time came for us to go to the country a few months later, his unpopularity with the Créditistes was still too fresh in people's minds, and as a result he failed to win the nomination as Liberal candidate, one that had my personal backing and in provision for which he had even announced his resignation as president of his union central. Our organizers, who were scared stiff of Social Credit, managed to persuade Lesage that he should reject a candidate whose presence in our ranks might be interpreted as a provocation. Not only did I protest in vain against this excess of faint-heartedness, but Marchand, thinking I had dropped him, and one can see why, never quite forgave me. I have often thought about this painful episode since, telling myself that the history of the past twenty years might have been considerably different if we hadn't been so afraid of the Créditistes! A great subject for a work of politico-fiction.

While the regional context went against our party's grain, Daniel Johnson knew how to exploit it with awesome efficiency. Promising to raise the minimum wage and to help people with modest incomes in various ways, he racked up points. But his policies of tiny, shy, little steps backfired when he tried to apply them to the main election issue. He shouted from the rooftops that nationalization would be the ruin of us, that it would cost a billion dollars – a figure that scares off people who get dizzy looking at all those zeros. He brought in some obscure businessman from the American Middle West who solemnly announced that if we were re-elected he would never again invest a red cent in Quebec. Even though we showed the man up as a featherweight, his words still had some effect. "The liar from afar has a better chance of getting away with it."

And then Johnson made his big error. His instinct told him that in spite of everything our message was getting through, so in a panic he invented a kind of cut-rate nationalization. If my memory serves me accurately, he included the Nord-Ouest and Bas-Saint-Laurent companies, that is, the most shabby of them and the ones that promised to cost the most to update, but left out the big, flourishing enterprises without whose support the operation lost any hope of profit. All we had to do was point out that this would just be a way to play the people of Quebec for suckers – the losses for us, the profits for them. No one could accept that.

The other factor was the Anglophones. Ever since Duplessis had let them know, and on many occasions had proved, he could do without them, they had, luckily, become almost automatically Liberal. They were again this time, but not without bursts of mumbling and grumbling, particularly among those middle-management tyros whose calm superiority complex was ruffled by our entrance on the scene, men like the beefy redhead, for example, who waved his glass under my nose one evening in a house in west-end Montreal where I had been invited after a meeting. "But Lévesque," he kept on repeating in a voice coloured by several whiskeys, "how can people like you imagine you can run Shawinigan Water and Power?"

"People like you." Or better still, people like you Québécois. This was exactly the way the British and French had treated the Egyptians a few years before: how the devil did "people like that" think they could run the Suez Canal?

"My friend," I replied, "just wait a little and you will see what you will see."

The first thing that could be seen on November 14, 1962, was our very clear election victory, more decisive than the previous one. We won 63 seats, twelve more than in 1960. The Union Nationale lost that many and found itself with 31 instead of 43. But we couldn't talk of a clean sweep. Johnson had managed to hold on to his rural strength. It was the city that swung the balance. Isn't it there, for that matter, that revolutions, be they large or small, quiet or noisy, always break out, especially among the middle classes who have time to become interested in the clash of ideas? From Paris to St. Petersburg and from Prague to Manila, always such things begin in cities. So it was in Montreal, if we can compare our little events with bigger ones.

On our quiet scale, big things were happening just the same, full of portents for the future and continuing to rush forward at a dizzying pace. In several months the nationalization of our electric resources became a reality and it cost very little more than the $600 million that had been anticipated. Thanks to the contacts Lesage had made with financial markets in the U.S., a loan of $300 million was arranged without difficulty. It was striking evidence of the confidence Quebec and its hydroelectric power inspired in the States, for never since World War I had the Americans lent such a large sum abroad. No one has better summarized this chapter in our history than Douglas Fullerton,* the well-known economist and administrator who wrote shortly after the event: "The nationalization of electricity was one of the most rational and best executed

---

* Fullerton, who had helped us tune up the operation in 1962, became from 1976 on one of our most pitiless adversaries. It should be said that this was about quite a different matter.

financial transactions I have had the privilege to see in my whole career."

The results of this operation were equally rapid and beneficial. Where rates had been exorbitant, they were quickly reduced to reasonable levels, which has not prevented various lame-brains over the years from reproaching me for having gone back on a promise they invented themselves out of thin air, that is, that we would supply them with *free* electricity! I had the inordinate pleasure of receiving a motley group of businessmen who had fought us fiercely and who, "now that hydro is ours," were coming around to inquire about line maintenance, the purchase of vehicles, or accounting and inspection services, all domains the old companies had never entrusted to anyone but their closest kin, most often living in Ontario. We took the opportunity to repatriate the maximum of goods and services at the same time as we put the whole distribution system into good working order.

Two names deserve special mention, Jean-Paul Gignac, an engineer from Shawinigan, and Georges Gauvreau, a notary who had opened an office in my native village in Gaspésie. They were named together to the commission that ran Hydro-Québec in those days and showed themselves, during this period of special effervescence and expansion as well as for years afterwards, to be tireless servants of the enterprise as well as staunch promoters of the necessity for *Québécisation*, which was fortunately accomplished without too much commotion and with full respect for the human factor. There were even some amusing incidents, like the arrival, one fine morning after these events, of a boss of the ex-Shawinigan Water and Power Company.

"Bien le bonjour, Mademoiselle!" he said to the receptionist. "Quel beau temps aujourd'hui!"

"God bless me," the young woman said afterwards, "it's the first time I ever heard him speak French. And without an accent either!"

I could go on indefinitely invoking the place Hydro held in my life for so many years, not to mention the place it also held and must continue to hold in the life of Quebec. "If you knew how boring it is to be at La Manic!" Find me another business capable of inspiring a song on the hit parade! A propos of La Manic, I remember the first steps in making French the language of work when, seeing "coffer dam" translated as "bâtardeau," one of the old men on the crew asked with a sceptical shake of the head: "Ouais, bâtardeau! That's just great, but are you sure it's going to work as well?"

In this respect as in so many others, Hydro became, to use an expression I've already used to death, the flagship of our development. From 1963-64 this seedbed of new skills was already producing a dramatic increase in the number of electrical engineers. And progressing from stage to stage these skills have gained such a reputation for Hydro-Québec that it is recognized today as the champion in its field, and these experts manage for us the vastest reserves of clean energy on the continent.

But I must stop this. We're still in the years 1962, 1963, and 1964, at the apogee of a period when the people of Quebec set their clocks to the time of the twentieth century. I don't think there's another place in the world that has ever witnessed such a catching up touching so many domains in such a short time. And from that part of our society that had become aware of our backwardness, there arose such a pressure that it literally pushed us forward and often dictated our decisions for us.

I remember the collective shiver produced by the awesome Parent Report on education. In 1964 (*scarcely twenty years ago!*) four-fifths of our adult population hadn't gone beyond, and many hadn't even finished, elementary school! Discussion on this subject turned around the following alternatives: either we should give ourselves the several years necessary to educate qualified teachers, or we should immediately recruit the best candidates available and, following the old adage, "It's in cobbling you learn to be a cobbler," expect them to learn on the job. The climate of urgency was such that we had no difficulty choosing the second option. So, neither better nor worse than elsewhere, our apprentices became teachers and permitted us to pretty well catch up to the average North American level of instruction. It is in this generation of teachers – and it was only to be expected – that today we are discovering cases of burn-out at forty or forty-five.

Let's pass quickly over the opening, on the eve of the election, of the Société Générale de Financement, and also the creation of a Ministry of Federal-Provincial Affairs, the direct ancestor of Inter-govermental Affairs today, and likewise the appearance of camping sites in the province, which Duplessis had refused to have anything to do with because he still thought of Québécois as destructive children.

But let's pause to remember the arrival in the House in 1961 of Claire Kirkland-Casgrain, our first female MP, and another novelty the same year, the opening of a Maison du Québec in Paris. Here's a little anecdote on that subject. Buttoned into my rented tux and stuck at the end of the table, I only had a distant echo of the animated discussion going on around De Gaulle and Lesage, who sat face to face in the middle of the immense ceremonial banquet hall in the Elysée Palace. From there, in descending order of rank and service, our ministers and MNAs were mingled with French guests. Two ladies who had been installed on either side of André Malraux followed, agog with admiration, the heaving fire, punctuated by feverish tics, of the famous author's monologue, the only style of conversation he deigned to practise. All of a sudden Malraux paused to draw breath. As often happens in such circumstances, everyone else stopped talking at the same time, and in the general silence a feminine voice with a strong Quebec accent struck up: "Honestly, Monsieur *Marleau*, you talk so well you should try writing some day!"

An event of more consequence was Eric Kierans joining the government in 1963. In short order and almost single-handedly this remarkable buccaneer succeeded in at last breaking the monopoly the dynasty of A.E. Ames & Sons had held on provincial loans. Besides getting rich at our expense, this company had the misfortune to be essentially WASP from way back, which made it a choice target for this self-made man who was Irish into the bargain.

At the same time as we advanced case by case, and like as not in catch-as-catch-can fashion, toward a certain measure of decolonization, we simultaneously attacked the problem of wresting a vital minimum of democratization for our lamentable electoral practices. This reform was such a crying need it was undertaken in a joint committee with the opposition, which had immediately agreed to participate. The new law gave the vote to eighteen-year-olds and put a ceiling on electoral expenses for both parties and candidates while leaving the door open to substantial reimbursements. There was still a lot of ground left to cover, but from then on Quebec was catching up with the most advanced democratic societies.

As for the rise of trade unions, it was also in 1964 that we not only went farther than everyone else but maybe even a little beyond the limit. Hospital employees, teachers, and then civil servants under the new Labour Code got the right to collective bargaining and the right to strike.

In another of those grandiloquent statements that he had to swallow afterwards, Lesage had begun by proclaiming majestically: "The Queen does not negotiate with her subjects!"

I must confess, I have wondered more than once whether the poor sovereign shouldn't have made them sing a bit longer for their supper, particularly her "hospital subjects" whose subsequent behaviour was little short of barbarous. But at the time the Queen was an illusion. In the first rank of those who, one hand on the Bible, assured us, swore up and down that never, never would they use such a powerful weapon as the right to strike, was Jean Marchand, who was putting in his last months as union leader. Twenty years later, what would the same man say about this experience that was characterized by a boldness, or should one say rashness, unequalled anywhere?

Recalling that he is talking about the man who "personally negotiated granting the right to strike to state employees with Premier Jean Lesage in 1964," journalist Jean-Claude Rivard attributes the following opinions to Marchand in an article in *Le Soleil* (April 17, 1985). These views, in the light of what we now know, we can only subscribe to wholeheartedly:

> By bringing together around the same table union centrals that are often rivals, and by opening the door to general strikes that are political in nature, common fronts have altered the rules of the game.
>
> We have strayed from union principles . . . designed to avoid situations leading to union monopolies. And if the incidents that have occurred in hospitals over the past years were planned, they should be denounced as criminal offences. . . .
>
> [Mr. Marchand] also believes that if union members wish to regain credibility . . . they should make the public realize that their leaders are sometimes far from speaking for the membership at large. . . .

When all was said and done, however, despite excessive press coverage that sometimes blurred the issues, between 1960 and 1964 Quebec lived through the most exalting and fruitful *aggiornamento*. And I must state for the record that Jean Lesage showed himself to be a great government leader. Of course he had his faults. Who hasn't? With his height and those regular features that earned him the title of "the handsomest man in Canada," he was so candidly and incommensurably vain that it was possible, though dangerous, to forget the deadly keenness of his wit and his truly superhuman capacity for hard work. When I was an apprentice minister I even had to defend myself against the early-riser's abuse of power when this workaholic would telephone my hotel at seven or eight in the morning to drag some sleepy agreement from me.

"Dear old René," he would begin in a tone of hateful joviality, "I'm sure you'll be in favour of this amendment that I'm going to propose. I think it will settle the problem. Don't you?"

In actual fact I had serious doubts about it. But he who retires late is defenceless in the morning. So I would give in just to be left alone and be able to drop back on the pillow again until, conscience forbidding me rest, I would haul myself out of bed cursing both my own weakness and the man exploiting it. It reached a point where I was reduced to warning the receptionist: "You'd better watch out next time you put through a call from that practical joker passing himself off as Jean Lesage!"

It was the victory of 1962 that brought us close together. Although I was being spoken of as a possible successor, Lesage knew that didn't interest me in the slightest. Not only had I told him so myself, but he was sharp enough to realize I had absolutely no partisan ambition. He came to put his confidence in me to a point I often found excessive. More than my share of times, I would be sent into the front lines when some project got bogged down in the House, or sent out into the field when some business or other was going under and we had to save the furniture.

Back in my own bailiwick, leaving Hydro to get on quietly with adjusting to its new enormous size, I plunged into my mining dossier. Even in New Quebec the Duplessis heritage was not as disastrous as Lapalme had let on when he described foreign cargo ships sailing past Quebec City laden down with our iron ore at "one cent a ton!" But it wasn't Peru either, far from it, especially for a people and a state that had been used to letting themselves be had like happy cuckolds.

The worst thing was the supreme arrogance of the colonizer paraded by all those big and little "bwanas" of the mining industry. I didn't always resist the temptation to tell them to their faces that the day was coming when Quebec was going to rid itself of the Rhodesian climate they cultivated in this sector. Among others, I remember an ex-president of Noranda Mines with whom I was to examine two possible sites for the building of a zinc smelter. I had my preference and he had his. The various possibilities deserved to be discussed on their merits, and I was enthusiastically trundling out my arguments when he shrugged his shoulders with a peevish air: "My dear fellow, that's enough. Everything you are saying is perfectly irrelevant."

"How's that?" I replied. "It seems to me on the contrary, that nothing could be more pertinent. It's a big decision."

"That's right, a big decision. And just so, the company's already taken it. You see."

I boiled over, gave a furious blow to the table, and had the pleasure of seeing its glass top shatter. That was a relief, even if I almost fractured my wrist.

What was even more of a relief, though much less than I would have wished, was the laboriously technical work that led to an increase in government royalties and a complete overhaul of basic mining law in Quebec, which had been gathering dust for decades. Linked to these rather modest gestures, the creation of SOQUEM (Société québécoise d'exploration minière) also served as a reminder to interested parties that the subsoil was not their patrimony but ours. But real sharks never let go. "Babble on, little man," they mutter, "governments pass, but we will still be here." And, as far as that was concerned, they spared no pains to make us feel just that.

But these little vexations were not too hard to bear because of the multiple successes we were scoring, the high point being the battle of the pension plans. Ottawa had concocted an American-style scheme of the pay-as-you-go type, that is, contributions each year cut off at the level of what was paid out. One has only to see the catastrophic situation of social security in the States to understand that, a very small mouse compared to this elephant, we wouldn't have lasted long under such a system.

As luck would have it, we had a plan of our own up our sleeve, one that counted on contributions being large enough to allow a considerable part of them to accumulate in a bank whose mission would be, as well as to administer these funds prudently, to serve as an instrument for economic development. Here again we were venturing out into new and unexplored territory. But we had a team that was far superior to the federal one, for Lesage knew how to surround himself with the right people. To bring off this unprecedented project he had gathered together such men as Parizeau, whom he had learned to appreciate in the nationalization move in

1962, Claude Morin, who had become one of his deputy ministers, and, as always, his inseparable special adviser, Louis-Philippe Pigeon. This gentleman, you may remember, had kicked me out of his course in those long-gone days of my brief university career. But now I was in the government and, always showing me a profound respect, the great jurist would never speak to me without laying on a heavy "Monsieur le ministre." Since I was nevertheless an admirer of his, I often used to chat with him in his little office, where he disappeared behind piles of dossiers mounting to the ceiling. In the midst of this mess, one day I noticed an incongruous collection of *Popular Mechanics* and other publications of the same ilk.

"Well, you see, Monsieur le ministre," he explained in his high-pitched voice, "in my youth I dreamed of becoming an engineer. But there wasn't any room for French Canadians in those days. So I resigned myself to the law. It was either that or become priest or doctor to minister to the spiritual or corporeal needs of the cheap labour force we were then."

Needless to say, each step we took forward seemed to him to be a kind of personal progress. And every one of us in his or her own way reacted similarly. In the battle over pensions we had good sense on our side, too. There was no question of giving in, and since the federal side refused as doggedly to yield an inch, talks broke off. For a good ten days it was very like a real breakdown in diplomatic relations. Although Lesage was federalist to the point of harbouring the ambition of becoming Prime Minister in Ottawa before too long, he was still purebred Québécois and saw clearly that in this particular case our long-range interests forbade him to give in.

Then, as rapidly as it had gone sour, the conflict resolved itself. Summoning me to his office, Lesage suggested that to get there I should take a hidden entrance; then Paul Gérin-Lajoie came along by the same mysterious path. Gleefully, Lesage told us that the federal government had at last consented to give a little and that two emissaries had just arrived at L'Ancienne-Lorette – in an unmarked plane! Any more of this and I'd have thought I was back in Korea! But the important thing was that this arm-wrestling had worked out in our favour and that Quebec, followed more or less by the rest of Canada, was free to set up its own pension plan and its investment bank, the Caisse de dépôt.

Carried to the pinnacle of success as he deserved to be, Lesage had become the dominant figure in the world of Canadian as well as Quebec politics. And he knew it. Probably he knew it too well, to the point of forgetting that the Tarpeian rock is situated just at the edge of the Capitol. Moreover, back there in the Old Country there was this General setting a dangerous example . . . and not everyone who wants to can be a General De Gaulle.

28. The Decline

I STILL MISS the Easter holiday I never had in 1966.

I barely had time to install my family in a hotel in Bermuda near one of those matchless white beaches washed by water so limpid that with the naked eye you can watch the smallest stone sink twelve metres to the ocean floor. Pleasantly excited, we were on the point of renting our "mopeds" – the only motor vehicles the wise islanders permit tourists to use – when the telegram I was dreading arrived.

Adieu farniente. I had been summoned to Florida, to Miami, a city I detest more than any other but where Lesage, a golf addict, often set up his winter camp and sometimes his spring headquarters, too. This time, as I knew, it was plans for the next election he had just finished brewing. Well, one has to take the rough with the smooth, I told myself with gloomy resignation, and, having no other solution than to hitchhike by air, managed to get as far as the Bahamas without too much trouble. There I had to wait for hours before getting a seat on one of those casino-shuttles that on the return flight is full of losers, creating an atmosphere that matched my mood perfectly.

Indeed, in the state we were in, plunged into depression on top of the fatigue of six years of government, one couldn't have recognized the "fireball team" of 1960 and 1962.

Among these weary heroes there was no one whose morale was lower than mine. Little by little, beginning at the end of 1964, then continuing all the following year, the rhythm had slowed down. For example, the study of a project to set up a Quebec steel industry dragged on and on. It was needed to bring down the price of steel, dictated in the Great Lakes region, which held up our own industrial development while favouring that of Ontario. The only good memory I have of that business is the funny way I got to know Paul Desmarais. Rather than begin from scratch, we planned to buy an existing plant so we could rely on standing equipment and, even more important, a nucleus of experienced manpower for the first stage in our production. We had our eye on Dosco, the Quebec operation of a company that was a leftover from imperial times, established in Nova Scotia but still controlled from England. Desmarais, who was not yet the potentate he was to become, had agreed to go to London as the *honest broker* for the government, but first we had to examine the plan of action he had drawn up for himself. Lesage got Kierans to check the figures while I was given the mission of observing our potential emissary attentively. We remained in closed session for two or three days with the eminent financier and one of his advisers, meeting among ourselves every evening to try to sort out an incredible tangle that kept getting more complicated the more they explained it. Finally Kierans discovered the snag. As planned, the operation would have resulted, once the transaction had been tied up at government expense, in giving our agent effective control of the enterprise. It had been so ingeniously concocted that Kierans might very well have passed over the ruse, and it was in a tone of half-admiring reproach that he advised Desmarais of his discovery.

"Well, baptême!" the latter replied, bursting into laughter, "so you finally found it! Good for you, boys. Let's go and have a drink."[*]

We went on marking time in metallurgical matters, as well as in most of the other economic dossiers. During 1965 I was getting so exasperated I was thinking of packing it in. If I am elected, I had told myself five years earlier, I'll quit politics, whatever happens, at the end of my second term. That time was drawing near. But at the very moment I was moving toward my decision – so visibly so that rumours were already circulating in the corridors – an opportunity presented itself to accept a new challenge which, there was no doubt in my mind, would be the last.

Outstripping me in my intentions, our colleague Émilien Lafrance, that indefatigable follower of Lacordaire's teetotallers but "too good" to be a minister, suddenly left the post he had begun to feel profoundly unhappy in. Lesage at once proposed that I should replace him in the ministry then designated as Family and Welfare. At the same time he advised me that Eric Kierans would

---

[*] For better and for worse, Dosco finally became Sidbec-Dosco, but under another government . . . and in a different way.

"Something like a great people" first mandate, November 15, 1976.

Swearing-in ceremony: "I, René Lévesque,
swear that I will fulfil . . ."

Space command post, cabinet room in the bunker building,
Quebec City.

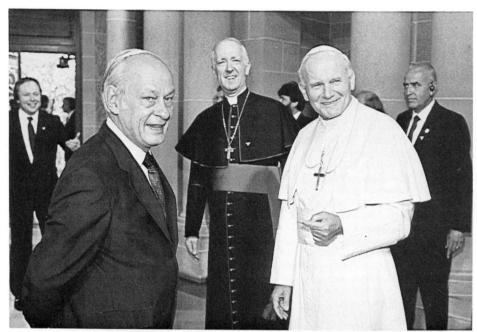

With Pope John Paul II and Cardinal Vachon,
Quebec City, 1985.

"Why keep it simple when it can be made complicated." (Shaddock)

Side by side but not closer.

Jean Drapeau listens intently, but ...

With Javier Perez de Cuellar, UN secretary general.

With Hon. "Tip" O'Neil, King of the House of Representatives,
Washington.

be taking over Health, where another good man, Dr. Alphonse Couturier, had also come to the end of his road.

In getting rid of two of "the old guard," economically speaking, the boss had opened up to me a vast field that to all intents and purposes had been left fallow. In the social sector, since 1963 we had been in possession of the Boucher Report, whose unsparing analysis ended in a set of recommendations that constituted the basic framework of a real social welfare policy. But how short the time was getting, while the stages left to cover stretched before us out of sight!

And there were psychological stages among others, always the hardest to get through. In those days, in far too many corners of Quebec, people still harboured old notions, fatalistic to the point of inhumanity, according to which the poor deserved their fate and the worst suffering had to be accepted as a product of divine will, if not of divine benevolence. I remember a dismal drive in the Beauce with Robert Cliche, who, as we went along the back roads, kept pointing out houses where in an attic, a cellar, sometimes even a barn, mongoloid or handicapped children were kept by families who considered them "punishments from the Good Lord." They were hidden away, never let out for years on end, sometimes not from birth. Doing a first tour of the institutions that fell under the ministry's jurisdiction, one day in a little town in the Lower St. Lawrence I came upon an indescribable private old people's "home" where, as soon as you entered, the smell of dirt and sourness was enough to turn your stomach. I can still see, right out in the open exposed to all eyes, an old woman drawing her last breaths and scrabbling at her filthy sheets. I made a special note of the fact that the three-storey building was a wooden structure whose walls were tinder-dry, a regular firetrap.*

In short, we had a long road to travel in a society where "public assistance" and pensions for "needy mothers" still cowered in an ungodly meanness of soul. Drawing inspiration from the Boucher Report, I proposed to substitute for this meagre maintenance of

---

* I ordered the establishment closed, but the election campaign came along and made me forget the follow-up on this decision. As soon as the Johnson government was sworn in, then, I left an urgent note for my successor, Jean-Paul Cloutier. Too late. I read in the newspaper the same week that a fire had destroyed the building so quickly that most of the inhabitants were burned alive.

misery a policy of investment in our human resources whose cornerstone would be a regime of Quebec family allowances better structured and more flexible than the Ottawa plan. At a federal-provincial conference held at the beginning of 1966 I presented a report showing (as it would be possible to show again today) that social affairs, for reasons of efficiency as much as of difference, should logically be administered in Quebec. So we quite simply asked the federal government to transfer family allowances to us at the earliest opportunity, that is, to give up issuing cheques guaranteeing high federal visibility every month in so many households! Needless to say, my proposal bit the dust, and any other fate would have greatly surprised me. Pearson spoke of my "sense of humour," but what wasn't so funny was that behind this hardening of attitude we were already beginning to sense the influence of the "three doves" who had finally made their landing in the House of Commons. There was no longer any question of yielding an inch, since from then on Quebec interests would be so much better served by the new "French power" whose chief architect was Pierre Elliott Trudeau.

Yet it was Marchand again who had been the first to be approached, and of the three he was the only one they were really keen on having. And here I have a painful confession to make. It turns out that I personally contributed, in however small a way, to Trudeau's entry into politics. It all happened in Newfoundland where that immovable little Father of Confederation, Premier Joey Smallwood, had invited me to take part in a big conference I've forgotten everything about long since. Judy LaMarsh and Maurice Sauvé, both federal ministers, had also come to strut their stuff. At one point Sauvé received an urgent call from Ottawa. Informing me that in just a few hours a general election would be announced, he added that the "doves" were running into unforeseen difficulties in getting nominated as candidates, and that it was certainly Marchand calling to tell him the results of the latest negotiations. I went up to his room with him and, sure enough, it was Marchand on the line.

"I've just come from seeing Pearson," he said in a strained voice, "and things aren't going too well. As for myself, there's no problem, they're dying to get me. They're ready to take Pelletier, too. But as far as Trudeau is concerned, it's no soap. In their eyes he's nothing but a little drawing-room socialist who had the nerve not so long ago to call them a bunch of idiots."

"Lévesque's with me," said Sauvé. "He's on the other line."

"Okay. Well, what do you think, both of you? But make it snappy, I've got to see Pearson again in five minutes. To tell you the honest truth, I'm beginning to get fed up."

Sauvé encouraged him not to give up, assuring him that Pearson would come around in the end and bring his colleagues with him. As for me, I tossed in this little sentiment on solidarity: "You went up there together, and it's together they have to take you. All three or nobody. And since they need you . . . "

The result is well known. Maybe I ought to have foreseen it.

Decidedly, my mind must have taken a strange twist. After this mistake in judgement and my defeat at the hands of Ottawa, I now managed to get myself caught in a magnificent mess.

Having endorsed the Fulton-Favreau amending formula (one of those lucubrations federal-provincial kitchen history is riddled with) without thinking too much about it, Lesage woke up next morning to a hue and cry in protest, most of it centred at the Université de Montréal. Since I was generally well received in those circles, I was requested to go and bring them the good word. Constitutional quibbles in those days (and still today) being one of the most junior of my preoccupations, I wasn't overly enthusiastic. But Lesage, who was becoming something of a despot, insisted so strongly, to the point of almost making it an ultimatum, that I tired of resisting and finally resigned myself to jump into the lions' den, together with Pierre Laporte.

Unluckily, I did not appear to treat the subject with the seriousness the audience expected. In my brief introduction I asserted that, in my humble opinion, constitutions were of a relatively secondary importance. What counts above all in a democracy, I said, is the will of the people, who alone have the power to accept or unmake such learned structures that someone is always trying to lock us into for all eternity. Therefore . . .

Therefore I was singled out, taxed with being unpardonably frivolous, and ferociously cut into little pieces by an eminent professor of constitutional law, who modestly accepted the acclamations of the crowd after seeing me thoroughly booed. (This professor, who went by the name of Jacques-Yvan Morin, will, I trust, permit me to reveal that many years later, at the time of a certain unilateral and fundamentally undemocratic operation launched by the Right Honourable P.E. Trudeau, he admitted that when you came right down to it perhaps I wasn't entirely wrong that particular night.)

That night, too, I remember coming out of the auditorium into a raging sleet storm and suddenly, through the opaque curtain, seeing the monastic silhouette of Mr. Claude Ryan surge forth. I offered to give him a lift home.

"Monsieur Lévesque," said he, taking that self-sufficient tone that is his trademark, "it seems to me that it would be in your own best interest, n'est-ce pas, to spend a little more time on constitutional matters . . . " This was, admittedly, excellent advice, which I unfortunately have not much practised, and never in the sense that the learned journalist intended.

So it was chewing over these lugubrious memories that I at last reached Miami, where nightfall and drizzle combined to provide a welcome well suited to my mood. I went around to the address on Sunset Avenue where Lesage used to lodge and was just about to ring when a hand seized my arm. Emerging from under the hedge and his umbrella stood Montreal lawyer Claude Ducharme, who loved to play the Machiavelli of the troupe.

"Lesage has gone to bed," he said. "Come over to my place. I've got something very interesting to show you."

It was a poll taken with a view to a possible election. Dozens of detailed tables divided Québécois up according to age, sex, profession . . . all done to justify the cost of the operation. But as usual, the real meat of the survey only took one page, the one that showed "voters' intentions."

"Look at this," said Ducharme, "it's as good as in the bag!"

Without pretending to quote the exact figures so long afterwards, I remember they ran roughly like this: something like 37 to 40 per cent for us, less than 30 per cent for the Union Nationale, about 4 per cent for the new indépendantiste parties, and finally a large bloc of about 30 per cent undecided.

"As for them," my informant affirmed, "they'll surely spread out proportionally. So right now we can count on 50 per cent or more. Maybe a clean sweep."

In my ignorance that seemed convincing. It was only afterwards, looking at the results, that I learned a lesson I've never forgotten. As election day approaches, when there is still such a big number of undecided voters, nothing is more presumptuous than to think you can divide them up in a purely linear fashion. Those voters are most often people who will be affected by the climate of the election, and they are waiting, a moistened finger held in the air, to see which way the wind is blowing. In this instance, sniffing the wind himself, Ducharme came to a pat conclusion I found a little surprising.

"No mistake about it," he said, closing the big folder, "this time we should go for a De Gaulle-style campaign!"

At the time the implications of this expression escaped me completely. But once the "Florida" election was announced and I had returned to Montreal, I learned what it was all about. While we rushed to draw up a new political program that nobody had thought very much about (I spent a whole night, alone, drafting the final text), our first campaign posters began to appear. They were certainly very De Gaulle-like, in the pejorative sense, and I'm not sure the General himself would have dared monopolize the image to that degree. On walls, in the papers, on TV, there was nothing but Lesage – Lesage served up in every possible sauce: Lesage with workers, with women, with youth, with farmers. Carefully prepared weeks ahead, these portraits of a solitary chief amidst groups of anonymous people at one stroke served to efface any notion of teamwork. There was not the least allusion, even visually, to the team of associates whose names and deeds had so filled people's minds since 1960. This time Lesage wanted a victory that would have only one father, and he naturally expected that thereafter his personal power would be incontestable.

This splendid isolation was confirmed during the official opening of the campaign at a big regional rally in Sherbrooke in the Eastern Townships at the beginning of May. Not having received the customary invitation and wondering if it might be an oversight, I called Paul Gérin-Lajoie only to discover that he was in the same boat. It was obviously intentional. Visibly put out, Paul swore he wouldn't set foot in the Townships. After thinking it over, I decided to go down anyway. It was a fine spring afternoon and I took my time, stopping here and there to chat with the locals and even dusting off the old reporter to the point of looking in on a rival meeting taking place a few blocks away from our own. I finally turned up in the middle of the speech by the Sherbrooke candidate, the only person authorized to share the platform with Lesage. Catching sight of me, an organizer grabbed me and, keeping close to the walls, courteously led me to the very back of the stage where I couldn't see anything and would remain invisible myself.

I got the message. Thereafter I agreed to do a little secondary campaigning, but my heart wasn't in it, even less so because the news was far from good. Lesage was very tired and his nerves were shot. He would get up on his high horse whenever anyone interrupted him, and when this aggressiveness rubbed off on his audiences he was soon at bay like a winded bull.

After a month the reports in the papers and what people had been saying left no doubt in my mind – we were headed straight for defeat. I cut short my road trips and, with my inseparable Jean Rougeau, like everyone else fell back on my home riding.

As in 1962, the atmosphere of the city contrasted favourably with that of the country. Although rural voters had seemed "fed up" and secretly hostile, in Montreal one still felt at home and the disaffection hadn't spread there yet. In the central committee, that kettle where one can immediately check the level of tension on the faces of the volunteers, everything was running smoothly. In charge of the organization, which had been rebuilt after the patronage follies of the early years, was one character in particular, "Ti-Loup" Gauthier, who will always stand out in the memories of those who knew him. Yves Gauthier was a notary but lived first for politics and then for painting, where his generosity to young artists bordered on blindness. These two passions, which equalled each other in intensity, were nourished by his professsional practice, which also furnished him his three, four, or five meals a day. Here's how he entered into my life. Thickset and seemingly short because of his extra width, he presented himself with the assurance of an old campaigner, depositing his notary's attaché case on a chair and drawing out of it a huge apron-serviette that covered him down to the waist.

"And now," he proclaimed, "you don't have to worry yourself about the ratings" (those so frequently misleading impressions based on the incessant intriguing gossip that citizens are subjected to). "I'm going to look after all that till election day. My fee? A large pizza with everything on it, every time you see my plate half-empty!"

That was all he ever asked for giving us the benefit of a crafty intuition whose like I have never seen, either before or since. Added to this innate gift was a finely tuned, encyclopedic knowledge of the vagaries of electoral behaviour. In this department he knew the whole of Quebec by heart, as I had been able to witness myself in 1963 or 1964 in the Mauricie where I had been asked to help out with a by-election and where, out of the blue, Ti-Loup caught up with me in Shawinigan.

"Poll XYZ," he said, addressing the organizers, "I hope somebody's looking into it this time. Yes, yes, yes, you know the one, that little outpost on the edge of the riding where you've been losing forever because you don't know how to handle it. Anyway, I'm going to look after things this time." He was very impressive, but did he really manage to win the famous little outpost? Unless I'm mistaken, he never spoke of it again.

But this time, on the contrary, he assured us a good bill of health in Laurier. For that matter, after a few campaigns you can do your own rating. The people who look you in the eye when they shake your hand and, maybe just as important, those murderous looks lavished on you by the other camp can tell you more than the best analyses. All that remained to be done, then, was to prepare for the big day itself, those few incredibly long hours when you can lose your deposit if you can't "get the vote out." Teams telephone all day encouraging the faithful, the promptings getting sharper and sharper as the day wears on. A fleet of cars crisscrosses the riding endlessly to pick up "our" old people and supply babysitters for harried mothers. As soon as this ultimate effort gets under way the candidate is made to feel that he is superfluous. He is requested to go and expose himself elsewhere, at the snack bar, at the Golden Age Club, or at the door of the presumably undecided voter, anywhere except in the committee rooms where serious people are at work.

Without saying a word to anyone, I took this opportunity to execute a modest project I had been strongly discouraged from trying and went to see how things were going at the headquarters of my indépendantiste adversary, Mme. Andrée Ferretti, who at that time was a fervent follower of the Rassemblement pour l'Indépendance Nationale, the RIN.

This party was certainly the most promising fruit of that variegated flowering the sixties had seen rise from a native soil that had never before been so thoroughly stirred up. We had, pell-mell, a Parti Républicain, a Parti Socialiste, a Regroupement National, and, just on the eve of the elections, a Ralliement National . . . so many improvisations condemned to miscarry after a period of more or less brief activity. Only the RIN had a semblance of structure and a coherent philosophy, which, unfortunately, one heard less about than one did of the fulminations of its leader, Pierre Bourgault, an orator whose style was more nervous, and necessarily more radical, than Lesage's, though no less theatrical.

I had been too preoccupied by my own task to give much serious thought to these phenomena, though I had followed the political effervescence with more interest than I professed to publicly, that is to say, just enough to make me suspect, both among the Liberals, for whom I was too curious, and among the indépendantistes, who denounced the sinful indecisiveness of my remarks. I couldn't have said that either party was exactly wrong. I rediscover this divided attitude even as early as 1964 in the caption to a photograph in *La Presse* of May 11, 1964, which showed me with students from Collège Sainte-Marie:

> M. Lévesque asserted that only one alternative was open to a Quebec presently stifled in the toils of confederation – either it becomes an associate state endowed with a truly special status, or Quebec will separate. The second solution, according to the Minister, should be implemented only if it has been proven that the first is unrealizable.

Why this beating about the bush? As I have often repeated, I am less given to working things out in the privacy of my room than to thinking aloud about questions that bother me. Since our political orientation for the future appeared to me to be the most important of all these questions, I kept turning it every which way, seeking my own answer, which naturally ended up irritating everyone.

But if it was true that I talked about it too much, or not enough, I wasn't wrong, I think, to sound out such an uncertain future, orienting myself by several major landmarks that were pretty easy to see.

We formed a people who were distinct and consequently unique in the world. We, that is, we French-speaking Québécois, are not French, or at least haven't been so for centuries. Observers of the French regime had recognized this fact well before the Conquest. A new continent had already forged a new and original type of man, and the small interest the Old Country showed in him only reinforced his spirit of independence. During the last century this same man rose against the Empire of Her Britannic Majesty in 1837-38 in a hopeless combat, yet it emphasized his refusal simply to disappear. And now we were in a position to establish that, warmed under the sun of the Quiet Revolution, the same sap that ran in his veins was feeding all kinds of expressions of a true national community, one that nothing could prevent from aspiring to break its bonds to reach full realization of its potential.

But was it necessary to cut all formal ties with Canada? Even though Confederation, which was never really a true one, gave us dangerously little breathing space at the very time we felt the need for ever-increasing room to manoeuvre, didn't it remain conceivable that the framework could be readjusted in such a way as to let Quebec live and develop freely?

Like many others, I tried out the various formulas then current: special status, or particular status, opting out (the right to withdraw, with financial compensation, from various federal programs), and finally a new or renewed federalism within which we would constitute an associate state, free from dependence as a minority. With regard to all these concepts one idea stood out: equal rights for the two collectivities, an idea that Daniel Johnson had expressed in a striking slogan, "Equality or independence." This alternative, which I had clumsily evoked myself, suited me perfectly. It appeared to me to be a legitimate ultimatum and one that had some chance of shaking up the musty rigidity of the federal regime.

For the RIN, what was required was not "Equality *or* independence" but equality *and*, or better still, equality through independence. In other words, straight ahead, and right now. I didn't agree with that, not that "clean, hard" independence didn't represent a valid option, or that it was excessive in itself in a world where, since 1945, dozens of peoples, small, middle-sized, and numerous, had acceded to full, absolute sovereignty. And it was certainly not a question of my preferring the more abstract perspective of "large ensembles" that people like Trudeau were proposing, claiming they promised a prosperity and a democratic well-being that "little tribes" like ours could never attain alone. This proposition was frankly quite droll when our large-ensemble-promoter listed Canada among his protective mastodons, that same Canada that, except for its immense size, is an extremely narrow dwelling in every other respect, in terms of population, markets, and (history shows it only too well) in narrowness of mind as well.

But without entertaining the least passion for this false large ensemble, I had difficulty seeing us "Pakistanizing" Canada by cutting the Maritimes off from the rest, and I dreaded the long quarrels and, even more I must confess, the surliness manifested by the RIN itself. Already they were speaking of denying Anglo-Québécois the right to their own schools, imitating in that an attitude that had been inflicted on our own minorities everywhere else. Injustice as a response to injustice did not appear to me then, any more than it does today, as a very promising solution. Didn't it risk leading to other excesses that no one can ignore the danger of?

Indeed, violence had erupted in Quebec several years before, directed against essentially Anglophone and federal targets. Among other incidents I remembered the explosions that in May, 1963, had interrupted one of those evenings we intermittently spent together at Gérard Pelletier's place. With the reflex of the old journalist, he had decided to go and have a look, and we went with him – his wife Andrée, André Laurendeau, and myself. Our investigation led us to Sherbrooke Street West where some unfledged terrorists had this time blown up a series of mail boxes, one bomb exploding when the police tried to defuse it, mutilating a man for the rest of his life.

"I am a nationalist," I declared some time later, "if that means being, for oneself, fiercely for or against something or against a given situation. But never against someone. Nationalism that means racism or fascism makes me vomit."

I would be called upon to make other professions of faith in the years ahead. Marked for life by the abuses that various "isms" had led to throughout the world, I dreaded anything that resembled them, near or far, like the plague. Knowing our people well, I was sure we would never descend to similar iniquities. Just the same, an ounce of prevention . . . And human speech, when the tone becomes incendiary, always reminds me of André Maurois's prescription: "Every dictionary should carry a sticker marked 'EXPLOSIVE'."

In short, the verbal radicalism of the RIN didn't say a thing to me. In the eyes of the young RIN militants, who welcomed my impromptu visit like that of a dog to a putting green, I was nothing but a kind of wet blanket whose appeals for realism seemed ridiculously outmoded. Until further notice, I told myself on leaving them, we just weren't made to get along. I vaguely regretted this, for I couldn't help admiring their burning idealism and the formidable energy it generated. Joined to this idealism were many illusions, granted, but wasn't that better than to be threatened with the loss of both illusions and ideals together?

Luckily, I was soon going to have time to get my thoughts in order. In the last stages of the election one might have said that Lesage was really working to ensure defeat. Arriving in Montreal two days before the vote for the big traditional rally in the old Palais du Commerce, he was in pitiful shape. Eric Kierans and I, who for this last evening had the signal honour to share the platform with him, found him exhausted, vacant, thick-voiced. He had been asked to make his appearance by nine o'clock at the latest. He promised to be there for sure. But when 9:30 came, then 9:45, and I was obliged to spin out interminably a speech that was getting progressively gloomier, we sent out inquiries only to discover that Lesage, who had heard there were some empty rows, said he was not leaving the hotel until they were full! He finally came to his senses and turned up a little after ten. Fifteen minutes later he had to take what he deserved and see the whole auditorium start to empty.

Did he also deserve the sad fate of being beaten in seats, 50 to 56, when the government led the Union Nationale by a large majority in the popular vote, more than 47 per cent against less than 41 per cent? Yes, up to a point he did, since his advisers had backed off before a real reform of the electoral map, leaving many ridings in the rural regions whose demographic weight hardly justified their existence. Besides, the two indépendantiste groups, although none of their candidates was elected, had polled 8 per cent of the vote, which was enough to shake us seriously in the metropolitan region.

Lesage took all this very badly. He even claimed he was going to contest the election, though he knew perfectly well that power necessarily goes to the majority. He finally resigned himself to making the best of a bad job and went over to the opposition benches. But politically he was finished. It was hardly the end one would have wished for the Premier of 1960-64, the man who had presided with such mastery over the entry of Quebec into the modern world. History will surely reserve him a choice place, even if this chapter had to end on such a mournful note, a note to which I may be allowed to add a brief postscript recalling a scene that will serve both as a transition and a commentary.

A week or so after that fifth of June, 1966, now that I had become a "simple" MNA again I was going up (or down, since one can say either) to Quebec City to pick up from the ministry my personal belongings and a few documents I wanted to keep. My little housekeeping chore was quickly dispatched and coming out on the Grande-Allée, where my brother-in-law who had offered his services as chauffeur was waiting, I noticed a crowd forming in front of the parliament, blocking the street from one sidewalk to the other.

"Who are all the people?" I asked. "The elections are supposed to be over."

"Come on," said my brother-in-law, "today's the day Daniel is due in Quebec City and everyone's waiting for him at the Renaissance Club. If you like, we'll just make a small detour around them."

"You go ahead," I replied, "but I want to have a closer look. I'll meet you in five minutes."

There they were, all of them, lawyers, engineers, entrepreneurs, suppliers, everyone who, a month earlier, had been enthusiastically licking our boots. Raising their eyebrows at this intruder examining them one by one with a bemused smile, some consented to make a microscopic sign of the hand in lieu of greeting, others elbowed their way out of the danger zone, and most turned their heads away as if avoiding an indecent spectacle. *Sic transit* . . . .

VI

OPTION QUEBEC

*"Most often one is born in a homeland; frequently, alas, one must
also conquer it."*
JACQUES MADAULE

---

29. "Oui, oui, oui, De Gaulle said free!"

YOU COULD SEE it coming.

His landing at l'Anse-au-Foulon, the port of Quebec, reminded me of his entry into Paris in 1944. Here, too, though in another way, he was coming to wipe out bad memories. As soon as he appeared in the little square where the whole of Quebec seemed jammed, you could feel a current running through the acclamations of the crowd, a current that had been intensifying from village to village along the King's Highway, le Chemin du Roi, leading to Montreal, nourished by the sure escalation of his rhetoric. So when he strode forth into that other square packed with people where the mayor of Montreal was waiting for him in front of his city hall, everyone was saying, "If he goes on at this rate, something's going to happen that our grandchildren will still be talking about!"

The same presentiment must have been haunting Jean Drapeau, so when the General expressed a desire to step out on the little balcony to greet the wildly enthusiastic crowd, the Mayor hastily excused himself, saying the microphone wasn't hooked up.

"But Monsieur le Maire," said my good friend Bouchard, the devoted technician who was always with the Radio-Canada team, "it's no big deal," and added with his customary obligingness, " I can fix that for you in a jiffy."

"Then do so, my friend," said De Gaulle, "do so."

And off they went, the three of them, the technician glad to be of service, the Mayor rather apprehensive, and the General exuding an air of lofty serenity.

Behind the city hall, among the guests waiting patiently on a large terrace, two MNAs, Yves Michaud and I, he elected for the first time, I re-elected the previous year, stood regretting the fact that we were no longer journalists at this historic moment and watching in some frustration as De Gaulle appeared on a TV set, stepping onto the balcony on the other side of the building. When he began speaking "confidentially" of a certain climate of liberation, in one instinctive movement we drew closer to the screen, crouched low so as not to block other people's view.

It was in this posture that his "Vive le Québec . . . libre!" held us paralysed a few instants. Then, hearing the deathly silence that reigned behind us, we turned around to face the rest of the guests. It is rare to have such an opportunity to see the two Montreals so clearly. In a state of shock, frozen in a fury that as yet was only emitting a few anticipatory rumblings, stood the Anglophone city. As for French Montreal, except for those constrained by office or acquaintance to reserve, they did not hide broad, complicit smiles, or even, in the background, gestures more discreet but just as enthusiastic as those of the crowd in the street.

What followed was a classical little triangular situation. In the name of the federal government Lester Pearson replied that night in scathing tones. On his side, the Premier of Quebec for less than a year, "mon ami Jonsonne" as the General called him, was walking on eggs. In spite of the name he owed to an Irish father, Johnson's formation and inclinations were so French that he no longer spoke English very well and, more to the point, he had become a nationalist who wasn't scared into nightmares by the word "independence," though the deed might have been something else. He was even suspected, probably quite correctly, to have made a pact with the indépendantiste groups permitting them to approach De Gaulle to their hearts' content as long as there was no roughhouse. As for the illustrious author of the incident, after calmly touring the Expo site, he cancelled his visit to Ottawa and the next day, replying to Drapeau's friendly criticism with a final witticism, telling him to take no heed of "scrabblers, toadies, and scribblers," and flew off to Paris to discover they were already scribbling away there furiously.

During this month of July, 1967, Expo's success was taking on the proportions of a triumph and many celebrities were turning up in Montreal, so the explosive little phrase of the last of the great Western leaders was destined to set up worldwide reverberations. But it also cost him dearly.

A few years later, speaking of the last years of the retired hero, Claude Mauriac wrote: "It was doubtless his 'Vive le Québec libre!' that caused the most uproar. In his exile the General's thoughts turned occasionally, painfully, to what had been said and written on his return from this voyage. 'What a rage the bourgeois French have to eclipse France at any price. . . . The Quebec business was a perfect illustration of this on every level, from *Le Figaro* to *L'Humanité*. Frenchmen reaching out their hands to France. . . . It was incredible. . . . And they even went so far as to suggest that I wasn't all there. . . . How could anyone imagine De Gaulle remaining indifferent before those French Canadians shouting "Vive la France!" and singing "La Marseillaise" while the band played "God Save the Queen," and after so many years of ingratitude on our part!' "*

Mauriac adds that on that day, as on many other occasions, De Gaulle had felt "carried along by events." What we must remain grateful to him for is, by the same stroke, to have carried the name of Quebec into the most unlikely corners of the world. A Montreal student reported that the next day in a Peruvian *barrio* where he had been sent by the Canadian government to spend the summer working on community projects, the Indians had come to tell him about the event, saying that from then on they knew that Quebec existed, too.

Even if his ecumenical vision sometimes led him to consider us as Frenchmen of the diaspora, never once did De Gaulle misjudge the heart of the matter. In one of those dazzling monologues he used to preface his press conferences with, he demonstrated, shortly after his return, that he had the Quebec dossier at his fingertips and was fully acquainted with its nuances. And like his successors, each

---

* Claude Mauriac, *Mort du Général de Gaulle* (Paris, 1972).

in his own style, when the occasion warranted it he never undertook to give us more support than we ourselves would have requested.

So the seismic effects of the balcony scene eventually died down. But for some of us, myself included, it had been a red alert. And rather premature. We weren't ready to imitate those young people marching in the street chanting:

"Québec libre, oui, oui, oui!
Québec libre, De Gaulle l'a dit!"

In fact, their exuberance filled me with a vague uneasiness, for it did not seem to me to be at all advisable to have recourse to some external authority, no matter how prestigious. This feeling was confirmed in a special emergency meeting of the Liberal caucus that Lesage called shortly thereafter.

For one member of our group, François Aquin, there could be no choice but to approve the General's attitude, whereas, at the other extreme, the Anglophone wing and their allies insisted that the guilty party be severely chastised. Seeing that Lesage was also inclined to take the hard line, Aquin threatened to resign. We tried in vain to dissuade him, arguing that the time was not ripe and that De Gaulle's gesture should encourage us to wait rather than to rush ahead. But our colleague refused to listen and, carrying out his threat, became for a time the first and only Gaullist member of the Quebec parliament.

As for the rest of us, we saw the future differently. We were ready to bide our time and let the dust settle. Québec libre, by all means, but who wanted that liberty to seem an imported product? In this country dominated by an Anglophone majority, the emancipation of our minority people would have to be the result of a purely indigenous movement, or nothing. In the same way that a conceded liberty is often illusory, a liberation that has to count on others to help it get started stands every chance of never getting off the ground. Consequently, we must neither take nor seem to take our inspiration from sources outside the country. When the day came, it would be up to Québécois alone to decide, to seize their fate with a firm hand, and on that basis go forward, already free.

It took me almost the whole of a year during 1966-67 to become definitely convinced that the future lay in that direction and, in attempting to move from dream to reality, to succeed finally in drawing up a coherent project to follow. During the pause that De Gaulle imposed on the process, in concert with the coming of the summer dog days, the rough draft had time to settle down into a text that was more or less acceptable. After that, what? I hadn't the slightest idea. The only thing I became sure of as I worked on my ideas was that the party wouldn't go along with them. Still being a Liberal, I was well placed to know this, for among ourselves, quietly but not secretly, we had been seeking our path since our defeat in the last election.

To begin with we hadn't been more than a handful of veterans chewing over their memories like a branch of the hot-stove league. There were François Aquin, the future Gaullist, Yves Michaud, the lawyer Marc Brière, and a few other survivors of the Political Committee of the party. This committee, which considered itself with just cause as the "thinking wing," had known its last triumph in 1964 at a party congress where the provincial Liberals had accepted by a narrow margin to cut free from the federal big brother, thereby giving themselves an autonomy that did not prevent anyone, be he minister or the most obscure organizer, from being red on both levels like the upper and lower plates of a good denture. For that matter it had only been a Pyrrhic victory, for Lesage, who had given in under duress, wasted no time in taking over control of the committee to pack it with unwavering supporters, which until the recent election defeat had made it an apparently burgeoning autocracy given to bloat.

Okay. What's over is over, we said. But since we haven't reached the memoir-writing stage yet, where do we go from here? For me the answer was simple. As MNA for Laurier I would serve my third term and, God willing, go back to journalism in four years' time. That way, from 1960 to 1970, from age 37 to 47, I would have given ten of my best years to the service of my fellow citizens. For six of these years I would have had the pleasure and pain, equally intense, of being part of a government whose highs and lows had accompanied an historic breakthrough, one which was also, alas, very incomplete. I was torn by two major deceptions: Hydro, the Caisse de dépôt, SOQUEM, the SGF, and our metallurgical dabblings had only slightly lightened the economic yoke that one day Quebec would have to free itself from forever; and the political domination of the federal government, which we had really only loosened a little, had recently been firming up again.

Now the ball was in Daniel Johnson's court. We, his loyal opposition, would keep an eye on him, of course, and would keep him going with some good, brand new ideas. But after all, what ideas? The Liberals, as they stepped down, were drained, with nothing better to offer than the makeshift program the electorate had just thrown into the garbage can. The most urgent need was to tank up again.

We set about doing so in the autumn of 1966. Several dozen and soon nearly a hundred members of the old "thinking wing" seized this occasion to rediscover the heady atmosphere of those long discussions spent reinventing the world. Besides Yves Michaud, another newly elected MNA, Robert Bourassa, had joined the group. Gérin-Lajoie, Kierans, and I naturally served as resource persons. Since most of us were his friends, Lapalme would sometimes come in to enliven our meetings with his caustic humour, which the décor of our meetings suited admirably. The room we met in was in the now defunct Saint-Denis Club and was dominated by a frightful, murky old oil painting showing the sea casting up a drowned corpse; the room was called the Shipwreck Salon! The setting was ideal for inspiring that favourite pastime of the defeated, the eternal post-mortem. But we soon resigned ourselves to dropping such an easy and practically inexhaustible subject and began to look toward the future.

What would it be like? That's probably the hardest question members of yesterday's government can ask themselves. To answer it they have to abandon their old style, which doesn't come easily, and then define a new role for themselves by sifting through their reflexions and learning to exchange mastery of government dossiers – a skill that quickly fades – for a solid effort of research and imagination.

How laborious it was, especially since we had to come to terms with the permanent theme of the Quebec situation that is generally encompassed in the catch-all expression "the national question." What made it even harder was that we had before us a declaration by Daniel Johnson, who in mid-September had used a meeting in Ottawa as an occasion to run up his own colours. Not only had he not spared the mustard, but from the start his remarks had gone beyond what are traditionally called (another cliché) "traditional claims." In his opening statement he proclaimed:

We believe there exists in Canada, in the sociological sense of the term, a French-speaking nation whose heartland is Quebec. This nation has the firm intention to continue to affirm itself by acquiring, in an orderly and just way, all instruments necessary for its development.

Speaking more precisely, what does Quebec want? As fulcrum for its nationhood, it wants to be master of decisions that relate to the human growth of its citizens (that is to say, that relate to education, to social security and health in every form), to their economic affirmation. . . , to their cultural expansion (that is to say, not only in arts and letters but also as pertains to the French language), and to the representation of the Quebec community (that is to say, with certain countries and international organizations).

Focusing on the subject of the meeting, which marked Johnson's entry into the federal-provincial club, he rapidly outlined his position on joint programs established by Ottawa but financed by the two governments. He described them as an increasingly troublesome tangle and, for Quebec in particular, a permanent obstacle to the free choice of priorities and a forced reduction of budgetary autonomy. Together with the basic principles he had just enunciated, this criticism led him logically to demand a new sharing formula whose key was the famous "100-100-100," that is:

. . . to reserve for Quebec the entire use, that is, 100 per cent, of sources of fiscal revenue to which it has a constitutional right – income tax, corporation taxes, and succession duties. We have calculated, in fact, that the revenues the federal government will draw from these three sources in Quebec in 1971-72 correspond almost exactly to the sum that Quebec should receive that same year either as a a direct transfer payment to cover the difference between its present responsibilities and its present sources of revenue, or in the form of fiscal compensation for new functions Quebec has assumed, or as equalization payments.

Placing himself in a "waiting posture," he closed his declaration in the form of a diptych, speaking first of us, then of us and the others.

Quebec insists . . . that as soon as possible the present constitution be replaced by one that recognizes fully the existence within Canada of a

French-speaking nation with all the rights that pertain thereto.

These demands by Quebec do not aim to destoy Canada. On the contrary, they will assure our country, if they are met in time, a much more stable equilibrium than the one it knows today. English-speaking Canadians and French-speaking Canadians will then be able to live in harmony. Close collaboration between governments will become possible wherever the needs of interdependence make it really necessary. . . .

Johnson had us in a nice fix. His position went quite a lot farther than the Liberal Party's, so unless we simply wanted to parrot him, there was no alternative but to stay behind or forge ahead. Behind? No question of that. Ahead then. Yes, but how and how far? The more we talked, the more we went round in circles. So we did what is generally recommended in such cases: we put off the decision until later, agreeing to go on thinking about it in the meantime.

The annual party congress arrived at just the right time to provide a counter-irritant. We decided to put up three candidates for the executive, with Eric Kierans as president. In no time the climate turned sour. With very few exceptions our group was from Montreal and moreover had dared attack the old internal structure of the party treasury, the pillars of which stood foursquare around the faction from Quebec City that supported Lesage. As well as being a confrontation between the capital and the metropolis, it was also something of a quarrel between Ancients and Moderns. On one side were the more conservative members, in whose view the government had been beaten because of the excessive rhythm of change we had introduced; opposite was our clan, persuaded that the contrary was true and that even more avenues of reform should be explored. On both sides, however, we felt that the moment of truth had not yet arrived. Bargaining took place and a Solomon-style compromise was reached. Kierans was allowed to become president, but his running mates were dumped. Everything took place in the classical context of a party deceived and dejected by the loss of power and looking around for a scapegoat.

For the Quebec City faction that propitiatory victim was me. I had long been their favourite crypto-separatist, particularly because of my frequent attacks on the federal government. Also pretending to take me for the Machiavellian organizer of the inter-city match we had just witnessed, they even began to whisper that Kierans was nothing more than Lévesque's marionette. Collecting this bad blood into a furious diatribe, the outgoing president went so far as to suggest that there was no longer a place for me in the Liberal Party, or anywhere else in politics for that matter. I deserved neither this excess of honour, nor this indignity, both spurred on quite simply by the dark suspicions that were beginning to arise around the question of the party leadership, for which some, quite wrong-headedly, cast me in the role of candidate.

Lesage himself knew perfectly well that the danger, if one can call it that, lay elsewhere. Nor did he ignore the fact that none of his true potential successors had the inclination or the means to declare themselves openly. He was sure he knew them all, but I discovered that he was wrong. It was, if I am not mistaken, a day in the winter session at the end of 1966 or the beginning of 1967. In one of the modest offices we had been assigned under the eaves of parliament, the discussion was going strong among the official dauphin, Paul Gérin-Lajoie, the new and voracious candidate that Claude Wagner, the "Hanging Judge," had become, and Pierre Laporte, whose patient organizational work could not be entirely disinterested. Playing agent provocateur, I had just mentioned the goal of leadership they all pretended was the last thing on their minds, when suddenly at the back of the room I perceived our fifth conspirator sitting on a desk swinging his legs. A discreet flush suffused his face and his eyes held signs of some inner tumult.

"Well, what do you know!" I said, turning toward him. "There's someone here who's at least as interested as the rest of you."

"Come on now, René," Robert Bourassa replied with a start, "you're making fun of me. Where did you get that idea?"

But he didn't say no, and only went on getting redder.

He continued to attend the meetings of our Montreal group, which after the Christmas break had slowly begun again. The horizon remained blocked. We couldn't agree on any important issues. Some, concluding it was all a waste of time, came less and less frequently and finally disappeared altogether. We were headed for chaos unless someone extracted himself from the muddle to try to clear things up by himself, in silence, the only place one can hear oneself think.

I remembered that Daniel Johnson's declaration of the preceding autumn had left me with a vague impression of something unfinished. Looking up his text and the notes I had scribbled in the margin, I realized in a single evening that my unconscious had completed my reflexion on this matter. Johnson had spoken of the need to recognize a nation and for this had demanded a wide range of exclusive rights. If we were to claim we were leading and not following him on the road to emancipation, why the devil wouldn't we go all the way, all the way to sovereignty rather than this half-way house where at best a larger share of autonomy would still be exposed to all the traps set for it in Ottawa and elsewhere? Why wouldn't the nation that had been rediscovering itself with such zest since 1960 find the natural fulfilment of its belated renaissance in just such a challenge? Johnson had also spoken of inevitable interdependence. Wouldn't such ties be less difficult to define between people who could discuss and accept them freely, as equal to equal, leaving behind the old constraints?

The more I thought about this project, the more it seemed logical and easy to articulate. Its main lines were beautifully simple and there was a paradoxical added advantage that was far from revolutionary. In fact, it was almost banal, for here and there throughout the world it had served to draw together people who, while determined to be masters in their own house, had found it worthwhile to enter into associations of various kinds with others. So association it was to be, a concept that had figured for a long time in our own vocabulary and a word that would marry well with sovereignty, sovereignty-association making a euphonious pair. Independence-association, on the other hand, with its marriage of opposites would be like bad Racine minus even the poetic effect of "These serpents hissing o'er our heads." Above all, and more seriously, the notion of independence had been so dragged through the streets by the RIN, acquiring an absolute, rigid character from demonstration to demonstration as if independence were an end in itself, that the name was not much more, alas, than an invitation to the riot squad! Like the rose, however, wouldn't it smell as sweet by any other name?

The structure of the project was completely contemporary; and now all it lacked was the indispensable motor of political will. At our next get-together, however, it soon became evident that this wasn't going to materialize tomorrow. We were just leaving winter behind, but the further I advanced in my exposé, the paler all those spring smiles grew and the more lenten faces became. In the general rout that followed I understood, first, that my days as a Liberal were numbered and, second, that the "separatist" aspect of sovereignty-association was perhaps less innocuous than I had thought. Kierans, Laporte, and Gérin-Lajoie soon rejoined the orthodox flock and those of us who were left fit easily into Robert Bourassa's basement.

So at the time De Gaulle arrived to send us off on our summer holiday we could count our numbers on our fingers, but we did have a valid project in hand.

30. A Country That Must Be Made

HOW LONG IT SEEMED, that aisle dividing the immense auditorium of the Château Frontenac, down which I walked in quitting the Liberal Party. From one row to the next, I recognized a throng of familiar faces. Some discreetly made friendly little signs, but most, feeling the eyes of the party vigilantes upon them, acted as though I had ceased to exist. Only Gérin-Lajoie dared cross the psychological barrier and step forward with outstretched hand to say good-bye. This pause allowed me to realize that a handful of accomplices had followed and that I wouldn't be completely alone at the exit.

As foreseeable as it had become, this departure cost me something. I recognized members from every region in Quebec along with certain workmates who had crossed over to the opposition with me, remembering all those successes and failures we had shared! We had covered a lot of ground from April, 1960, to October, 1967, and now it was the parting of the ways. I felt a twinge in my heart. As far as the party was concerned, I was frankly relieved to be leaving it. I had never been a real partisan. Maybe I should say straight off that I believe I could never be a party man, no more Péquiste than Liberal. For me any political party is basically just a necessary evil, one of the instruments a democratic society needs when the time comes to delegate to elected representatives the responsibility of looking after its common interests. But parties that last generally age poorly. They have a tendency to transform themselves into lay churches with power to loose and to bind and can turn out to be quite insupportable. In the long run sclerosis of ideas sets in and political opportunism takes over. Every new party should, in my opinion, write into its statutes a clause anticipating its disappearance after a certain time, perhaps after a generation, certainly no longer. If it goes on past this, no matter how much plastic surgery it undergoes to restore its beauty, one day it will be nothing more than a worn-out old thing blocking the horizon and preventing the future from breaking through.

In any event, that's how I had come to see the Liberal Party. There was nothing traumatic about it; I wasn't breaking up with my family, just an old, outmoded party fallen into sterility. It had used me as long as I had seemed profitable to it, and I had used the platform and other means it provided to realize or at least to advance things I believed in. We were quits, all the more so because right up until the last moment I had followed the fundamental rule that requires every member to work loyally within the party framework as long as his conscience will permit.

In the normal line of things I had first tried out my ideas on my Laurier riding association, where the sovereignty-association project went down with the greatest of ease, almost unanimously. That surprised me, but it moved me even more. For this neighbourhood assembly, made up of good souls who boasted no more than their title as ordinary citizens, my plan was a question of common sense as well as a perspective on the future that the party should not hesitate to underwrite. In no time, interdictions and threats of excommunication would begin to ring in their ears, and I was sure that many of them would resign themselves to make due apology and request absolution, but for the meantime what could be more encouraging than this spontaneous adhesion by a hundred or so Québécois simply following their reason and their instinct.

Once this stage was passed, the project was officially out in the open, together with the names of those who had worked so hard to articulate it. There could be no doubt that they would be subjected to continuous pressure, or that certain of them would find themselves plunged into a cruel dilemma: either a dive into these untried waters or the very legitimate hope of a more certain and accelerated career.

Nothing guaranteed that a final examination of the project wouldn't reveal risks or weaknesses that hadn't been anticipated clearly enough. That's the reason Robert Bourassa gave for leaving us. At the decisive moment he discovered that the monetary question (which, in all fairness, was to remain one of his most deep-seated obsessions right up to 1976) hadn't been scrutinized thoroughly enough for him. Then, one of the very last, Yves Michaud withdrew, almost bringing tears to our eyes with his evocation of the Rocky Mountains, a part of his patrimony it seemed to him as impossible to abandon as his urge to go there one day seemed improbable to the rest of us.

After the usual editorial cacophony, I drew fire from the big guns. Lesage proclaimed that never – and this time a "never" as solid as rock! – would he accept to direct a separatist organization. Eric Kierans let it be known that it was him or me, and that if it was me, he'd leave, slamming the door. Nothing was more predictable than this reflex from an Anglophone who was more Canadian than Québécois. Back when he'd been accused of being the "marionette" of the chief suspect, hadn't he rushed to clear his name? Quebec still wasn't capable of going it alone, he explained, curiously, and even if that changed, he'd still be against the idea! It was the natural slope of his mind, and it ultimately led him to Ottawa, where Trudeau made short work of him.

Opposed by both the leader and the president of the party, I didn't stand much chance. Right up to the eve of my departure, however, I had hoped we would have a proper debate and that perhaps with our skeleton crew of supporters we might rally, say, 10 per cent of the vote. For that, they'd have had to accept a secret ballot. Not only did they refuse to hold one, but as I entered the auditorium I saw Lesage sitting right next to the microphone, on the lookout for trouble. According to rumours circulating in the corridors, it wasn't what I said that was going to be discussed, but my head, and apparently it wasn't even going at a very good price. So when my right to speak to the group one last time was recognized, I expressed myself approximately as follows.

> I want to thank those who have at least allowed our proposition to become a full-fledged motion so that you can see what it says. But I know it has no chance of being studied on its own merits. Without holding anything against those who want to make a scarecrow of it, I think that one day they will see they were wrong. Now all that remains for me to do is to leave, taking with me my share of our common memories and the regret that things had to end this way.

I had left in a deathly silence. Two hours later I found myself in another room whose walls seemed ready to burst. Several hundred exuberant people were crowded in there, young people mostly, making an infernal racket. I couldn't hear myself think and was struck by the fact that even without the delirium the same spirit of spontaneous adhesion was there as with the crowd in my riding association. Carried by this current, I promised that things wouldn't stop there.

It was a bold impulse. If it meant anything more than words in the air, such a promise could only signify one thing – a new political commitment. Scarcely demobilized, was I going to re-enlist so quickly? And so completely? They wanted me as provisional leader of a provisional group that intimated I should take over the no less provisional committee that had just been established. They wanted me, first because I was the most widely known of the bunch, and then because I had started the ball rolling. My acts were catching up with me. "Bah!" I said to myself, wasn't I resigned to go on till 1970 anyway? I would just cross the floor from the Liberal benches to that particular purgatory the House reserves for independent members, that was all.

But it was most urgent to consolidate the provisional before it frittered itself away, as it was eminently likely to do if we didn't take care. In a few weeks we were ready to give birth to a new movement, not a party, just a simple gathering with a minimum of very supple controls to keep it as open and welcoming as possible. That way we would have time to wait for a response that only the population as a whole was capable of supplying. Would it be, as Claude Ryan wrote in *Le Devoir*, the end of a "time of ambiguity"? Or would it be the little "separatist adventure" without a future that other journalists disdainfully foresaw?

The best way to see the situation more clearly was obviously to make public the text that had stirred up such a fuss and which the Liberal Party had buried so hastily it remained largely unknown. Without it, in fact, the name we had given ourselves – Mouvement Souveraineté-Association, or MSA to its friends – risked returning to limbo.

A small book, *Option Quebec*, was soon ready for the press and was launched early in 1968. Working at that speed, in order to bring the weight up to the respectable level required of a serious book, we had to devote more than half our 173 spacey pages to various appendices that mainly reproduced commentaries or statements of support signed by personalities who added a precious dose of credibility to our project.

One of these was none other than Jacques Parizeau. He had already been thinking of joining us when he was called to give a conference at Banff. He prepared his commentary on the transcontinental, the great empty spaces of the Prairies undoubtedly giving him extra inspiration. The text he stepped out of the train with, entitled "Quebec-Canada: A Blind Alley," remains one of the most cruelly exact portraits of the non-sense of the Canadian nation. On the one hand are nine provinces for whom, despite many historical and political differences, belonging together must inevitably exclude "a degree of decentralization that can only be ruinous. . . . As for Quebec, whatever could be offered would necessarily fall short, sooner or later, of what it wants, no matter how generous these propositions might seem at the outset. The answer lies in recognizing frankly that we are faced with two different societies, that efficient economic policies for one are not necessarily efficient for the other because values are different, and that there is no need to sacrifice efficiency for the larger society to accommodate the smaller one, which is likely in any case to be dissatisfied with the compromise."*

It was this same absurdity, seen by the economist under his specialized angle, that we attacked in the two "official" chapters of our thin volume. We locked in hand-to-hand combat with our adversaries, who hadn't hesitated in laying the stick to us at the same time as they dangled a few pale greenhouse carrots before the noses of the Quebec people, like the "biculturalism" that came out of the Laurendeau-Dunton report, which enticed a lot of nationalists whose appetites were modest. Daniel Johnson, for example, who had felt considerable pressure from the De Gaulle affair, made this the occasion to put a good deal of water in the wine of his "Equality or Independence." This slogan, as strong as it was politically sinuous, could be interpreted, according to the needs of the moment, either in the sense of global equality between two distinct nations, or else as so-called cultural equality between two so-called founding peoples. The Quebec Premier took the federal bon-ententist bait: "I have made a sort of bet," he declared, "on the future of Canada in a renewed federalism that rests on cultural duality. . . ."† His vocabulary was sadly outdated and erratic, and

* This and the following excerpts from *Option Quebec* can be found in René Lévesque, *An Option for Quebec* (Toronto, 1968).

† *Le Devoir*, December 1, 1967.

a later premier would try to freshen it up a little by daring to use the term cultural "sovereignty" . . . with the same amazing results!

The basis of these snares and delusions was and still is, for our obstinate ostriches, nothing less than the mirage of a bilingual Canada upon which Messrs. Trudeau and Company so shrewdly built their careers. Weren't there to be more and more French employees behind federal wickets? Weren't our minorities outside Quebec learning to let themselves be cuddled by Ottawa as never before despite or because of the fact that they were on the road to extinction?

"And now," I wrote on December 3, 1967 (and would write again today), "how can they get out of this situation? By obtaining, as a host of honest folk and others who are not so honest persist in imagining, advantages comparable to those already enjoyed by Anglo-Québécois? That would mean starting immediately with as good schools, from elementary to university, for minorities that are not well off, are often widely scattered, and, except for New Brunswick, do not make up even half the percentage of Anglophones in Quebec. And what would this incredible effort result in? In launching workers trained in French culture into a marketplace and a climate that is exclusively English. Or more probably in sending them here to Quebec as soon as they graduated (at least that much would be gained).

"In short, what they would like to substitute for the indispensable emancipation of Quebec is the pale shadow of a pious impossibility."

It was based on those assumptions that I had entitled my manifesto "A Country That Must Be Made." The eminently simple theme that I developed in twenty pages or so has had a reception that has always surprised me. For twenty years now it has been a political option that has never ceased to hold favour in many hearts, as well as in the polls. I may be a bad judge, but it seems to me that such persistency is significant. At the very least it shows that the idea is very much alive, even if the firemen of the status quo continue to do all they can to douse the fire under the ashes. Rereading it again for the first time in a long while, I tell myself, I can still live with that, and even, presumptuously, that the day will come when we will finally end up with something of the kind. It's up to the reader to judge.

We Are Québécois

If there is one thing time has never ceased to confirm progressively, it's the permanent truth of the identification I state in my title.

> That means first and foremost, and if need be exclusively, that we are attached to this one corner of the earth where we can be completely ourselves, this Quebec, the only place we have the unmistakable feeling, "here we can be really at home."
>
> Being ourselves is essentially a matter of keeping and developing a personality that has survived three and a half centuries. At the heart of this personality is the fact that we speak French. Everything else depends on this one essential element and follows from it or leads us infallibly back to it.

Then, having evoked the history that made us who we are and gave us the will and stubborn hope that permit us to survive and grow, the manifesto continued:

> Until recently in this difficult process of survival we enjoyed the protection of a certain degree of isolation. We lived a relatively sheltered life in a rural society in which a great measure of unanimity reigned, and in which poverty set its limits on change and aspiration alike.
>
> We are children of that society, in which the *habitant*, our father or grandfather, was still the key citizen. We are also heirs to a fantastic adventure – that early America that was almost entirely French. We are, even more intimately, heirs to the group obstinacy which has kept alive that portion of French America we call Quebec. . . .
>
> This is how we differ from other men and especially from other North Americans, with whom in all other areas we have so much in common. This basic "difference" we cannot surrender. . . .

It wasn't that there weren't plenty of opportunities to lose it. I had only to recall the waves of forced abdications that the other provinces and some of the American states had been forced to accept in difficult times, without counting internal exile, uprootings, assimilations . . . .

> For a small people such as we are, our minority position on an

Anglo-Saxon continent creates from the very beginning a permanent temptation to self-rejection, which has all the attractions of a gentle downward slope ending in comfortable submersion in the Great Whole. . . .

The only way to overcome the danger is to face up to this trying and thoughtless age and make it accept us as we are, succeeding somehow in making a proper and appropriate place for ourselves. . . . This means that we must build a society which, while it preserves an image that is our own, will be as progressive, as efficient, as "civilized" as any in the world.

In fact there are other small peoples who are showing us the way, demonstrating that size is in no way synonymous with maximum progress among human societies. . . .

But I was obliged to confess that we hadn't dared give ourselves this country of our own. We were always claiming that we were building it piece by piece, by means of partial recuperations of power, by statutes that were more or less "special" in tax matters, in social security, in the field of immigration, and in controlling the main instruments of mass culture (radio, television, cable-diffusion). And while we clutched in vain at these disjointed pieces, justice continued to be dislocated, corporate competency fragmented, and our financial networks troubled. Consequently, it was no great merit on my part to arrive at this common-sense conclusion:

> Order must be re-established in the chaos of a governmental structure created at a time when it was impossible to foresee the scientific and technical revolution in which we are now caught up, the endless changes it demands, the infinite variety of things produced, the concentration of enterprises, the crushing weight that the greatest of these impose on individual and collective life, the absolute necessity of having a state able to direct, co-ordinate, and above all humanize this infernal rhythm.

It required no great insight to trace the ceaseless see-saw of the Byzantine federal-provincial regime I had been involved in and to show that such an objective was simply a dream in the context of Canadian institutions.

From a purely revisionist point of view, our demands would seem to surpass both the best intentions displayed by the "other majority" and the very capacity of the regime to make concessions without an explosion. . . .

If Quebec were to begin negotiations to revise the present frame of reference, it would soon fall back on the old defensive struggle, the enfeebling skirmishes that make one forget where the real battle is, the half-victories that are celebrated between two defeats, the relapse into divisive federal-provincial electoral folly, the sorry consolations of verbal nationalism, and, above all – this must be said, and repeated, and shouted if need be – above all the incredible squandering of energy which certainly is for us the most disastrous aspect of the present regime. . . .

So many years later, in seeing what has passed, and in attending the most recent constitutional hagglings, wouldn't one have to admit that this description wasn't far from what we actually had to live through, or rather, what we inflicted upon ourselves? Wouldn't one have to admit also that it was below our dignity? By 1967 our people had already found the strength to catch up a distance that they would never have believed possible. From then on, our rising generations have had the same chance to be educated and skilled as young people in other advanced societies. In certain sectors of social planning and even in economic life, Québécois have quickly crossed obstacles that place them in the avant-garde in Canada, if not in the whole continent.

From all that, then, from the repeated failure of federal-provincial negotiations to the revelation of our striking new maturity, one could draw only one conclusion:

. . . Quebec must become sovereign as soon as possible.

Thus we finally would have within our grasp the security of our collective "being" which is so vital to us, a security which otherwise must remain uncertain and incomplete.

Then it will be up to us, and us alone, to establish calmly, without recrimination or discrimination, the priority for which we are now struggling feverishly but blindly, that of our language and culture.

Only then will we have the opportunity, and the obligation, to use our talents to the maximum in order to resolve without further excuses or evasions all the great problems that confront us [as well as] the form and evolution of the political structures we must create for ourselves. . . .

In other words, we had to take into our own hands the entire liberty of Quebec and affirm our right to the essential content of independence and the full control of each and every one of our principal decisions. In this way we would be rejoining one of the two major currents of our times: that of national emancipation. It would be, in fact, a double emancipation that might take place. The Anglo-Canadian majority would also at the same stroke be rid of constraints that our presence imposed upon it, would be free to reorganize its own institutions, and free to prove to itself that it really wanted to preserve a society distinct from that of the United States.

And if this is the case there is no reason why we, as future neighbours, should not voluntarily remain associates and partners in a common enterprise, which would conform to the second great trend of our times: the new economic groups, customs unions, common markets, etc.

Here we are talking about something which already exists, for it is composed of the bonds, the complementary activities, the many forms of economic co-operation within which we have learned to live. Nothing says that we must throw these things away; on the contrary, there is every reason to maintain the framework. If we destroyed it, interdependent as we are, we would only be obliged sooner or later to build it up again, and then with doubtful success. . . .

We are not sailing off into uncharted seas. Leaving out the gigantic model furnished by the evolution of the Common Market, we can take our inspiration from countries comparable in size to our own – Benelux or Scandinavia – among whom co-operation is highly advanced, and where it has promoted unprecedented progress in the member states without preventing any of them from continuing to live according to their own traditions and preferences.*

To sum up we propose a system that would allow our two majorities to extricate themselves from an archaic federal framework in which our two very distinct "personalities" paralyse each other by dint of pretending to have a third personality common to both.

* I had used two sentences from John Kenneth Galbraith as an epigraph: "There certainly exists a tendency which impels peoples to form ever-larger economic groups. But one sees in the world no equivalent tendency toward more extended political units." Time has confirmed this judgement made in 1967.

This new relationship of two nations, one with its homeland in Quebec and another free to rearrange the rest of the country at will, would be freely associated in a new adaptation of the current "common-market" formula, making up an entity which could perhaps – and if so, very precisely – be called a Canadian Union.

I was persuaded, need I say, that such a change would really be *the* solution. But I was nevertheless aware of the extreme difficulty of the enterprise. According to a maxim of Gramsci, which has become one of a few favourite mottos of mine, "Pessimism of the intelligence; optimism of the will."

The first half made me guess the fright that would seize many people at the thought of leaving a political dwelling that a very long habitation had almost made sacred. Indeed, this old house of "Confederation" constitutes one of the last vestiges of those ancient certainties that our times are constantly stripping us of. Without foreseeing the extent of the phenomenon or the quite extravagant excesses it would lead to, I knew that at the moment of decision certain people would fasten onto the status quo with that kind of panic energy that betrays more fear of the new than reasonable attachment to the old.

As for optimism of the will, it made me bet on that moment, despite the foregoing, because it would be a time "when courage and calm daring become the only proper form of prudence that a people can exercise in a crucial period of its existence. If it fails at these times to take the calculated risk of the great leap, it may miss its vocation forever, just as a man does who is afraid of life."

Hoping with all my heart to have been mistaken in that last sentence, this is what I continue to believe.

31. From Trudeaumania to La Manic

OUR ELOQUENT PREFACE-WRITER, Jean Blain, had seen in this option a balance between past and future "that inspires confidence . . . and that will perhaps make it one of the most important rallying points in our history."

By the time 1968 was barely a third over, this prediction was on the way to being fulfilled. Our little book was selling so quickly and so well that I was able to deposit the tidy sum of ten thousand dollars in royalties in the empty coffers of our movement. Even more important was the fact that our total membership had almost passed that figure.

May, 1968, was a month of social upheaval in France that deserved to be marked with a black stone or a white one, according to one's politics, what with unions and especially students taking to the barricades and threatening for a few days to topple even mighty De Gaulle. On this side of the Atlantic it was April, rather, that saw two turning points leading to events less violent than those in France but ones that promised more lasting consequences. One of them, to which I'll return later, was to shake our movement to its very foundations.

Chronological order is not the only thing that requires me to note the first date, April 6, when Trudeau became head of the federal Liberals. Hierarchical order also requires that I mention it first, at least as he explained it himself in a little compendium of his thought published when he was still only a minister.* "The small influence that I may have as Minister of Justice," he explained with becoming modesty, "is a greater influence than I would have had if I had remained in the province of Quebec. The laws I propose here not only govern the six million inhabitants of the province of Quebec, but the twenty million inhabitants of Canada."

* *Réponses de Pierre Elliott Trudeau* (Montréal, 1968).

At last he could dominate that "large ensemble" he represented to himself as all of a piece, peopled with citizens all cast in one and the same mould, people who would cease to be preoccupied with questions of language and culture as soon as he had realized his intention of transforming Canada into a country that was officially and generously bilingual. This way the idea of two nations would soon be forgotten. That idea got on his nerves so much that he jumped down Daniel Johnson's throat on the issue. Johnson had compared him to Lord Durham, author of the famous nineteenth-century report on the French-Canadian people, "a people without a history," he had called them, but a people just the same. "Monsieur Johnson does not know his history very well," the oracle replied. "He seems to ignore the fact that the Durham Report affirmed the existence of two nations, whereas I myself do not happen to believe in this *thesis*." This took place in a federal-provincial conference, one of that innumerable, repetitive lineage which this time had chosen to turn its attention to the extremely uncertain question of "Confederation Tomorrow." In 1967 the regime was celebrating its centenary with festivities eclipsed by Expo in Montreal, and by sponsoring a shower of "cultural centres" pattering down haphazardly from one ocean to the other (although contracts fell with uncanny regularity into the pockets of Liberal entrepreneurs). Behind it all lay vague collective yearnings that betrayed a vast, existential uncertainty. "What is a Canadian?" asked the *Atlantic Monthly*. The responses it received failed to describe a truly distinctive creature. After one century, *homo canadiensis* remained hazy, incapable of defining himself in any convincing fashion.

In a country that lacked consistency to this point, Trudeau was far from being the only one to refuse to recognize two nations, that is, the tough reality of ours compared to the relative non-existence of the Anglo-Canadian one. The new Quebec bothered them. It was beginning to make them frightened. All that was being asked of the "French Power" that had taken over the reigns in Ottawa was that it make this province that was getting a bit too uppity step back into line. For the group that had gone to Ottawa in 1965 in order to "counterbalance" Quebec nationalism, this was exactly the type of action they had in mind. One could see it clearly as soon as Trudeau, the new broom sweeping clean, precipitously launched his first election campaign. His platform had no substantial political content: a few pious generalizations about a juster society; a couple of jokes at the expense of Conservative leader, Robert Stanfield, who was promoting, with a good deal of common sense, a dose of price controls (which had to be applied two years afterwards); and nothing more. Trudeau only had to present himself as an elegant receptacle into which Canada could pour all its hidden hopes, among them the sneaking wish to see French Quebec put in its place. The unspoken but fiercely evident slogan that floated in the air everywhere was "Keep Quebec Quiet!"

In years gone by on the coast of Africa little Negro kings were tolerated because they could assure the security of the landing sites while the slave merchants pushed into the interior to make their raids. In the same way, from Laurier to St. Laurent to Trudeau, each time the Anglophone majority has given Québécois the signal honour of reigning in Ottawa, inevitably Quebec itself has had to pay the price – except that, luckily, the slave trade isn't much in fashion nowadays, and the chains are practically invisible to the naked eye . . .

While Trudeaumania took off with the greatest of ease, during that same month of April our own thrust experienced its first set-backs. Along with some twelve hundred delegates gathered in Montreal, we treated ourselves to a major confrontation. At the heart of the disagreement, as so often in our history as a minority, was the language question. Following the example of the RIN, our radical comrade François Aquin came forward to propose integral unilingualism whose point of departure would be the abolition of English schools. He had also been the first to draw the attention of the House to the alarming double phenomenon of the rapid fall in our birth rate and the galloping anglicization of the waves of post-war immigrants. This tendency was particularly visible among the main contingent of new arrivals, the Italians, who rushed to learn the language of the continent. One could understand their rationale, because it wasn't really in Quebec they had landed but in America. But from there to let ourselves be "continentalized" was quite a jump. There was a real danger here, and nothing illustrated it better than the incendiary situation in Saint Leonard. In this little town in the Montreal suburbs, things had reached the point where Anglo-Italians were claiming a redistribution of schools to serve their offspring better. A "School Integration Movement" had sprung up in opposition, demanding that children of immigrant families be obliged to attend French schools. This was a perfectly legitimate stand, except that the integrationists went from occupying school buildings to skirmishing, to issuing hate-filled declarations, which made me aware of another danger, a very grave one, in the temptation of intolerance to which we are all exposed.

Seeing the MSA assembly leaning toward Aquin's position, I resigned myself for the first time, but far from the last, to put my head on the line. The maintenance, not of excessive privilege, but of basic school rights for Quebec Anglophones appeared to me to be a test of our maturity and also of our aptitude to maintain proper relations with the rest of North America. I had my way, by the skin of my teeth, after coming under fire from the noisy, angry, and increasingly large group leaving the RIN to join us, bringing with them an unquenchable ardour guaranteed to keep the spirit alive, but also a kind of extremism which, it seemed to me, we could have done without.

Fortunately, we were also picking up support in greater and greater numbers from other quarters. From the North Shore to Montreal (where some fifty old friends had resisted Liberal pressures and had formed an "Association Laurier-Lévesque") our recruiting campaign was giving us a base that was more and more diversified. But what a constant effort it was, undoubtedly as arduous as anything in the annals of political action. From union meetings (warm but still hesitant) to student assemblies (as difficult to mobilize then as now), from township to township, from family to family, the extenuating missionary work went on, little by little weaving a tissue of conversions whose threads were still so fragile that at any instant they might give way before adverse winds or opinion.

Promoting a project like ours was like planting a crop in soil that is not used to receive it, and on many occasions it provoked a veritable rejection syndrome. In the Lower St. Lawrence, for instance, they refused to rent us a hall in Saint-Pascal, a corner of Kamouraska where, if I'm not mistaken, there are proportionately more Lévesques than anywhere else in Quebec! Never had I felt such a black sheep or so little a prophet in my own country. From there we went to that seedbed of the most fiery Quebec nationalism, the "Kingdom" of Saguenay–Lac Saint-Jean, where the trailers we used for our recruiting circuit at first only managed to empty the classrooms. If adults were conspicuous by their absence, at least the children succumbed to the magic of this gypsy caravan, and we in turn were fascinated by the marvellous little kids who crowded around us, their sparkling eyes and high cheekbones speaking of earlier frequentations between the native people and the handful of whites who had "opened" the region a little more than a century ago. It was a remarkable mixture that can be referred to without shame now that "The Savages' Entrance" at the National Assembly has been renamed "The Entrance of the Amerindian" and nothing is so chic as to have a little Indian blood in the family. It was a mixture I was all the more susceptible to since one of its most splendid exemplars, a certain Corinne with a slender face devoured by glowing eyes, had cast an irresistible spell on a man whom politics mostly, as it often does, had practically separated from his wife. In her regulation miniskirt, Corinne at first dissembled her fine intelligence, but she stepped into my life that day and has since shared good times and bad with me, making the former even better and the latter usually easier to bear.

This ray of sunshine certainly contributed to the optimism with which I gave my support then and there to a decision I had been somewhat fearful of taking, for it signified our crossing the Rubicon. That autumn the MSA was transformed into a political party, that is, an instrument of political power. This fact was not taken too seriously by everyone, least of all at that time. Many people shared Trudeau's view when he dismissed us with the back of his hand, calling our new party "a particle."

He could well afford such an attitude, for his first electoral attempt had produced a striking victory installing a majority government in Ottawa for the first time in ten years. The "balcony scene" surely had something to do with it, but one couldn't blame Trudeau for that. Voting day had been set for June 25 and he had come to Montreal the night before to attend the traditional Saint-Jean Baptiste parade. It would have been much better to ignore his provocative presence, but Pierre Bourgault and his militants got it into their heads that they should mount a noisy demonstration. As a result Trudeau, superbly conscious of the cameras turning only a few hours before the vote, remained almost alone on the reviewing stand under a shower of stones and bottles. These images had, it is said, a decisive effect on English Canada and very certainly caused the defeat in Montreal of Robert Cliche, head of the provincial NDP, a candidate whom we had supported to the full extent of our meagre resources.

Another result, which I must admit brought me a certain relief, was the interruption of talks we had opened with the RIN that were dragging lamentably anyway. This latest outburst, which revealed an extraordinary lack of political savvy, provided us an opportunity to put an end to these futile negotiations.

Happily for Quebec, these squabbles among "particles" only took up a small part of the political scene. Facing off with a triumphant Trudeau was "mon ami Jonsonne," who in his own right was living through a particularly stirring apotheosis. Who would have expected to see this man, long considered to be a second-string politician, spattered by the last Duplessis scandals, and saddled with the demeaning nickname "Danny Boy," become transformed into a popular idol and, on the somewhat narrow scale of the provincial arena, a true statesman? The trials he had to surmount had matured him and he had achieved a serenity in part explained, perhaps, by the fact that his health was becoming more precarious and his days were cruelly numbered.

To Ottawa's increasingly haughty expansionism he smilingly opposed a solid attachment to the interests of Quebec, which his new place in the people's affection gave considerable weight. In addition, "Vive le Québec libre!" had exposed him to the shock of opening himself to the world and the promises and pitfalls that implies. Reinforcing our links with the old country had led De Gaulle to raise the budget of Franco-Québécois co-operation from one to six million dollars. No doubt this relationship also had something to do with the Gabon affair, where a Quebec delegation had been received with the full honours normally reserved for sovereign countries, which pushed the offended federal government to the ridiculous decision of breaking diplomatic ties with the tiny African state.

Everything was going well for Johnson when sickness struck again. He left to convalesce and didn't return till September, bravely declaring that he felt "dangerously well." He had come back to preside over the inauguration of that masterpiece of hydroelectric engineering, Manic 5. Stuffed into a fleet of airplanes, several hundred guests flew off toward the North Shore. Even though I was only a mini-leader, I wasn't surprised to be counted among them since I was still an MNA, and especially because it was well known that the Manicouagan and I had had a real love affair. But I came within an ace of not seeing my old flame again. Last to leave, our plane ran into such a terrific storm that, groaning in every strut, it was obliged to land at Forestville. We chartered an old school bus to take us up to the dam site, way north of Baie Comeau on a road soaked and battered by squalls of wind and rain. It was nearly midnight when at last the gigantic floodlit arches of the dam appeared, stretching away with the delicacy of a work of art yet capable of holding back the waters of one of the largest artificial lakes in the world. No light showed in the sleeping camp except from the windows of the workers' cafeteria. Lost in this immense shed were several dozen people accompanied by Johnson, who had insisted on waiting for our arrival. He had even managed to keep early-to-bed Lesage up until this ungodly hour. Coming to meet me, he took my hand in one of his, caught Lesage's in the other, then, drawing the latter in to close the triangle, made us pose for one of the best photos in my collection.

The photo is unforgettable, too, because of what followed. Seeing his extended hand I had noticed Johnson's extreme fragility, given away by the bluish wrist that the light almost seemed to penetrate. Lesage soon left and, since it was so late, I made a move to go, too. Impossible. Johnson refused (feared?) to go to bed. With that simplicity and humour that tempered his sometimes biting wit, he began to talk about everything in general. Chuckling, he asked for my candid opinion on the speech he was going to give the next day. A few passages seemed rather weak to me, and as we began talking about them the president of Hydro-Québec, his old friend and my former accomplice, Roland Giroux, could no longer hide his impatience, which was underscored by anxiety.

"Daniel, for the love of God, go to bed. Honestly, do you want to catch your death?"

"All right, I'm coming," Johnson replied with a sigh of resignation. "As for the speech," he added, turning to me, "you'll have plenty of time to fix it up however you like, you and the others . . ."

In the morning it was the silence that woke me with a start. I looked at my watch. It was after eight and breakfast was supposed to be at seven-thirty. Then the door of the dormitory where we were sleeping opened with a bang and, from one cubicle to the next, I heard knocking followed by a few rapid words, always the same, though I couldn't quite make them out. I stepped out into the corridor and found myself face to face with one of Johnson's close collaborators.

"Daniel is dead," he said in an expressionless voice.

And then, without another word, he went on to knock at the door of the next cubicle.

32. A Defeat
with an Air of Victory

IN THE PARLIAMENTARY RESTAURANT where I sat sipping the solitary coffee of the independent MNA, Claude Morin came over to discreetly share a state secret with me. "The election," he said, "is for April 29."

The loyal deputy minister had waited until the eve of the official announcement before giving me these several hours' notice that wouldn't change anything anyway. It was, I told myself, the minimum of courtesy I was entitled to, because at the beginning of 1970 I was, counting my year with the MSA, the oldest of all party leaders.

Less than a month after Johnson's death, in mid-October, 1968, we had held our founding congress in Quebec City. I would have preferred to give the party a descriptive name such as "Parti Souverainiste" or even PSA. But while most of us were preoccupied with putting together a program and laboriously drawing up those bizarre tables of the law that were, alas, from the start, our statutes and regulations, Gilles Grégoire, a promoter with an hallucinating gift of the gab, was busy in the wings imposing his choice on us. He succeeded handily and all that remained for me was to get used to the name "Parti Québécois," which I nonetheless continued to find rather presumptuous.

Grégoire, who was unfortunately later to destroy himself, in those days was a strange customer. His father, Ernest Grégoire, long-time mayor of Quebec City after having fought the good fight with the old Action Libérale Nationale in the thirties, had left him a legacy of robust nationalist convictions. A stay with the Jesuits, whose cassock he wore for a time, added a crust of culture that he soon sloughed off on contact with Social Credit. They got him elected to Ottawa under Réal Caouette's banner, and I will never forget that one day in 1965, at a time when I was trying to get the federal government to recognize inadequate boundaries in Hudson Bay, he

was the sole MP from Quebec to telephone from the House of
Commons to offer me a hand. Once his Créditiste days were ended,
he became leader of the tiny, semi-rural extension of the independence movement, the Ralliement National, and, bringing it into the
ranks of the PQ before the founding congress, he had got himself
elected vice-president of the new party.

As for the RIN, which avoided the event though knowing perfectly well that its strength was continuing to dwindle to our benefit, after a couple of weeks' painful reflexion the party decided to
commit harakiri by inviting its last faithful members to join us.

The essential task was complete. We had managed to group
everyone in one party and all we lacked now was a multitude of
candidates. We quickly set up teams to look after organization and
recruiting, and the young Turks who were involved, wearing themselves to the bone for a pittance, progressively acquired such mastery of their jobs that one day our electoral "machine" would be
considered the best in the country. First there was Michel Carpentier,
whom I had met in a CEGEP languishing away teaching political
science when all he really wanted was a chance to switch from
theory to practice. No sooner had he thrown himself into the fray
than he developed into a regular workhorse and, doubly, a motiva-
tor whose efficiency, based on a subtle mixture of get-up-and-go
and self-effacement, quickly made him our *éminence grise*. There
were also, of course, the old indispensables Jean Rougeau and
"Ti-Loup" Gauthier and, among our few full-time workers, the
inexhaustible Jean Doré, who later would go on to complete his
law degree and end up in municipal politics. And finally, with the
approach of election day, the dizzying eruption of volunteers in the
midst of whom stood out the huge, hairy head of a frail little fellow
named Claude Charron, who was almost immediately to make his
political debut at my expense.

Now that I was deprived of Liberal unction, I would inevitably
be beaten from the start if I presented myself again in Laurier. In the
north, the Anglo and ethnic streets of Park Extension, peopled by
Italians clustered around their Casa d'Italia and an ever-increasing
number of Greeks, would give me no quarter. On the other hand,
in south-central Montreal there was a welcoming bunch of modest
people who had made us feel immediately at home. That gave us
a number of ridings that are described, though sometimes chancily,
as "sure." One of these was Saint-Jacques, a riding we had left open

in case we had to slot some important candidate there in the late stages of the campaign. Soon after the campaign began I learned, reluctantly, that the candidate in question was supposed to be me. But if I quit the riding that had elected me twice before, going off someplace else to save my skin, wouldn't that be interpreted as a sign of panic, and wouldn't our adversaries jump at the chance to sow disarray and even defeatism in our ranks? We didn't have a solid enough reputation to run that kind of risk. It seemed too bad, but I would stay on in my hazardous Laurier and somebody else would take Saint-Jacques. But who? A candidate had to be chosen that very evening, and we still had nobody lined up except a couple of willing but wobbly hopefuls.

"Talk about bad luck!" complained Carpentier. "And such a swell riding!"

"Is there really nobody else we could dig up?" I asked him.

"There's so little time left. I can't see anyone. Unless . . ."

"Unless?"

"Unless," he said in an uncertain voice, "we take a chance with Charron. I know he's been dreaming of it."

So we sent for the shock-headed Claude, who in less than a minute was ready for battle.

"Do you think you can win the nomination in Saint-Jacques?" Carpentier inquired. "It's tonight, and you've barely got two hours to get ready."

"I don't need that," the phenomenon replied, "I'm ready now."

With that he tore out of there so fast he almost forgot his manners. He had already gone out the door when he did us the honour to recall our existence.

"Thanks a lot," he said with the absent smile of someone who is already far away.

The rest is history. Claude Charron won the nomination, then the election, both in a breeze, and demonstrated gifts that situate him, in my opinion, in the front rank of the greatest orators I have known. He was eloquence itself, the kind of speaker who *feels* his public and gets in tune with them, then, moving at will from emotion to humour, to rhetorical developments of unparallelled strength and precision, holds them spellbound as long as he wants.

Now that the Saint-Jacques problem had been settled, and mine, too, by the same stroke, all that remained was to hit the campaign trail in hopes of picking up at least a few seats. We weren't asking for the moon, but it seemed to us, since the battlefield was more crowded than usual, since there were a new Liberal chief, a newly improvised provincial wing of the Créditistes, and a seriously weakened Union Nationale, that we had some chance, however modest, of making a breakthrough.

What had weakened the Union Nationale was obviously, in the first place, the sudden, upsetting death of Daniel Johnson. But it was also the disastrous public style of his successor. Affable and plump, Jean-Jacques Bertrand turned in quite a remarkable performance as head of government just the same. His decisiveness contrasted rather well with the Hamlet-like hesitations Johnson was constantly caught up in. So he was able, in less than two years, to put through a whole string of important laws, ranging from the establishment of civil marriage to the creation of a Ministry of Public Service and a National School of Administration. Succeeding where others before him had always had to admit failure, Bertrand had also – paying heavily, but it was worth the price – persuaded the Legislative Council, our ridiculous little out-of-date senate, to sign its own death warrant.

He showed an equal brio in taking over international affairs, first by opening the Franco-Québécois Office for Youth that was to prove a most valuable meeting place for the rising generation. Then, although Ottawa had launched an offensive in charm and dollars in Francophone Africa after having ignored that area for years, he succeeded in assuring the presence of an officially recognized Québécois delegation, distinct from the Canadian, when some thirty countries met at Niamey in Niger to consider an association something like a French commonwealth.

But despite everything he didn't pass the ramp. As soon as he was unlucky enough to open his mouth in public, his good-natured charm vanished in an old-fashioned, boring discourse that all too often became tangled to the point of gibberish. That damn style of his – which doesn't necessarily make the man, no matter what they say – made him seem awkward and almost stupid.

Even more damaging was the obstinacy that plunged him into the most catastrophic of all bills on the most treacherous of all subjects, the school question. Bill 63 was a notoriously clumsy text. While claiming to "promote" French, it offered everyone, immigrants included, free access to the school of their choice, in other words eliminating any defence against anglicization. Like pouring oil on the fire, this error transformed a few centres of protest already worked up by linguistic fears into a widespread conflagration. Soon thousands of demonstrators were taking shifts day after day around parliament, while inside a combat of David and Goliath was taking place. Squaring off against the stubborn majority and a Liberal camp largely in cahoots stood a microscopic opposition called "circumstantial" because, among others, Yves Michaud had joined the group in a gesture of temporary dissidence, as well as Jérôme Proulx, a government member whose defection earned him immediate expulsion from the inflexible Bertrand, and a couple of other members who had jumped the fence. Promoted leader of this curious amalgam, I became for the first and last time in my life a past master at parliamentary procedure. Jacques Parizeau, who had just entered the executive council of our party, rushed to Quebec City to work behind the scenes in the role of Napoleonic strategist he had always fancied. With his help we spent entire evenings concocting all sorts of motions imaginable. Never had House regulations been tortured to such a degree, but since it was for a good purpose, we continued to paralyse parliament for two full weeks. Then one evening I found myself face to face with Bertrand, who, like me, had stepped outside to grab a smoke "behind the throne." It was a man with a drawn face and trembling hands who called me over.

"René," he said in a broken voice, "this can't go on. Stop it, for the love of God. Even my children refuse to speak to me." There were tears in his eyes.

"If you ask me," I replied, "it should be up to you to stop it."

"I can't," he groaned. "I promised."

He continued to make it a point of honour, whatever happened, to keep that thoughtless promise he had made to some Anglophone circle, and finally the execrable law was passed. But from that day on it was certain knowledge that the Bertrand government was on its last legs.

As soon as the campaign began, then, it wasn't hard to see that the Liberal Party was on the road to an easy victory. Lesage, who had become the target of particularly lethal knives – those that are planted in the back – had retired from the leadership some months before. Since Gérin-Lajoie also decided to leave at just the wrong time, the field had remained practically empty except for the same Robert Bourassa in whom, back in 1968, I had thought I discerned the obsessive dream that he was now on the verge of realizing.

On our side, we, too, were growing more and more confident that we would achieve our modest objective. Our fight against Bill 63 had bolstered our credibility with decolonized voters. In another direction, a little more grist had been brought to our mill by the incredible event that had taken place at the Estates General, where the delegates, who had voted in favour of every stage leading up to independence, grew frightened at their own temerity and at the last minute voted down a formal declaration of independence.

In Montreal a small but very distinct current in our favour was becoming perceptible and nothing proved it better than the hysteria spreading through certain milieux that dreaded us like the plague. For example, one morning reporters were awakened at dawn expressly to witness a convoy of Brinks trucks* fleeing to Ontario carrying away millions of dollars that were really nothing but paper transfers but were terribly real for simple souls. Toward the end of the campaign an obscure weekly, *The Suburban*, knew its hour of glory by issuing a call for civil war in case the PQ won more support than we hoped for!

On the French side of the metropolis these crazy reactions naturally had a boomerang effect. But everywhere else one could tell the effect was negative, hardening even more or allowing only a feeble relief from "the old ice of our fears and complexes, the winter of our Quebec impotence," which I went around the country condemning. Especially in Abitibi where the Créditiste Mr. Big, Réal Caouette, in a speech supporting his new provincial party, set the tone in these apocalyptic terms: "If you don't want a bloody revolution in Quebec," he fulminated, "don't vote for the Parti Québécois. Vote for our future, not for socialism, communism, revolution, and blood in the streets!"

Caouettism was the law of the land in those parts, so it's hardly necessary to say our business wasn't booming there. It was so bad, in fact, that I jumped at a chance to travel dozens of kilometres from Rouyn to "plot" with a single family who lived in the little village of Palmarolle, a name whose Mediterranean music still lingers in my ear. There were four of them in the house, husband and wife and a couple of neighbours. I spent two hours in their company and another hour to get back to Rouyn, and what was the harvest? On election night, April 29, I made a special point of

---

* The recent purchase of Brinks by the Desjardins Movement strikes me as sweet, though tardy, revenge.

getting news from Palmarolle. We had three votes, I think. Three out of four, not so bad after all . . .

That night, encouraged by the overflowing halls multiplying throughout Montreal but worn out by a last campaign swing through the electoral desert of my native Gaspésie, from the Iles-de-la-Madeleine to Rimouski, passing through Gaspé, Chandler, Bonaventure, Cap Chat, Matane, and Mont Joli, I had nothing to do but be a man, like the son in Kipling's poem: "If you can meet with Triumph and Disaster / And treat those two impostors just the same . . ."

The most difficult thing to swallow was the enthusiasm of the volunteers getting more and more excited on the ground floor as excellent results accumulated from the lower part of the riding, while on the floor above some few of us waited stoically to hear the bell start tolling in the upper, Greco-Italian part of Laurier. Luckily, the result wasn't too long coming, and after consoling the mourners to the best of my ability, I left to join the crowd and congratulate our elected members in the Paul Sauvé Arena.

The atmosphere was explosive: so much conviction, so many efforts, so many votes, too, and all for so little. "The powers of money and the status quo and most of the traditional props of our people," I myself had growled in my opening commentary, "have obtained the reaction they hoped for. . . ." Behind the tears a great wave of anger was mounting. If it burst, it wouldn't have far to go to reach its target in the west of the city. I was completely bushed and couldn't find words to defuse the tension. But finally, just as our first elected members arrived, beaming, on the shoulders of their supporters, an idea came to me.

"Don't you find," I asked the crowd, "that it's a defeat with an air of victory about it?"

The least I can say is that it was a trifle forced, but it met that need for joyful release that is often all the stronger when the deception has been cruel. And when I thought about it, we had, after all, made our breakthrough. From zero to infinity, that is, seven full-fledged MNAs: Claude Charron, Camille Laurin, Robert Burns, Guy Joron, Marcel Léger, and Charles Tremblay, all Montrealers, and then, the only one from outside, Lucien Lessard, elected in the North Shore, which would subsequently be our second stronghold.

In the metropolis, however, it was really miraculous. In the Francophone east on our first try we had carried a good half of the votes. If one subtracted the Anglo-Québécois vote, which we had learned to count as 95 per cent against us, we even came close on the heels of the Liberals on the national level. On their heels is perhaps a little excessive, but in popular esteem, yes, certainly. In terms of strict parliamentary accounting, however, we were far off the mark. With the help, among other things, of the brilliant slogan-mirage "100,000 Jobs," and above all helped by Jean-Jacques Bertrand, Bourassa got 72 out of 108 seats.

Thanks to riding distribution that continued to favour rural areas to the detriment of the cities, the Union Nationale with only 20 per cent of the vote and the Créditistes with 12 per cent both had more seats than us. But seeing that our seven would represent among them nearly 24 per cent of Quebec citizens, I could still justly proclaim: "At any rate, we're the ones who are the official opposition in public opinion!"

Mission accomplished, then, and besides, the ten-year lease I had given myself had just expired at the very moment the voters sent me politely back to private life.

During the summer I began to readapt by trying my hand at some daily writing and rigging out a few projects for September. I had reached that point when, one after another, two terrorist acts, one springing from little clandestine cells, the other emanating from the State itself, burst upon us that autumn.

33. Je me souviens

IT WAS SATURDAY, the tenth of October. I can see that beautiful day as though it were yesterday, the sun lingering on the horizon, its slanting rays hovering gently over Lac L'Achigan. We slowly walked up to Marc Brière's chalet overlooking the lake to listen to the six o'clock declaration by the provincial Minister of Justice, Jérôme Choquette (later nicknamed "Two Gun" because he always had at least one on his person). He was to reply in the name of the State to the FLQ ultimatum. As soon as he got into the meat of the subject, after a pompous introduction, it was clear that it was going to be a refusal, but that was hardly surprising on the part of a tough customer whose following remarks reflected less the opinion of his own government than that of Ottawa.

There was nothing to do but wait and see. The evening was still so beautiful we went back down to the tennis court at the water's edge to play another set. We hadn't finished the first game when an excited voice reached us from the chalet, shouting something incomprehensible.

"What is it?"

"They've kidnapped Pierre Laporte."

Should I admit that my first reaction was to find the little guys pretty nervy. They must certainly have been young, as in all those other FLQ cells that had succeeded each other during the sixties. But this time, instead of explosives that kill blindly, their acts, while still remaining inexcusable, gave a chance to life.

First to the life of James Cross, the British commercial attaché who had been kidnapped a week before. Communiqués broadcast on the radio had laid down a series of conditions for his liberation: the freeing of a score of FLQ members picked up after previous crimes, a "voluntary" contribution of $500,000, and a plane for Cuba or Algeria. Taking the initiative from the start, the federal government drew the line, calling it blackmail and saying there was no question of giving in, except on one point. The kidnappers had also demanded that the text of their political manifesto be broadcast. Taking advantage of a certain diversity of opinion still prevailing in Ottawa, Gérard Pelletier, by then Secretary of State, had displayed a sort of favourable indifference to the request.

"No objection," he had dropped disdainfully. "It can't do much harm."

That was a grave error. On Thursday, October 8, when the manifesto hit the airwaves, a multitude of Québécois found themselves implicated. They certainly had no sympathy for the call, in coarse language, for a revolution to "strip their power to harm from the professionals of holdups and fraud: bankers, businessmen, judges, and sold-out politicians. . . ." But on the other hand, the long list of grievances that preceded this conclusion was far from unfounded. That Quebec accounted for 40 per cent of unemployment in Canada, that it was impossible for too many of our people to earn their living in French, that the east end of Montreal had its hovels and the west end its châteaus, who could deny it? By personalizing its audience ("Yes, there are reasons why you, Mr. Lachance of Sainte-Margeurite Street, went to drown your bitterness, your despair and your rage in beer . . ."), the FLQ also demonstrated a sense of psychology of the masses that Trudeau himself would use a few days later. In public opinion this homegrown terrorism suddenly seemed closer, even almost congenial. It had succeeded in forcing from the authorities the right to say loud and strong what many people had merely been muttering under their breaths.*

---

* Gérard Pelletier, however, had imagined the manifesto would have little effect. In his unsparing account of these events, which I have drawn from freely, Jean Provencher explains this by referring to a theory elaborated by a university scholar on our "external elite," that is, politicians and bureaucrats who leave Quebec to take up a career in Ottawa. "Even for the most Québécois of Québécois . . . it only takes eighteen months in Ottawa cut off from his own people for him to lose his footing and cease to live in tune with the population. Such an out-of-phase Québécois finds himself in the midst of a foreign country dealing with problems that are not his own and beset by preoccupations that are generally the opposite of those experienced by his fellow citizens. So he turns up his nose at Quebec, which he no longer understands. . . . A quick look at the history of Quebec and Canada shows this statement to be true and reveals that the most implacable adversaries of Quebec politicians are not Anglophones but expatriate Québécois who stubbornly try to impose their views on those who still live in Quebec." Jean Provencher, *La grande peur d'octobre 70* (Montréal, 1974).

A great deal of confusion reigned in a great many minds, to the point where one could hear people saying they supported the "objectives" of the FLQ. I felt called upon, in one of the daily columns I had begun to write, to make this clarification: "These objectives, what are they? Revolution, anarchy, obscene insults? For those who opened themselves on the radio, it was in no way a question of such objectives, but only of a statement of the facts: exploitation, electoral iniquities, cultural frustration, etc." (*Le Journal de Montréal*, November 5, 1970)

I was more obliged than others to keep a cool head because the manifesto had taken the liberty of using me as a sort of witness: "We believed once," the manifesto read, "that it was worth the effort to channel our energies and our impatience, as René Lévesque explains it so well, within the Parti Québécois; but the Liberal victory shows clearly that what is called a democracy in Quebec is, and always has been, nothing but a democracy of the rich. . . ." Had these unknown authors effectively worked and voted for us in the elections? I strongly doubted it, but could one be sure? Not bothering themselves with such questions, our adversaries wasted no time in transforming the allegation into a certainty and then into a slanderous slogan which, travelling from mouth to mouth and chalked up on walls, for several months did us incalculable harm: "PQ = FLQ! PQ = FLQ!"

This coincided with the campaign of intoxication launched as soon as the second kidnapping had provided the pretext that had been so impatiently desired. From the start the federal government had been frenetically seeking a way to condition public opinion. A few hours after the manifesto was broadcast, for instance, an impressive military convoy had left Valcartier army base in the suburbs of Quebec City to move on a wartime footing to Sainte Thérèse north of Montreal. That didn't prevent the FLQ text from provoking what was called in high places "an erosion of popular will." But as soon as Pierre Laporte was captured, the federal government at once seized the occasion to act, while the Quebec government, which in panic had taken refuge in the Queen Elizabeth Hotel in Montreal, was showing signs of shock. That same evening coming back from Lac L'Achigan I learned by radio that Robert Bourassa wanted to meet the leaders of opposition parties. Camille Laurin, whom we had named parliamentary leader, was charged with this mission. He came back with a devastating picture: one whole floor sealed off by squads of police, a premier who was hypertense and not a little depressed at the same time, his staff hysterical. And things got worse the next day with the arrival of the pathetic letter from Pierre Laporte addressed to his "dear colleague and friend" who had the power of decision, he said, "over my life or death." This was followed by long debate. We were to learn afterward that Jérôme Choquette, still under the Ottawa boot, had threatened to resign if there were any signs of weakening! Finally, very late that night, Bourassa delivered himself of a curious declaration, so ambiguous that it was not impossible to see in it a vague intention to negotiate. Afterwards, all during the fateful week that followed, he and his government remained literally buried in isolation and silence.

Grasping at the glimmer of hope they thought they could perceive and which the designation of a negotiator seemed to confirm, some honourable and well-known citizens, Claude Ryan among them, embarked on a search for a solution. They were even ready, it appears, to envisage the perspective of a coalition government to strengthen backbones that seemed visibly yielding on the Quebec side. Together with the same Claude Ryan, I ventured to assemble a dozen or so persons so that we could tell Bourassa with one voice that if he was really looking for a non-violent solution, he could count on our "complete and rapid" support. At the same time another group, called Friends of Pierre Laporte, reminded the government of a fact that any responsible society must never forget: "It is up to the government of the people of Quebec to find solutions to our present problems, solutions that cannot be imposed either from Ottawa, Toronto, or elsewhere. . . ."

Alas, it was exactly from Ottawa, Toronto, and elsewhere that the final offensive burst forth without delay, its fury transforming Quebec for some time into a Gulag and responsible citizens into a panicky flock of sheep.

"Just watch me!" Trudeau had replied to journalists asking him how far he was willing to go.

. . . As far as barefaced lying anyway, and that's the least of it, for he claimed to see, for instance, in the few meetings I have just described, "a parallel power . . . that threatens the elected representatives of the people."

. . . As far as caricatural excess, and thus, because "lies from afar (from Toronto) are more convincing," we heard from the mouth of the Premier of Ontario, John Robarts, that terrorism in Quebec had turned into general war and the time had come to rise up and fight!

. . . As far as the alarming confirmation that the newspaper *The Gazette* obtained immediately of a *secret* RCMP report according to which the FLQ, in addition to more than 130 members in active cells, could count on some 2,000 reservists ready to be mobilized at will.

. . . As far as ridicule when Ottawa announced that it was increasing security measures "because of the climate of violence afoot in Quebec and an important arms robbery perpetrated . . ." Where? In British Columbia, 5,000 kilometres away.

It was a climate scientifically made jungle-like. Big shots hired bodyguards; students were in the streets; medical specialists (who had the bright idea to go on strike in the middle of the crisis) left in droves for Ontario and the U.S., at least that's what the president of the Canadian Medical Association said, sheltered by 500 soldiers, "protecting the nation's capital against terrorists." In a madhouse like this, as inevitably happens in such cases, the police take over the power and dictate to the members of government, who have lost control.

That's the only excuse, if it is one, that can be found for Jean Drapeau and Robert Bourassa reaching the point of calling for the military occupation of Quebec. The mayor of Montreal, who was in the middle of an election campaign, laid it on to the degree of declaring: "It is because a revolution is brewing that we have asked a superior level of government for help." Still hidden away God knows where, the provincial Premier at first sent out word in a laconic communiqué, soon followed by a letter that had previously received the *imprimatur* of Marc Lalonde, Trudeau's chief of staff.

Thursday, October 15: the day of shame had arrived, or rather the night, hiding whatever it chooses and dramatizing the rest. Trucks loaded with soldiers rolled down the streets, making the houses tremble. On the flickering screen Bernard Derome, an unknown face announcing a new era, came on every quarter of an hour asking us to stay tuned. After a long period of carefully manipulated suspense it was at last announced that *The War Measures Act* had been proclaimed, just like that, over the head of the House of Commons. Immediately, in the small hours of the morning, "all the police in the Montreal area charged, head down. . . . Given the right to break down any doors and arrest whomsoever they chose, they struck in almost every quarter. . . . On Boulevard Saint Joseph numerous people telephoned radio station CKAC saying they had seen handcuffed prisoners taken away by the police. It is impossible to give a list of the persons who have been apprehended during the last few hours. . . ." (*La Presse*, October 16, 1970)

This was easily understandable when one realizes that the list of people arrested, without warrant, on the strength of suspicions, prejudice, or pure idiocy, exceeded the incredible number of four hundred. Indiscriminately, union leaders, artists, writers, whoever had dared cast doubt upon official verities, or simply those the unleashed bloodhounds didn't like the look of, were thrown into the paddy wagons and put away. Deprived of all their rights, beginning with *habeas corpus*, a great many of them were to remain in custody for days and weeks. As much as if not more than in 1917, when there was at least the excuse not of "apprehended insurrection" but of a real world war, the whole of Quebec found itself behind bars as Trudeau and company now attempted to justify their act before Parliament, the existence of which they seemed just to have remembered.

Minister Jean Marchand had no fear of overdoing it: "We know there is an organization that has thousands of rifles and machine guns in their possession, and dynamite enough, about 2,000 pounds, to blow up the heart of the city of Montreal." O tremble, mortals!

Just think, added Trudeau, addressing his good citizens at the end of the day, "that these kidnappers could have taken anybody, you, me, or even a child . . . ." Then he repeated it for those who might not have got it first time: "Tomorrow the victim might be a bank manager, a farmer, a child." Using for his own ends the technique of the FLQ manifesto, he gave a whole series of human faces to the fear he was spreading around so it would reach even those whom he hoped to prevent from killing their captives, at the same time as they received a safe-conduct that Robert Bourassa had been permitted to offer *in extremis*.

It was what could be called nicely loading the dice: heads I win, tails you lose. If the hostages escaped alive, it would be the peaceful triumph of the sorcerer's apprentice who at the same stroke would have forced us Québécois back into our holes. If not, it would be proof that, whatever the "chicken-livered" and "bleeding hearts" said, the only response to terror is terror.

The next day Pierre Laporte was found strangled. The FLQ had made its choice, a barbarous, insane choice. One doesn't kill for a cause, whatever it is, so long as one is free to promote it democratically, even if for the time being democracy . . .

The wolves had been let loose. As always, the rabid sheep were even worse, and their wild bleating rose with the terrible unanimity of a collective nervous breakdown. Coming back home that night, skirting the dark little park near which the consulates stood, I saw threatening shadows everywhere. "With the intervention of the FLQ," wrote Fernand Dumont, "we didn't see blood running in the gutters as had been predicted, but fear, hatred and stupidity."*

Such paroxysms don't last long. The mind has its own instinct for survival. With the municipal elections of Ocotber 25, the FRAP (Front d'action politique), an opposition party that Jean Drapeau was bent on decrying as a wicked monster, disappeared without trace. To hear the Mayor berating those who "were preparing to install a revolutionary government," at the very moment he had been re-elected with fifty-two aldermen out of fifty-two, made it hard to take him seriously. That formidable tenacity he had brought to the service of the best causes, such as the realization of the Metro and Expo '67, which had made him the irreplaceable "Monsieur Montréal," was this time misapplied to a caricatural degree. But if one really thinks about it, that's where things began to get tragic again. Just how completely had we been had, after all?

Piloting that infamous law that bears his name through the House of Commons, John Turner had promised: "I hope that all the details of the information the government based itself upon before acting can one day be published, for until then, at all events, the population of Canada can never judge the action undertaken by the government." This was duly repeated in its own style by the honourable tape recorder in Quebec. It should be said in passing that in 1976 I tried to obtain this dossier that was supposed to "easily justify" everything. Needless to say, there was nothing to be found. Now, sixteen years later, the official line is, and has been for donkey's years, the response that Trudeau, speaking frankly for once, had begun to repeat endlessly: "The facts that motivated our decision are well known . . . and they are very clear facts."

Very clear indeed.

* Fernand Dumont, *The Vigil of Quebec*, translated by Sheila Fischman and Richard Howard (Toronto, 1974).

The headlong flight of medical specialists? Unless I am mistaken, none was absent when the National Assembly ordered them back to work.

The "parallel power" that led the wife of one minister to say that Ryan was "trying to overthrow the government"? A complete fraud.

The two or three thousand terrorists? In December, with Cross's kidnappers in exile and the assassins of Laporte locked up and their accomplices identified, they came to the grand total of some twenty-odd desperados.

The terrifying arsenal to blow up the heart of Montreal? At the beginning of the new year the government had to resign itself to provide the facts to NDP member Andrew Brewin: in the homes of the hundreds of persons arrested since October, the police had found thirty-one firearms (revolvers included) and twenty-one offensive weapons (hunting knives, machetes, bayonettes, and three smoke bombs). As for the mountain of dynamite, it was only a squib. . . .

It is meagre consolation, but on the essential points I hadn't been far wrong when, on October 16, at a time there was still hope that the worst might be avoided, I had dared make an analysis in which, without mincing my words, I had still tried to use my reason right through to the end.

Quebec no longer has a government.

The stump of a one we did have was swept away at the first really hard blow. Bourassa's cabinet has turned in its hand and is no longer anything but a puppet of the federal rulers.

It is now clear that from the very beginning of this tragic period marked by the kidnapping of Mr. Cross, this government has only had a bit player's role. During the pseudo-negotiations initiated last Sunday by Mr. Bourassa, we were, alas, obliged to conclude that it had accepted to serve simply as the instrument of a policy conceived and determined outside its control; that it played the card of compromise while knowing all the time about the intransigent stand that was being taken in Ottawa; that in fact it was preparing the present climate by letting the situation drag on and grow rotten while pretending to ponder what to do; and, finally, that last night it was this government that backed the extreme move of the Trudeau regime in placing the whole of Quebec under military occupation until next spring. . . .

Nor can we help thinking and saying that this degradation of Quebec was willed, very consciously by some, instinctively by others.

The determining factors of this conduct spring from two forms of extremism.

The first is very official and judicially legitimate, stemming from the federal Establishment and the forces, economic and other, that uphold it. That is the source of the first suggestions of the eventual use of every possible means, including military force, to contain Quebec and, if need be, to put her in her place.

This is the source, and has been for years, of the attempt to stifle all Quebec's aspirations, even the most moderately evolutionist, by drowning them in a swamp of learned committees, conferences, and eternal rebeginnings. Also, as we cannot help but see, it is from the very highest levels of this Establishment that orders are issued to promulgate propaganda, constantly, by every available means, to deform and caricature every aspect of, and every stand taken by democratic nationalism in Quebec, even to having recourse to the basest calumny in associating it with subversion and terrorism.

At the other extreme are those who have thrown themselves desperately, body and lost soul, into a career tragically contrary to the interests of our people. Let us hope they at least realize today that they have stupidly made themselves the forerunners of the military regime and the placing in peril of the essential rights of all Québécois.

We have said it before countless times, neither bombs, nor even less kidnappings, are morally, humanly, or politically justifiable in a society which, until yesterday, permitted the expression and organization of all kinds of desire for change, no matter how difficult this expression had been rendered by the vested interests of that society and the authorities who represent them. Such terrorism is a terrifying form of rootlessness, especially among members of the new, educated generation, and their most ardent impatience does not make it excusable. Nor will any of our numerous and terribly neglected socio-economic ills be healed thereby. . . . (*Journal de Montréal*, October 17, 1970)

Without forgetting Quebec journalists, who in the main, with whatever means they had, saved their honour by performing an impossible task honestly, I leave the last word to Fernand Dumont. With an irony made even more biting by his serenely objective tone, here is what he wrote some time after about the Ottawa clan:

"They are fond of saying that if the people disagree with their attitudes, they have only to kick them out at the next election. As a principle it is undeniable but inadequate; we had already said so, *along with Mr. Trudeau*, in the days when it was Duplessis who held legitimate power. Taken on its own, this principle could lead to the following: once elected, you can do whatever you want between elections."*

Yes, but even if one can't undo, at least one can regret such abuses and excuse oneself for them. Did any of the protagonists of the drama do so, particularly the Right Honourable P.E. Trudeau? Never, as far as I know. And has the federal Parliament, ridiculed and led like sheep, ever recognized its fault like other democratic bodies have after much less bloody errors? Again, never.

If I am not mistaken, of all whose good faith had been deceived, only the Conservative leader, Robert Stanfield, published a confession after several months, which I read in French in a little review appropriately named *Credo*. It ran approximately as follows: If it were to do again, I would not do it. But the pressure was so strong at the time that we couldn't resist. Besides, we were on the eve of elections in New Brunswick, and our friend Dick Hatfield would have had to pay dearly if we had resisted. . . .

Who cares what happened to Hatfield? It was certainly less surprising than what happened to us on February 8, 1971. In the riding of the late Pierre Laporte, and despite all the "PQ = FLQs," Pierre Marois of the Parti Québécois lost a by-election but managed to better his standing of 1970. The worst was over.

But *je me souviens*.

---

* Dumont, *The Vigil of Quebec.*

34. The Long March

FEBRUARY, 1971, TO AUTUMN, 1976: if one had to enter that forest of sixty-five months or some 2,000 days to clear out the brush and examine the trees in detail, there'd be no end to it. But don't worry, I'm not going to try it.

When I think back from the heights of memory, leaning out to cast an impressionistic look over what seems an interminable expanse almost six years long, how it shrinks all of a sudden! It's nothing more than a little grove undistinguishable from the immense forests rolling away before and behind it, much less than Pascal's instant between two eternities.

What's there to see? A sort of mist at first, floating over the whole countryside. An upside-down world, since that's the way it always is. But above all, a world squatting in its own mediocrity. Next door, in the capital of the Western world, lacklustre figures succeed each other on the throne: Nixon, meeting his miserable Waterloo in the files of Watergate; then Ford, colourless, odourless, tasting of old chewing gum; the legions returning gloomily from Vietnam; in the third Rome, my "comrade" Khrushchev (at last a tsar dead in his bed) replaced by Brezhnev, painfully hoisting himself into power to begin the valetudinarian period; in Peking, Mao dwindling and his legend with him, only to be reborn, purified, after his death, for the time being a living illustration of this judgement by De Gaulle, that other colossus of our times: "Old age is a shipwreck." As for Pompidou, De Gaulle's successor, sickness sinks him before his time, while in England . . . but is there still an England left while waiting for Mrs. Thatcher to come along and tweak Britannia's hair?

And what can be said of the Canadian sub-product, languishing from sea to sea, from the fogs of Halifax to the mists of Vancouver? One can say that once upon a time in those monotonous skies there appeared three doves, friends of the human race, who were transformed by the events of October into hawks inspiring fear, though they lost some tail feathers in the process. We had seen enough of them, or almost. Reduced to minority status in 1972, they hung on until Quebec helped put them back in the saddle again, and again paid dearly for it.

The Quebec they had so cruelly humbled might have had good reason to sink into the general morass, but this was not to be. The impression left by our overview of this northern forest is, on the contrary, one of persistent effort to catch up, of aspirations as stubborn as ever and still expanding. The new educated élites especially exerted pressure on the government, forcing it to pull itself together after its collapse of 1970. One remarkable minister, Claude Castonguay (I can find only one), used the opportunity to push social reforms that were to make a lasting impression and at the same time mounted guard over our national identity. He served in this capacity until he no longer felt capable of endorsing the corruption into which the government began to sink about 1973. Luckily, the civil service, a product of the Quiet Revolution, remained on the job and these loyal servants of the State kept the damage to a minimum.

Even if most of the time the effervescence of the sixties seemed only to be simmering on the back burner, it hadn't completely died out. Like things that happen on a deep level, though sometimes imperceptible it continued to work through society. Change continued, in every corner of the country, but even more in people's minds. Slowly but surely the collective project, which had sprung from the rich turmoil of the previous decade and which the setback brought on by federal abuse had in some respects given a second start, kept relentlessly gaining ground. Sovereignty and independence were not a reality, far from it, but those who persisted in mocking the idea would soon be laughing on the wrong side of their mouths.

Had we who had been custodians of the project during this crossing of the desert – so long to live through day by day, so short, however, when one looks back on it – had we been worthy of it? No more than one is ever worthy of a great cause that surpasses oneself. But the same cause also held us together, and without it that heterogeneous assembly called the Parti Québécois might have burst apart on many occasions. This was not true in parliament, where the small number of our members dictated a solidarity very capably captained by Camille Laurin for the first three years, then by Jacques-Yvan Morin, who took over from him as parliamentary chief in

1973. It was a tiny team that owed a great deal of its bite and efficiency to a tireless worker whose arrival in our ranks deserves special mention.

In 1970, two weeks after the election, I had come back to Quebec City to pick up my ex-MNA's baggage. Once this dreary task was over, I had grabbed a sandwich and was on my way to get the car when I heard a voice saying "Good luck!" and felt a hand on my shoulder. Turning around I recognized Louis Bernard, an assistant deputy minister, one of those busy young technocrats who always seem a bit distant and who was said to be one of Robert Bourassa's intimates.

"Good luck!" he repeated. "I just wanted to say it's no time to give up. The way I see it, the results weren't all that bad."

More surprised than comforted, I thanked him and left to join Camille Laurin, who, barely installed yet, was waiting for me accompanied by Jacques Parizeau, like myself a defeated candidate. The first item on the agenda was who to name as chief of staff. To back up our seven debutants we would need an experienced person for this post, a rare bird for a third party to find since it could neither offer much money nor, in all probability, much future. We were just on the point of giving up when I mentioned, without holding out much hope, my chance encounter of that afternoon.

"Ho-ho-ho!" laughed Jacques Parizeau in his inalterably self-assured way, "don't go getting ideas. Louis Bernard is something like Bourassa's alter ego!"

"Dr. Laurin," said the secretary entering the room, "telephone for you."

"It was Louis Bernard," said Camille Laurin coming back two minutes later. "He wants to see me about the subject we were just discussing . . ."

Parizeau wasn't laughing any more. The business was quickly settled and the new chief of staff explained his decision in terms that could be summarized as follows: "Bourassa would have liked to keep me, but I didn't have much confidence in his government and I told him so. Besides, I've been an indépendantiste for a good while now and it seems to me the time has come to do my part. I've talked it over with my wife and she agrees one hundred per cent. As for the money, we'll make do."

With several thousand dollars less than his salary as senior civil servant, he did make do until 1976, showing an enthusiasm and a capacity for work that were truly phenomenal, and after that, without ever hiding his colours, became one of the great servants of the State of whom Quebec can be proud.

As for the "militant" wing of the party, as everyone else liked to call themselves, things were much less simple. It wasn't easy to get over a first defeat, soon followed by another that at first sight seemed even more discouraging. The global image I have of all those national council meetings and congresses that followed is of so many stations of the cross. Twice condemned to prolong its stay in the opposition, marking time after having given its all, the party wasn't thick-skinned yet and was unavoidably subjected to internal strains that can even lead to dislocation. This is particularly true of a party working with ideas rather than with material interests. Moving from one crisis to the next, torn between the "purists" and the "vote-getters," trying to reconcile social priorities with national commitments and to maintain as stable a balance as possible between the parliamentarians always on the firing line and the long-distance runners working on membership and financing, we still felt, miraculously, in the midst of all these cross-purposes, that we were making progress. This was due above all to a handful of tireless apostles whose zeal was equalled only by their selflessness. They were now present in every riding, even in ones where we didn't stand a chance. Working patiently without ever being put off by the initial aridity of the soil, they managed during those years to de-Montrealize our party and give us solid roots in nearly every region in the country.

As for my own performance over this period, it seems to me to have been a saw-toothed affair. Beaten, then beaten again in the elections, asking myself every six months what I was still doing in this madhouse, I had finally consented, reluctantly, to accept a modest salary as one of the party's permanent staff. As a result, besides being hard up, I found myself in the abominable position of the man who is the employee of the people he is leading. Certain critics did not hesitate to rub this in, and I often became so ill-humoured I reached the stage where one realizes that one is quite hateful. There were complaints about this, but they put up with me all the same. On the hypothesis that the game I was getting into was worth the candle (which I'll let others decide), I owed my staying power to the unflinching support of a few close collaborators, and to the admirable equanimity of certain members of the executive of the party in calming storms. Among them I must single out Claude

Morin and Pierre Renaud, the former arriving from the upper echelons of administration where he was used to the exercise of patience, the latter from the RIN where he had learned to cut a cent into four parts and how to defend the treasury of a poor party with his life.

With that much as general background, I feel it would not be amiss to focus on some of the principal events that held our attention during this period. My choice, which is obviously arbitrary, singles out just one topic for each of these years. Lacking a personal diary, which I have never been able to keep except episodically, I have before me, together with scattered souvenirs, certain of my published opinions from those days. Not seeing anything in them I would disown today, I present them for whatever instruction they may provide, or at least for their aura of déjà vu.

1971: THE CONSTITUTIONAL PLAYOFFS

(It was the year of the grand finale . . . until the sombre resumption of talks in 1981-82. On the bargaining table, besides the eternal question of the amending formula, was the question of jurisdiction in the domain of social policies, a question that fifteen years have now rolled over, like water off a duck's back.)

February 1, 1971

Last Tuesday, January 26, I made an easy prophecy:

Mr. Castonguay will leave for Ottawa with this monument under his arm, I said, referring to the Castonguay-Nepveu report . . . he will laboriously lay claim to "if not exclusive, at least preponderate powers for Quebec," and he will come back empty-handed, as before.

It's done.

"Negotiations have broken off between Minister Castonguay and his federal counterpart, John Munro, over the question of social policies," Jacques Guay, correspondent for this paper, reported on Saturday, January 30.

"The governments of Ottawa and Quebec," added Marcel Dupré of *La Presse* of the same day, "were not able to reach agreement on the way to discuss the question!"

It was such an easily foreseeable failure after so many others that it's depressing to predict it without running the slightest risk, and fastidious to rub it in afterwards while waiting for the next one. But it must be done as long as Quebec goes on banging its head against the wall of this imprisoning regime and is satisfied to sit back idiotically and count its bumps afterwards.

P.E. Trudeau and his machine are rigorously logical on this point: a province is only a province and it can call itself "State" or "national homeland" as much as it likes, or give itself an Assembly also called "National," but it will never be more than a purely verbal shadow of the political entity it is not. And there is no question of letting it become half or three-quarters responsible as long as it claims at the same time to remain part of the federal system.

A veteran of the Ottawa scene, John Gray of the *Montreal Star*, pointed out in his own article on Saturday, January 30, the real and precise reasons why Ottawa is blocking any major increase of Quebec power in the social field or in any other:

"The administration of such programs from Ottawa both permits a certain income redistribution across the country and gives the federal government a visible presence. . . . Also, committing a further large portion of income tax to the provinces would deprive Ottawa of an important instrument of economic policy."

In other words, Ottawa clings to its power and wants to be visible, dominant, and unquestioned everywhere. It is either naive or cynical to think that anything is going to lead it angelically to reduce that power, that is, to act against its own nature, for the most basic characteristic of any established power in any age and under any regime has always been to extend power, never to give it up.

This evident truth, which most commentators and most of our traditional leaders refuse to see, was already accepted in the MSA manifesto of 1967:

"The current attitudes of the federal government, the painful efforts to understand made by opposition parties, and the reactions of the most influential Anglo-Canadian circles, all lead us to foresee more and more difficult confrontations. . . ."

(Months passed and we tried to forget until finally the super-game opened in Victoria.)

May 18, 1971

I am going to have to talk again shortly about the constitutional question, and it's not too terribly stimulating.

Dare I admit that, personally, I find it a subject that plunges me into the depths of boredom? Just like the language question, for that matter.

Let's get this straight: I'm not talking about language itself or about the obvious need for a national society to give itself, as much as possible freely and drafted by its own people, a framework of basic institutions that is to the collectivity what a charter is to a company and its shareholders.

But the Quebec language problem – a terribly localized problem, for it is shared by only a tiny handful of protracted or crypto-colonies and shackled minorities – is absurd. It's the problem of an idiom that is not at home in its own house, like a spineless landlord who lets himself be locked in the basement by noisy, self-confident tenants. And it will only extricate itself the day it stands up, mounts the stairs, and calmly takes over the living room and the kitchen, imposing its own recipes and its own choice of furniture and curtains. That day will never come through blows struck by slogans ("Priority to French, language of everyday, language of work,") or because of commissions of inquiry that go on scratching the epidermis when it's cancer of the will the patient is dying from. . . .

That day will come when we're at home in our own house and our language with us . . . like five million Danes in Denmark (which doesn't prevent a great many of them from also speaking English) or five million Finns in Finland (which doesn't prevent them from also speaking Swedish when necessary). . . .

It's the same thing for the constitution.

Two-thirds of the life of a man of my generation – since the centralizing ploys of Rowell-Sirois and the leonine arrogance of the wartime government – have been periodically punctuated, more or less heavily, nearly always uselessly, by the tug-of-war between Ottawa and Quebec, each seeing itself the "senior" government of our torn and tortured people.

It is in this rousing atmosphere that they are now preparing to leave for Victoria for the sixth game in the current series, started in 1967, of the constitutional playoffs, the dullest spectacle that has ever put an audience to sleep.

After six or seven years they are scheduled to take up again the far-fetched question of repatriating a colonial text 104 years old that journalist Guy Cormier described very well when he compared it to "a child born with only one leg, six pairs of eyes, a wallet in place of a heart, no ears, and very little brain." (*La Presse*, March 30, 1971)

This is the monster they want us to bring triumphally back from Westminster. But first they'll have to agree on what transplants, plastic surgery, and other desperate treatments they want to perform once they're stuck with it. So once again they're pushing an amending formula. . . .

"Miss Turner-Trudeau"

That's a facile title and it's a little out of style . . . it's just a peg to hang my memory on, I know it won't make my fortune.

But no matter what nickname you give it, or whether it's finally given an anonymous grave, the important thing for Quebec is that the amending formula concocted by the Trudeau regime and peddled by his travelling salesman, Mr. John Turner, die a natural death and become forgotten as quickly as the Fulton-Favreau one was in 1964.

That one at least had a brief brilliant career: under the name "Miss Fulfa" it suggested some kind of enticing striptease. . . .

Now here we are seven years later. Once again the head of a Quebec government has apparently been sucked in. Last February, at the time of those secret preliminary sessions with Mr. Turner, or perhaps even before, it was already evident that Mr. Robert Bourassa had let himself be inveigled into giving, if not an unequivocal "yes," at least a kind of "n . . . yes" good enough to get the others' hopes up. . . .

Which is why they are pushing so hard. Mr. Trudeau even went on television recently to declare that in actual fact Mr. Bourassa had endorsed the text that came out of the February conference. The Quebec Premier hastily denied this. It has reached the point where you don't know if it's one or the other, or perhaps both at once, who are trying to make monkeys out of us a couple of times a week. . . .

But, adds Mr. Bourassa, the formula is nevertheless "susceptible to lead to agreement. . . ." Putting the advantages it "might have" in parallel with "questions of substance like social security," he has been speaking about the possibility of some kind of bargain. That takes us right back to what Mr. Claude Ryan was talking about at the start, on the eighth of February last, as some "incredible package-deal." In other words, give me a big chunk of social security to keep Mr. Castonguay from growling, and let me seem to be a bit of a champion, and then maybe I'll swallow the formula.

No citizen the least aware of the fundamental interests of Quebec could condone the dangerous temptation of such political simplemindedness.

For a federalism of the "special status" kind, this represents a closing of the door on any major extension of Quebec powers, since in the future decisions will have to be sanctioned first by Ottawa and five other provinces. Farewell to Quebec's aspirations!

(The final consummation: Robert Bourassa, O wonder of wonders, has at last condescended to speak clearly, and it's "No!" English Canada is grumbling . . . and understands.)

June 25, 1971

Reading the Toronto papers yesterday, I was struck by the kind of surly resignation that emanated from all of them. "Bourassa backs down before a few reactionary intellectuals." (What happened to the "wonderful" little fellow he was in October?) What difference does it make anyway? "The average French Canadian is not much interested in constitutional games." (Freely translated: with a little effort we'll overtake them as usual at election time!). . . .

But, basically, the commentators seem to lack conviction, for Liberal credibility has gone down the drain. On Wednesday the title of the *Toronto Star* editorial read: "Separatists rejoice – Bourassa's 'No' is ominous for Canada." The Ottawa correspondent, commenting on "the dead-end of constitutional revision," with realistic lucidity arrived at the following conclusion:

"[Nationalist] pressures are increasing all the time as the politically conscious young French-Canadians educated during the sixties climb towards positions of power. . . . In English Canada there seems to be a growing feeling that Quebec is hell-bent for separation and a willingness to let it find its own way there. This undercurrent was evident among English-speaking delegates at Victoria. . . ."

As for the *Globe and Mail*, it lets its Ottawa correspondent, Stanley McDowell, spell this out in black and white:

"Mr. Bourassa has reluctantly become the first Quebec premier . . . who can hold out to his people no convincing hope that constitutional bargaining will bring Quebec all the powers it has been talking about since the early sixties.

"That door may always have been closed, but a succession of Quebec premiers based much of their political strategy on making it seem open. . . . Ottawa can claim success in closing a door on the special status school of Quebec Nationalists whose aims it has always seen as a disguised or unconscious form of separatism.

"The undisguised separatists who know what they want, want it now, and say so, are multiplying behind another door. There is no democratic way that door can be locked."*

. . . In short, as you said to Mr. Bourassa: it's your play, Mr. Trudeau! (Alas, they got us in the end after all.)

1972: THE COMMUNISTS WOULDN'T DO THAT

July

Here we are in Paris. For the first and the last time the party has the means to send me as a delegate to France, accompanied by Bernard Landry. We look up Louise Beaudoin, who already knows everybody and proves it by fixing up three or four meetings a day . . . in the best restaurants if possible. Admiral De Gaulle invites us to Chez Voisin. He's a timid man, not like his father, but he seems to be a good sort, and so faithful to the overwhelming memory. Chez Drouant, next door to the Goncourt's literary salon, it's Jorgensen's turn. He's one of the big shots in the French Foreign Office and will surely be a good friend. A small problem arises, however: he hasn't really invited us, and we only have a travel budget of $2,500 for the whole trip. Just before the bill comes we have to invent an urgent rendezvous and, all three crowding into the microscopic elevator, take French leave like the freeloaders we are. . . .†
On the other hand, our encounter with Michel Rocard is one of equal to equal, for the Socialist Party he represents isn't any richer than the PQ. He receives us without show in his proletarian basement in the suburbs. He's bubbling over with vitality and is as informal as a Québécois. . . . He'll go far.

I also see Yves Michaud again. For him, as for Louise Beaudoin, and they'll have a chance to show it very helpfully one day, Paris is a

---

* *Le Journal de Montréal*, February 1, May 18 and 19, and June 25, 1971.

† This same man, today a French ambassador, was victim of a scam some years later in which he was supposed to have been involved with us in some shady international money deals. Our cut was said to be in the neighbourhood of $50,000. If only we'd had one-tenth of that sum, plus the excellent lunch!

second home. That's presumably one of the reasons, now he had broken his pan-Canadian ties, that he has decided, he tells me, to drop his career and take the plunge with us.

And last but not least, a stopover at the central of the Labour Confederation, where, since they don't hide their political affiliations, we find a Communist MP waiting for us as well as several members of the permanent staff. And straight off, right in the middle of the presentations, it's the Communist cold shoulder.

"So you come from Quebec? That's the oddball country where they throw union leaders into prison, isn't it?"

It had happened, what, two or three months ago. The Common Front had closed the hospitals, not only closed them but mounted siege on them. I had seen Red Cross trucks stopped at "security" barriers and forced to turn back with their deliveries of plasma, maintenance workers turned away, too, and visitors begging passes to go and see sick relatives. The courts had ordered an end to the strike. When the three union leaders defied the court order, they were sent to prison at Orsainville . . . with weekend leave. Inhuman repression, that's what they called the sentence far and wide, and the news had got as far as Paris.

"Unfortunately, it's only too true," I replied. "They did a spell in jail. But, by the way, tell me, how do you orthodox Marxist-Leninists and proponents of class war deal with hospitals?"

"With hospitals?"

"Yes, when there's a general strike, for example, what role do the hospital unions play? Seeing as work stoppages seldom last more than twenty-four or forty-eight hours, do you order them to shut down the hospitals?"

"Never on your life! We just ask them to supply a few bodies to carry placards in the demonstrations. It would really be too stupid to close the hospitals. That would stir up public opinion against us."

"Well, here's what happened in Quebec . . ."

After our account the astonished representative of the extreme left preferred to change the subject.

1973: THE BUDGET OF YEAR I

late October
This time we won almost one-third of the votes instead of the bare quarter of 1970. But at the same stroke we lost a seat in parliament!

Now we had only six out of 108: 5 per cent representation for 31 per cent of the vote. Ever since the defeat of Lesage in 1966, despite his winning a popular majority, the dangerous absurdity of voter distribution has never been so clear. Now is the time to demand more strongly than ever some form of proportional representation, even if excellent political scientists like the late Jean Meynaud tell you, with a certain cynicism, "Don't let it worry you. One day the shoe will be on the other foot, and it will be your turn to profit from it." As it is, with our six elected members we are the *official* opposition. When our turn comes . . .

But in the meantime, it's a pain in the neck. Some are already immersed in the classical exercise of post-mortem. Whose fault was it? It was the fault of the "Budget for the Year I," so they want Jacques Parizeau's hide. Several of us have to act together to calm the pack down and remind them that we were all in favour of that project, and that it was even approved unanimously. But when things go wrong, the first thing to be thrown overboard is solidarity. It can always be put back together again piece by piece, since it must be . . . after people have happily massacred each other. . . .

And yet that darned budget was perfectly logical, and even quite conservative. Basically, it was a pedagogical instrument designed to counteract if not cure one of the most pernicious economic aspects of our old inferiority complex, you know, the complaint that's always served up whenever we're just the family together: "A sovereign Quebec? Impossible. We're not capable. We'd never have what it takes." Of course, this means we'll just have to go on being propped up by Canada, which is exactly the way they want us to think, and they can always find uprooted French Canadians ready to prove it to us, like Trudeau himself when he began to worry about saving his skin when the end of his term was coming up. He laid it on shamelessly and thus betrayed the extremely low esteem he holds us in. I jotted down one of his remarks that's so simplistic it's insulting: "Quebec pays about 26 per cent of Canadian taxes," he said, "whereas the federal government pays the province something like 30 per cent of family allowances. . . ."

Lucky Québécois! A big 4 per cent to the good! – as long as the rapid decline in birth rate isn't registered in the budget. But what's the use of talking about that? As with children, we should stick to simple statements and, above all, not go complicating things by reminding them that nothing is crookeder than using one isolated budget item like this.

For its 26 per cent contribution in taxes, for example, what was the Quebec part of old age pensions, or of the billion-dollar wastage of defence spending, or of a Ministry of Trade and Commerce perpetually obsessed with Western wheat? . . . In short, what is our *global* return for being tied to the federal government? Like La Fontaine's dog, will we at least get a good pittance for being tied up? The official figures that Mr. Robert Bourassa has just made public show that Quebec is very probably a loser right down the line, particularly if one takes into account, beyond any apparent sharing, the astronomical cost of double administration, the interference of measures that are incoherent and often contradictory, and the incalculable loss of time and energy.

But let's return to family allowances just long enough to listen to the final little refrain, every bit as repugnant as the kind of fears that were being sown in April and October, 1970.

"If Quebec took over control it would be children, old people, and the needy who would suffer. . . ."

Isn't it clear as crystal that with the same money, which is our own anyway, Quebec would necessarily forget to look after these unfortunates who are watched over by the Good Lord in Ottawa? For is it necessary to say that Quebec is evil and backward? No, it's much better just to insinuate it. . . .

But what in God's name have we done to deserve such indignities?*

That was the reason for the budget: to reply to those who were holding us down in the shit, because they despise us, and who will despise us all the more as long as we let them go on holding us down in the shit! We explained all this without pulling any punches in our last manifesto: "We must present a budget project for an independent Quebec that will clearly show the falseness of the image the federal government is trying to spread, namely that the multitude of subsidies paid to Québécois come to them as gifts from the rest of Canada. In fact, Québécois themselves are paying for this so-called 'charity' without being aware of it. . . ."

Well, now there are thousands more who realize what's going on, and they won't forget it. We have to believe it was worth the price, but it cost us plenty: Jacques Parizeau, Claude Morin, Camille Laurin, Pierre Marois, and Bernard Landry and ninety-one others

* *Le Journal de Montréal*, June 23, 1972.

beaten in the elections. And me, too, need I add. And also poor old Michaud, who will be missing the opening of parliament. . . .

But he'll have plenty to keep him busy. He has convinced us to start a newspaper, a daily, if you please, to be called *Le Jour*. We haven't got a cent, but at last we'll have our own paper! All we have to do now is find a way to make it live.[*]

1974: FROM 63 TO 22 WHILE WAITING FOR 101

Big surprise! In May the Bourassa government at last decided to make a move on the linguistic front. It immediately drew fire from both sides. For Anglophones Bill 22 was a horror. By making French the official language, for the first time it established their status as a minority, and a shrinking one at that since immigrants' children whose language was neither French nor English were henceforth required to go to French schools. The only exceptions were children who could demonstrate "a sufficient knowledge" of English. So tests were imposed on little shavers six and seven years old isolated from their parents who were boiling mad at the whole business. Without going quite that far, I wasn't very hot on the plan myself. Did I tell Robert Bourassa as much in one of those interminable consultations he liked to cook up and which he deigned invite me to just before picking up this particular hot potato? I don't remember. One thing is certain, my reaction was not the same as that of the hardliners from the Mouvement Québec Français, which boiled down to one word: betrayal.

If one thinks back to sad old Bill 63, the "free choice" Bill that Jean-Jacques Bertrand left in heritage to his successor, and recalls the fact that the Liberals are the "English party" and that Bourassa's government reflects this amply, I consider that for once the Premier showed real courage.

---

[*] And we did – much longer than *Métro-Express* and *Le Nouveau Journal*, which gobbled up the millions of the Brillant and DuTremblay families – thanks to a team that knew how to turn out a good combat journal before sinking into the suicidal experience of auto-administration. Among all those who contributed, I'd like to single out three persons whose talent and integrity situate them at the very top of my list: Evelyne Dumas, Paule Beaugrand-Champagne, and Alain Pontaut, without forgetting our priceless Michaud who, begging support here, keeping the printer patient there, spent two years directing this lay version of the multiplication of loaves and fishes.

For that matter, his proposed Bill wasn't so different from our own way of looking at things. Even in 1976 the résumé of our election platform followed the same general lines, though more insistently:

> In everyday life, at work, at school, in leisure activities, and in all the services they receive, Quebec citizens must feel at home and must be able to assert and fulfil themselves following their own nature and identity.
>
> Under a Parti Québécois government French will therefore become the only language of the State, municipalities, school commissions and all public institutions, social welfare agencies, and outdoor advertising.
>
> In all businesses collective agreements will be negotiated and drawn up in French and it will be obligatory for communications between persons affected by collective agreements and their administrations to be conducted in French.
>
> But this presupposes as well that the teaching of the language in our own schools, and even in English schools, be seriously re-evaluated and improved.

You will notice, as I do myself with a certain astonishment, that the language of advertising didn't seem to us to be worth making a big fuss about. If it has caused so much ink to flow since, and has remained, to quote R. Bourassa, "a bloody big headache," it's because Bill 22 was allowed to turn into such a sad farce in this regard. It had been planned that outdoor advertising would be at least bilingual, with French holding priority status. But the follow-up on this provision was to all intents and purposes non-existent. Here, as in other cases, political will quickly crumbled, and unilingual English signs continued to appear shamelessly on many facades, including those of some of the most arrogant big companies.

As always happens when a law is permitted to be trampled underfoot like wastepaper, one risks seeing the question resurface some later day with serious consequences.

1975: ONE CASE OUT OF MANY

(But it was in highly visible hanky-panky rather than in foolish muddle that the Liberal government was preparing its own demise.

Here is an example from the holiday season that describes in a nutshell the insatiable appetites of little states within the State.)

December 23, 1975

Just A Hint Of Graft

When the names of those honourable companies that are the exclusive furnishers of jugs and bottles to the Quebec liquor board (Société des Alcools du Québec) are mentioned in the press, one word comes up repeatedly: "listing."

I have never seen a satisfactory French translation that renders the word "listing" with eloquence, clarity, and precision. Not being up on the internal jargon of the SAQ, I don't know exactly how they'd describe it . . . embezzlement, perhaps? At any rate, that's the only adequate synonym I can come up with.

A "listing," naturally, is the making of a list of brand names at the foot of which appears the name of the intermediary through whom you have to pass to get your products into the SAQ: Polarin Inc., Desautels Ltd., Société Générale d'Importation Inc., etc., etc.

And if you have to pass through these little operators whose appetites may be incorporated but are certainly not limited, it's obviously no free ride. It costs something. And if it costs, the additional and perfectly parasitical markup gets stuck onto the price the consumer has to pay (or else it would disappear from treasury profits.) In short, all these nice little wards of the State are getting fat doing nothing at the expense of us citizens.

On top of that, it's perfectly evident that in order to bleed the public this way what's needed is the kind of ministerial backing that puts them beyond question, to be specific, the support of the Ministry of Finance, or its close associates, upon which the SAQ depends. Now, it's that very same Ministry of Finance that has been recently swearing up, down, and centre that it hasn't "obliged" anybody to go through any particular channel. As if it wasn't enough that the thing should be delicately indicated, suggested, whispered. And in the same breath, without cracking a smile, the same ministry has been broadcasting how proud it is of the "reforms" it has put in place over the last couple of years. Doubtless the bookkeeping on graft is more carefully done (with fewer traces) than before.

Yet it should be possible for the government and the State to extract themselves from such gerrymandering, which has caused their credibility, already terribly undermined, to sink even lower. Does Mr. Bourassa think for a minute that anyone takes him seriously when he tells us, to fend off further questions, that, parasite for parasite, he prefers his own to somebody else's?

The only real solution, once and for all, would be to draw up the full picture of this big folkloric patronage scheme and then, having exposed it, make a firm commitment to get rid of it, giving the SAQ back its normal task of dealing, under correct administrative supervision but without artificial intermediaries, directly with the producers of wines and spirits. And if it turned out to be impossible to assure the integrity of the monopoly under these conditions, then the State would have to think seriously about getting out of the business, while still maintaining the tax revenues it collects.

Only this would give us, will give us, a government that would not, will not, be immersed up to the neck in the present system. *

* *Le Jour*, December 23, 1975.

VII

FIRST TERM OF OFFICE

"The government of a country is not the nation, still less la patrie."
LACORDAIRE

---

35. That Night, Something Like a Great People

IZZIED AND DISHEVELLED, we had finally managed to work our way through the uncontrollable mob spilling out of Paul Sauvé Arena and spreading its frenzy into the streets. As soon as the result of the election had been confirmed, a group of athletic young men I had never seen before surrounded me and drove, wedge-like, through the crowd, dragging me with them. We moved so fast I barely had time to shake the hand of my son, Claude, whose look betrayed as much commiseration as joy, and then Corinne and I and the few members of our team whose legs still held up were piloted out a side door where two black automobiles were waiting. The leader of the unknown squad barked a brief command: "Everybody get in!"

We were shoved aboard, the doors slammed, and turning toward me the leader signalled me to duck down.

"You'll have to hide, Mr. Lévesque, because if they see you we'll never get out of here."

Doubled up in the back seat I couldn't see anything, but I could hear excited voices ragging us and the thuds of placards bouncing off the roof. When I finally did raise my head I saw in the front seat a very young man whom the others were staring at suspiciously. In his embarrassment his hand slid toward his pocket. Immediately the leader moved as if to pull a gun. Realizing this, the youngster whined: "Hey, listen, it's not my fault. I was just standing there trying to get into the arena, when all of a sudden somebody says, 'Everybody get in!' So I got in. But all I want now is to get out. Please, drop me at the next corner."

And that is how, on the night of November 15, 1976, I made my first acquaintance with the role of premier and with the escort that was from then on to control the limits of my liberty. At that particular moment, I, too, would very much have liked to get out at the next corner. . . .

But it was too late. The "miracle" had happened. I had three pieces of paper I had been scribbling notes on since that morning, and "miracle" was the only one I hadn't written anything on. There was nothing much on the one headed "defeat" either, by which I meant another smattering of seats as in 1970 and 1973. I had really only been thinking seriously about "victory." Except for my "burnt-child" prudence that made me underestimate the extent of our success ("we hope to break the sound barrier and get a minimum of thirty seats"), I remain quite proud of the analysis I had made of the situation a few weeks before in an interview with Jean Paré for the magazine *L'Actualité*:

"You say electors consider you more and more as people who deserve to take power. In your opinion which districts seem most favourable to you?"

" . . . Except for the Anglophone bloc in west Montreal, I don't see any region where we're not ahead of the Liberals. We're running at between 35 and 40 per cent."

"You've said that before!"

"Apart from the natural optimism dictated by election campaigns, I've never said what I'm saying this year. You can check it out. The Union Nationale is a nuisance element that is mainly going to hurt the Liberals. . . . If they pick up the 20 per cent they'd like to get and don't give up the ghost, we're home free. . . ."

Give or take a little, I was right on. Enraged by Bill 22, which they nevertheless scoffed at every day of the week, and incapable of voting for the "separatists," Montreal Anglophones switched to the Union Nationale in sufficient numbers to ensure the "miracle." This was the way they made Robert Bourassa pay for what they considered a betrayal, though it had really been the most courageous act of his two terms of office, which just goes to show that in this imperfect world one has to be prepared to be punished for one's good deeds.

Since there is also an element of justice inherent in every defeat, however, and since a defeated government almost invariably deserves to lose, if only because it's been around too long, it must be said that the Liberals had really been asking for the good thrashing French Quebec administered them. And to use the old cliché that covers electoral upsets, it was really time for a change.

It wasn't just a question of six years of wear and tear, but of general rot that had spread into too many sectors. Its sickening odour found an illustration in the public mind with the "tainted meat" scandal, the widespread sale of beef unfit for human consumption that had taken years to uncover. For the past three years a hypertrophic majority of 102 seats out of 110 had at the same time engendered a great deal of frustration among many MNAs who in the normal course of events would have stood a chance of a ministry but who now had to wait in vain. As well, that majority encouraged appetites so numerous and so insatiable that the administration seemed little short of a free-for-all. From the more-or-less profitable concessions of Loto-Québec attributed to more-or-less deserving parasites to nominations of judges and attorneys, to the granting of the least little contract, we had witnessed an exploitation of public funds as bad as the most indecent practices of the past. Even the Olympic catastrophe of that same summer, which an honourable commission of inquiry was to lay entirely at Jean Drapeau's doorstep, was also largely attributable to the stupefying negligence of a government that could not have ignored the fact that sooner or later it would have to pick up the pieces.

It had reached such a point of unconsciousness that the Premier himself was caught out in a radio debate that opposed the two of us at the beginning of the campaign. Knowing he was very proud of his image as an amateur economist, we anticipated that he would try to trip me up in this field. It so happened that our paper, *Le Jour*, had finally gone down, due to overzealous auto-administration, and had been forced into an honest liquidation. Just in case, I asked to have a rejoinder prepared if questioned on this subject, and told Claude Malette, our researcher emeritus who was to be with me in the studio, to pass it over to me if I stretched out my hand.

"Some people claim to be capable of governing Quebec," snickered my opponent, "and they can't even run a miserable little newspaper!"

He had fallen into our trap. I stretched out my hand, he saw the gesture and the note Malette passed me, his eyes clouded with anxiety, and he lost track for a long moment.

"Some people," I replied, "aren't even capable of running their own party's miserable Reform Club and have just put it up for bankruptcy in very fishy circumstances. That's even more bothersome, wouldn't you say, Mr. Bourassa?"

Bagatelle for bagatelle. Bourassa's own assistant, that cheerful cynic Jean-Claude Rivest, gave me the thumbs-up sign to say I had just scored: 1–0. Right up to the end the Liberal campaign followed this drift, running the gamut from imprudence to panic to full flight. When he had only used up three years of his second term and everything seemed to indicate he would be better off to wait, why did Bourassa go sticking his neck out like this? I still wonder today. Was it excess of confidence, typical of the man who is prematurely lucky? A little, no doubt. Did he hope to surprise us, as the saying goes, with our pants down? Very much so. But, unless I am wrong, he was mainly motivated by a well-justified fear stemming from a budget situation that was extremely worrisome, one that had been developing covertly since the first shock of the oil crisis and which he had no wish to reveal until after his re-election.

Whatever it was, the Liberals kept on multiplying their errors, as almost inevitably happens when one feels things going from bad to worse, while on our side we ran an impeccable campaign, due principally to a feeling of serene invincibility that put the wind in our sails. For instance, we had prepared a list of our immediate "commitments" in an election platform that was concrete and solidly structured. Every item took the Liberals by surprise, forcing them to split hairs or, even better, to display their paucity of ideas by borrowing ours. It was also a very happy surprise to see, from one district to the next, the exceptional quality of a host of new candidates, even among eleventh-hour recruits who are generally considered simply to be stopgaps.

Yves Bérubé was one of these. A native of Matane but a long-time resident of Quebec City, this young university professor and distinguished scientist had humbly offered his services to Claude Morin . . . to paste up election posters! For this job he had invented a glue that was so adhesive that years afterwards it was still sticking! In Matane, which, like so many others, had suddenly become one of our "good" ridings, the projected candidate had left us in the lurch at the last minute. That invariably happens on the eve of a battle reputed to be difficult if not impossible to win, and in this case the timorous soul had plenty of time to regret his decision afterwards. A propos, I remember a delicious anecdote of Daniel Johnson's after his unexpected victory of 1966. Some of the notables who had dropped him flat, hopping onto the victory wagon a little late in the day, came around to beg him to "retire" some of the elected members to make room for them! Well, we were stuck with this no-show candidate a few hours before the close of nominations when, as a last resort, someone remembered Yves Bérubé, the displaced Matanais who perhaps would . . . I was persuaded to telephone him, but it was a woman's voice that answered, in a tone something less than enthusiastic.

"You gave me a bad night there," the victim reproached me, calling back the next morning.

"If you can stand to run an additional risk," I replied, "you'd better get down to Matane before tonight."

"Okay. But on one condition: you've got to come to one of my meetings."

At the risk of my life I kept my promise, and in our little campaign aircraft piloted by my friend Aurèle Dionne, a real breakneck northern bush pilot, we scraped past the Gaspé cliffs and landed in a raging storm, shaving a few rooftops on the way down. It had been a fruitful flight just the same, because between his chattering teeth the irreplaceable Jean-Roch Boivin, a former candidate from the lean years and now our legal and political adviser, had helped me jot down the ABCs of the very important commitment we were to make in the field of automobile insurance.

Soaked to the skin and tired to death, we entered the crowded hall at the precise moment our catapulted candidate was starting his speech. We hadn't many illusions: how the devil could he be accepted by the public on such short notice? Well, believe me, from forestry questions to mining problems, and from tourist potential to the decay of the back country, not only did he have an astonishing grasp on every dossier but he also possessed the art of painting a lively picture of the situation and, more surprising still, showed an easy familiarity with people who a month earlier had been unaware of his existence.

As for me, I told myself, there's an MNA-to-be who'll perhaps make an outstanding minister one day. But then I superstitiously chased the thought away for future reference. (And now, anticipating, I hasten to add that behind those thick glasses and that curious little goatee, as behind that sometimes pushy self-assurance that hides a modest and passionate seeker after truth, was one of the most remarkable politicians I have ever worked with, a man who, I hope, will one day want to give himself once again to the service of his fellow citizens.)

So in Matane as elsewhere "victory" became assured. Formerly so hostile, this land suddenly became as fertile as during the best seasons of the sixties, bearing a rich harvest, ripening by the hour under the grey November sky. Nothing revealed this better than the way our adversaries were behaving. The dollar, which had levelled off ridiculously far above its American counterpart, had the misfortune to lose a third of a cent in the very last days of the campaign. Bourassa jumped to hold us responsible and, declaring that *la patrie* was in danger, demanded an emergency debate on the poisonous monetary consequences of separatism. I refused categorically to take the bait (which was really poison) and set off on a final campaign swing that, as luck would have it, saw us leaving Trois-Rivières at the same time the Liberal chief's airplane landed. When our party crossed the path of that ineffable Jean-Claude Rivest, I couldn't help poking a little fun at him.

"So how are things in the Cassandra camp? I have the vague impression that playing with fear is less and less effective. The last monetary bombshell sort of fizzled out, didn't it?

"Ho-ho!" laughed the loyal sceptic, "it's just too bad if we run up against the law of diminishing returns!"

On the night of the fifteenth, our victory was confirmed within an hour. When the TV announced we had carried Deux-Montagnes, where the strong Anglophone minority had led us to write it off as a "lost" riding, Michel Carpentier turned to me. "You'd better do a little thinking about the 'miracle,'" he said.

Shortly after, it was announced that we had indeed won the election. Not able to believe my eyes or ears, and incapable of finding a single word to put down on the blank page, I went into hiding while waiting to hear what fate held in store for me in my own riding.

Finally, one of the last as usual, I was told about the second miracle. I, too, had been elected. Even me. It was really a sweep then! After a five-minute stop in a hall so incandescent with excitement I wasn't able to thank the electors of Taillon as I would have liked to, we painfully forced our way to the Paul Sauvé Arena, and then, even more painfully, to the stage at the back of which, in big exuberant numbers, were displayed the almost final results. We had won 71 seats and the Liberals had lost exactly the same number. It was more than a sweep, it was a tidal wave, breaking in from everywhere to carry away the joyful crowd of adults laughing with tears in their eyes, children perched on their shoulders thrilled and amazed at this political Christmas party, the fleur de lys floating triumphally over the sea of faces, all our veterans elected and re-elected, crazy artist-types welcoming the poet Gérald Godin, who had just tasted sweet revenge by defeating the man who had him locked up in October, 1970. . . . But there was nothing mean about it; it made you think rather of a very pure, hot first day, the "beginning of a new age" we were singing about without really daring to believe it was true.

It was so strong that, forgetting for a moment the weight that was already beginning to bear down on me, I did find words that were truly new, words that weren't really my usual style at all and that must have come from beyond my own thoughts, or most probably were dictated by that collective unconscious palpitating out there before me.

"I've never been so proud to be Québécois! We're not a little people, we're closer to something like a great people!"

Beyond that instant, I thought I could make out the form that the project we had extracted from our old dreams would take in reality some day in the not-too-distant future. Everything seemed possible . . . even probable . . . and, why not, assured! Hadn't Félix Leclerc in his song "The Night of the 15th of November" tallied "six million greetings from the two sides of the river"? And Gilles Vigneault chimed in with: "I hear you, tomorrow, talking of liberty. . . ."

Tomorrow, alas, is perhaps a figure of speech, but as someone once said, the future lasts a long, long time. . . .

For the time being, and for tomorrow in the strict sense of the word, we had to get our feet back on the ground and, trying to look fresh and rested, start tackling the innumerable demands on our time, the urgent as well as the trivial (the barber, the new suit, the "image") that would never taper off from now on.

But first, as is customary, I had to go and salute my predecessor. I don't know what ordinarily takes place on such occasions since it only happened to me once. . . . Robert Bourassa was waiting for me on the seventeenth floor of the Hydro-Québec building, the same floor where, as Minister of Natural Resources, I had been the first politician to move in with my tiny office and a reception area more modest still. When the Montrealer Daniel Johnson became head of government, he took over space all around this, creating a domain I now found myself a little lost in.

Tired, but relaxed and apparently relieved, the retiring Premier had no earth-shaking revelations for me. What comes to mind are mainly impressions. He had been beaten in his own riding. Did he hold it against me for having, ten years earlier, recommended that he choose the grassroots Francophone riding of Mercier rather than the Town of Mount Royal, where a Liberal can be ineradicable, even though he has no roots there? I was sure he didn't, for the man wasn't one to hold a grudge and had always seemed to have a certain fatalistic side to his nature, or, more precisely, a kind of congenital insensitivity to the caprices of fortune.

He told me that as soon as he resigned as party chief he was planning a long stay in Europe to make an in-depth study of the mechanisms of the Common Market, which, though on a much larger scale, had been a distant inspiration for the sovereignty-association project he himself had vaguely adhered to in days gone by. I could only encourage him strongly while doubting, just as strongly, that he would last long in this studious exile. His whole life had been governed by political ambition. All during his career, from his first steps as a brilliant young adviser and researcher, in Ottawa as in Quebec City, he had never strayed from this one-way path.

Entirely devoted to this single-minded objective, but with a mind constantly on the lookout for short-term advantage, he appeared to me to be a long-distance runner performing like a sprinter. In 1970 he used the "100,000 Jobs" slogan, he admitted later, just to dramatize the situation. . . . When we were being called social democrats, it was all aboard for social democracy, and he would try that hat on, too. Were we talking about sovereignty? So would he, but he would stick a cautious qualifier on it, speaking of cultural sovereignty. It wouldn't be sovereignty then, but autonomy; no less than that, but no more either.

For Quebec this "no less" is certainly (and this is all I will allow myself to say for the moment) a minimal guarantee, the one our nationalist governments have always offered, except for times when Big Brother has found or created an opportunity to put the squeeze on them: Godbout in 1940, Bourassa in 1970 . . . .

But will we one day have the surprise of discovering behind this remarkable destiny a design worthy of the name?

Enough said. Let's get back to yesterday.

36. Penelope's Weaving

HYPOTHESIS A . . . LIST B . . . into the wastebasket. And begin again. There is nothing easier to begin with than to put together a cabinet. The first names drop into place all by themselves. But who does what? And who's left over to do the rest? That's the tough part.

I had taken refuge with a handful of advisers in a little inn at North Hatley. Among them were two who possessed special information for us, Louis Bernard and Michel Carpentier, the former on the needs of the State, the latter on the potentials of our elected party members. The operation had started smoothly enough, beginning with some self-evident facts. Like Lesage in 1960, I was the only one to have a certain experience of government. To this, Jacques Parizeau and Claude Morin would add their vast and more recent expertise as civil servants. So now we were three. Then came our two successive parliamentary chiefs, Camille Laurin and Jacques-Yvan Morin, plus two other particularly valuable members drawn from our House veterans, Robert Burns and Marc-André Bédard. So now we were seven, with five from Montreal. We would have to broaden the base, regionalize it. But first, who would look after agriculture, a vital portfolio with ramifications everywhere, one that was hypersensitive and had always been a real ministerial abattoir. Luckily, the president of the Union Catholique des Cultivateurs, Paul Couture, had telephoned me just after the election.

"Don't go appointing another agronomist," he advised me, "nor a farmer either, apart from the fact that I don't see all that many of them among your electeds!"

"All right, but who then?"

"I'm going to surprise you. We're up against such a tangle of laws, regulations, and red tape of all sorts, as well as being drowned in figures, what we need to help us see clear is a lawyer. You ought to be able to find one somewhere, an intelligent one who knows how to count and understands concrete things. . . ."

So with Jean Garon, who on top of everything else had the perfect build for the job, that made eight.

278

To this we added two "regionalists" also capable of speaking for Quebec as a whole, Yves Duhaime and Yves Bérubé, then two old campaigners who had shared our birth pangs and our first defeats, Pierre Marois and Bernard Landry. So we were twelve.

And now what? Deadlock. Our first choice absolutely refused to touch the job we offered, as did our second choice. In our cheerful innocence we had thought the post would suit them perfectly. But they were solid personalities, and workers of the first hour besides, and there was no pushing them around. There was one good thing – they knew what they wanted. But as for our plan, there was no end to redesigning it. What made the task even more complicated was a new idea adapted from Ontario practice and advanced by Louis Bernard, who stubbornly insisted until he had sold me on it. Like our neighbours, we were to have ministers of state, that is, ministers without ministries. They were to be chosen from among the heavyweights and would be charged with planning, as far as that was possible, and with co-ordinating work in the major development sectors, in economics, social and cultural affairs, and territorial matters, flimsy labels covering fields that continually overlapped. To co-ordinate the co-ordinators we created a Committee on Priorities. And to avoid frustrations apparent in the Ontario system where the super-ministers suffered the worst fate that can befall a politician, that of invisibility, we decided to give ours precise mandates that would permit them to show their stuff by creating and presenting their own projects without trespassing too much on their colleagues' territory. But in the long run nothing can replace the palpable pleasure, analagous to running one's own business, of the daily management of a ministry. So despite some remarkable achievements, we eventually had to drop this structure and after several years came back to the traditional system where each minister retains his bit of concrete authority, administrative as well as political, the only one forbidden this luxury being your humble servant. . . .

We had allowed ourselves ten days or so to complete this baroque but essential task of laboriously matching names and portfolios, a job that with each cabinet shuffle over the next nine years I came to consider more and more as a veritable punishment from heaven. To blend old and new talents as well as possible, to maintain an acceptable balance between Montreal and Quebec City without forgetting the rest of the country, and beyond these normal requirements to try to place everyone in a post that suits him, is really like trying to square the circle. The result is never more than fair to middling, but one can't do better.

In the Quebec City hotel where I had set up shop, it was only a few hours before the deadline when I put the finishing touches to this piece of Penelope-like weaving. Among last-minute appointments, two amuse me still every time I think about them. First, Claude Charron's astonishment at being entrusted with what we called the High Commissariat of Youth, Leisure and Sport, when he had severely contested my leadership a few months earlier. And so what? Contrary to certain mumblings for whatever reason, I don't know anything more childish than vengeful vanity, the slight scrape that takes itself for the mortal wound. One of the most striking victims of this must be the economist Rodrigue Tremblay, who first became a candidate, then a minister, by mistake. At the beginning of the election campaign he showed up one day saying he had come in response to a telephone call from me. In reality the call had been from his boss, also called René Lévesque, but our man, hearing only his own inner voices, had precipitously rushed to join us. He was a well-known university professor, a "prestige candidate" as they say in the jargon of the trade. Seeing that he obviously took himself for the cat's pyjamas, I should have thought twice before offering him a ministry. I lived to regret the day. Boasting an IQ "in the top three in Quebec," and never ceasing to preach unless it was to criticize, this extraordinary colleague became so perfectly insupportable that I soon could hardly wait for the chance to send him back to join the rank and file. And as long as he remained in the House he continued to look down his nose at us ignoramuses who hadn't known how to appreciate his true worth.

There are some people who, for various reasons (an excess of self-esteem being just one example), are not really cut out for public life. At the risk of being taken for a heretic at a time when the supermarket-state has established a lifestyle as imperative as it is bound to be short-lived, I think this is generally true of businessmen. Of course, there is no rule that doesn't have its exception, but so far I have only known one: Rodrigue Biron, whose fertile imagination and constant availability made him stand head and shoulders above most of his fellows. Nothing is more deceptive than the apparent similarity often superficially noted between the public and private sectors, or more slippery than the confusion that can quickly result from such comparisons. In business, profit is the iron law; in public affairs it never applies, and even in fields where the State operates its own commercial or industrial enterprises, it only applies to a relative degree. Even more important, the two types of behaviour can never be the same. A minister must take into account the permanence of his principal collaborators and a whole unwritten code that dictates a myriad of ways of doing and not doing things. The boss of a private company, on the other hand, usually steps into government with the self-assurance that his own brand of success has given him and an attitude of being just one rank below God. This carries its own type of etiquette but doesn't fit in all that well with the demands of service to the State, so those who avoid falling flat on their faces in this post, at the same time so close and so different from a job in private business, are rare birds indeed.

One might think we had nothing to fear on this score, since in our first government there wasn't a single emanation from the business world! To make up for it, what an array of talent, what a display of deep learning braced on the bedrock of that good old general culture that business itself, when it is the least bit intelligent, is beginning to call on again as in former times. For nothing is more flexible or more durable than the foundation of a "well-formed mind" in a world where the most impressive professional diplomas have a half-life that is steadily diminishing.

So here was I, the dropout, with a team more than half of which had completed graduate work in the States or Europe, saying to myself with a mixture of pride and apprehension: "Of all the cabinets we have known, we have never seen the like. How will I be able to keep charge of the helm when the crew is made up of so many potential captains?" After nine years I was still asking the same question.

Thoughts like these were present when, on November 26, 1976, I had to introduce this government that people had been waiting for with such incertitude and impatience and upon which so many citizens had placed such a heavy burden of hope.

> If we were to deceive our fellow Québécois, [I declared, going straight to the heart of the matter,] it would be our confidence in ourselves as a people that would be at stake. It is quite simple, we haven't the right to fail. . . . I call upon each and every one of you to make the necessary effort, not only to help lift Quebec out of economic and social difficulties that we know only too well, but also

to assure our fellow citizens peace, well-being, and pride, which is also an essential commodity they have a right to.

If everyone puts forth his best effort we can make Quebec a country that is a happy place to live in, a country that cultivates harmonious relations with its neighbours, a country that treats its minorities with justice and equity, a country that develops its resources while respecting its environment, a country that gives tangible recognition to its elders because they have earned it over a long life, and cares constantly for its more unfortunate members because they need such care, a country that lodges its families decently, and assures its workers not only jobs but also adequate working conditions. . . .

Rereading this idealistic statement tinged with utopian dreams, I realize all too well that we fell a long way short of these objectives, but I can also affirm that we never lost sight of them. However, man proposes and often it's circumstances that dispose. And in the Canadian context circumstances are also the others.

In Ottawa, where our accession to power traumatized the whole of Parliament Hill, Trudeau sketched out his reactions on three separate occasions – three times in ten days, that was quite something. "At least it shows," I said, replying to a journalist's question, "a sudden and very flattering intensification of interest in the evolution of Quebec." The disconnected nature of his remarks, however, showed also that the results of the fifteenth of November had triggered "an agonizing reappraisal" in those quarters. This painful search for a new way of looking at things did contain some positive aspects. For instance, to put an end to a rumour that had been given free reign to arouse childish fears, according to which a collective decision on the part of the people of Quebec might throw them back into the same ignoble mess as in 1970, the federal Prime Minister at last admitted that in a democracy a political regime could not be maintained by force. Since War Measures were now excluded, how did they plan to check us when the referendum came around? The reply was there between the lines. Trudeau described me as surrounded by my "blood brothers." So once again, as always, he resorted to the facile allusion to tribalism, to the narrow and inevitably isolated ghetto where we would find ourselves deprived of the inestimable benefits of the "large ensemble." Already one could define quite accurately the alternative that would be proposed in the debate, even if one could not foresee the unspeakable dishonesty with which it would be applied.

At any rate, we hadn't time to think seriously about such things now. The most urgent task was, so to speak, to decolonize ourselves day by day, proving to ourselves and to others that we were as capable as anyone of running our own affairs, at least that part of them we were permitted to look after ourselves.

37. A Real Government

OUR FIRST PREOCCUPATIONS were economic ones. The fact that we had no recognized representative of the business world in our government gave certain prima donnas from this milieu, the Conseil du Patronat in particular, a chance to harp on the same string for several years running, and to hear themselves parroted endlessly. To listen to them we were just a bunch of arts students who knew nothing about figures. One must be dishonest or crassly ignorant not to see that no government can survive in our era without being constantly concerned about this essential dimension of our collective life. Since the end of the crazy fifties and sixties one could even say that economic questions in all their aspects – business, jobs, budget, finance – touched every realm.

We had scarcely been sworn in when we were told that the city of Montreal, following its great Olympic orgy, would have to correct its financial situation by imposing a special tax; if not, goodbye credit rating. At the same time that an emergency session was called to deal with this problem, ministers of finance, then provincial premiers spelled each other off in Ottawa trying to sort out the inextricably tangled skein of federal-provincial fiscal arrangements. Less than a month after the vote, these meetings gave our counterparts from the other provinces a chance to test the seriousness of our basic option. Now they're in power, several of them said, they'll quickly settle down and get back into line. But when they discovered this was not to be, they showed their resentment by breaking the common front put together to better resist Ottawa and accepted for the next five years a billion dollars less than the sum they were entitled to. It was the first time I saw them ready to penalize themselves in order to exclude Quebec. It wouldn't be the last. . . .

The year 1976 hadn't come to an end before a working committee, grouped under Bernard Landry, was established with an urgent mandate to improvise if necessary but to start up work-creation programs to respond to the dramatic increase in unemployment. The "Operation de Stimulation Economique," with its exuberant acronym OSE ("dare"), was an effort that was to be pursued relentlessly, first creating more occasional work than lasting jobs, but little by little getting the right range and gaining concrete experience for us that we would so badly need during the economic crisis of 1981-83.

This way, from the very beginning, we tried to act like that "real government" that we had insisted on promising, to emphasize the contrast with the pitiful end of our predecessors. It was with this perspective in mind that, during the electoral campaign, we had established a list of specific commitments. One of these was specially important to me, to such a degree that I insisted on making it public less than a week after the election had been announced:

> Speaking in the name of his party, Mr. René Lévesque made a formal commitment to abolish secret campaign funding as soon as he came to power.
> Mr. Bourassa had promised as much on April 29, 1970, but did not keep his word, Mr. Lévesque declared. . . . "But I would keep my promise because my party has already proved that it can finance itself democratically. . . ."

In fact, in this domain we had succeeded in maintaining, and even in progressively tightening, unprecedented regulations. At the very first, when we were nothing more than a laughable "particle," we accepted a few substantial gifts. But as soon as our base broadened, we introduced measures that were more and more strict. From 1972 on, when 24,000 people subscribed some $600,000 during our first well-organized funding campaign, we never counted on anyone but Quebec citizens to keep us alive. From year to year, hundreds and then thousands of canvassers, after making their own contributions, would spread out for a month through every corner of Quebec, insisting more on the gesture than on the sum collected. I went from quarter to quarter like everyone else, well received not only among party members but also by unknown sympathizers who felt our concern for integrity deserved to become contagious. I remember one old couple calculating their resources before writing out a cheque on the corner of the kitchen table, and in another case welfare recipients excusing themselves for not having more than a meagre two or three dollars to give us. Moments like those were among the most rewarding of my public life.

Now that we were elected I was impatient to make this way of doing things compulsory, perhaps for fear that if we didn't hurry, some devil would come and push us into the same old malpractice. I knew that sceptics were saying there's nothing easier than to be virtuous when one is in the opposition, especially when we had hardly any access to financial circles, and now that we held power we would soon be pushing our way to the trough like the rest. We had to give them the lie without delay. So the democratic financing of political parties was our number-one commitment and was the second bill of the new government, though it was in fact our first major accomplishment.

From then on parties were obliged to make their financial statements public. Contributions were no longer to come from companies or interested groups but only from individuals, they were not to exceed $3,000 a year, and, to begin with, any gift of over $100 had to be declared. At the same time we encouraged citizens to become involved by letting them deduct these modest contributions from income tax.

At various times I have explained this law in other provinces, in the States, and in Europe where, unless I am mistaken, no similar system has ever been tried. On such occasions I have read in the astonished and often incredulous eyes of my interlocutors the thought that I must be some kind of political Martian. But in Ottawa, as in other world capitals, financial scandals remain everyday fare and draw public life under the fire of public scorn, yet not once did we have to wallow in that mire. Of all the reforms we were able to push through, this is the one I will always be the proudest of. It is also the one that will cost the most if one day someone lets it fall into disrepute.

> . . . At the first regular session following the election of a Parti
> Québécois government we will propose to the National
> Assembly a new automobile insurance plan. . . . This plan . . .
> will not only guarantee better protection of victims, but also a
> reduction in premiums.

This, too, was an urgent matter, but it was another kettle of fish. Who would be so base as to publicly oppose cleaning up the Augean stables that party funding had become? With automobile insurance, however, we were attacking a milch cow whose sticky tits fed some extremely honourable and articulate segments of society. This was particularly true of the bar, whose members sometimes made as much as half their salaries out of automobile accidents and who frequently did not hesitate to strike a deal with the insurance company to spin legal procedures out forever, until the client became discouraged and finally dropped the claim or settled for a pittance. In our own ranks we had a few lawyers who for some time were not insensitive to the powerful lobby determined to paralyse us as it had the previous government. I can remember one day, when the discussion was going hot and heavy, finding myself together with Lise Payette almost alone against a consensus of nervous members demanding that the project be put off a year or two, which was the same as burying it for good. It was thanks to Lise Payette and her fierce energy, I must stress, that we finally managed to break the ice-jam and pass a law people had been waiting for in vain since 1970. The Bourassa government had dodged its promises by naming a commission of inquiry, the Gauvin Commission, whose report sat on the shelf for three years. The verdict of the commissioners had been really shocking. Lise Payette had studied their report thoroughly and then, as she liked to say, started out, pilgrim's staff in hand. Helped by her fame as a TV personality, she led a vigorous whirlwind campaign and won the day.

Since memory is the faculty that forgets, and people who forget always risk repeating the same errors, it might not be a bad idea to recall briefly certain features of a past that is still recent. It was a time when the higher the damages, the less the compensation was adequate, even for victims who were completely innocent; it was a time when only three-fifths the value of Quebec premiums, which were the highest in Canada, were paid out as indemnities; it was a time when a twenty-five-year-old single male, driving a model of the current year, was held up to ransom to the tune of $1,800 per annum – if he could find a company willing to insure him! As a result *one vehicle in five* on Quebec roads was being operated without insurance, like so many time bombs.

"People before anything" was the slogan we embedded in the law that at last took us out of the Middle Ages as far as the automobile was concerned. In addition, rates remained sheltered from inflation for three years. If we had shown as much determination as our American neighbours in enforcing road safety, Quebec today would be first among Western nations in this domain, too.

Quebec must be as French
as Ontario is English.

Could I say the same as far as language is concerned? Can I be as enthusiastic speaking about Bill 101, which, at the same time as it corrected previous legislation, installed the defence and promotion of French in an unshakable structure? No, of course not, since what was involved this time was an instrument that only a colonial society would have to provide for itself.

Everywhere outdoor advertising continued to throw down on us the unilingual sneer of a dominant minority. Nothing seemed able to stop the assimilation of immigrants. Our economic inferiority continued to be carefully maintained from the highest echelons to the level of simple foreman. We weren't told to "Speak white!" any more but we were still obliged to do so in many cases, right here in our own home. One day, if we wanted it badly enough, French would be at home everywhere in Quebec and, as in any normal country, we could finally toss aside the crutches of legislation that have always seemed to me to be deeply humiliating. But for the time being, the prosthesis remained necessary.

This medical vocabulary comes spontaneously to mind when I think of Dr. Laurin, of his steel-forged gentleness, of his rich culture entirely directed to the passionate love of this country, of his epicurean tastes submerged under his slave-like laboriousness. A demigod for some, pure demon for others, he was first, and sometimes somewhat ostentatiously, an eminent therapist.

He made it his job to cure our language ills, to bring our speech back, whether we liked it or not, to a good state of health. For months on end, backed up by a group of clinicians as ardent as himself – Fernand Dumont, Guy Rocher, Gaston Cholette – he literally remained day and night at his patient's bedside, article by article concocting the prescription that first took the form of a White Paper, then of a first law, some of the dispositions of which were unfortunately too rough and ready a remedy. The opposition immediately stuck us with a filibuster, that interminable logorrhoea that can, perfectly democratically, paralyse the House. In *Le Devoir* Claude Ryan, who was not yet leader of the Liberal Party and would ultimately be quite happy to become a minister, at once withdrew the prudent benediction he had accorded us at the time of the election and gave us a good dressing down, which I must admit we deserved a little.

René and Corinne Lévesque, Brian Mulroney,
Ronald Reagan and his wife.

Juan Carlos, King of Spain.

Corinne and René Lévesque with Laurent Fabius, prime minister of France, and his wife, Françoise.

October, 1984, with the Mayor of Shanghai, Mr. Wang.

With Andréas Papandréou, prime minister of Greece.

Pierre Mauroy, prime minister of France, hosts René Lévesque at
Matignon, December 6, 1983.

At the Élysée Palace, with French President, François Mitterrand,
June 29, 1983.

On December 15, 1980, Mr. René Lévesque receives an honorary
degree from the Sorbonne, in the presence of Mr. Raymond Barre,
prime minister of France, and Mrs. Saumier-Seite,
minister of universities.

Paris Mayor Jacques Chirac and his wife host René and
Corinne Lévesque at Paris City Hall.

With Valery Giscard d'Estaing, French President in 1980.

Djao Dziang, prime minister of China, Montreal, 1984.

So the project was withdrawn, purged of some of its excessively authoritarian passages, and introduced in a new version under the key word "reciprocity," an invention of one of our colleagues that might have opened a very rich perspective to the rest of Canada. In order to control admission of children to our English schools, we had begun by setting up a rule commonly known as "the Quebec clause," according to which at least one of the parents had to have gone to English elementary school in Quebec. For my own part, I would have preferred "the Canada clause," which would have respected the constant flow of internal immigration by extending the right to English schooling to all Canadian children whose parents were authentic Anglophones. Short of this, as suggested by the word "reciprocity," we would permit a sort of tit-for-tat approach: with provinces that would assure our French minorities school rights more or less comparable to those enjoyed by Anglo-Québécois, we would be ready to draw up agreements guaranteeing the same advantages for their own residents coming to Quebec.

When the linguistic debate resumed in the National Assembly in July, 1977, I had a chance to go and test this excellent idea in New Brunswick, where the Premiers' Conference was taking place. However, when I arrived fresh and eager with my reciprocity formulas under my arm, I ran straight into a wall of indifference that Richard Hatfield, with the aid of federal officials in the wings, had erected especially for me.

"For the love of Heaven," I protested, "I have the impression that nobody here has even taken the trouble to read our propositions. Couldn't you at least take a look at them?"

Instead, Bill Davis, Premier of Ontario, who all during his long reign was the expert manipulator of these reunions, presented a virtuous resolution, neither fish nor fowl, in which we all agreed to pay special attention to our minorities and to do our best to improve their lot. Business as usual. . . .

The reciprocity clause remained in Bill 101 just the same. It's still there, like the preview of a future as uncertain as ever. On the other hand, I reluctantly consented to see article 133 of the constitution struck out, the one that concerns bilingualism as it applies to laws and tribunals. This move was bound to wind up in the Supreme Court and be struck down in turn. When that happened, as you may remember, our valorous tribunal of the last instance found itself obliged to enforce the same treatment on Manitoba where a law that, with a stroke of the pen, had eliminated the use of French and pushed our minorities to the brink of extinction had been quietly in force *for the past ninety years!*

Two major aspects of Bill 101 that seem to me to require constant and close attention are advertising and francisation of business enterprises. In Montreal especially (though we might ease up in certain residential areas), we must never again let the city centre take on that bastard look we tolerated far too long with servile passivity. Also, and even more important, the policy of francisation must be maintained in all important enterprises.

Three years ago I revisited a multinational company on Montreal's south shore where, at the time of my first visit around 1977, I had struggled in a totally alienating atmosphere. Then, the rare Francophone foremen they could dig up were obliged to speak English; now, all these "little bosses" had to know French and use it. Little by little, a handful of Francophones had also reached administrative posts, and there were even one or two in the highest executive offices, and not only in public relations, the traditional refuge of token Québécois.

When one says multinationals, one thinks first of Americans, then of Europeans or Asiatics who have invaded every continent. These people establish their own game rules and never hesitate to make governments and populations toe the line, but at least their experience of the world has taught them to respect the linguistic contexts in which they function. This is not the case for Anglo-Canadians who set up business in Quebec. Often narrowly provincial themselves, they arrive in their internal colony where their despicable imperialism has been practised since the Conquest and where Anglo-Canadians have acquired most of the faults of the white man in a nation of coloured people. First our election victory set their world on its ear, then Bill 101 made them furious. Fired up by hysterical Montreal Anglophones, the Toronto press went overboard. From one phrase to the next we were metamorphosed from "ridiculous shrimps" to dangerous "revolutionary fanatics" and then, for the benefit of a United States still haunted by the spectre of the Communist bear, into "Castros of the north."

There is nothing more pernicious, in fact, than the facility with which this language community permits Toronto outlets, who supply New York and Chicago, to deform the facts and disparage us at will the length and breadth of the continent. It is less well known that there are numerous English Canadians whose careers have established them south of the border and who, much easier than blacks integrating white circles, transform themselves into impeccable Yankees while continuing to propagate their anti-Québécois prejudices. An example is that Ontarian who published a continuous stream of nonsense about us in a weekly business review. This underhanded propaganda had invaded the New York Economic Club, where I was invited at the beginning of 1977 to explain our political intentions, and it contributed to making my first contact with our American neighbours a monumental flop. I must add that on that occasion, for the first and last time, I had consented to read a text prepared by a team whose talents were definitely not on the American wavelength and who put into my mouth certain awkward expressions destined to grate on my audience's corporate ear. But I remain convinced that it was thanks to our well-camouflaged Canadians that these details were later blown up out of all proportion.

Just now, leafing through a Sunday paper, I came across an excellent article reminding us that the Sun Life Assurance Company built our first Montreal skyscraper, which at that time was the biggest building in the British Empire. I was delighted to learn that this architectural chef-d'oeuvre was decorated with syenite marble columns on bases of black Belgian marble and that the walls and staircases were in pink Italian marble while the floors were in pink Tennessee; that the architects and contractors were Messrs. Darling, Pearson, Cleveland, Cook and Lietch; and that besides its skyscraper, the company had also been so kind as to offer us a monument to commemorate the Diamond Jubilee of Queen Victoria in 1898, and, for Expo '67, an electromechanical carillon that is one of the wonders of the world. All that was really missing from this account was one single chapter that is also, doubtless, unique in the world. Here it is.

On January 6, 1978, the president of Sun Life, Thomas Galt, announced that its central offices would quit their skyscraper and take refuge in Toronto where a meeting of shareholders had boldly been called (500 kilometres from Montreal) to ratify the decision. The official motive of this departure was none other than Bill 101, which, Mr. Galt said, threatened to interfere with "the recruitment and maintenance of competent employees possessing the knowledge of English required for the daily operation of the company. . . ." This knowledge was, in fact, all the more indispensable because

Thomas Galt himself, after some thirty years in Quebec, did not speak a word of French, and more than 80 per cent of his employees were unilingual Anglophones. "The Sun Life is not leaving us," quipped our colleague Denis de Belleval, "because one can claim, without caricatural exaggeration, that it was never really part of Quebec society in the first place!" This was illustrated more fully in the company's investment portfolio: 41 cents of every dollar taken out of Quebec pockets were invested here, as compared to $1.20 in Ontario, $1.07 in the Prairies, and $1.71 in British Columbia. Good riddance, we told ourselves along with numerous Québécois who showed their indignation by transferring their insurance to other companies. Good Lord, what nice forgetful people we are! After a short penance, Sun Life, like various other companies that had taken the same road, had no difficulty recapturing the lost ground and continued to grow fat at our expense.

Just compare these dealings with the attitude of the American company, Prudential Life, whose internal newsletter, *Contact*, for October-November, 1977, first noted that the company's capital investment in Quebec was three-and-a-half times its obligations to its policy-holders. "Immediately after the election," the article continued, "members of our board of governors contacted the highest authorities of the Quebec government, including Premier Lévesque. . . . The measures taken by the new government were also analysed and appear to be perfectly reasonable. . . . *Even the language bill presents no particular difficulties for our business. . . . We have already adopted a good many of its provisions and will do what is necessary to implement the others*."

For that matter, the Pépin-Robarts Commission was to indicate a little later (in a report that Trudeau trashed for this reason among others) that Bill 101 in no way prevented Anglo-Québécois from being treated, like other minorities if not better, in a perfectly civilized fashion. So while its detractors went around terrorizing tourists by conjuring up the unspeakable intolerance we were reserving for them, in Montreal *The Gazette* and "Channel 12" continued to be among the most profitable media outlets in the country. Quebec City, the capital, also continued to offer an extravagant menu of radio-television fare to its English-speaking one-twentieth or one-twenty-fifth of the urban population, while an army of cable distributors from below the border went on inundating us on every side. I would like to know where else in the world (let alone in Canada) minorities have their public education from kindergarten to university paid for according to the same norms as the majority. These same minorities call the tune in a good half of the economic transactions in our country and, come what may, can communicate in English with the rest of the continent to run us down.

I want to be well understood on this point. I am very glad we were able to be more than exemplary in this matter, but I am less glad when I think of the long road decolonization still has to travel, though it has now crossed hurdles that formerly would have been unthinkable.

. . . With the participation of representatives of agricultural producers [we will set up] a zoning policy aimed at protecting our best farmland. . . .

Taking up our election commitments once again and getting my feet back on the ground in the most literal sense, I want to refer briefly to this simple reform, dictated by common sense, which for the future of our soil and those who live off it by making us live, represented nothing short of a mini-Quiet Revolution.

Before we intervened it used to be said that we were having the rug pulled out from under us. Delivered up to speculators everywhere, our fields had been waiting for years to have someone recognize the peril this mismanagement had put us into. We are a northern people; four-fifths of our land has been described as "the land that God gave Cain"; the arable acreage is scarcely as big as Belgium, and the growing season is less than six months a year. Luckily, just south of the St. Lawrence, barely beyond the suburbs of Montreal, is a black-earth belt that rivals the best land in the world and is avidly sought out by the matchless market gardeners who come here from the old countries. But it is precisely this rich patrimony that the proximity of the metropolis threatens to bury forever under shopping plazas and other wildcat developments. With tax laws that persisted in blocking successions from father to son, how could the farmer resist promoters who offered him hundreds of thousands and sometimes up to a million dollars for his farm? To give an example, in my own riding on the edge of this agricultural granary, the city of Saint-Hubert told me that almost half its property taxes were collected from owners who could only be reached through post office boxes in Zurich or Hong Kong! More rigorous than any law of the kind I know, the bill for the protection of arable land, or the zoning law as it is commonly called, put a stop to the dilapidation of this primary resource and re-established that minimum equilibrium between city and country, and between the city dweller constantly on the move and the rural citizen whose roots go deep, that is essential if human society is not to succumb to an anaemia more pernicious than simple food shortages. I am ready to admit that this law suffered from sometimes obtusely severe legal interpretation, almost inhuman on occasion, but one must also admit that we had a long way to go. I should add that in a few brief years our rate of auto-sufficiency, that is, the proportion between the export of surpluses and the cost of goods we cannot produce ourselves, climbed from less than 40 to more than 70 per cent. Roots and productivity are of equal concern, and so it should be when one considers our world of five billion among whom there are so many children who haven't even the strength to cry out for help; anything else would be dishonourable. In short, concern for profitability went hand in hand with an evident question of principle, a combination that, whenever it occurs, stimulates the will to act prodigiously.

This was precisely the formidable combination the federal government was obliging enough to create for us in 1978 by raising the thorny question of the sales tax in its budget. That inalienable jewel of the Ontario crown, the position of Minister of Finance, had just gone to Jean Chrétien, who, feeling his oats, had the great idea to strike a bold blow. Keeping the stick and the carrot going together, he offered provinces that would reduce their sales tax a reimbursement of up to 3 per cent. On the one hand, this would inject a little adrenalin into a sluggish economy, and at the same time it would let Ottawa step with its big boots into a fiscal field exclusively reserved to the provinces. One by one, despite a little grumbling, all the provinces accepted this clever federal yoke . . . except Quebec. Cleverer still, Jacques Parizeau had taken his time and, moving skilfully from one discussion to another, had carefully avoided giving his consent. Thinking we were bound to follow the flock, Chrétien announced that if we would lower our sales tax, too, we would have the right to the reimbursement. Parizeau immediately called his team together and asked, what's 3 per cent? The reply: $226 million. Were we willing to spread this sum across the board in a blind detaxation affecting Cadillacs and mink coats as well as the necessities of life? Falling into the federal trap would make us miss an unhoped for chance to make some progress on the social as well as the economic front. Our primary industries were untouchable, but certain of the "soft" sectors – furniture, textiles, clothing, and footwear – attracted our attention immediately because they produced goods that corresponded to the basic needs of the average family. By removing the sales tax from these commodities, not only partially but completely, we would reach more than $200 million, if luxury items were excluded. By coquetry or meticulousness Parizeau was determined to have his $226 million, and not a penny less. Eureka! Someone thought of eliminating the tax on hotel rooms, an exorbitant one that was seriously hurting the tourist industry, and there we were, right on target.

As soon as this socio-economic kit was made public, it not only received enthusiastic support but also put the laugh on our side. Chrétien was furious and reacted by refusing us our $226 million. He preferred to cover himself deeper in ridicule by sending $85 to every Quebec taxpayer, a sum that Parizeau quickly recuperated in income tax!

Our fragile industries and even the majority of families had Ottawa to thank, then, for this largesse, particularly during the hard times to follow, and it was from this moment on that Jacques Parizeau established his solid reputation as a financial wizard.

But over and above that image, one that he nursed tenderly, he was in my opinion the most efficient as well as the most progressive of all great Quebec treasurers. From old bourgeois stock, "and proud of it," he was nevertheless extremely sensitive to the iniquities of fate, a feeling his budgets tried to reflect. Not satisfied with taxing the wealthy more, he managed little by little to reduce the load of humble folk, too, until finally comparison with Ontario, so often a masochistic exercise, turned out to be strikingly in our favour. There, it was still the little people who were being bled white and the rich who were spared, while here it had come to be precisely the reverse.*

Parizeau was a superb minister and also a disarming character possessed of an incredibly vivacious mind and perhaps knowing it a little too well. A former student of François Perroux and other

---

* It was during this period that the deficit began to increase. How could we forget that when it's been drummed into us for so long! Yet it must be that such a trend was inevitable, for despite all the subsequent paring the providential State has been subjected to, even today the government can do no better than remain at the ceiling we set ourselves when the crisis was on.

illustrious masters, he had been marked as well by the London School of Economics, where he picked up the mannerisms of The City. He could be both amusing and totally irritating. He was ambitious, certainly, and spent much time organizing a network of followers around him, but he also took pride in being "the good soldier" whose loyalty remains beyond question. This, at any rate, is the man I knew all those years until the day when soberly, brutally, following his absolute indépendantisme which had already been cruelly shaken by the referendum, he left us, slamming the door behind him.

Independence must come about in a democratic fashion,
that is, with the consent of the population.
– 1976 Platform

In 1979 we all still held to the one great hope that had been the motivation of our action for the past twelve years. However, time was passing. Without further delay we had to start assiduously to meet our supreme commitment.

With that fake indignation that characterizes the discourse of all opposition parties, our adversaries accused us of having neglected daily problems for the sake of our main option. But in reality we had had to leave it aside almost entirely for nearly three years. In Ottawa, task forces, working committees, the Prime Minister's Office, and the rag-tag-and-bobtail of propagandists for Canadian unity had known no rest since the end of 1976. On our side only Claude Morin and his ministry, whose federal-provincial role clearly encompassed this responsibility, had been able to devote themselves to the task. But from now on it was to be everyone's business. To the law on referendums, a key instrument we had provided ourselves with in advance, we next added, in the spring of 1979, a White Paper entitled *Quebec-Canada: A New Entente: Equal to Equal* from which we would draw the substance of our campaign. For me, this contained the essence of sovereignty-association; I felt full of beans and ready to open the campaign. But first we had to wait for two big roadblocks to disappear.

I had decided we should avoid mixing the referendum debate with the excitement of an election. Knowing this, and also seeing himself doomed to almost certain defeat, Trudeau spun out his term of office from month to month. At last he had to resign himself to take the plunge, and in May was beaten hands down, except in Quebec. At last, we thought with relief, we were going to see an end to the mirage of "French Power" that had so long maintained the illusion of a sort of all-powerful Quebec presence in Ottawa. With English Canada recuperating the power it had never really given up, appearances were restored to reality.

The other hurdle was the Common Front and the triennial confrontation with its blasé old union chiefs, with their jargon, their utopian demands, and their bloated oratory. In 1978 we had naively thought to give a good example by freezing our own salaries for twelve months and limiting future increases to 6 or 7 per cent per annum. Were our friends in the public sector, who had just that same year pocketed 20 per cent and more, impressed by this moderation? Not on your life. This time they wanted 30 per cent! Some have claimed that, like our predecessors, we let them walk away with the bank. I can affirm the contrary. We even managed to impose, here as in tax reforms, the start of a return to equity, the highest paid having to bear the brunt of a considerable raise in the minimum wage. But we hadn't reached the worst of the crisis yet and appetites remained limitless, as did the cynicism of those who became used to holding the public as hostages. Here and there hospitals were closed. Public transport was paralysed in Montreal. Once again peace had to be purchased for a price, though less ruinous than during the previous round of negotiations.

It was really to our merit, it should be added, that we succeeded in limiting the damage somewhat. Right in the middle of the hullabaloo and all those inconveniences the public instinctively blames on the government came by-elections in three ridings: Prévost, Beauce-sud, and above all Maisonneuve, one of our strongholds in popular Montreal where Robert Burns had quit the party bitterly, giving me a final kick as he went. There's no need to recall what happened next, because everyone knows that never, but *never*, in nine years were we destined to win a single by-election. Well, you can't have everything, as my grandmother used to say.

But the most depressing memory I have of this period is of the pre-referendum blackmail the unions indulged in so shamelessly. Our answer to you is a "Non," they proclaimed, laying stress on the *non*. Certain of their spokesmen went so far as to tell us openly that if we wanted to count on them, we would have to loosen the purse strings "always more" – an historic vote against a handful of dollars.

38. Heartbreak

ON DECEMBER 19, 1979, toward the end of the afternoon, the cabinet was meeting in that room where the indirect lighting and the wart-shaped vault give one the impression of being in a space capsule. Cut off from the world like this, we had to concentrate as never before in order to come up, a few hours hence, with the referendum question, at the same time as we tried to put out of our minds the unexpected turn of events that had just occurred.

Less than a week before, poor Joe Clark, that worthy westerner who had gone to all sorts of trouble to learn French but who was dogged by bad luck to the point of being the butt of scores of jokes and caricatures, had known the ultimate misfortune of losing a vote of confidence in the Commons by a narrow margin. Although he had announced his own departure from politics the previous month and had admitted that "a new man" was needed to replace him, nobody doubted for an instant that Trudeau would fail to seize this unhoped for chance to be born again from his still hot cinders.

Here was a double complication. First, federal elections might get mixed up with the referendum debate. Should we wait longer? But we were entering our fourth year in office, we had a commitment to fulfil, and the troops were mobilizing already, all the faster for having strained at the leash for so long. Besides, we undoubtedly risked finding ourselves with the phoenix of renewed federalism to contend with again; in fact, it was a dead certainty since in a "farewell" interview Trudeau had clearly indicated his intention to intervene. Wouldn't it be better, for that matter, to come to grips with this stiff and Manichean opponent rather than have to put on kid gloves to deal with a nice, basically broad-minded guy like Joe Clark?

So what about the question? During the three years we'd been waiting everyone had had time to formulate his own idea of what it should be, but only three people had received specific instructions to explore the *terra incognita* of popular consultation. Flanked by the demanding Louis Bernard and Daniel Latouche, a political adviser whose young university career hadn't had time to stifle his imagination, Claude Morin had been in charge of sifting the subject, refining their thoughts in several drafts, and finally coming up with *the* question.

Many decisions had to be made. For example, should we, as the United Kingdom did when preparing its entry into the Common Market, pass a "sovereignty-association law" that citizens would then ratify or reject by vote? But what palaver there would be over each clause, and what nit-picking the Liberals would indulge in! So we decided to fall back on the type of question that is really a question, one that, having clearly described what was at stake, would ask Québécois . . . . Well, just what would we ask them? An idea that came quite naturally was to solicit a mandate to negotiate, since the perspective of a new association necessarily implied talks with Ottawa and the rest of Canada. In that case, like any scrupulous bargaining agent, we would then have to report on the success or failure of the negotiations. Consequently, we would have to plan to go to the people again afterwards. That was realistic, it seemed to us, and more reassuring for those who were still hesitant to stick their toes in the water.

Could Claude Morin be called one of these? That was the dark suspicion the stringent integrationist wing of the party cast on him. This had begun back in 1974 at the congress where he had become the "father" of the referendum. Until then we had simply thought that with a parliamentary majority a PQ government would speedily declare independence without any other formal process. That would have been in keeping with the old saw that says Parliament can do anything except change a man into a woman. Still, that would have been a little too quick and more than a little risky. If we had won the election with less than half the popular vote, a very probable result and precisely the one we got in 1976, what kind of a welcome would the federal government hold in store for such a unilateral declaration of independence? Nothing more likely than a furious rejection of official recognition, the only way a country can be entered in the international registry of nations. It would have an easy time of it, too, considering the large family of post-colonial states that still maintained many smaller peoples within their boundaries and thus were condemned to fear any form of separatism like the plague. To extract an encircled province like Quebec from within the federal structure, it would be absolutely necessary to obtain an incontestable mandate first. What we needed was a "maître chez nous" type of statement affirming our collective determination on this precise point. Seeing the good sense of this line of reasoning, the party agreed without too much grumbling to include a referendum in its platform.

But because he had piloted us around this bend, Claude Morin became suspect in the eyes of disappointed radicals who now saw in him a camouflaged federalist, or at the very least a faint-hearted stage-by-stage negotiator, an "étapiste." This tag used to drive him crazy, as happens to anyone when others stupidly blame us for being logical and using our common sense. It was that very logic that inspired Morin's favourite metaphor: "No matter how much you tug at it, the flower won't grow any faster." It was also the same logical mind that led him to construct his thought in interminable syllogisms of the kind: Small a.) Think of this; small b). Add that; small c.) Without forgetting . . . etc., etc., a process that obviously tickled his vanity. For people who couldn't stand him, this was enough to put him in the class of drawing-room Machiavellis, whereas in reality he was a tireless and sharp-witted journeyman constantly on guard against traps Ottawa might be laying for us, and consequently execrated by the feds with cordial intensity.

It eventually fell to my lot to propose to cabinet the question that our meticulous trio had been sweating blood over. I had worked on it a few days myself to flesh it out a little while trying to avoid making it heavier. But it goes without saying that no formulation was going to get quick approval from a group that is getting ready to stake all or nothing on a few lines. Patiently assuming the role of stenographer that a chairman is bound to fill, I noted a word too many according to this member, an expression that didn't ring true according to that one. We subtracted, we added. Unforeseen doubts hove into view. For instance, why ask for a mandate to negotiate instead of one to go right ahead? As for the idea of a second referendum, it literally brought Jacques Parizeau to a boil, since even the first wasn't easy for him to swallow! Tension was building up too much so I adjourned the meeting for an hour. By midnight we were approaching a fairly solid consensus. And so we continued until the small hours, when our jurists were called upon to weigh our words in the delicate balance-pans of legality. Then next morning, a night's sleep unluckily having allowed time for second thoughts, I arranged with Morin and Bernard to change two words at a place where Parizeau had been especially upset, and more unluckily still, one thinking the other had done it, neither of us told him, which he almost took for a foul blow. Everyone's nerves were shot.

You can imagine the great relief it was, now that the die had been cast, to rise at the opening of the session and unveil the famous question to the House:

> The government of Quebec has made public its proposal to negotiate a new agreement with the rest of Canada, based on the equality of nations;
>
> this agreement would enable Quebec to acquire the exclusive power to make its laws, levy its taxes and establish relations abroad – in other words, sovereignty – and at the same time to maintain with Canada an economic association including a common currency;
>
> no change in political status resulting from these negotiations will be effected without approval by the people through another referendum; on these terms do you give the Government of Quebec the mandate to negotiate the proposed agreement between Quebec and Canada?

It was rather long and heavy but, to use a word that is fashionable today, it was perfectly "transparent." In three short paragraphs and some hundred words the essence was there for anyone who knew how to read.

The holiday season gave all a chance to talk it over in their families, and seeing that on the whole the question was pretty well received, we began to look forward confidently to the debate that would mark the real opening of the campaign in February.

A first leitmotif would naturally be a critical analysis of the federal regime. But the most important theme, one that everyone would have to explore according to his or her own feelings and experience, was the promise sovereignty-association held for the future. On this score what was required of our elected members was nothing short of the best performance of their careers. I never saw such discipline in our ranks nor such willingness to work. With the help of a battalion of research assistants we had mobilized, even the least articulate MNAs strove like slaves, absolutely determined to surpass themselves. And they succeeded. We had really thought of everything, right down to crash courses for those who didn't "come across" on TV. From delivery to dress, everything was impeccable, for everyone knew how crucial the issue was, and for once there was no absenteeism.

Nor was there the least false note. Day after day on our side one could witness the most extraordinary performances. An unprecedented flood of tight arguments backed by stunning examples soon began to flow from this marvellous teamwork, contributing to an atmosphere that was emotional and almost euphoric. Claude Charron, who had replaced Robert Burns as parliamentary chief, patrolled the ranks handing out advice and encouragement, an administrative task that did not prevent him from turning in one of his most unforgettable speeches. Emulation constantly improved our output.

What a contrast to the disarray in the opposite camp. Elected party leader in 1978, and just recently MNA for Argenteuil, Claude Ryan was as awkward as a debutante and, worse still, showed sure signs of inebriation at being close to the goal of political power. Since his party had been winning by-elections handily, he was beginning to see himself as head of government already. But although he was sure of himself, he was skimpily and poorly prepared for the debate. Content to harp away that the referendum question was dishonest and must surely hide sinister intentions, from the start he took the path of pure and simple demagoguery. There is nothing old veterans of the House like better, accustomed as they are to playing with clichés rather than ideas, so his Liberal cohorts followed his example with relish. In reply to dense and passionate statements on our side, they sat back and croaked "séparatisses, séparatisses." Our determination to situate ourselves on a level worthy of the subject was met by mean-minded, repetitive, and most often childish refrains. The merciless eye of the camera revealed a Claude Ryan staring about vacantly while the rest of the herd, floored by the steady broadside we directed at them, no longer managed to conceal their confusion.

The public could see very well what was going on. Rarely has a political debate been anticipated so impatiently and then followed so closely by so many Québécois, and they got our message all the better because our adversaries could only conjure up the most trivial contradictions.

The polls were not slow to confirm that we had won this first round hands down. I have before me one from the beginning of April, 1980: six weeks before the big day we had taken a comfortable lead.

The Referendum Question: All of Quebec

	Oui	Non	Undecided
A) March-April	46%	43%	11%

B) Commentary:
– important gains for the "Oui" in March.
– compared to February when the distribution of valid votes was 48% for the "Oui" and 52% for the "Non," this represents an increase of 3% for the "Oui."
– even if the race remains very close, one can foresee a majority for the "Oui". . . .

Constitutional Variants: Francophones Only

– Sovereignty-association (55%) is now, for the first time, more popular than renewed federalism (46%).
– The three principal constituents of sovereignty-association obtain majority support, i.e., Quebec should be responsible for:

	Oui	Non
All laws	51%	41%
All taxes	63%	29%
International representation	54%	35%

Voters' Intentions: By Age

	18-24	25-34	35-44	45-54	55-64	65+
Oui	69%	66%	54%	51%	40%	37%
Non	27%	27%	36%	40%	44%	45%
Undecided	4%	7%	10%	9%	16%	18%

At 55 per cent *of Francophones only* the "Oui" side was still a few points below the barrier we would have to cross. Considering the monolithic "Non" that could be expected from Anglo-Québécois, the French majority would have to come up to approximately 62 per cent in favour of the "Oui." At the time it wasn't at all inconceivable. Hadn't we seen, elsewhere in the world, people deliver a unanimous or almost unanimous vote on similar occasions?

Keyed up by the clear victory we had won in the National

Assembly, "Committees for the Oui" spread throughout the country like wildfire. There was at least one in every riding. In many businesses employees had their own groups, too. One after another we saw "Economists for the Oui," "Lawyers for the Oui," "Scientists for the Oui." Crowning the pyramid, the "Regroupement National" could boast spectacular members: senior civil servants like Thérèse Baron, military heroes like General Allard, writers and artists like Marie-Claire Blais and Fabienne Thibault, an important collection of former ministers and members of both the federal and provincial parliaments, front-line combatants like the Association des Gens de l'Air, well-known university figures like the Rector of Sherbrooke, Yves Martin, and the Vice-Dean of Laval, Christine Piette, and a good number of the most respected spokesmen for rural Quebec. Painting a moving picture of the future he hoped to assure his children by his option, the leader of the Union Nationale, Rodrigue Biron, also joined our ranks.

The eminent businessman and veteran indépendantiste Fernand Paré was in charge of the "Foundation for the Oui" that was to collect more than three and a half million dollars. Its vice-president was Madeleine Ferron, wife of the late Robert Cliche, who shortly before his death had written these prophetic words: "In my view, one of the gravest dangers would be a Non in the referendum. English Canada would believe that the crisis was over and would slip back into its lethargy."

And what precisely was happening in English Canada? Forget for the time being the Quebec branch of the Anglo establishment where the halt, the sick, the lame, and the dead were being conscripted for the "Non" and where the exceptionally rare dissidents, huddled together in their CASA (Comité Anglophone pour la Souveraineté-Association), risked the same fate as that meted out to former Liberal minister Kevin Drummond, whose "Oui" had cost him the loss of friends and a rift in his family.

Outside Quebec, on the contrary, opinion was less entrenched. The situation appeared to be still quite fluid. Bill Davis and his Ontario government might refuse in advance to negotiate as much as they liked, but they were far from reflecting the opinion of people most directly concerned. Since they had always been the principal beneficiaries of the federal regime, the leaders of Ontario society obviously preferred to retain the status quo, but if Quebec said "Oui," wouldn't they come to terms to maintain a hold on the common market of association? This, at any rate, was the conclusion a team of researchers from York University came to when a solid majority of decision-makers chosen from every sector of society admitted that in the event of a victory for the "Oui" they would opt for accommodation. In the Atlantic Provinces there wasn't the least hesitation. Quoting a study made for the Task Force on Canadian Unity, the *Globe and Mail* noted that they "would be favourable to economic union between their region and an independent Quebec. In the same breath 65% of those polled said that if a 'free and democratic' vote went in this direction, Quebec should be authorized to quit the Canadian federation."

Economist Abraham Rotstein provided figures that eloquently describe the economic interdependence that binds a great number of Canadians: "In Ontario no less than 105,800 jobs depend directly on the Quebec market. Ontario enterprises annually export 4.6 billion dollars worth of manufactured goods to Quebec. . . . [Rotstein] estimates that there are 9,000 workers in the Maritimes whose salaries depend on sales to Quebec. The Prairies sell $432,000,000 in consumer goods to Quebec (particularly beef they are unable to sell elsewhere in America) which supports some 10,000 jobs. Finally, 3,000 persons in B.C. have jobs related to exports to Quebec. In the reverse direction the number of jobs is approximately identical."*

Could Québécois have been right, then, when at the end of March they replied 71 per cent "Oui" and only 16 per cent "Non" to the question: Will Canada negotiate? Perhaps they were, as long as one kept in mind, applying it to the present context, the judgement Mazzini passed on the British in the last century, a view that has been constantly confirmed by history since: "From time immemorial it has been English policy [read Anglo-Canadian] to put obstacles in the path of any factor that might seem to introduce a new element into the European [Canadian] picture, and then to accept it as soon as it has been solemnly accomplished. . . ."

As could be expected, we, too, were to be presented with every kind of obstacle imaginable. But just the same, we felt that a great many of our people, perhaps even that small majority the polls indicated, expected to see the "Oui" succeed and, though they did not always show it openly, had actually come to hope it would.

This was all the more so because in Ottawa, as among provin-

* *Le Devoir*, December 19, 1979.

cial federalists, the situation remained fluid. When the multi-billion-dollar decision came up whether to build the F-16 fighter plane, the economic benefits of which would go principally to Quebec, or the F-18, with 80 or 90 per cent of contracts going to Ontario, Trudeau's government was faced with turbulence in its Quebec caucus. Claude Ryan's cohorts, meanwhile, continued in the depression caused by their parliamentary discomfiture. The "Non" were feverishly seeking a strike force but, failing to discover a trigger mechanism, seemed incapable of inventing one.

It was we, alas, who were going to give them the booster they needed. One day in March in a modest meeting that would normally have sunk quietly beneath the sands of time, Lise Payette got caught up in one of those feminist declarations prompted by her job as Minister of the Status of Women. In the most logical way imaginable she had set about exposing a school text presenting two great incarnations of traditional sexism – little Guy, future champion and perfect macho, and little Yvette, model miniature housewife, broken in to be perfectly submissive. So far so good. But carried away by her subject and "pushed by some devil," our colleague dropped a remark to the effect that Quebec women would have to learn to sit up and sit still if ever Claude Ryan took power because he was married to a protracted "Yvette." This was not only in poor taste but untrue and Lise Payette soon heard about it, for several journalists made a point of enumerating Madame Ryan's exceptional accomplishments and made it a duty to execute the guilty party in the public square.

This deplorable slip was a small enough cause, but it was destined to have resounding effects. Toward the end of March, well supported by Liberals, several hundred "Yvettes" met in Quebec City. And when, on April 7, thousands more filled the Montreal Forum waving the Canadian flag in one hand and the fleur-de-lys in the other, having quickly forgotten the incident that had served as a pretext to launch their reinvigorated "Non," we understood that the opposition machine had finally got off the ground.

The next forty days that took us up to May 20 deserve to be described in detail, hour by hour, for the edification of future generations, if not for those who were steamrollered by them.

It was an unqualifiable deluge of lies, threats, and blackmail. The federal Minister of Energy, Marc Lalonde, promised a sovereign Quebec an energy deficit of exactly $16.6 billion. His colleague in social affairs, Monique Bégin, predicted a phenomenally high level of taxation just to be able to maintain old age pensions and family allowances. Taking what could be called the "low road" and hitting shamelessly below the belt, unscrupulous terrorists infiltrated the weakest sectors of society, for example, an old folks home where one of them, seeing some oranges in a bowl, had the gall to tell the senior citizens sitting around: "Watch out now, if the separatists win, you'll never see any more oranges in Quebec." No one knew how to evoke this pitiful, down-at-heel Quebec with more verve than Jean Chrétien, belching out in conclusion his caricature of Claude Morin, promoted ambassador of some equally under-developed country driving around in a Cadillac "avec le flag su'l'hood."

Despite rules that we had legitimately established but that had been rapidly trampled underfoot, the "Non" camp had no scruples about floating their campaign on floods of money, the exact total of which, unless I am mistaken, will never be known. The tribunals we addressed prudently sidestepped the issue with a few remarks that amounted to placing federal public funds beyond the reach of any Quebec law. How many millions were swallowed up in Ottawa back offices where all the "Non" propaganda was prepared, including material used by the provincial Liberals? How much more to paper the media and every corner of the country with "Me? I'm staying in . . . for my own good," and that "NON merci" that even cropped up in anti-alcoholic advertising from Honourable Madame Bégin's Ministry of Health and Welfare?

Nerves and stomach pinched and pummelled by such savage blows, public resolution began to falter. In the most fragile strata, among seniors and "floaters," who are always like a feather in the wind, the hurricane of "Non" propaganda wreaked havoc. It seemed to be irresistible and dealt in fear. From West to East, from Blakeney in Saskatchewan to Hatfield in New Brunswick, came the heralds of the Anglo-Canadian refusal. Sniffing their victory to be, they felt free now to write us off in the most callous tones. By the end of April everyone knew, in Ottawa as in Quebec, that we would not reach our 62 per cent and that even a straight majority was no longer a sure thing in French Quebec.

It was at this point that Trudeau, who had become prime minister again the month before, decided to step on stage and participate without risk in the last act. First on May 2, 1980, presenting himself before the receptive audience of the Chamber of Commerce, he began by indulging in heavy irony, citing our cowardice, saying we hadn't dared to go straight to the goal, machine gun in hand . . . like Zimbabwe or Algeria. Seeing that he was on the wrong track he fell back on another analogy, less explosive though just as misplaced. "Suppose," he said, "that Cuba or Haiti came proposing to associate with us, because down there they like Canadian prosperity, the Canadian countryside, Canadian women . . . So they vote on it and agree, massively, yes, we want association with Canada. Would we, in the name of democracy, be obliged to accept them? Would our only choice, in the name of fair play, be to consent: 'Well, yes, they voted for it, so we don't have anything to say in the matter'? (*Much laughter and sustained applause.*)" Finally, betraying both his peevishness and his relief, our improviser imagined the care with which a Castro or a Duvalier would have felt out the ground in order to avoid simply being told "Go and get lost!"

To my mind such remarks deserve a choice place in a little manual entitled "The Way to Insult People Without Risk Who Don't Think the Way You Do." It would be a very thin volume, for history doesn't record many who have treated their fellows so grossly. As for the anthology of political duplicity that would fill several fat volumes, the historic encounter of the following week certainly deserves to be enshrined there.

On May 14, one week before the vote, here, in résumé, is how Trudeau, before thousands of Montrealers and addressing the whole of Quebec, proclaimed that he and his were ready to put their heads on the block: "We, MPs from Quebec, ask Québécois to vote Non, and at the same time we warn Canadians in other provinces that this Non should not be interpreted as proof that all is well here, or that there are not changes to be made. On the contrary, it is with the aim of getting things changed that we are putting our seats on the line."

Change, okay. But what change? That remained a mystery. Considering the past and so many claims so often reiterated, any right-minded person couldn't help thinking that nothing less than greater autonomy and better guarantees for Quebec were in question. If not, it was just an airy promise, or else something no democratic politician could permit himself at this moment – sheer deceit.

Every chance we had to speak in public over the next days we demanded specifics. In vain. The sphinx kept his secret, knowing full well that if he revealed the true nature of his thought, innumerable

Québécois would turn away in disgust. He was biding his time while we spent our last strength trying to reach that vital minimum of a strong majority French vote. Describing the instinctive and perfectly comprehensible solidarity Anglophones showed in throwing their support massively to the other side, I went around begging our people to show the same solidarity for once in our history. But it was too late. Or perhaps it wasn't yet time . . .

To this day no one knows if our two-fifths vote for the "Oui" represented 49 or 51 per cent of French Quebec that night. On the other hand, the three-fifths vote for the "Non" was sadly incontestable. And hard to swallow, I had to add when speaking to some 5,000 partisans who had gathered at the Paul Sauvé Arena just the same. At the back of the platform, side by side, stood Corinne holding back her tears and Lise Payette dressed in black like a penitent; before me swam a sea of faces that no other defeat had thrown into such dejection.

"The day will come, however," I said, trying to convince myself, "and we will be here to greet it. But I must admit that tonight I would be hard pressed to tell you when or how. In the meantime we must live together. . . ." To cut words short I struck up the Vigneault song that had practically become our anthem, "Gens du pays," off-key, as usual. Then I took my leave with "A la prochaine!" – a sentiment that was also a bit off-key but might at least help forget the present a little.

In Ottawa Trudeau lost no time in transforming himself into the wheedling healer full of solicitude for the downtrodden, pretending to spread balm on our wounds by praising our sense of democracy, a perfect Tartufe as we would soon discover, once again.

As for Claude Ryan, I am told that he gave the victory a sinister turn by conjuring up invisible sceptics and making a long show, in a strangely vengeful voice, of enumerating every county and even every town that had followed him, conveniently forgetting the twelve ridings that stuck by us in the tempest: Taillon, L'Assomption (Parizeau), Louis-Hébert (Morin), Rivière-du-Loup, Saguenay, Maisonneuve, Sainte-Marie, Abitibi-est, and every one of the five electoral districts of Saguenay–Lac St.-Jean, which were to hear from the lips of this same man one day that they had been deprived of the proper information. Decidedly, in normal times as an adversary he would hardly make more than a mouthful, but that was small consolation.

39. Out of Fashion

THIRTEEN YEARS OF HIGH HOPES and "optimism of the will" had just collapsed. That hurt. Yet it was more hurtful to see the heavy curtain that had fallen, closing off the horizon. For the first time, during those few hours of May 20, our people had had a say in their own destiny, the same people who had been so pushed around by history, from the French regime to the English occupation, from the beginnings of self-government to the Union, and to Confederation. How many people are there in the world who have refused such a chance to acquire full powers for themselves peacefully and democratically?

The worst of it was not to have missed a victory of heart and reason, but to find oneself faced, first and foremost, by the triumph of fear. Aggravated by propaganda that no regime that felt at all self-confident would have permitted, it was fear, the fear Roosevelt had described, "There is nothing to fear but fear itself," that had won the day.

We hadn't dared, hadn't been numerous enough to dare cast off our moorings. We hadn't even gone as far as giving that clear, decisive "Oui" from French Quebec that might have been the means to force certain restoration work in the old federal homestead. Strictly speaking, we would have to continue living there as dependants in an increasingly minority situation. As I have often said, it wasn't exactly hell, far from that; it was more like some painless purgatory where our development would be whittled down, where we would live torn between what the Inuit used to call the "Little" and the "Big" government. Since the latter didn't belong to us, there wasn't much sense crying over spilled milk. But such a context will never let us know the self-realization that the full range of our resources would justify. Never under this system can we push to the full limit of our capacities.

I know very well that the subject isn't fashionable any more. The days of decolonization are behind us, so they say. The nation-state isn't any more popular than the welfare-state. That's all right by me, except that I can't help observing that states, whether nation-states or not, don't often consent to any substantial reduction in their decision-making powers. Even the poorest and deepest in debt manage to stand up against the dictates of the rich. And it's by standing up to others, as if by some kind of visceral reflex, that all sorts of nationalisms, even ones that are hard to take seriously, come alive. Faced by the American violation of *our* Arctic waters, for example, and even more by the leonine attitude of our powerful neighbour in free trade matters, didn't we hear a sudden rumble from the usually sputtering motor of Canadian nationalism?

I am only referring here to nationalisms that have had the time to live their independence as they saw fit, well or poorly, it doesn't matter which, but long enough to become a bit blasé about it. This is not the case with us. I promise not to come back to the subject again, at least not in this book, but I must say one last time that so long as we haven't passed through that stage we will never be more, in many respects, than a potential people. I want to return for a moment to those days when the obstacles before us seemed nothing more than so many new challenges, and when, like legendary Lancelots in a real world, we strode forth in search of our grail, which I persist in believing was no illusion.

"There is in any drive toward independence," I proclaimed in 1972, "a privileged moment, a unique opportunity for movement and renewal. The experience of a host of other countries proves this, and one would have to be terribly despondent to think that we would not know this moment, too. In the life of a nation it is a chance that, by definition, occurs only once and does not come back again, but which permits one, like no other opportunity, if it isn't missed, to achieve veritable revolution that is peaceful and fruitful at the same time. . . .

"Men and women of Quebec wouldn't recognize themselves. Belonging to a people entirely responsible for themselves can only engender a totally new sense of responsibility and develop the spirit of initiative as never before. One doesn't have to think about some impossible mutation that would change human nature along with a change in political structures. We are simply talking about an 'enrichment of soul' that is infallibly accorded the members of a national community when they attain that supreme goal. All people who gain sovereignty experience this, even those whose lack of preparation or under-development prevents normal and durable progress beyond the initial euphoria.

"In short, independence is a true move into action. All the rest, for the past three hundred years and more, will only have been a too-long training period. . . ."*

On this note I will go on seeing us as future champions, come what may, though keeping my word I will now pass on to what follows, a continuation that I really don't feel much like tackling, particularly when the time comes, as it soon will, to go into the consequences of the referendum.

One thing was certain, the "Non" vote was going to cost us plenty. Just how much, no one could really say, but knowing the permanent aims of the federal establishment and the fixed ideas of the man who was directing it again, we could be sure we would get our comeuppance. We didn't have to wait long. In September, 1980, we were to learn the true sense of his "putting his seat on the line" and of his grand promises of renewal. During discussions in Ottawa on division of powers, that eternal deaf man's debate, a sensational leak revealed that once again we were going nowhere. What turned up was a memo from Michael Kirby, one of Trudeau's most intimate henchmen. Studded with quotations from Machiavelli, this text explained with limitless cynicism that negotiations had only been opened for show and at the appropriate moment would simply be shut down. Like my provincial counterparts, I was incensed. But Trudeau, not in the least put out at the discovery of his scheme, simply rang the curtain down on the farce and shortly after decided to reveal the depths of his thought: since our miserable little provincial governments so obstinately opposed him, The Prince was going to settle the business in London, as "equal to equal" with Her Majesty's Parliament.

Since I must, I will tell this ugly story as I lived it, trying to bring to it the rigour of honest reporting. But since the climax of all this only came late in 1981, I must first speak about the astonishing victory we won in the interval. Was it a bad luck victory? Many times I have secretly asked myself that very question.

* Extract from the manifesto "Quand nous serons vraiment chez nous" (Québec: Editions du Parti Québécois, 1972).

VIII

WINNER LOSE ALL

"A collective hope cannot be put down. Every shoot cut back springs up again stronger and more beautiful. Despair in politics is absolute stupidity."
CHARLES MAURRAS

---

40. When the Opposition Regains Power

"MONSIEUR LE PREMIER MINISTRE," the dean asked in a tone full of compassion, "could you tell us how you see the next elections?"

I had my answer ready, an answer I only half believed.

Three months earlier everyone had us slated to lose, to such an extent that in the autumn of 1980, near the end of our fourth year, neither ministers nor MNAs could get together on the date for the election. Discussion followed by a vote ended on two separate occasions in an astounding result: an even draw. One half were resigned to get it over with right away, the other preferred to put off taking the bitter cup, even if that meant putting up with diatribes from an opposition that already saw itself in power and jibes from all quarters calling us cowards.

In the end the caucus turned to me. To tell the truth, I literally flipped a coin.

"Things can't get any worse," I said, "consequently they might get better. We'll see, come spring."

It was true that we were taken to be the ones who had lost our nerve, though we did get a little commiseration in the necrologies that were being written for us. Still unable to win the least by-election, marked by the loss of colleagues who had left broken-hearted after the referendum defeat, trailing far behind the Liberals in the polls, all that remained for us, it seemed, was to receive the electoral extreme unction. I had registered this sentiment even as far as Paris where, in December, on what would undoubtedly be my last official visit, the parting handshakes were accompanied by professions of friendship that sounded like farewells: "We'll miss you, you know . . ." Even President Giscard d'Estaing conveyed this message, expressing it with great diffidence since he was superbly confident of his own re-election.

"No, I am in no hurry to launch an election campaign," he said. "I prefer to look after government business as long as possible. That's what the people want, I think."

Lucky you, I thought to myself.

"But two terms of seven years, Monsieur le Président, that's quite a lease!"

"Yes, it is doubtless too long. I am very seriously considering reducing the mandate, from seven to five years, perhaps, or even four as in the United States. But one thing at a time. First the election, then we'll think about it." Except, as the poet says, that the best laid plans of mice and men . . .

Christmas came and went, that key season when sometimes a spectacular alchemy affects public opinion. One day in February at about the time Giscard d'Estaing was beginning to condescend to get a little concerned about the future, Michel Lepage burst into my office to tell me the results of the latest polls. A wizard at this métier that is also an art, and capable of transforming dozens of volunteers into a team of experts, he had never led us astray yet. But this time I was sure he must be off his rocker.

"But no matter how I calculate it," he said, "it always comes out the same. If things go on like this we'll pick up almost 50 per cent of the vote, in 79 or 80 ridings."

A few days later it was my annual meeting with the consular service. The dean had just asked his question . . .

"Well," I replied, "I'm no prophet, of course, but if the vote were held today or tomorrow, I think we could count on the same number of seats as the last time, at least 72, perhaps 75."

With the courtesy common to good diplomats, the consuls swallowed down this preposterous statement unruffled. Less discreet, a couple of journalists, who had been hiding in a cupboard in order to "respect" the closed-door nature of the meeting, rushed out choking with laughter to spread the news, so that when I left the room the whole media gang was there waiting for me, splitting their sides.

But Lepage was right. The turnaround had indeed taken place. After our autumn hesitations the party organizers had worked nonstop. Sniffing victory in the wind, the team was full of self-confidence and champing at the bit. By March 11, if I may be permitted to motorize my metaphor, the machine took off with a squeal of tires.

Of the seven election campaigns I've been through, this was by far the easiest. Unlike those of 1962 or 1976, when my nerves were stretched to the breaking point, this one seemed more like a month's holiday. People were visibly happy to see us again. Did this warmth hide a wish to console us? Maybe a vague remorse had infiltrated many minds since that sad evening of May 20, 1980. To know for sure I would have had to be able to delve the recesses of the human heart like the Arab angel.

What did become clear from the first week on was that people were pretty satisfied with the work we had done in the last four years. Bill 101 stood like a formidable rampart protecting our language and our national future itself. Too well, probably. I still wonder whether this feeling of complacent security didn't contribute in some sly way to weaken the referendum "Oui."

Though they had been much discussed, automobile insurance and agricultural zoning were now two of our major trumps. Guy Joron and his team had left us a plan for autonomy in the energy field that is still valid today. The same holds true for the main lines of the "Build Quebec" policy for industrial development set up by Bernard Landry's group. Since our first "summit" held at Pointe-au-Pic as early as 1977, we had improved our relations with the business community, particularly with the small and medium-sized enterprises which in Quebec, as in every advanced economy, remain the principal sources of employment. From trying to seize so many problems – including cultural industries, housing, consumer protection, measures favouring the elderly, aid to municipalities – our grip was undoubtedly too slack in certain cases, but I don't believe we neglected any important area. Even the partial nationalization of the asbestos industry, where recession and boycott would eventually darken the horizon, seemed at the time to be fulfilling promises Yves Bérubé and I had made four years earlier, assuring Québécois a piece of property we had never owned, as well as transformations in the industry that in the past had been well nigh non-existent.

Above all, and this had never been seen either, in every corner of the administration we had been incorruptible right down the line. Just like the defence of liberty, this requires eternal vigilance, so I would not be particularly surprised if, looking hard, one might turn up a few spots of dust, but we had really done a big housecleaning job and had come out of it with clean hands. *

Added to the fact that we had been seen to do our best to fulfil our commitments from the preceding campaign, our constant concern for integrity did not go unnoticed. Nor did the simple good sense we showed in promising that "without detours or evasions we intend to respect the decision of May, 1980. . . . Since the will of the majority of the population was expressed a year ago, the government undertakes not to hold a referendum on sovereignty-association during a second term of office."

Once again we were proposing a whole new raft of concrete measures, which experience now helped us formulate with great

---

* Of course, our opponents tried to manufacture some scandals for us. Funnily enough, these came out of authentically dirty deals left behind by our predecessors, which we had decided to clean up. Since 1972, for instance, the case of the destruction caused at the James Bay dam site had been dragging on in the courts. In going over the dossier we realized that the unions involved were practically insolvent and that to collect even a fraction of the enormous damages that were being claimed we would have to pursue them through the maze of their head offices and the American courts. To reach a speedy solution we twisted Hydro-Québec's arm a little and negotiated the least unfavourable settlement, which in any event was one hundred times better than an interminable cascade of ruinous legal proceedings.

For some time we were also reproached with getting a friend to make overly hasty "major repairs" to some high-rises that had been built by regular bandits, brand new buildings whose roofs and walls collapsed and whose basements flooded. Our friend was a specialist in this type of renovation and not only made the repairs in record time but saved us several million dollars into the bargain. But alas, as many contractors do, he had the misfortune to give his son, a student, a small summer job, and the "scandal" was blown up to such proportions and was kept alive so long that it left him bitter and raw.

precision. I will restrict myself to mentioning one of these, the continuing importance of which still recalls the dramatic appropriateness of our action.

> The wish to own one's own home is widespread among young families with children. The growing needs of growing youngsters are an incentive to find larger houses and better environments. Acquiring property is the best way to increase savings and stimulate construction in the domestic field. . . . To this end the government plans to set up without delay a program to help young Quebec families acquire property.

Several thousand young couples were soon to take advantage of this policy, one of the most striking effects of which was to give impetus to the healthy transformation of a people of tenants into a people of property owners. That subsidies granted at the birth of additional children were intended to encourage growth of the population, I cannot deny. Nor do I regret it at a time when our birth rate continues its steep decline, when the aging of our population promises us an extremely problematic close to this century, and when, in addition, one sees the multiplication of dwellings and condominiums designed for people who are unwilling to "become encumbered" with more than one child, if that. Obviously, children cannot be bought any more, as they were in the days of Mussolini, and the "revenge of the cradles" belongs to a past age. But that's no reason to sit by, arms folded, before such a demographic collapse.

The true causes of our re-election, however, were not this or that fine and noble project. They lay outside us, I'm convinced of that, out there, ironically, among the federal Liberals and their branch-line Quebec party. In Ottawa Trudeau was back in power again. Were we going to vote Liberal-red in Quebec too? Put all our eggs in the same old basket? As usual, the voter thought twice about such things.

But our greatest luck was to be matched up with a Claude Ryan who, ever since the revealing ferocity of that referendum night, had taken off on a power trip of disconcerting intensity. He spoke and acted like someone dreaming, not only of power – as far as he was concerned, he had it already – but of autocracy, to a distressing degree. Lording it over his party like Duplessis reincarnated as the Grand Inquisitor, almost requiring a confession slip from his candidates, obstinately keeping in his treasury the large sums contributed earlier by the profiteers of the Olympic fiasco, he seriously risked collapsing in ridicule.

Everyone agreed, however, himself the first among them, that he would be premier just the same. As for me, I was already nothing more than a poor little leader of the opposition fighting like the devil to ward off disaster. When the election came around, however, what a heaven-sent gift it was to have been perceived for months as the guaranteed loser, and even as the one who had already lost, while still benefiting from all the advantages conferred by remaining the government. The ideal situation is to find oneself able to attack rather than having to fall back on the defensive. For us, the all-too-visible arrogance and funny tricks of the "Ryan government" combined to become the most determining factor in our victory, so true it is that the voter always votes "against" as much as "for" something.

Does it follow that for this reversal of expectations we had no price to pay? No way. All autumn long and then a good part of the winter we struggled along, grinding our teeth, through a veritable valley of humiliation. One station of the cross in particular has remained branded as with a red-hot iron in my memory.

As I said above, as soon as he had his "Non" safely in his pocket, Trudeau rushed on to bring up his big guns. What he now demanded was nothing less than the hasty repatriation of the constitution, to which he also wished to graft his pet project, a Charter of Rights that had the singular virtue of giving everybody the goose pimples. Such was the case, on our side, because we knew that it would be an instrument to reduce the powers of Quebec, and so it was on the side of the Anglo-Canadian provinces because this kind of American-style "Bill of Rights" is completely foreign to the unwritten tradition of British institutions.

Intransigent as always, The Prince had spurned us and decided to apply directly to London, calling on the Parliament at Westminster to affix his Charter to the old BNA Act and to repatriate the whole thing without delay. The least that one can say is that the English were not very keen on the idea. Many took offence at this cavalier way of proceeding and didn't hide their feelings. "If they don't like the smell," Trudeau proclaimed, insulting them further, "all they have to do is hold their noses and vote."

It was at this point that we made our appeal to the National

Assembly. When the supreme interests of the nation are clearly at stake, most parliaments, putting aside their partisan blinkers, almost always find a way to reach agreement. The Quebec Liberals could not ignore the fact that a unanimous reaction would carry considerable weight with the British. To our way of thinking, they should have been even less hesitant to support us since Claude Ryan himself had quickly denounced Trudeau's attitude, and in its essential points our motion actually borrowed many of his own terms.

So there was nothing contentious in the text of our motion before the Assembly. It was merely a question of signalling our opposition to the federal gesture, which, for that matter, had been contested by a clear majority of the other provinces. What we were asking was that the two parliaments, one in Ottawa, the other in London, condemn Trudeau's manoeuvre since it was obviously contrary to the very nature of federalism, above all to the established rule that had always required that all provinces consent to any constitutional modification.

Logically this should have taken about ten minutes. But we were in November, 1980. The PQ government was at its lowest ebb. Not content to see us on the canvas, the Liberals were, one might say, out for blood. So they cooked up a truly inconceivable amendment. To obtain their unanimity, we, the trammelled, would have to endorse a statement acknowledging the "attachment" Québécois felt for the federal regime and its "advantages," while rejecting sovereignty-association. "Bow lower still," we were enjoined, "and accept the yoke of humiliation!" I begged Ryan not to push us to the wall like this. I asked him to put himself in my place. A little more and I would have gone down on my knees to him. But, murmuring a few soothing words, the Liberal chief was quite content to let me stew in my own juice. Beneath his ingratiating exterior one could perceive a hint of voluptuous sadism.

Despite some last-minute manoeuvring, all that remained was for us to register the divided vote that sadly undermined our position. Trying awkwardly to explain their action, the Liberals only sank in deeper. According to Léon Dion, the constitutional expert, it was a day of mourning, and he attributed the entire responsibility to "an act of betrayal [of the national interest] that was both subjective and objective."

That was exactly my sentiment. It was at this moment that I swore to myself I would concentrate all my energies on this election and would try to make it the best campaign of my career. That's the way I am: the worse things are, the more I generally feel in my element. Nothing could have galvanized me more surely than the spectacle we had just been subjected to: people bartering away a golden opportunity to serve Quebec because of the meanest, most underhand parliamentary trickery.

In this regard I think I recognize my own prose in this passage taken from our election platform, where, maintaining that "we must remain strong in Quebec," we asked: "Which of the parties is exclusively Québécois enough to demand as a vital minimum in any resumption of [constitutional] talks the explicit recognition of a distinct national society whose homeland is Quebec, its inalienable right to dispose freely of its own future, and exclusive rights in the matter of the language of education? Quite simply we believe that to ask the question is to know the answer."

This is the way voters also came to see things, and basically, the die was cast. Claude Ryan could do nothing but improve our chances, and he didn't miss a trick. To his power-drunk behaviour as Premier before the fact, he foreseeably added that of a man who, too sure of himself, hasn't taken the trouble to prepare his campaign in advance.

We were following a rigorous plan of action, while poor Ryan was soon reduced to the most haphazard lucubrations. After proclaiming he would never lower himself to handing out "candies," he quickly perceived that our precise commitments were being well received and began scattering half-baked promises right and left. While our slate of candidates was active everywhere, as solid as ever nationally, and richer and better balanced in most regions, Ryan on the contrary, like Lesage in 1966, thought he was strong enough to win without anyone's help. Taking himself for some local Kissinger, he was really only a lonely cowboy galloping off into his own sunset. The most amazing thing was that he appeared to be unconscious of the danger until two weeks before the vote, when the polls brutally unsealed his eyes and threw him into a frenzy of despair. We might even have felt somewhat sorry for him had it not been for the self-indulgent way, when he was on top of the heap, that he had kept riding us down. Without going so far as to say, "Now it's your turn," we did feel he had deserved his lesson.

For the last two weeks all we had to do was surfboard down the wave that swelled magnificently under us, then, on the evening of April 13, 1981, await the inevitable. The result was such a sure thing that for once the traditional cabal of Liberal gamblers, who had opened the campaign by tossing a showy wager on the table, were nowhere to be found when, toward the end, our own players obligingly offered to raise the ante.*

Yet the evening began by putting us into a cold sweat. As if to prove that the machine can never quite replace the human brain, Télé-métropole's computer insisted for a good hour in maintaining that the Union Nationale had come back from the grave and that good old Roch Lasalle should be thinking about forming the next government, on condition that he was willing to make an alliance with the extreme left, which was also making dizzying . . . electronic . . . gains!

We had already switched channels long before the producers admitted that the joke had gone on long enough, so it was in English that I learned the extent of our victory. We had won a good 49 per cent of the vote, and not 72, not 75, but 80 seats. It was what they call, erroneously, a comfortable majority, for the more Indians there are, the more aspiring chiefs there will be, and there is no way of keeping them all happy. But just try to suggest such an inherent problem to the voters to moderate their support . . . .

Later that evening I heard Claude Ryan congratulate us sincerely and wish us good luck after saying that he bowed "without the slightest reservation" to this cruel popular verdict. A reversal, I noted, suited him decidedly better than a triumph. Setbacks, as I myself had learned long before, often have salutary effects. While putting us in our place, they oblige us to look inward and take account of our relative insignificance. The thing one must guard against above all is the attitude of the victorious frog who speedily deludes himself into thinking he can be as big as an ox. But as will be seen, I scarcely had time, let alone the inclination, to give in to this particular temptation.

---

* Was it overscrupulousness, or fear of tempting fate, or more likely the state of my finances? Whatever the cause, that's the only form of gambling I have systematically deprived myself of.

41. A November Nocturne

IT SEEMS TO ME, when I look back on the four years that followed, that politically that was my last night of unmixed joy. We felt the euphoria of the resurrected whom most people had written off as dead and buried such a short time before. Yet I had to remind the thousands of supporters come to celebrate this rising from the tomb that it would fade with the dawn.

"Whoop it up now," I told them, "because tomorrow it's back to work!"

This was strictly true. I had only one day off, if you can call it that, to bone up on those mind-boggling constitutional dossiers, then the next day it was off to Ottawa to join the seven godfathers of the "Vancouver Formula."

At this point a brief flashback is necessary, for I must begin by describing a situation whose evolution had obviously not been interrupted by the Quebec election.

In Ottawa, Trudeau had been urging the Commons to hurry up and pass his constitutional "kit" unilaterally before the summer recess, but Joe Clark and the Conservative opposition absolutely refused to play along and used every method possible to drag things out. In London, too, a good many British parliamentarians found that Trudeau's bad manners stuck in their craws.

Besides, seven of the provinces were going all out to stir up public opinion against federal highhandedness. They had quickly realized, however, that they wouldn't get very far if they adopted a purely negative attitude. The trouble was that this damned "repatriation" created the image of some kind of treasure on the verge of being brought home after long exile. Even in Quebec quite a few people were beginning to fall for the magic of this symbol, though whether the old imperial text went on sleeping in Westminster or was bedded down under the Peace Tower didn't change much, if the truth were known.

"But don't forget," Trudeau and his friends proudly clamoured, "we will never again have to go to London to change our constitution."

"What's so great about that?" we asked. "The British Parliament is just a rubber stamp anyway."

"Yes, but that stamp is the last vestige of our ancient dependency."

So, as Napoleon had discovered years ago, we learned again that baubles can still sway the minds of men.

The seven dissident provinces, all the others except Ontario and New Brunswick, had met in Vancouver to work out their own constitutional proposal, the cornerstone of which was to be the inevitable repatriation feature. They eliminated the embarrassing Charter of Rights but, of course, still drew up an amending formula.

I have never hidden the fact that constitutional law has always seemed to me to be eminently soporific, and all too frequently I have demonstrated my sketchy knowledge of the subject. I do know enough about it, however, to affirm that if people are talking about giving themselves a constitution they intend to be lords and masters of, they must at the same time provide a way to modify it. If not, the constitution is nothing more than a block of granite incapable of responding to the imperatives of change, which is why, from the Fulton-Favreau project to the Victoria plan, every time we have talked about repatriation we have always run into the problem of the amending formula.

Briefly, what the proposal concocted in Vancouver put forward was that any modification should obtain approval in the federal parliament as well as in at least seven provincial legislatures representing 50 per cent of the population. Under these conditions no province, and Quebec was no exception, could exercise the famous right of veto. On the other hand, any province that didn't wish to subscribe to such and such an amendment would be free to "opt out." At the risk of passing for a heretic, I admit that on the whole this perspective seemed rather sympathetic to me and I didn't hesitate to say so during a conference call that Bill Bennett, then chairman of our interprovincial summit, set up in the middle of our election campaign.

"Except that, quite frankly," I added, "we would have some pretty important objections to put forward."

"Well then," someone interjected, "what would you say to meeting in Ottawa on . . . your elections are on April 13, eh? What about the 14th?"

"Whoa boys! Let's not count our chickens! If, and I repeat *if* we are re-elected, okay, I'll be there. But for the love of God, not the 14th! Give us time to catch our breath a little."

The feeling of urgency was so great I really had to tweak their ears to get them to give me a couple of days' grace. But by the time I arrived at the meeting on April 16 with Claude Morin and Louis Bernard, the tension had visibly lessened. In the meantime the Newfoundland Court of Appeal – which these neighbours of ours, as fond of ambitious expressions as we are, called their "Supreme Court" – had declared that in its opinion Trudeau's proposal was clearly illegal. The federal government was therefore obliged to refer to the "real" Supreme Court . . . whose judges are named by the federal government. We could breathe a little more.

I used most of this reprieve, the rest of the day and far into the night, for talking non-stop about the objections I had mentioned on the phone. The first and most basic one to my mind was that our seven counterparts had not foreseen any financial compensation in case of opting out.

"Suppose," I said to them, "a majority of you, or perhaps all, came to the conclusion that one of the fields under your jurisdiction was costing you too much and you decided to offer it to Ottawa. Okay, good luck to you, but we have fought so hard to keep the federal government out of our flower beds that in all probability any transfer of this kind would be unthinkable for us. If there wasn't any compensation, you can see what the result would be: you could wipe out budget items that we would have to maintain while still continuing to pay our part of the burden you had shucked off. Just a minute now . . ."

On this first point they had to agree with me. But our second objection ran into a brick wall. In their formula the seven had provided that in order to exercise its right to opt out a province would have to obtain the consent of two-thirds of its parliament. I have always believed that in a democracy, except in certain extreme cases, a simple majority should carry the vote. So from the start I had a hard time understanding how, when allowing a right, they insisted on making it so difficult to exercise. Yet the reason was very simple. My two companions, Morin and Bernard, whom I was reporting to every quarter of an hour, soon put me straight on this.

For the other provinces the most important thing was that their project should be acceptable to the federal government; consequently, they had made the opting-out provision a tough one. For that matter, even if Trudeau's attitude drove them up the wall, they themselves were still attached to the notion of "national unity" which, in the last analysis, an Anglo-Canadian puts before provincial autonomy. That is why, on principle as much as by strategy, they were holding so firmly to the requirement of a two-thirds majority.

For us, too, principle and strategy met very precisely, but applied in the opposite direction. For Quebec, which in all likelihood would have to use it more often than the others, the exercise of the opting-out provision should be made as easy as possible. This way, I speculated, might we not, little by little, be able to build the associate state we had been refused? I was no more forward with these thoughts than the others were with theirs, but we understood each other very well. So well, in fact, that we remained locked in close discussion until two in the morning. I was ready to spend all night at it if they wanted, but luckily the seven had had the imprudence to call a morning press conference to announce the agreement that would make us "The Gang of Eight." Seeing that I would not give in, they at last resigned themselves to dropping their two-thirds, making me promise, in return, to solemnly affix my signature in the right place on an historic document headed up by the maple leaf flag! It seemed a small inconvenience compared to the importance of the result.

Faced with a common front of eight provinces out of ten, Trudeau didn't stand a chance . . . as long as everyone stuck to his guns and respected his signature.

But Quebec would be deprived of its right of veto.* I should perhaps admit that this old obsession has never turned me on. A veto can be an obstacle to development as much as an instrument of defence. If Quebec had it, Ontario and perhaps other provinces would surely ask for it, too. And, as in Victoria in 1971, it would be possible to block change and in protecting oneself paralyse others, leaving everyone way ahead . . . or behind.

---

* On this subject, as everyone remembers, the Supreme Court ruled in December, 1982, that in its opinion the right of veto did not exist and had never been more than a fiction. But no matter how hard one might try to revive it politically, I can't see the Anglophone provinces, and even less the federal government, renouncing this judgement, which is right down their alley. At all events, going down this path does not appear to me to be the most promising direction for our political future.

On the other hand, the right to opt out, which we had learned to use in the sixties – the best example being the creation of the Caisse de dépôt – is in my view a much superior weapon, at one and the same time more flexible and more dynamic. "You wish to take this or that path we are not ready to follow? Very well, my friends, go ahead. But without us." From stage to stage, I repeat, we could create something very like a country in that fashion.

Certain cases could arise, of course, whose extreme gravity might require a refusal of a more dramatic nature, the abuse of force in constitutional matters, for example. But I'm anticipating.

Still, while I'm at it, I'd like to anticipate a little more, if only to stress how much we were cornered by events. While in the depths of the constitutional drama we were beginning, in a confused way, to perceive that another crisis was on its way. At first it didn't seem to be more than a small cloud, the forerunner of a spring storm, but then it began to swell and as we watched the whole economic horizon began to darken. Reading over the speech I delivered less than two months after the election to open a brief spring session, I am struck today by the long passage near the beginning that I devoted to this unnerving prospect. What would tomorrow hold in store? We didn't know exactly, but one could foresee,

> . . . and not only for the present year, that the time of widespread growth is past. Also the time of the automatic growth of the economy, as well as the time of an equivalent growth of expenditures. Like all societies without exception, Quebec from now on will be confronted with limits . . . that will be absolutely impossible to ignore. . . .
>
> We will therefore have to navigate these treacherous waters of the eighties with great caution. While we maintain and increase measures taken since 1976 for cleaning up and cutting down on our expenses, we will also have to choose each of our new programs with the greatest care, realizing that it has become unthinkable to go on endlessly adding to existing ones as was done in the past. More than ever these sometimes painful choices must be "transparent," clearly explained and justified. It is on this condition alone that a democratic society can consent to such discipline, however necessary it may be seen to be.

Five years later, now that recession has come to confirm our suspicions, I think everyone would have to admit I had good grounds for making these remarks. Could I say the same for the end of this speech, where I returned to the constitutional confrontation? It was my opinion then, as now, and I continue to propose it today to whomsoever wants to share it.

The very great threat Ottawa's plan represents for Quebec has unfortunately not been removed. We are presently awaiting the opinion of the Supreme Court as regards the legality of this unilateral reshuffling. But whatever the judgement is, as far as we are concerned, the plan will continue to be absolutely illegitimate, that is, politically unjustifiable and even immoral, which is why we must go on opposing it by every means until we have blocked it. . . .

This people will never accept to have their essential rights taken away. They would not have endured it in 1867, and after such efforts to survive and such collective self-affirmation, they will not endure it in 1981. . . .

Under the pretext of giving citizens a new Charter of Rights, the Ottawa project is, in fact, an unprecedented attack on the powers of the National Assembly of Quebec, designed to limit and restrict it, especially with regard to the language of education.

So that's where we were, waiting for the Supreme Court to deign to give its opinion on three questions that three provinces, Quebec included, had submitted to it. In keeping with the rule that the higher the tribunal, the less speedy it is, the nine powerful gentlemen kept us on tenterhooks until the very end of September.

I remember the day as if it were yesterday, the Supreme Court's decision being so unforgettably well orchestrated.

Basically we had asked them three questions. The first a school child could have answered: Would the federal proposal affect the powers of the provinces? Yes, 9–0. With the second we got into the meat of the subject: Did there exist a "convention" in virtue of which Ottawa should first obtain the consent of the provinces? Yes, 6–3. The real snag was the third question: Was the consent of the provinces necessary? According to "convention," yes, 6–3. But according to law, no, 7–2.

What did this hocus-pocus amount to coming on top of all the hair-splitting we were already embroiled in? Issuing from the English tradition where well-established precedents so often replace written law, "conventions may have more weight than the law itself," these federal Solomons told us. "This is why one can say that the violation of a convention is an unconstitutional act, even if inconsequential in terms of strict legality."

In other words, Trudeau's goals might be unconstitutional, illegitimate, and even "go against the principles of federalism," but they were legal! On hearing that I was reminded of another bit of old English wisdom: "The law is an ass."

All the more so since this "legality" was not required to be based on a consensus of the provinces. To retain a semblance of decency, of course, it would have to claim a certain amount of support. But how much exactly? No opinion would be proffered on that subject, the tribunal unctuously concluded, implying: "You can very well see that politics is beneath us." Baloney.

Now that he knew his constitutional monster was legal after all, Trudeau had to find a way to get the other provinces to adopt it. He couldn't turn up at Westminster flanked by Bill Davis and Dick Hatfield and nobody else. The latter, who is less a government leader than Minister of this, that, and everything, was certainly one of the commandos commissioned to do in the "Gang of Eight." But the main part of the job was confided to three men who might be considered as three "dauphins" of their respective governments. Jean Chrétien was in some respects Trudeau's handyman. Roy McMurtry of Ontario and Roy Romanow of Saskatchewan played similar roles for their bosses. Romanow's job was particularly delicate because he and his chief, Allan Blakeney, were busy sapping the common front from inside. Despite the underhandedness and, when necessary, outright lies, we soon had a pretty good idea of what was being plotted.

But what to do? Keep in touch, as Claude Morin assiduously did amid mounting doubts; urge Gilles Loiselle in London to intensify even more his admirable campaign of "disintoxication" for the benefit of British parliamentarians; obtain, though very late in the day, the almost unanimous support of the National Assembly, thanks to the lucidity that defeat had re-awakened in Claude Ryan. It was better than nothing, even though a group of Liberals from the West Island, prisoners of an electorate that was more federal than Québécois, refused to follow Ryan, which abruptly revealed the fragility of his leadership.

A few days from the opening of the final round of talks, which had been set for November 2, all these efforts had not been enough to prevent a worsening erosion. We were already getting signals that two or three of our allies were becoming shaky and that secret transactions were taking place in the wings.

As usual, the opening session was a series of carefully prepared solo performances. Trudeau began by stating his three objectives again: repatriation, an amending formula, and his inseparable Charter of Rights. He also took the opportunity to attack the right of opting out, saying that in his opinion it constituted a permanent negation of "national will," since a single province would be able to oppose a consensus of the others and go off in its own direction. He was looking straight ahead as he talked, but it was obvious who and what he meant. Davis followed with his habitual "noble father" patter, the sole aim of which was to reinforce the federal position a little.

Then it was my turn, according to the rule that gives the floor to "First Ministers"* in order of the seniority of their provinces. I didn't mince my words. Stressing the fact that Trudeau had no mandate to act unilaterally, I defied him to put his plan to the voters. Forgetting Hatfield, who was simply a ventriloquist's dummy, I next listened to our seven counterparts with the strictest attention. None failed to underline the unconstitutional character of the federal project, but first Bennett, then, naturally, Blakeney, started mixing discreet advances in with their well-justified reproaches. They seemed to be saying to Trudeau: "Find something or other, if you possibly can, to let us reach a compromise." The common front was decidedly beginning to crack.

The next day, Tuesday, it fell to Bill Davis, who adored posing as the honest mediator, to launch the decisive phase of the discussions. He tabled a compromise motion. If Trudeau would accept the "Vancouver formula," couldn't the eight dissidents resign themselves to put up with his Charter? For us there was no question of endorsing this hypocritical verbiage essentially aimed at wresting from Quebec its sovereign authority in education. Without taking such an absolute stand, several other provinces also had strong reservations. Reminding the meeting that England had done very well without any such legalistic yoke and nonetheless had not sup-

---

* In English the title "Prime Minister" is reserved for the federal government, the provinces only having the right to "Premiers." So, translating from French, they had invented this new appellation which, semantically, put us all on the same footing.

329

pressed its citizens' human rights, our Anglo-Canadian fellows were leery of this "government by judges" that was to be installed above parliament. I shared this point of view, all the more so since Quebec already possessed its own charter of rights, and especially since my wise old friend, Judge Pigeon, had also given me his views on the subject.

"This American-style project," he had said in essence, "does not conform at all to the logic of our institutions. It risks providing more tensions than solutions. In addition, as I am well placed to know, having experienced the great slowness of the courts, I am very much afraid that this new and complex responsibility will just multiply the delays and confusion."

Seeing his precious Charter so fiercely attacked, Trudeau, it appears, spent a good part of the night bringing up his big guns. As for us, all we could do was touch wood, knowing that we could expect the worst.

The following morning, at a breakfast meeting, one didn't have to be very perceptive to see that now there were only seven of us left. Blakeney had drawn up a "new" formula whose sole originality was that it purely and simply eliminated the opting-out clause. Since this treachery was backed by a thick document, it was certainly not the fruit of nocturnal inspiration. On top of this, as I realized shortly after, our chairman, Bill Bennett, was not standing exactly square on his feet. I had given him the text of the statement we had prepared for the public meeting, but he had simply mislaid it – "So sorry!" – and didn't seem to be in any great hurry to find it again. Whereupon I had only to pick out around the table several other pairs of averted eyes to conclude that the "Gang of Eight" had decidedly had its day.

It was then that Trudeau, toward the end of the morning when there was scarcely any time left for explanations, pulled the rabbit out of the hat. If there was no agreement, he announced, he would settle for repatriation alone, and then we would have two years more to reach agreement on the Charter and amending formula. After which, if the impasse persisted, the litigious question would be submitted to a pan-Canadian referendum.

Trudeau had put on his exacerbated air, clearly implying that this time he had reached his limit. Our ex-allies drew back a step, almost in horror. They didn't want a referendum any more than a charter of rights, less, in fact, because they were scared stiff of having to oppose something Trudeau was sure of passing off as being as virtuous as apple pie.

As for me, I was trying to weigh the pros and cons. Our common front was a dead issue. For the time being, then, we didn't have much to lose, and two years down the road . . . who could tell? Besides, if the whole population had a chance to vote on such a fundamental subject, wouldn't that be democratically more respectable than all this intriguing that ended up poisoning the atmosphere?

In an insinuating and provocative tone, Trudeau pushed me to the wall. "You, the great democrat," he said, "don't tell me you're afraid to fight . . ."

At the time he really seemed sincere.

"All right," I said.

After lunch, however, we were to discover that in reality it was a politician's trick of a rather repugnant kind. An "explanatory" text had been distributed that squirmed with almost incomprehensible subtleties, but its underlying import was as clear as day. Before a referendum could take place, consent would have to be obtained *from each and every province*! Behind his Oriental impassivity one could feel Trudeau literally rejoicing. He had put one over on us. To each his own concept of democracy. In his concept, from the word "go" the end justified the means. He had just given us one more proof of that.

At any rate, his manoeuvre served to drive a last nail in the coffin of the late common front. I couldn't even be bothered wondering who'd look after the burial.

Just the same, before going back to the Hotel de la Chaudière on the Quebec side of the river, Claude Morin and I took the precaution, as a formality, of giving our telephone number to two or three of the others who, as usual, were staying in Ottawa.

"If anything new comes up, don't forget to call us."

"No problem," they replied, but they had trouble looking us in the eye.

We have been reproached since for staying in Hull that night. Did they expect us to snoop around the corridors of the Château Laurier, listening at keyholes perhaps?

Toward one in the morning, since no one had called except to remind us of the frightful breakfast at eight-thirty, I turned in.

Reliving the adventure that had absorbed us since spring and that was now drawing ineluctably to its close, I had some trouble getting to sleep.

Thursday, November 5, 1981. Because we had to cross the river in the middle of rush hour, I got there late. Brian Peckford, who had been chosen to bell the cat, said, showing me a sheet of paper that had been put beside my plate, "We've put together a final proposition. It's very short, it only takes a couple of minutes to read."

It was short all right, but no less clear for all that.

They had taken advantage of our absence to eliminate the most crucial of our demands, that is, the right to financial compensation in case of opting out. It was the stab in the dark.

For giving their consent, the others had managed to wring concessions from the federal government that seriously weakened several dispositions of the Charter. In short, all this shady dealing, presided over in some kitchen apparently by the Chrétien-McMurtry-Romanow trio, had resulted in a dish that was basically mediocre in which Trudeau's initial designs had been considerably diluted. It was said, for that matter, that he was furious to have to put so much water in his wine. He was even more so, I am sure, when he found himself obliged, to make partial amends for the unspeakable wrong he had done us, to give Quebec back its right to financial compensation in the fields of education and culture.

Fruit of a great deal of trickery, palmed off on a country that once again the authorities had not deigned to consult openly on the question, this constitutional monument was already beginning to show foundation cracks and wouldn't last eternally. The only thing that seriously bothered us was that Ottawa would now have the power to reduce the scope of Bill 101 to the benefit of Anglo-Québécois, though this would in no way put our basic positions in danger.

It was the procedure much more than the content that was intolerable. May 20, 1980, had been an infinitely sad day of mourning. November 5, 1981, was the day of anger and shame.

We had been betrayed, in secret, by men who hadn't hesitated to tear up their own signatures, and without their even taking the trouble to warn us. We knew that for them it had gone against the grain to accept certain of our conditions in April. But they had put their signatures to it. For us that was as good as a signed contract. But for them . . . one could see now that it had been nothing but a simple instrument used to pressure the federal government. Their signatures had never had the weight we gave ours. As I have read somewhere, although the Englishman may seem to be impeccably scrupulous in private life, one should always keep a close eye on him when it comes to public issues. I therefore swore that . . . but a little later . . .

Tricked by Trudeau, dropped by the others, all we could do was tell them briefly our way of looking at things before returning to Quebec. All around the big conference table, except at our place, it was congratulations and hearty laughter, some even going so far as to toast this doubtful victory.

"I am infinitely sorry," I told them, "to see Quebec back in the place the federal regime has traditionally reserved for us: once again Quebec is all alone. It will be up to our own people to draw what conclusions they can. When they have done that, I think you may feel a little less joyful than you seem to be now."

The next day I gave our MNAs a blistering account of these proceedings. They reacted in kind, full of fury laced with a strong feeling of humiliation. At the opening of parliament on November 9, I put all the vitriol I could muster into my inaugural remarks. As for Claude Morin, whose character did not permit such outbursts, he merely wrote to his counterparts and ex-partners expressing his bitterness. Now, he concluded, all that remained for the Anglophone-dominated federal government and the nine Anglo-Canadian provinces was to ask London, another no less Anglophone government, "to diminish, without our consent, the integrity and jurisdiction of the only French-language government in North America." So ended a good twenty years of intensive and constantly perilous labour in the constitutional minefields. It was a cruel deception and it was certainly largely responsible for his decision shortly after to abandon politics.

For my part, calling on all the resources of my vocabulary, I continued to rage and storm. From "the night of the long knives" to "the most despicable betrayal," I couldn't find words strong enough to express my burning resentment. For the first time, I even went so far as to suggest that we might think of administering to Anglo-Québécois some of the "school medicine" our minorities were forced to swallow in the rest of Canada.

It was a release I badly needed, but it became excessive. Begging ministers and backbenchers to do likewise, I tried, without too much success, to apply the soft pedal. At the very beginning of December there was a party congress and we had begun to receive several truly incendiary motions. We would have to stop throwing oil on the fire. But it was already too late.

As soon as the congress opened the 2,500 delegates showed themselves to be both disillusioned and full of bitterness, harbouring a fierce desire for violence. The deep wound of the referendum was far from healed. The constitutional dirty-dealing had poured acid on the wound. Defeated in 1980, swindled in 1981, it was just too much. From the start, what grew out of that climate of grinding frustration was an unprecedented feeling of hostility toward English Canada. They didn't want anything to do with such neighbours. The contrary would have been surprising. Carried away by resentment, I made the mistake of going for easy applause. I shouted, "No more games with a regime that always loads the dice!"

I did take the precaution to stress that the principal agents of our misfortunes were none other than "those eminent Québécois named Trudeau and Chrétien." Trying to divert attention to difficulties of another more disturbing order, I also spoke about the economic crisis that had now settled in firmly and which we would have to cross before we could seriously go on talking about our political future.

It had no effect. The activists had only one idea in mind, to wipe out every vestige of our plans for co-operation with the rest of the country. And to begin with, to hell with "association." Hadn't this concept given people like Blakeney at the time of the referendum opportunities to refuse our option for perfectly ridiculous reasons but ones that many nervous people had taken for valid arguments? I was obliged to agree on that point. I also agreed to let the famous hyphen drop from "sovereignty-association." Once this marriage that until now had been insoluble was broken, we would concentrate first and foremost on sovereignty. That way any agreement we offered freely to the others would no longer provide an opportunity for blackmail.

But from there to simply strike out the word "association" and eliminate any idea of interdependence from our minds and from our program was a step I refused to take. With a few colleagues who were also getting more and more worried, I did everything I could to turn things around. But it wasn't possible any more. In an atmosphere that was turning distressingly ugly, "association" was thrown in the garbage. The confusion was such that, toward the end, Jacques Parizeau could be seen going up to the platform where the anti-associationists were holding forth, then changing his mind and going back to his seat with the very pale excuse that he had gone to the wrong microphone.

The next day the congress completed the job in a jiffy. Without bothering to consult the public by referendum, hereafter a government would only need a simple parliamentary majority to proclaim independence. After fifteen years it was Mr. Hyde replacing Dr. Jekyll. While the Parti Québécois finished wiping itself out, it was the implacable face of the old RIN that was reappearing, accompanied by pure, tough, inaccessible independence.

In the little office where I had withdrawn to give some thought to the traditional closing address, I had barely had time to scribble down a few notes when suddenly a startling incident happened to cap the disaster. Someone had proposed an apparently harmless motion asking that former members of the FLQ, now held in federal penitentiaries, be transferred to Quebec prisons. Surging through the crowd like a red-headed devil, a stocky young man made his way to the microphone. It was Jacques Rose, one of the cell that had assassinated Pierre Laporte in 1970. Not only was he permitted to speak in favour of the motion, but when he went on unduly, the chairman showed great deference in finally asking him to stop, and together with the applause that broke out in pockets came a voice feverishly saluting one of the "true pioneers of the liberation"!

That was the limit. I didn't have to hunt for my words any more. I kept my notes, inadvertently no doubt, but I will spare you all but the conclusion.

Having summarized these facts, I will permit myself only one commentary: putting myself in the shoes of the voter, I would have some difficulty in voting for me under these conditions! For from the foregoing it follows: first, that the party risks until further notice (and I am saying what I think) losing an important part of that precious political capital I referred to in opening this congress; and second, that as president of the party who has generously been given a certain role as spokesman for all, I find myself in a very awkward situation.

It will surprise nobody, and for that matter it is no great secret, to learn that last night I spontaneously thought of relinquishing this role and stepping down from the presidency. But then, I told myself, there are people here who would be just too happy to see that. So I thought things over. And I am still thinking. Such an investment, on top of so many others, fifteen years of effort and exhausting hope, that doesn't permit one to take a decision too hotheadedly under the impress of emotion alone, or as the result of some sort of depression, no matter how normal that might be.

So you'll have to excuse me when I assure you I haven't the least intention of fabricating artificial suspense, but I will have to ask you to let me go on thinking about it for a few more days.

These few days gave rise to an idea that wasn't mine. One of our colleagues from the executive committee of the party proposed that we should hold a referendum on the matter, not only asking the opinion of a group of delegates under pressure, but getting the calm, considered response of the 300,000 members of the party. Having seen our congresses all too often cut off from reality by the deluge of motions that kept growing year by year, and having just witnessed totally absurd scenes where a well-directed shouting match could lead to irrationality, I rallied to this suggestion without the slightest hesitation.

Democracy by delegation is terribly easy to manipulate, sometimes reaching a point of the purest anti-democracy, so why not, for once, try direct democracy and give the right of response to those citizens who are generally so little consulted?

The three questions to be asked in this referendum (pejoratively known in unwritten history as the "renérendum") were rapidly drawn up by an ad hoc committee. The first two concerned fundamental points the congress had been split on.

> 1. In order to proceed democratically, should Quebec's accession to sovereignty be approved by a majority of citizens?
> 2. Even if the obligatory link between sovereignty and association which our option has upheld until now were dropped, should our program contain a concrete offer of association with Canada?

As for the last question, it was prompted by signs of intolerance that had broken out during the congress.

> 3. Should the party reaffirm its respect and openness toward all Québécois, whatever their ethnic or cultural origin, and in particular

336

the right of the Anglophone minority to its essential institutions, educational and other?

Of 292,888 questionnaires sent out, almost half, some 48.8 per cent, were duly filled out and returned to the secretary of the party. Of this number, 95 per cent had replied "yes" to the three questions.

As had been planned long before, the second half of the repudiated congress took place in February, 1982. The delegates, the same ones for the most part, stepped back into line. I did my own modest best at replastering. But everyone knew very well that Band-Aids wouldn't really be enough to cure us.

As is so often the case, events from outside gave the impetus to make us, for better or for worse, hang together again for two more years.

42. The Butcher of New Carlisle

I T WAS ENOUGH TO DRIVE ANYONE CRAZY. From April, 1981, to February, 1982, we had to face not one but two crises at the same time. For those ten interminable months the constitutional catastrophe and its harrowing consequences were accompanied, step by step, by economic collapse, and we found ourselves whirled away like straws in the wind. It was enough to make a cat kitten, and the reader must admit that it's not much easier to handle things today. Since I'm certainly not expected to turn every stone, I am tempted to forget this period that was quite painful enough to live through, and so close to us anyway that real historians are only just beginning to sift it.

Having made these reservations, however, I feel obliged to sketch in the backdrop and single out certain stages in this chaotic descent into hell that may serve as landmarks for what follows.

All during 1981 that small cloud we had noticed at the beginning of the year continued to grow and finally gave birth to a hurricane whose violence reminded older people of the blackest days of the depression. Canada, the whole of North America, and Western Europe, all were or would soon be hit. But in Quebec the situation was deteriorating fastest. Our economy, open as few others are and hypersensitive to any ill wind, had caught pneumonia while others were generally only suffering from a nasty 'flu.

That spring the situation already seemed so bad we judged it necessary, even before launching the campaign, to present a budget that contained certain very unelection-like features, bound to make many people unhappy. In return for some minor relief that really only served to sweeten the medicine, citizens had to absorb nearly a billion dollars in cuts – a word that was soon to become familiar – as well as this cutting judgement from Jacques Parizeau: "We must modify the structure of our tax revenues so it can bring in more, and at the same time seriously reduce the rhythm of rising expenses."

For all that, the accumulated deficit was mounting toward $4 billion. We were living dangerously beyond our means.

This is why, immediately after our re-election, I had to resolve to take drastic action. For five years Parizeau had been both Minister of Finance and President of the Treasury Board. In the view of some colleagues, that was a lot of power, too much for one man. Besides, the excessive extent of this double responsibility had recently become much more onerous. Anyone's capacity for work has its limits, and Parizeau wasn't able to deal with the Treasury post with more than his left hand. Considering the unusual rigour we were now constrained to practise, it was evident that we needed a full-time treasurer who would jealously, night and day, watch over the use made of public funds. But in such circumstances men are like children whose toys have been taken away. Even if basically he must have known as well as I did that it was necessary, Parizeau first took the news quite badly and then, with that art of suspense whose secret he had mastered, kept me eating my heart out for two days before his good sense and proverbial loyalty got the upper hand and he finally came around.

I immediately asked Yves Bérubé to quit his beloved and fascinating domain of Energy and Resources for the colourless post that Treasury is generally considered to be.

"So here I am condemned to non-existence," the victim sighed. "But so what, there are certainly things to be learned there as much as anywhere. Since I must, I'll become the invisible man."

"It's not things to learn you'll be short of," I replied. "And as for visibility, I bet that before long you'll have plenty of that!"

I couldn't have spoken truer words. For three whole years, calculator constantly within reach, he combined unyielding administrative discipline and attention to the least detail with an extraordinary aptitude for grasping the general picture and presenting it with great clarity. Often reviled but always respected, not only did he carve out a solid reputation in this perilous post, but he was without doubt the one who contributed the most efficiently to keep us afloat until the end of the storm.

Parizeau and he shared a mutual respect and quickly learned to complement each other, so it was in tandem that in November, 1981, they unleashed "Operation Big Stick," which was the beginning of a period of crisis management. Parizeau, not content to double the gasoline tax, tied it to that famous "elevator" that made it climb automatically every time there was a price hike, while Bérubé brutally sliced hundreds more millions off ministry budgets.

Unless I'm mistaken, our government was the first to take such decisive action against the economic downturn. Not that we were more far-sighted than others – we simply didn't have the choice. Even strengths we were proudest of were switched around and became weaknesses. Those prodigious small and medium-sized businesses, which since 1977 had allowed us to establish record growth, had started to drop like flies and were leaving a distressingly large number of people out of work. A lot of these businesses started by the up-and-coming generation were still young and poor in capital and had had to finance themselves by borrowing heavily, and the dizzying rise of interest rates had broken their backs.

Like desperate firemen fighting an uncontrollable blaze, we had sent out an SOS to Ottawa well before Christmas, because these murderous interest rates of 18, 19, and sometimes even more than 20 per cent were being set there. But when Quebec is the only one to cry out, Ottawa always turns a deaf ear. It was only after two long months, after the general alert had sounded in the rest of Canada, that finally a federal-provincial conference on the emergency was called in February, 1982.

To our surprise we discovered on arriving that apparently the real master of the Canadian government was no longer Pierre Elliott Trudeau but a powerful manitou by the name of Gerald Bouey. Governor of the Bank of Canada, this manipulator of monetary masses, like a spider in his web, had stubbornly, month by month, been weaving this blind policy that threatened to stifle our economic life completely.

I can still see the meeting, with Trudeau, putting on the airs of a simple spectator, letting us discuss in vain with his guru. No argument managed to ruffle the Olympian indifference with which Mr. Bouey seemed to contemplate the disappearance of so many businesses and the loss of so many jobs from one day to the next.

"It's inflation we have to bring down first," he kept on repeating endlessly. To listen to him, the cost of borrowing money had to be maintained far above the American rates in order to prevent runaway inflation, which we should dread above all else.

"That's fine," we replied, "but what about this runaway unemployment we've got that gobbles up so much activity and so many hopes? Isn't that just as dreadful? Without counting the fact that it's quite simply inhuman not to . . ."

340

"I grant you that," the oracle would reply, "but inflation first."

"Very well, but how come our rates are so much higher than our neighbour's? Couldn't we let them come down a bit from that stratosphere where everyone is becoming asphyxiated? What we need is more time to reduce inflation. Besides, if you don't use anything but a hammer to repair the house, you end up bringing the whole building down. There are plenty of other tools in the chest . . ."

"But we must also think about the dollar . . ."

Just so, we were thinking about it. I can't remember whether it was Peter Lougheed or I who first suggested the supreme heresy.

"Okay then, let's talk about the dollar. Instead of keeping it, too, far above its real value, why don't we help it find a level that suits it better? That might be 75, or maybe even 70 cents!"

Our interlocutor's reaction, betraying a mixture of horror and amusement, made me think of the expression grownups put on when one of the kids lets out some enormity. The discussion stopped flat. We had conjured up the inconceivable: a Canadian dollar in only a few months losing 15 or 16 per cent of its weight! And who would have thought of evoking the relative depths (still not enough today) that it would finally reach, though much too late. I will just give one example of what other countries have done in this regard. In the autumn of that same year Sweden, without bothering to act progressively, put into effect the exact operation we had been proposing. By chance I have here a number of the French review *L'Expansion* that describes how the Swedish economy, as well as those of a handful of other intelligent countries, managed to get through the crisis almost without mishap: "Announced on October 8, 1982, just after the Social Democrats returned to power, *a devaluation of 16 per cent* achieved its aim all the more effectively since the international climate was favourable . . . and the U.S. dollar was rising steadily. . . . A gift to business? Of course. The Social Democrats do not hesitate to admit as much, because without good industrial performance the Swedish model would not be viable. . . ."*

Alas, in Ottawa all we had was an arthritic government and technocrats like those old families "who have never learned anything and have never forgotten anything," so we had to settle for the old Canadian model with its incoherence, its sacred cows, and

* "Modèle suédois pas mort!" *L'Expansion*, February 22-March 7, 1985.

its capital that has often reminded me of a lay Vatican, the seat of the most arrogant false infallibilities.

The superb incarnation of all that, Trudeau, visibly bored, had attended the long, sterile confrontation between his man who knew everything and we who knew nothing. What was he thinking about with that absent air of his? About the delicious convolutions of his constitutional schemes? Or about those new low blows he and his teammates had just delivered us in the form of two particularly odious bills, one designed to hinder the sensational development of the activities of our Caisse de dépôt (abusive because Québécois), the other, more ridiculous than insulting, claiming to expropriate a corridor running straight across our territory for the benefit of Newfoundland? It had reached the point where I had almost become persuaded that for these people the same thing always applied: nothing interested them unless at the same time it furnished an opportunity to hurt Quebec. I was exaggerating. But not much. So it was stripped of illusions that I asked them for a bit of *our* federal money to improve measures to encourage employment that we had just put the finishing touches to. Even if they refused to abandon their ruinous monetary obsession, wouldn't they at least condescend to help attenuate its effects? We were told we would have to put up with our own troubles. Decidedly, we could only count on ourselves.

But all that was, in the long run, a sideline to the real crisis, so far to the side, in fact, that when we left Ottawa we had the impression we had been living for two or three days outside the real world. Perhaps it is not entirely useless, however, to remind people that in this ivory tower we had found mentalities comfortably ensconced in the calm possession of their dehumanized verities, whereas a true "national" government would have busied itself at that conjuncture, and even long before, to provide some help for a people at bay.

In Quebec on April 5, 6, and 7 a "summit" meeting took place that was at one and the same time a moment of self-appraisal, a sort of calm before the storm, and the beginning of two years of torment that were going to drive us up the wall, two years of absurd but understandable cruelty, interrupted by a few exciting times that revealed in a good part of Quebec unexpected reserves of energy and generosity.

All the powers and potentates and socio-economic decision-makers, sensing the gravity of the times, had made a point of turning up. Sitting around the big central table were the leaders of the four major trade unions representing hundreds of thousands of workers in the public and private sectors, the presidents of two unions representing the municipalities of Quebec, the leaders of the Union Catholique des Cultivateurs there to speak for the farmers, then employers' associations, women's organizations, and spokesmen for consumers. The chief financial power of the country, the Mouvement Desjardins, was there represented by its president, Raymond Blais, that stout little man whose handicapped walk just emphasizes the liveliness of his mind and an imagination that sees far while remaining firmly planted on the ground. Behind them, dozens of assistants and advisers and observers and journalists complete the picture and make up a full house.

I am the one who is to provide the spectacle of opening this meeting. Experts from the Ministry of Finance and the Treasury Board have prepared a ruthless report for me, backed up by statistics that reveal the alarming extent of the collapse. We will soon have lost 200,000 jobs – everything gained during the good years. Bankruptcies and shutdowns succeed each other in an infernal rhythm. Except for the well-off, is there a single family in the whole of the private sector that has not been plunged into unprecedented insecurity? As well as innumerable families who have already lost their breadwinner and will soon begin to slide from unemployment insurance to welfare, there are thousands who fear for tomorrow. And then there are all those workers who are being asked to give up not only wage increases but often advantages won after long, hard battles. And lastly there are those young people between fifteen and twenty-five for whom an unemployment rate of 23 per cent constitutes a human tragedy as well as an economic one.

This crisis that had come from elsewhere had quickly spread because of certain weaknesses inherent in our economy, and since federal irresponsibility had washed its hands of us, we would just have to take it, as we had taken other crises. And we would have to find the way to get out of it, too. We were capable of that, but it would demand enormous efforts, an unusual dose of solidarity, and also, perhaps the most difficult thing because we had lost the habit, some sacrifices.

Who would have the dubious honour of prescribing and administering this inevitably unpopular cure? I didn't have to ask the question. Every time things decide to go really badly, people automatically turn to the State. All right, that's what we were elected for, for that above all else when you think about it. But I also had to remind my audience that we would never make it alone.

"It's got to concern you every bit as much as us," I told them, "because we can't tackle the job empty-handed, and here's the financial situation of the government at this very moment. . . ."

It was a vicious circle. Not only did all those people out of work pay no income tax, they cost the State more, so the ravages of the crisis never stopped swelling the astronomical sums we were already devoting to the regular "clientele" of our social services. Nor was there any question, for that matter, of severely curtailing the essential services furnished by hospitals, old people's homes, and educational establishments.

None of this, however, had prevented Bérubé's scissors, wherever possible, from making cuts that made people squeal. Not knowing that the worst was yet to come, everyone also griped about the increase in taxes we had announced. But in spite of all these efforts, we were still in a very bad way. Grabbing a thick black pencil and writing on a sheet of paper someone slid in front of me, I projected onto a screen the enormous figure I had to etch in my audience's minds.

"700,000,000 dollars! For the upcoming year, that's the financial gap we're faced with, 700,000,000 dollars. Where are we going to find them? By raising taxes again? Yes, sure, but you can't go on squeezing the lemon for a sum like that. Cut programs and services to the quick, really to the bone? If ever that becomes necessary, we'll have to resolve to do it, but only as a very last resort. So what now?"

The answer was the main point of this long preamble and since it might prove to be explosive, it was no time for oratory.

"Well," I said in my most neutral voice, "there is one thing left. I hardly dare bring it up, but I must. There is a possible third choice to get us out of this impasse, and a third question to ask ourselves: Could we envisage a total or partial freeze in remuneration in the public and parapublic sectors?"

It was at once an invitation and a warning that we had long contemplated. On July 1, in three months' time, very large salary increases were due to be paid, averaging something like 12 per cent. The $700-million hole I had spoken of was there. Such salary hikes were already excesssive back in 1979 when the last collective agreement had been signed, but like our predecessors we still believed then in unlimited growth. Now, however, when we were in a period of sharp decline, they were perfectly indecent. They would deprive us of the money we most urgently needed to bring a little relief to whole sections of society that were continuing to crumble and fall down on the heads of the workers. It seemed to us that people in the public and parapublic sectors, with their lifetime job security, should be able to understand and feel that this was a chance for them to do their part . . .

. . . All eyes were turned on the union leaders, especially the CSN (Confédération des Syndicats Nationaux) and the CEQ (Corporation des Enseignants du Québec), whose power extended over all institutions of public health and the whole network of elementary and secondary schools. How would they react? If my memory serves me right, they sat there icily, content to shrug their shoulders while waiting for someone to have the good idea to change the subject.

It wasn't going to be easy, we knew that from the start, because these same unions had been asked a little earlier to give up another $100 million that was their due by virtue of a clause in their contract that the present state of affairs had turned into black humour: it was an "enrichment clause" . . . at a time when society was growing poorer by the minute! Two pillars of the CSN whom I explicitly wish to single out, Marcel Gilbert and Jean-François Munn, who had already been pleading for moderation in demands, tried to convince their fellows to take this opportunity to show that the union movement was not devoid of all sense of social conscience. They ran into a wall.

It was one of the union leaders, however, during that summit of April, 1982, who put forward a genial and pertinent proposition which, once the audience had got over its initial surprise, was seized upon by everyone as if it had been the invention of the wheel.

Louis Laberge, the indestructible president of the FTQ (Fédération des Travailleurs du Québec) whose members formed the backbone of the construction industry, knew better than any of us that things weren't going at all well in his field. So this colourful character, whose torrential delivery and blunt style sometimes, for those who don't know him, hide his fierce attachment for Quebec, as well as the wily ways of a sly old fox, decided to do something about it.

The plan he put forward united these two characteristics beautifully. To rapidly dispel the stagnation that had seen building starts plunge to 23,000 for the current year, he recommended neither more nor less than an incredible injection of 50,000 additional homes as quickly as possible. This way all our regions, and every one was experiencing the same desperate need, would see a certain upsurge of activity while the construction trade, it should be noted in passing, would also get a healthy shot in the arm . . . an eventuality the crafty old proposer had not failed to foresee.

"My members have authorized me," he said, "to immediately table the contribution they are ready to make. Every one of them will pay one cent for every hour of work the plan brings in. Obviously, that's far from enough. The thing has to become like the 'corvée' of the old days when everybody put their shoulder to the wheel. But you've got our one cent per hour. Who can top that?"

Raymond Blais was the first to respond with the assurance that we could doubtless count on the Caisses Populaires. Building contractors, who could hardly have stood aside, promised a percentage of their turnover. Getting into the game, the mayors spoke about the possibility of subsidies for the purchase of building lots, then architects and engineers offered a cut in fees . . . .

It was one of those exciting moments I was talking about. Everyone knows the follow-up. "Corvée Habitation" building sites didn't spring up like mushrooms; first the operation had to be organized. Headed up by a board where all participants had their say with the aim of maintaining a climate of good will and willingness to work, it turned out to be a true concertation (another buzz word of the time) between people who were more used to meeting nose to nose than to working shoulder to shoulder.

Co-ordinating the whole thing in the name of the government, which was in a sense the chief contractor and guarantor of the enterprise, was Guy Tardif, Minister of Housing. He took on a colossal task and handled it with the skill of an accomplished organizer combined with that of a career diplomat. This tireless workhorse, for whom holidays were just a waste of time, is one of the most devoted and productive men I have ever known in public life.

In a few months he had so efficiently launched this original project that housing starts increased from 23,000 in 1982 to 40,000 in 1983 and 42,000 in 1984. At the same time he invented from scratch a program designed for old people called "Loginove," which in three years saw the renovation of some 140,000 decrepit dwellings.

It should also be remembered that it was principally thanks to his initiative that the number of low-cost housing units, which was 16,000 in 1976 and had been marking time for years, rose to more than double that figure in 1983.

But despite the old saying "When construction is booming, so does everything else," it ain't necessarily so. The crisis continued to make unimaginable inroads on small and medium-sized businesses, and it was more than high time to provide some of the support measures we had announced. In May, 1982, attacking the most urgent issue first, the government decided to assume a substantial portion of the interest rate itself, thus spreading a sort of safety net under these businesses. Commonly known as the Biron Plan, after our ingenious Minister of Industry and Commerce, in two years this program allowed us to save some 800 businesses and several thousand jobs.

In the meantime, our $700-million hole had not disappeared. On the contrary, all the efforts we were making could only aggravate the situation. The bank was drying up. The May, 1982, budget didn't beat about the bush. The sales tax rose from 9 to 10 per cent and tax on tobacco from 45 to 50 per cent. Besides, doctors' fees and salaries of senior civil servants were frozen until further notice, decisions that only drained off a thin trickle of water from an ocean of needs but which served as yet another warning to the 300,000 union members in the public and parapublic sectors. In the depths of this period of collective trials, with public financial resources stretched beyond their limit, there was no question of granting the exorbitant salary increases negotiated three years earlier. In all conscience it was our duty, and we were absolutely sure of this, to put those hundreds of millions of dollars to the service of the whole of the population.

But how to go about it? Some wanted us to repeat the action we had taken with the civil service administrators and doctors, that is, freeze salaries after having simply annulled the increases. Thinking about it afterwards, I have often said to myself that perhaps that is what we should have done. After a few bad bumps, the summer would have come along to calm the atmosphere and by autumn we probably would have been able to talk about something else.

But there was a problem. The unions' collective agreement still had seven months to run, until December 31, 1982. We were looking at the signature we had put to the contract and we didn't feel we had the right to tear it up, as others had so recently done, at our expense. But how could we honour our commitment until the expiration of the contract without losing those astronomical sums that the Treasury absolutely could not do without?

That's how Bill 70 came into being. We agreed to pay the contracted increases from July to December, but afterwards, by salary cuts that ran as high as 20 per cent, we would recuperate the money in three months, from January to April, 1983.

That was the source of the drama we were soon swept up in, and which I admit had been more clearly foreseen by our critics than by ourselves. Taxing us with naiveté, they wondered how the devil we could imagine that after three months, when all this money would not only have been collected but largely spent, it would be all that easy to recuperate. God knows, as we were to learn, they weren't wrong. Others, pursuing the same line of thought, couldn't believe we were really serious. "When the time comes," they said, "they'll never dare." For them Bill 70 was pure bluff. I have the impression that, unluckily, this was also the opinion that soon began to infiltrate the union negotiating team and made them think too long that solemn and hallowed precedent would make us back off in the end.

That's what certain factions within the party thought, too, mainly in the "left wing" where union links were often stronger than parliamentary solidarity. Two MNAs demonstrated this clearly toward the end of the debate on the law, Louise Harel simply voting against it, Guy Bisaillon handing in his resignation to boot.

These flurries might have spread farther had it not been for the summer recess that sent us all back to our ridings. During the two months' pause, listening to the voters, meeting their own families who had not been spared either, the members were forced to see that, economically, Quebec was a disaster area. Hundreds of thousands of families were in desperate straits. It was a great downfall after all those years when everything had seemed possible, if not easy. A veritable psychological rout was beginning to take place in people's minds, and a feeling of revolt, as well, against the injustice of fate, against the government, too, and against the unions every bit as much. The government had no more been able to stem this tidal wave of economic misfortune than had governments in Ottawa, Paris, or elsewhere, where similar grumblings could be heard. As for the unions, the idea that a privileged caste could have the right to demand still more from a society that couldn't give any more was something people didn't buy. It wasn't hard to see that an overwhelming majority of them stood behind those men and women who all summer long had sought us out to tell us, in a tone that is usually reserved for giving orders, "Whatever happens, don't give up!"

When parliament opened again, the last hesitations had evaporated. Ministers and backbenchers alike came back with the unalterable determination to go through with our plan, overturning all obstacles that stood in the way, if necessary. I say "if necessary" because we hadn't given up hope of finding a compromise solution; that was one of the reasons that had led us to run the risk of Bill 70 in the first place.

We still had three months to go before the deadline of December 31, time enough for reflection before it was too late. From the depths of that insecurity that was gnawing at their foundations and before the economic woes that were afflicting so many of their members, wouldn't the private unions find the right words to say to their fellows in the public sector? It took courage, but some tried, emphasizing, for example, that when you enjoyed absolute job security, enviable paid vacations, a retirement plan, and a rich spread of other benefits, it became almost immoral, when your neighbour was down and out, to go on as if nothing was happening, demanding "always more." They were told to go and get lost.

All during the autumn, however, we refused to stop trying. While Yves Bérubé stumped the country meeting all sorts of audiences, even the most hostile, with the same imperturbable calm, developing his "crisis pedagogy," back in Quebec City we tried to reopen discussions with the leaders of the Common Front. We looked for any kind of gangplank to cross the rift that separated us. September turned into October, and by November we had to face up to the facts. The Common Front was preparing a general mobilization. The rift had become a chasm. There was now a gulf of *seven billion dollars* between us! That was the end!

At mid-November I resigned myself to issue an ultimatum. If after three more weeks we found ourselves still in the same situation, the National Assembly would be called upon to settle the question. No response. A confrontation was inevitable.

On December 11, 1982, the decisions we had held in reserve since spring were finally applied. They were almost exactly those Bill 70 had set forth: they would permit us to eliminate more than $600 million of the $700-million budgetary shortfall, but this sum would be collected keeping the strain to a minimum. We had established a sliding scale that completely spared those in the lower wage brackets, only slightly affected those in the intermediary range, and applied fully, up to 20 per cent of salary, to the highest paid union members. Many times we had asked the unions to work with us to humanize the operation. Since they had refused, all we could do was to proceed unilaterally.

The law, renumbered Bill 105, established by decree some 109 collective agreements, detailing working conditions for all unions. Because of the unbelievable mess that had accumulated from one set of negotiations to another over the past twenty years, some regulations going so far as to stipulate teachers' workloads to the last minute, the combined documents made a mountain of 80,000 pages. This ridiculous quantity doubtless inspired in certain commentators – our colleague Louise Harel, being true to herself, among them – judgements condemning the law for its "grotesqueness" and its "brutality."

In reality, opinion was curiously divided. For some, the employees of the State were victims of an odious holdup; for others, it served them right. A certain ambiguity was also perceivable in the ranks of the Common Front. At the same time that the unions were calling for a general strike at the end of January, representatives of the nurses, as combative a group but more realistic, had gone back to the bargaining table and were negotiating hard in order to gain concessions in some aspects of their decree. And a good number of union militants had discreetly let us know at various times during the conflict that they were beginning to find this rigid and insatiable corporatism into which they had been dragged more than embarrassing.

Here is a letter, for example, which was accompanied by a cheque made out to the Minister of Revenue:

Monsieur le Premier Ministre,
    I am a Québécois teacher, father of four children. I enclose a cheque for 300 dollars which represents part of what I am counting on paying to the State of Quebec. The collective agreement that sets my salary gives me a raise that I consider too generous, considering the economic crisis . . . .

You would think that here and there you would see movements of collaboration and sympathy springing up in view of the grave dangers we are running. No . . . People aren't aware that Quebec is living beyond its means. . . . Workers in the public sector earn 15 to 20 per cent more than those in the private sector . . . [and] despite the present situation they refuse to reopen their contracts. As a union member and a citizen, I object to them taking the State of Quebec for a milch cow. . . .

Hugues A.

It was an exceptional case, but we were discovering more and more of them. For the great majority, however, the dominant trait was a somewhat cynical attitude that a long period of too profitable labour disputes had turned into an ingrained habit. An example of this was that other teacher, a very active member of the party, whom I reproached with embarking on a strike lost in advance.

"I know," he said, "it won't be one of our best ones. But who can tell? Don't forget, they've always paid off in the past . . ."

Though they must have known this one could scarcely be profitable, the hardliners of the Common Front busied themselves just the same preparing for the big showdown. In the CSN and the CEQ especially, real power had for years been concentrated in the hands of the middle echelons, often dominated by permanent staffers for whom the strike, that orgastic moment, constituted the supreme justification of their existence.

The mass of the members, on the other hand, seemed resigned and didn't evince much enthusiasm for a fight for the sake of honour that would automatically force them into civil disobedience. To whip up the troops, the Common Front unleashed a frantic propaganda campaign, telling people, for example, that everyone was to be stripped of 20 per cent of salary, and not just for three months but for eternity, or almost. Worse still, it oozed ill will that easily disintegrated into the most outrageous insults. A choice target, I suddenly saw myself in demonstrations guillotined, my head on the end of a pike, my face streaming with long locks of blood-red streamers. The news at that time was full of stories about the war criminal nicknamed "The Butcher of Lyon." Some inspired union publicist had the brilliant idea to make up a poster calling me "The

Butcher of New Carlisle"! It was a bit forced, but amusing just the same – in a sad way.

No less sad, the strike came, led off rather tepidly by the teachers and the hospital workers, who seemed much less caught up in this ritualistic ceremony than they had been in the past. Work stoppages began, all perfectly illegal, with students and, above all, old people paying the price as usual. But after several days, seeing that they were gaining nothing but public censure, the hospital employees lay down their arms and joined the nurses who, having signed their contract, luckily had stayed on the job. That left the teachers in the CEQ. After several more days we had to pull our last weapon out of the drawer, a law only to be used very exceptionally that the jurists called "the atomic bomb."

We were violently upbraided for Bill 111 in various circles where union sympathies went hand in hand with an excessively punctilious interpretation of civil rights. Our requiring an immediate return to work and providing drastic sanctions in case of refusal didn't go against the rules. No, what caused all the uproar was article 28, which stated that, for specific purposes under this law alone, the Quebec Charter of Human Rights was suspended. In the middle of the ensuing outcry, a journalist got worked up to the point of finding in this paragraph "a moral equivalent to the War Measures Act of 1970"! In fact, similar dispositions had been taken without stirring up much flak in a good number of previous laws. Our Liberal predecessors had used them, too, but memory being the faculty that helps especially the opposition to forget, they raised a hell of a stink, quite overblown with very democratic indignation.

Then, brusquely, the CEQ collapsed like an exhausted runner. At the end of a week classes were back to normal.

There was, however, a last pocket of resistance that felt the need of an ultimate release. On May 5, 1983, at Hotel Concorde in Quebec City, where we were holding a meeting of the national council of the party, several hundred hotheads were waiting to welcome us. Since they were blocking the main entrance, we went around toward the garage. My car was briskly battered and clubbed, and the ones following had their windows smashed. Unfortunately for him, Camille Laurin had recognized some of *his* teachers in the crowd, and smilingly stepped out into the middle of the mob. He had cause to regret it. He barely escaped, face bruised and legs so badly beaten with sticks he was half crippled.

When this savage scene was reported in the media, it did have a beneficial effect. Seeing that it was getting an even worse beating, the union movement withdrew into its tent.

But we weren't proud either. Many of the union members had formerly been among our best militants. Full of bitterness, all they could think of now was to make us pay dearly for this, their first big defeat in twenty years. As for public opinion, already quite shaken by the economic troubles, it had more than it could stomach with these additional shocks. It had the classical reaction: once the alarm was past, it blamed everyone indifferently. In a poll taken about that time, public opinion didn't even give us 20 per cent. We had hit bottom.

Paradoxically, I felt in excellent shape. After two years of heavy vexations and intolerable tension, I could at last see the light at the end of the tunnel.

43. Exit: This Way

COMPARED TO THAT GLEAM OF HOPE, even the worst polls didn't count for much.

An invigorating breeze was blowing from the south. The American economy had started up again, and since its recovery is as contagious to us as its illnesses, we soon began to sense an upturn beginning in Quebec, too.

For the rest of 1983 not a day went by without our being at the bedside of our convalescent patient. What if there's a relapse, we said to ourselves, once bitten twice shy.

Parizeau consequently directed his budget to vigorously stimulating the economy and bringing it back to life. "A business budget," the sourpusses said disdainfully. It was true. There was really nothing in it for anyone except for industry, for the sole and excellent reason that this was the only place our return to health could come from, and from there would come the return of all those lost jobs.

The next stages are easier to find on the map than in the memory: Mont Ste-Anne, Pointe-au-Pic, and finally, Compton. From there we fired off progressive salvos, growing stronger as our ideas and intuitions learned how to transform themselves into projects, which amounted to a whole battery of provisions aimed not just at recovery but at a permanent enrichment of our economic situation. Not all these remedies laid claim to originality, for after all, such questions are basically a matter of common sense. What could be more traditional, for example, than subsidies? In the mining sector, however, we focused them on the opening of new sites and in several months our $120 million generated almost $700 million in investments, and when I visited Abitibi, people were saying they hadn't seen such feverish activity in twenty years.

The same was true for the program to modernize pulp and paper operations launched four years earlier and supported almost single-handedly by Yves Bérubé, whose portfolio it was. These efforts had finally affected the whole industry, moving it from a state of decrepitude back to one of competitiveness. Now, to add to this, we had an extraordinarily accelerated program of reforestation. Knowing that our forests had been outrageously plundered for so many years, we had already quadrupled new tree planting. It was far from adequate. During these exciting months of 1983 we decided to raise the annual rate of reforestation from 65 to 300 million trees before 1988, thus assuring the perpetual renewal of our forest patrimony, Scandinavian style. It's an objective we must absolutely meet if we don't want things to degenerate as before.

I have in hand a memo dating from 1985 summarizing the spectacular result of another decision taken in those days: "a policy of rate reductions designed to favour companies that are large consumers of electricity . . . . Hydro-electric power first at the service of our own development rather than being massively exported to create jobs . . . elsewhere, in the South. In doing so we are attracting enterprises of the future, like aluminum plants – Pechiney at Bécancour, Reynolds at Baie-Comeau, Alcan at Laterrière – and Quebec is rising in this domain to the level of the biggest world producers. Besides, we are getting in on the ground floor of tomorrow's technologies, like production of hydrogen by electrolysis in the pilot plant at Shawinigan."

Tomorrow's technologies . . . like Dickens's "best of times and worst of times," they promise the best and the worst of things. What the panic of the last two years prevented us from seeing was that the crisis signalled a revolutionary metamorphosis. A complete range of practices and equipment was sinking to the bottom like a moulting lobster's shell. The economy was changing its skin. Henceforth no efficient enterprise could do without all those inventions that continually reduce production time, but, on the other hand, reduce the number of jobs just as dramatically.

At the time of the announcement of the new aluminum plant, I managed to wring this confession from an Alcan representative only after much insistence: "An up-to-date plant will increase productivity enormously," he repeated for the nth time.

"Yes, great, but what about jobs?"

"Jobs? Uh . . . well . . . Yeah, jobs . . . Well, maybe not so many as before. But not that many less, just the same."

The same number of jobs, then. Maybe. And one day surely many more, once the economy is robotized, computerized, and has taken off resolutely for the year 2000. But in many cases the jobs won't be the same and will demand a different preparation that is quite a bit more specialized than any we have considered satisfactory up to this point.

So we are going to have to upgrade our manpower. Young people especially are going to have to train like champions to carve themselves out a place in this new pitiless and unknown world. Let's get our ideas straight on what we mean by young people. Nothing disgusts me more than naysayers who take a gloomy pleasure in running down today's youth, beginning with those juvenile Cassandras themselves whining in advance over their "lost generation." In reality youth is an entity as complex as society itself, since tomorrow – it stands to reason – it will be society. Now, among the fifteen to twenty-five-year-olds of today, nine-tenths of them make out, all things considered, as well as if not better than we did at their age, and they have a marvellous aptitude for anticipating all these transformations and all the demands that will be made upon them, and for making their way through them.

Those who, because they lack seniority, are the first to be laid off when hard times come are also the first to be hired back when the sun begins to shine again. Much more to be pitied are those in their forties and fifties who have the handicap of costing more and being less adaptable and who are often trashed, along with their families.

I will stop. For all my colleagues, I am sure, this year must remain, as for me, one of the most staggering we lived through. But if I set about recounting it in detail, it would soon become fastidious for the average reader, which I am fast rebecoming myself. At the time, however, every dossier on a new project, even the driest of them, had the gift of completely absorbing me, because I saw each skeleton phrase swarming with jobs. In fact, all this had little enough to do with us. As it had for everyone else, the crisis had given us a cruel lesson in humility, and we no longer took ourselves for anything but what we were. We had learned to acknowledge the frailty of government before this cataclysm that had whirled us away like a cockle-shell, just barely allowing us time to bring down the sails and save the mast, while in the hold the crew suffered dreadfully. And when the wind turned fair again and began first to blow in our quarter – immanently just because the recession had entered Canada via Quebec – we had to admit that it hadn't sprung up at our signal. All we could be modestly proud of was to have used all our strength to avoid irreparable damage and to be ready now to get things moving again.

With this end in view, in September we decided to delay the opening of parliament, a decision that our "friends" on the other side of the House welcomed with their usual braying. But we needed those few weeks to adjust the ambitious development program that was the fruit of all our efforts. At the same time I announced that $30 million would be available immediately.

"Pooh!" snooted the know-it-alls, "that won't go far!"

Decidedly, it was hard to break the mould and get started going uphill again. This was even more evident when, shortly after, we brought down a forecast for hundreds of millions, not counting the "Biron Plan II" that offered businesses up to $2 billion in guarantees. All we got for our pains was silence, the minimum recognition allowed such reprobates. Working like dogs we had been able in full recession to fulfil, at least in part, nearly all our 1981 commitments, from job creation for youth just entering active life to "Logirente" for old people on the threshold of leaving it, and from a determined plunge into the impetuous waves of the new scientific and technological revolution to the more mundane cleaning up of our rivers and lakes after an eternity of neglect. Despite all obstacles, the worst of which is stubborn prejudice, we had tried whenever it was possible to encourage the advancement of women toward more and more important posts while knowing very well it was too little and too late.

But what's the sense in talking about the good fare of the day before to someone who's no longer hungry, or in proposing this or that dish for tomorrow when he no longer likes your cuisine? The day was coming when we'd be asked to hang up our aprons. All this past year spent sweating over the stoves of economic recovery had, for that matter, used up most of our energies.

Physically exhausted, emptied of that generous strength that had allowed him to give so freely of himself, Pierre Marois, white-haired now, had just left us, all of a sudden, with the apparent coldness that sensitive people clothe themselves in at times like that. I looked around at the other veterans of 1976 and before and was startled in turn at the sight of myself in the mirror. Good God but we'd grown old! Tiredness aiding, our great spring shape had blown away and on the barometer of sense of humour our smiles had stuck on "Very Dry."

For the first time in my life, with the exception of a few fugitive and narcissistic experiments when young, I began, more or less, to keep a diary. I started out with the heavy clumsiness of the man who isn't used to it and, although a new year was beginning, I began without any hoopla or many illusions about what lay ahead. In truth, I had the feeling that maybe I was starting the final countdown.

Sunday, January 22, 1984

It's a perilous practice, I know. Even when I wasn't hitting it off all that well with Lesage in 1964–1965 and let the rumour out just to stir up a little uncertainty, I had all the trouble in the world to scribble down a few scattered notes.

Because it's surely dangerous to start following oneself like this. It can create a "memoirist's" mentality, a sort of clearing the way for the exit.

But that's just it. I have the impression that 1984 threatens to be . . . but no, the word threatens is too strong for such a natural perspective. So what? I surprise myself more and more often dreaming of what comes next. Not making any plans yet, I can't do that because that would mean I'd really decided. But the temptation is there and it's starting to seem like fun.

God knows there's no shortage of good reasons these days. The media smell the kill. I haven't checked it out scientifically, but you can see and hear a curious parallelism developing. On the Anglo-Canadian side it's Trudeau and the federal Liberals who can't do anything right, even if it's just passing the time of day. Same for us in the French news in Quebec (how I hate the "-phone" jargon), which for that matter keeps its eyes and ears closed to everything our Ottawa Liberals are up to. Is it discretion at the deathbed of "French Power"?

Whatever it is, it seems the trough of the wave we're in has persisted beyond the holidays. Anyway, no one is sparing us. For example, the meanmindedness of our journalists, rivalling the Liberal pack on this score, at the news of Yves Michaud's nomination to president of Montreal's Palais des Congrès, until we began getting numerous reports from high sources overseas on the quality of his work there, whereupon the denigrators fell back into a prudent silence . . . but not before they had heavily underscored his *monstrous* salary of $82,000.

It was about this time that good old Jean Marchand left the Senate to be promoted to president of the Federal Transport Commission, a big raise. Plus how much more in pension benefits?

And do you imagine any of our lynx-eyed journalistic sleuths showed any interest in the question? Not so. It's true that over there, on the other side of the Ottawa River . . .

So here we are at the end of January. Not doing so hot. With election defeats in Mégantic-Compton, and especially in Jonquière, that makes seven by-elections lost since our 1981 win. And it seems quite clear that even an old tugboat like me isn't pulling the weight he used to. According to the confidential memo I was given for Christmas, even what I'm leaving in my wake is not all that palatable: "even your most faithful supporters are wondering what's going on," I read. "We can feel you are easily irritable, less open to suggestions . . . more and more isolated." The worst of it is that it's true, I can feel it.

Wednesday, January 25

There's a little statistical war going on between Parizeau and Bourassa. The latter got his knuckles rapped over the 121,000 jobs recuperated in 1983. At the time, we were working so hard I had forgotten to take note of his return to the leadership of the Liberals.

Here's a report from New York that drops into our laps like a gift from the gods, which just goes to show that the unexpected always happens and that the only political strategist worthy of the name is good old General Time. Here's what Mr. Honan, vice-president of a big U.S. financial institution, says after finishing an elogious study of Hydro-Québec.

1. That its rating is considerably inferior to what the management of the enterprise really merits . . . and the exemplary way the government has respected its autonomy!

2. That there is nothing more dangerous than Bourassa's super-projects at a time when we're swimming in surplus electricity. "In 1973," the report reminds us, "the first phase of the James Bay project was undertaken without any strategy for commercialization. The situation was saved by the oil crisis of 1978 . . . ." There you go! How often have we said the same thing, but it's so much more serious repeated in English by Americans.

3. That furthermore, and this tops everything, "even if Quebec became independent, this would probably have no effect on the financial situation of Hydro-Québec. On the contrary, investors might well be attracted by the fact that Hydro, in an independent Quebec, would turn more and more toward the United States."

Whereupon somebody came up with a little slogan that has been going the rounds since: "Americans are more afraid of incompetence than independence!"

This morning my first press conference in far too long. Everyone is agreed, we've got to get out and show ourselves, particularly to push plans for recovery and development and inject a maximum of that essential ingredient, confidence, into the system. I think it was Edison who said that genius was 90 per cent sweat and 10 per cent inspiration; I'm sure that for prosperity the proportions are the same, but that the 90 per cent is confidence.

Consequently, this week I'm doing my bit. Monday it was a pretty lively encounter with students from the aero-technical school at St. Hubert. I knew it went well when two young Liberals passing me on the staircase as I went out shouted: "To the showers with him!" Tomorrow I'm attending the opening of a branch of the industrial research centre (Centre de recherche industrielle) in Montreal.

So this morning there was this press conference with the blasé and basically lazy parliamentary press gallery. Rather than treat a specific theme, since in a way it was renewing acquaintance, it had been suggested that I survey the political horizon and then field questions. What a joke! In one hour I was pushed into at least forty-five minutes of remasticating the national question, the referendum, and so on, and so forth. A subject that has been talked to death is so much easier to spin out. I should also add that various colleagues, who hadn't opened their mouths at yesterday's cabinet meeting, let themselves go with joyful abandon as they came out, so-and-so in favour of an all-out election, so-and-so dismissing the question forever, and so-and-so coming back to the stage-by-stage approach . . . which is why it always pays to be a little less gabby.

The weekend is for thinking, in a relaxed way. I think that's what saved me for many years, this capacity to blot everything out by doing something else – reading, for example, reading anything except last week's news warmed over. I happened to pick up a book by Henry Cabot Lodge, the first of the name, a nineteenth-century biography of Alexander Hamilton. It's a re-edition of an old series on the founding fathers of the United States, one volume each for Washington, the three Adamses, Madison, Jackson, Marshall, Daniel Webster, Jefferson, Burr, Randolph, etc. Never since ancient Greece has a country seen such a collection of genius bending over its cradle.

Geniuses are consequently insufferable and contrary but with a vitality and a variety of talents that are breathtaking. This is true of Hamilton as well, and even the pedestrian style and preternatural conservatism and snobbishness of his young biographer can't rob his story of frenetic tempo and the ferment of ideas that marked him to his end, so typical of his times, a duel and death "on the field of honour."

But what struck me most, because one can't really escape one's own preoccupations, is the indescribable turmoil of those first years: the bankruptcy, the revolutionary army disbanded without getting a cent of their pay, the perpetual collisions between personal vanity and state rights in the fragile infant Confederacy, the general impoverishment leading to riots that a single gesture from Washington could have turned toward dictatorship. . . . It was a real Latin American-style show that the haughty powers of old Europe, beginning with vengeful England, expected to degenerate into such a mess that all they would have to do would be walk in and divide the spoils. But they pulled through in the end. When I think of us today, twice as numerous as they were then, and of all the advantages we have that they could never have imagined . . . it makes one think that maybe we need a life-or-death situation to be able to understand that there's nothing to lose . . . on the contrary.

Okay. It's already past six and I find myself facing at least one big problem. One after the other, Louis-Marie Dubé, our matchless riding secretary, and Jean-Roch Boivin himself have just come in to tell me that they're leaving. Two irreplaceable people who are going to have to be replaced just the same. I can understand Louis-Marie perfectly. It's killing to have to play the role of "vicar" to the most absentee MNA of them all. As for Jean-Roch, he's going to stay on a little, but I didn't dare hold on to him as I should have. I've been too aware of his discouragement and, what's more serious, his detachment toward me for some time now. Could it be that my own low period is rubbing off on him? But above all, seven years of stress, the dreadful wear and tear of the economic crisis, then the fall-out from all that bad luck, without counting all those years up to 1976

361

when we were laboriously building the party, that's enough to account for it, and then some. But if it's true for J.-R., it must be true for me, too.

It's an ill wind, etc. I've just stumbled across a replacement: Martine Tremblay, a miniature woman, so small she makes me feel like a giant! But what a going concern! She has a solid formation of political experience at the base, then administrative, and what a restless curiosity, and above all an unshakable loyalty. Loyalty to the State, certainly, but first to Quebec. She'll be the first woman to fill this post. She'll just have to make us sorry it's been so.

A brief official meeting with our two new "ambassadors" disguised as consuls-general, a curious status and no less flattering to us, though the motives behind the two roles are very different, even diametrically opposed.

If the Americans keep such an observation post in the provincial capital, it's precisely because our provincialism doubtless seems a little fragile to them and, despite the referendum, perhaps even transitory. Whatever the case, Uncle Sam is keeping an eye on us and I bet my bottom dollar that the CIA is permanently installed in the corridors.

As for France, its quasi-embassy is a legacy from De Gaulle's days. *Mutatis mutandis*, it could be compared to our own delegation in Paris: a listening post, a centre for co-operation and – if one can compare small and big – a place for high-level contacts. After two typical career officers, Messieurs Marcel Baux and Henri Réthoré, ultrasympathetic but discreet to the point of self-effacement, now we have been delegated to a phenomenal activist, Renaud Vignal. His appetite is insatiable and he is gobbling up Quebec, which he already knows remarkably well through other persons. His superb young wife, Anne, also jumped right into things. Registered at a CEGEP to study computer science, she is amazed at all the riches in hardware she discovered there. We're at least in the running as far as equipment goes!

As for our own "ambassadress," Louise Beaudoin, her nomination to Paris hasn't caused any repercussions, contrary to what some people feared and others certainly hoped to see. Besides her competence, which cannot be questioned, she has behind her the diffuse but enormous weight of the women's rights lobby that is beginning to scare people more and more. So much the better if she churns things up now and then!

A heavy cabinet meeting today, almost seven hours, three big items of business.

A whole series of investments in fisheries: in the Iles de la Madeleine, in Newport in Gaspésie, and in Natashquan and Blanc-Sablon on the North Shore. Good, hard-driving work and well done, like most of Garon's projects. But to sew up the business, will he finally win his sniping war with the ineffable de Bané and his Ottawa gang? In Ottawa it's terminal panic for the Liberals, who are going strong, spending wildly, buying up anything and anyone . . . especially in Quebec, of course.

Then the massive dossier on the new policy on adult education. We okayed publication and were particularly glad to note a firm intention, with the sums allotted, to really open up a first-priority fight against the running sore of illiteracy. It's an ailment we share with the rest of the continent, it's true, but one that gives you the shivers just the same.

Next come three projects Pauline Marois put together in record time to help destitute youth. Starting with the same perspectives that Pierre Marois, her homonym and predecessor, had abandoned in a generous haze, she came up with three clear, coherent, and apparently operational instruments: first, a mid-job training program for people who need to learn a trade while beginning to earn a salary; second, one for those inevitable community work projects designed to help the worst of the badly-off to become functional again; and third, for the greatest possible number of dropouts, a program to help them go back to school. I say "apparently operational" because of the often enormous distance, caused by the administrative machinery, between the paperwork and concrete results. If she succeeds in taming this paralysing monster, Pauline Marois will perhaps turn out to be one of our best "men" – as Ben Gurion used to call Golda Meir! It has to work. And we must finally correct this wastage of people, especially young people, as well as the staggering sums of money spent that in the long run only serve to sponsor more or less forced inactivity and lock victims up in a subcultural Gulag.

Tuesday, February 7
I've been reading over some articles about us.

In a learned examination of all my potential successors and the way various "camps" are organizing in the wings, Gilles Lesage in *Le Devoir* tosses off as though it were self-evident the opinion that we are "a government mined by opportunism." He's the perfect example of a man with "unfavourable prejudices." Errors, even blunders, and too frequent attacks of that mortal malady that is the arrogance of power, I grant all that. But opportunism! It's rather the contrary that is dangerously true: reforms here, reforms there, the whole team still assailed by an inextinguishable thirst for change, renewal, the real "clear cut" as Jean Paré wrote much more justly in the current issue of *l'Actualité* . . . school reform, adult education, tax reform, etc., etc. Opportunism, my foot! I really think that's what we lack the most!

A prize for lucidity should go to Louis Falardeau for his perceptive remarks on the "Common Front" of restaurant owners against the tipping law. Observing that when a government is unpopular "even good laws can be successfully overturned," he adds that if we don't get around to improving our public opinion rating, "the united opposition could very well force us to back down." That's first-rate analysis. This, indeed, is a deleterious temptation that has been creeping up on us more and more lately. When you're in a position of strength, certain retreats are often seen as signs of wisdom; but when you're in bad shape they open the door to public massacre.

Wednesday, February 8
I must be a prophet. As an excellent illustration of yesterday's last sentence, *Le Devoir* is running a headline stating: "Since October Quebec has been holding a police report incriminating Jean-Roch Boivin." A delicious media tidbit, but one wonders what it's all about. Can't find anything in Quebec City. Finally, from Montreal the chief deputy crown attorney confirms that there does exist an insignificant dossier that a policeman turned in last year and – for what noble motives one can imagine – that he has just slipped to the newspaper. The opinion of the chief deputy: "A little before Christmas I sat in on a discussion of this dossier and the conclusion we all came to was that the facts contained in the report in no way constitute any criminal act." Do you think this "definitive" legal opinion will keep the dogs at bay? Then you don't know them. The only sure thing is that this time Boivin is really going to pack it in. This low blow has visibly finished him.

Cute to the last, Trudeau chose this leap-year Wednesday to announce his new departure. One happy result: for once the cabinet meeting was very short. Nobody was listening to anybody. I adjourned the meeting for lunch, then somehow or other we got through the agenda. I ended the session about three by asking for suggestions for the press conference I had to give. A few good ideas, among them Jean Garon's on the "shipwrecked dream" of a bilingual Canada, a generous dream in Trudeau's centralizing perspective, but one that would only have been imposed in part, and by force, in Quebec alone.

What else can I say? That I remember having commented on another departure a few years ago? If then, *if* it's definitive today, it's the end of a long and important chapter in political history. It's also the probable end of a government that had become ultra-personal and is now conspued by the whole of English Canada.

Then in the House I spoke of the intelligence of this personality, dared speak of his brutality, and stressed that to have succeeded for so many years in imprinting his mark on the country he had to be very strong. "However that may be," I added, "what was called 'French Power,' a phenomenon we won't see again in the foreseeable future, will one day have to be weighed and judged for what it gained for us and what it cost us."

In short, I held back. It was no time to talk of the way a democrat can end up in the skin of a little potentate, or of the lack of concern shown about looking into, or rather, overlooking, the fall of the Canadian standard of living from second to twelfth or thirteenth rank, or, above all, about abuse of power and the slow decadence of a reign that had lasted too long. Historians will take care of·that. For today, *de mortuis . . .*

Two long days wasted in Ottawa attending the failure of the second conference on native rights. Trudeau spoke a couple of times, casting off his last rays, and showed himself to be more eloquent and persuasive than ever, a curious sort of Québécois who can defend the "national" rights of the Inuit and the Indians with zeal but when it comes to the no less undeniable rights of the nation called French Quebec he becomes completely blocked. As far as native peoples are concerned, we don't have to take a back seat to anyone. "Almost without exception," writes John Price in a study that is still contemporary, "comparisons show that Indian people live better in Quebec than anywhere else in Canada."*

April

Here, "April snow makes green peas grow." But in Paris and London it was as hot as July all Easter week.

And it's the same in Saint-Malo, our 1534 cradle, where we went to open the 450th anniversary celebrations. The old city is a wonder, built on its promontory, destroyed from top to bottom during the war, then reconstructed stone by stone by its adoring citizens . . . and contractors whose pursestrings were closer to their heartstrings. The harbour and the bay are magnificent: small whitecaps whipped up by a sharp breeze, swarms of sailboats, from tiny to fair-sized, then a few three-masters modestly surrounding the Polish training ship, a veritable floating cathedral with all its sails flying, taking us back to the days of Surcouf and Jean Bart and our own d'Iberville.

Paris, the female city par excellence, with her chestnut trees and new leaves and flowers everywhere, is decked out in her most brilliant spring attire.

Dinner with Pierre Mauroy, together with Louise Beaudoin and Clément Richard. Mauroy is solid as a rock, at least apparently so, despite the battering his government is taking from the economic winter storm in which he serves (for how long?) as Mitterand's icebreaker.

As usual we talk over memories of good times shared these last few years. The Socialists have simply assumed the Franco-Québécois heritage and made it work for them. It is a continuity that no change, on one side or the other, has interrupted. Going back even further, I think of the good-natured subtlety of Raymond Barre steering between the Charybdis of Ottawa and the Scylla of Quebec, and of Jacques Chirac's passionate character that made him seem more Québécois than ourselves, and right back to President Giscard giving me the Legion of Honour that De Gaulle, too late, had intended to award to his friend Daniel "Jonsonne" . . .

* John Price, *Indians of Canada* (Toronto, 1979).

Between Frenchmen and Québécois we'll go on becoming closer and closer knit.

The miracle continues! London, too, is at the height of its spring beauty. But the traffic slows, finally stops completely for a long time in front of Buckingham Palace. You can tell something is going on. A tense policeman refuses to tell us what's coming in on his walkie-talkie. It's only on arriving at the Savoy Hotel that we learn about the Libyan killers and at the same time a call from Paris informs us that, according to some far-fetched news release originating God knows where, I'm supposed to have been the victim of the attack! Then Reuters telephones to find out if it's true and I answer myself, which settles the question.

Lunch with the big wheels of the British Canadian Board of Trade, among whom, besides some "Londonized" Canadians, a good number of truly eminent bosses of big companies who do business with us. The fact they are here is a marvellous illustration of the subject of my address: outside America, good old Albion is still our biggest client, and we are one of her most important partners.

Back to Paris, just an hour before a random bomb in this same airport caused four deaths. Misfortunes never come singly. Stepping out of the plane we found ourselves confronted by two "special officers" of the French police whose mission was to shadow Corinne and me constantly thanks to new threats or rumours. Aren't we lucky not to live under the infernal tension terrorism is inflicting on the old countries. Touch wood.*

May

Our financial campaign isn't doing so well. Not that the militants are grumbling; on the contrary, their spirits seem to be improving everywhere and confidence has returned to the party ranks. At the same time we're betting on a new sovereignty campaign, which seems to me to be more and more chancy because those of us who were relying on an upswing – and I was one – have had to change their tune. Even if the mood is less surly than it was, dissatisfaction still persists, and so, equally, does disaffection.

Claude Morin, Pierre Marois, Claude Charron, then just recently

---

* It was only two weeks later that a certain Corporal Lortie made his bloody visit to the National Assembly.

Jacques-Yvan Morin . . . and how many others have left? I have the feeling I'm that tree Pamphile Lemay talks about, "an old tree forgotten in the plain."

September 2, 1986

"Thoughts take wing," writes Julien Green, "but words travel by foot." It's midnight. The wing droops, the words crawl. I've almost no more paper and no time left at all.

Afterword

Graham Fraser

T HE MEMOIRS END SO abruptly, it is as if the paper had been snatched from his hand. Reread now, almost ten years after his resignation and eight years after his death, there is something movingly plaintive about the sudden surprising coda to his book that echoes the end of his life, only a year later.

René Lévesque never lost that capacity to surprise. It was part of his inherent understanding of drama, which came from his experience in television, his personal impatience with ritual, his reflexive desire to choose the unexpected, to short-circuit any routine and evade any institution that he felt was designed to limit or confine him. He hated meetings, doctors, dinner jackets, protocols and procedures; he loved poker, cigarettes, late nights, foreign travel and good biographies of of interesting people; he preferred London to Paris, the United States to English Canada, the seashore to the lakeshore. He was always curious. He was always hungry for the new.

His political obituary was written many times: when he left the Liberal Party in 1967; when he was defeated in Laurier in 1970 and again in 1973; when he lost the referendum in 1980; when his party, in response to his rage in 1981 after the deal was struck between Pierre Trudeau and the nine other premiers, voted against his cherished dream of sovereignty-association; and when a third of his cabinet quit his government in 1984. Each time, he managed to elude the political oblivion that was predicted for him. Each time, he confounded prediction, and managed, somehow, to astonish.

I first met him in 1968. He had left the Liberal Party a few months earlier and was sitting as an independent; I was a student, writing a paper on the Radio-Canada producers' strike of a decade earlier. He was in Toronto making a speech, and at first he said he didn't have time to talk to me; then he said, "What the hell, come on back to my hotel." So we sat in his room and talked, late into the night.

369

Then, in 1969, shortly after I started in journalism, I followed him for a week as he travelled alone visiting university campuses in English-Canada. One night in Saskatoon, he spoke after a long, tiring day, during which he had repeated his speech three or four times.

He told the audience that he'd given his speech often enough that day, and that instead of the speech, he would simply tell some stories: "The making of a separatist."

He told of his upbringing in the Gaspé, of his anger that French-language schooling in New Carlisle ended at Grade 8 while the English high school led on to university, of his career in television, and of his entry into politics and government.

Then he told of his shock and shame at discovering that all the subcontracts for a major Hydro-Quebec project would be going to U.S. firms, and that key engineering experience for Quebeckers would be lost.

It was part, Lévesque told the audience, "of the slush fund tradition . . . they had a list of firms that contributed to the party. One firm had bridges in Montreal, another had roads – and this Boston firm had power plants."

He tried to get the decision changed at cabinet.

"Do you know how long it took me to fight that through?" he asked. "Two months! As soon as I brought up the issue in cabinet, I got a call from the senior lawyer of the Liberal Party, the chief fund-raiser – who was also a corporate counsel for this goddam Boston firm!"*

There was something moving about his rage.

At the end of the speech, a man in the audience got up and said, "Mr. Lévesque, supposing you lose. Suppose your party goes nowhere, and you are resoundingly defeated. In that case," and he paused for effect, "would you consider coming to Saskatchewan and running for office?" The room exploded with laughter and applause.

In fact, René Lévesque felt more passionate about political corruption than he did about Quebec independence. His commitment to democracy was greater than his commitment to sovereignty-association, the formula he had devised himself, and to which he was much more committed than his colleagues ever understood.

---

* Quoted in *PQ: René Lévesque and the Parti Québécois in Power,* Graham Fraser, Macmillan of Canada, 1984, pp. 26-27.

Thus, the piece of legislation that he was most proud of during his years as premier was the law that changed the financing of political parties, the first draft legislation presented by the new P.Q. government. (Although the first, it was numbered Bill 2, in order to preserve the symbolic number one for the language law. Ultimately, it didn't matter; a procedural wrangle meant that Bill 1 became Bill 101.) Quebec is one of the few jurisdictions where only voters can contribute to political parties – a rigorous limitation that not only ended the notorious corrupt practices of previous Quebec provincial governments, but also transformed political parties in Quebec.

Some of those who designed the election financing law believed that the Liberal Party was so dependent on corporate contributions that their elimination would reduce it to penury and starvation. Instead, the party was transformed into an organization with a mass base. Rather than starving the Liberal Party, Lévesque forced it to reform and, in the process, changed the nature of provincial political parties in Quebec forever.

Paradoxically, while Lévesque was committed to democracy, he disliked political parties – in particular, his own. He was suspicious of people who liked to go to meetings, who rose on points of order, who spent their weekends poring over resolutions and haggling over amendments. He saw them, correctly, as trying to limit his own ability to act and be decisive – even while he knew that the tedium and irritation of the political party process was critical to making democracy work. He had entered politics to get things done, and he would be remembered as a crucial figure in Quebec history even if he had left politics in 1966. For his energy was part of the driving force of the Quiet Revolution, and the development of Hydro-Quebec stands as a permanent record of his achievement.

There is an irony in his legacy as premier. One of the lasting, transformational acts of his government was the Quebec language law, Camille Laurin's Bill 101. Lévesque made no secret of the fact that he was uncomfortable with it: he didn't like its coercive measures, and said that he found the need for it humiliating. It wasn't until the Supreme Court began to find parts of the legislation unconstitutional that Lévesque became a defender of the law. Yet, despite Lévesque's discomfort, the language legislation has had a more far-reaching and profound effect on Quebec society than any other act of his government, literally changing the face of Quebec. The legislation has been amended, and may well be changed significantly in the future, but more than anything else, it symbolized and accelerated the process through which Quebec became a French-speaking society.

In 1976, a few months before the Parti Québécois was elected, I moved to Quebec and covered his government for the nine years he was premier. Over the years, he dealt with me in various ways: with openness, distance, fondness, exasperation, frankness, suspicion, candour, irritation and friendly teasing. That mercurial mixture was not a reflection on me; it was a reflection of his restless vitality. This was not always pleasant: he never forgot a slight; his mouth would tighten and his eyes become angry slits when an old wound was touched. He distrusted many of the people around him and could be distant, suspicious and stubborn. In cabinet meetings, he could not sit still when a minister whom he did not take seriously was talking, and would twitch impatiently.

He was a restless, solitary man, often more comfortable in the isolation of centre stage than with people who wanted an intimacy he shrank from. His closest boyhood friend, Raymond Bourget, died in the Second World War near Caen, accidentally killed by fire from Allied planes. Lévesque had to identify his friend's body, and some have speculated that this loss made him withdraw from the close bonds of friendship.

But, at the same time, he could be open, warm, witty, and, above all, curious. He read constantly and widely, in English and in French, and would emerge from his shyness by questioning people with a seductive intensity. At times, formal dinners would become awkward as he focused all his charm, attention and interest on the attractive wife of a junior official.

At the heart of his proposal for Quebec was a profound ambivalence: sovereignty-association. Many of his colleagues wrongly assumed that the ambivalence was merely a reflection of his understanding of the uncertainties and fears in the Quebec public. While he did personify many of the apparently contradictory feelings in Quebec, his commitment to the concept he had developed was no strategic device: he really believed in the idea as an alternative to both the limitations of federalism and the isolation of independence. Lévesque also understood the political obligation to reassure the Quebec public, which feared the consequences of rupture.

At first glance his moderating influence in the Parti Québécois went into decline as his leadership of the party weakened in the early

1980s. His authority in the party did not survive the wrenching debate of the fall of 1984; his health and stability were shaken by the schism in the party. But despite all the zig-zags of his shaky last six months in office, he still managed to catch everyone off guard with his resignation.

Writing this book on his return from the trip to Europe was part of his effort to redirect his life. Few memoirs are entirely candid, and this is no exception. After his death, doctors reported that he had suffered three or four small heart attacks; a few years later, it emerged that one of these may have occurred when he was told that one of his ministers, Claude Morin, was an RCMP informer. In the memoirs, he skates over just how traumatic and ugly his hospitalization was. In fact, the "details" that he declines to go into involved a nasty incident in which he exploded with rage, punching his most senior civil servant, Clerk of the Executive Council Louis Bernard, and had to be subdued by two cabinet ministers, Pierre Marc Johnson and Bernard Landry. They summoned a doctor who gave Lévesque a tranquillizer and sent him to hospital. However, he was released the next day, and the official word went out that he was simply suffering from extreme fatigue.

But writing the memoirs enabled him, literally, to turn the page on politics. Back in 1969, he had said that if Quebec became independent, he would not stay on in politics, but would either become an ambassador or return to journalism. His return, when it came, was to journalism.

He met his late-July 1986 deadline, and, when the book was published, he embarked on an extensive book tour. That tour revealed another of the paradoxes of his career: the man who had given the Quebec independence movement the respectability and legitimacy it had never enjoyed before was adored in English Canada. Thousands of people stood in long lines in front of bookstores to meet him and shake his hand.

On Friday, October 30, 1987, Lévesque attended a fund-raising dinner for Canadian authors in Montreal, and bumped into Trudeau. Lévesque was full of the projects he was embarking on: television documentaries in countries he had never managed to visit before, political reporting of one kind or another. For once, Trudeau seemed less vigorous; he had had knee surgery shortly before, and was still using a cane to walk. It occurred to him that Lévesque was taking on too much.

On Sunday, November 1, Lévesque complained of indigestion. His wife urged him to go to the hospital, but, ever suspicious of hospitals, he would have none of it. During dinner, about 8 pm, he collapsed. Frantically, Corinne Côté-Lévesque telephoned Urgences-Santé, the emergency ambulance service, and, as a nurse stayed on the line, began giving mouth-to-mouth resuscitation and chest massage. The ambulance was stuck in traffic, but a doctor arrived separately ten minutes after the call and tried to revive him.

At 8:35, twenty-two minutes after the call, the ambulance arrived, and the paramedics worked for another forty-five minutes before carrying him to hospital. He was dead when the ambulance arrived.

René Lévesque's death was an enormous shock, both in Quebec and in the rest of Canada. Thousands stood in line for hours in Montreal to pay their respects, and, when the coffin was removed from where he had been lying in state to be brought to Quebec City for a state funeral, there was spontaneous applause, a last inarticulate gesture of respect, affection and grief.

For millions of Quebeckers, he was a cultural symbol as much as a partisan figure: a little guy, whose weaknesses and strengths were a reflection of all the contradictions in French-speaking Quebec. He was full of paradoxes. A man who hated political parties and was suspicious of serious people who liked going to meetings presided over a party that was filled with them. The man who invented sovereignty-association hated labels and definitions; he played with them sometimes, hinting, teasing and flirting, but would slip away from their constraints. He entered politics to do things.

And, while death meant his oratory was suddenly stilled, and his sentences no longer floated like the wisps of cigarette smoke that constantly surrounded him, his achievements remained. Hydro-Quebec. The cleanest party fund-raising system in North America. A framework of progressive legislation, including agricultural zoning, anti-scab legislation, strong laws on health and safety in the workplace, provincial automobile insurance. A renewed strength of the French language in Quebec. But, above all, a commitment to democracy. For Lévesque set a number of critical precedents that shaped the political culture in Quebec: he committed the province to the rule that only voters can contribute to political parties; he established the principle that a mandate from a majority of the population in a referendum is required to change the political regime; and he accepted the results in 1980.

The shock in Quebec at Lévesque's death was not merely personal. Politically, it had the seismic effect of an earthquake. Pierre Marc Johnson, who had been in Paris when Lévesque died, was faced with a nationalist surge in his party; those who had left over the sovereignty issue in 1984-85 made it clear they were reclaiming the Parti Québécois. On November 11, Johnson stepped down from the leadership of the party; four months later, on March 18, 1988, Jacques Parizeau became leader, unopposed. Vowing to talk about sovereignty "before, during and after" elections, Parizeau re-energized the Parti Québécois, and in 1989, the party won ten additional seats.

Despite the crisis of morale, membership and fund-raising in the party that had taken place upon the departure of the separatist wing, and the revival in those three areas that occurred with Parizeau's leadership, the party's actual electoral performance did not alter much. In 1985, when Robert Bourassa returned to power, the Parti Québécois won nineteen seats and received 39 per cent of the popular vote under Johnson's leadership. In 1989, when the party congratulated itself on how well it had done under Parizeau, it received 40.2 per cent. And in 1994, after nine years of a Liberal government that had become tired and unpopular, the Parti Québécois formed a majority government with 44.7 per cent of the popular vote, only a hair ahead of the Liberals led by Daniel Johnson, which got 44.3 per cent. (In terms of parliamentary government, the percentages are irrelevant; in terms of a referendum, they are significant.)

Today, a decade after René Lévesque stepped down, and fifteen years after the 1980 referendum, the Parti Québecois is again poised to hold a referendum. In 1979, when the referendum question was announced, Jacques Parizeau made an elaborate show of pausing before rising to his feet to join in the ovation: a silent message of displeasure at the convoluted text.

In some ways, a great deal has changed since 1980. Quebec is more French, more confident, more entrepreneurial, less passionate about politics. Canada has a constitution with a Charter of Rights that has never been accepted by the Quebec National Assembly. There have been two wrenching, unsuccessful attempts to amend it: The Meech Lake accord, which failed in 1990, and the Charlottetown accord, which failed in 1992. It is hard to argue in 1995, as federalists did in 1980, that a No will mean a Yes to renewed federalism.

Neither Jacques Parizeau nor Jean Chrétien command the respect, affection or awe in Quebec that Lévesque and Trudeau did in 1980. If Lévesque resembled the French cartoon character Astérix – short, mischievous, wily – Parizeau is more like Obélix: large, ponderous, a little self-satisfied. (Or as Parizeau himself put it in an interview published in 1987, "I project the image of a thirties' politician in France. I look at some of my photos, and I say 'You could have defended the interests of the Bordeaux winegrowers in 1935!'")

At the same time, there are striking parallels. Jean Chrétien, who was minister of justice in 1980, is prime minister; Jacques Parizeau, who was Quebec's finance minister, is now premier. The tension that marked the combat between Trudeau and Lévesque is echoed in darker tones, without the residual bond of mutual respect that, despite its prickliness, characterized the relationship between the champions of 1980. Neither the supporters of Chrétien nor of Parizeau have forgotten their bitter, personal fight over the sales tax issue in 1978 (in which Chrétien felt he had been betrayed by Parizeau) or the referendum campaign in 1980 (in which Quebec nationalists felt they had been mocked by Chrétien).

In addition, a surprising amount of the ambivalence of Lévesque's vision for Quebec has survived. For while it seemed that sovereignty-association died with its author and the subsequent return to the Parti Québécois of the separatist wing of the party, Parizeau has rounded several of the rough edges of his policies. The legislation tabled in the National Assembly in December 1994 contains some significant parallels to the White Paper on Sovereignty-Association tabled in 1979: a proposal for a common currency with Canada, and Quebec membership in the Commonwealth, NATO, NORAD and the United Nations. Thus, exactly like Lévesque (who casually told *Barron's* in an interview two years later that the common currency ideas had been inserted for political expediency), Parizeau is proposing a country that would have a seat at the United Nations, but not its own currency; would collect all its own taxes, but not be able to control interest rates; pass all its own laws, but be unable to control the foreign-exchange value of the dollar. *Plus ça change . . .*

How would René Lévesque have responded to the renewal of the debate he had been so centrally involved in? All such speculations run the risk of being self-serving as the living enlist the dead in support of their analysis. When Jacques Parizeau tabled the legislation that turned Lévesque's process upside-down (passing legislation first and holding a referendum to ratify it rather than holding a referendum to get a mandate to negotiate), Liberal MNA Christos Sirros said the procedure being proposed "would make René Lévesque turn in his grave."

It is obviously impossible to tell, but nevertheless let me venture a comment. I doubt that he would have objected to the process Parizeau has proposed. After all, Lévesque tried to link his government's legislative record with the benefits he argued would flow from sovereignty-association and, like Parizeau, tried to reach beyond the P.Q. to nationalist politicians from other parties.

In a broader sense, I suspect that he would have been pleased that the rendezvous he had predicted on referendum night in 1980 was taking place as soon as it is, but disappointed that much of the passion for politics seems to have subsided in Quebec. He would have felt grimly vindicated, feeling that the closing of the Collège Militaire de Saint-Jean reflected his view of how federalism favours Ontario over Quebec. And he would have felt equally vindicated at seeing the similarities in the discourse that Jacques Parizeau's Parti Québécois has adopted for the 1995 referendum and the rhetoric he used in preparing and campaigning for the 1980 referendum.

Most of all, he would have been hoping to see things get done, and see Quebec move forward.

Graham Fraser is Washington bureau chief of *The Globe and Mail*. His book *PQ: René Lévesque and the Parti Québécois in Power* was published in 1984.

377